Death of a Nation

Critical American Studies Series

George Lipsitz, University of California–San Diego, Series Editor

Death of a Nation: American Culture and the End of Exceptionalism
David W. Noble

The Culture Concept: Writing and Difference in the Age of Realism
Michael A. Elliott

Not the Triumph but the Struggle:
The 1968 Olympics and the Making of the Black Athlete
Amy Bass

The New American Studies
John Carlos Rowe

Those without a Country: The Political Culture of Italian American Syndicalists
Michael Miller Topp

American Studies in a Moment of Danger
George Lipsitz

Death of a Nation

American Culture and the End of Exceptionalism

David W. Noble

Foreword by George Lipsitz

Critical American Studies

University of Minnesota Press
Minneapolis
London

Published by the University of Minnesota Press
111 Third Avenue South, Suite 290
Minneapolis, MN 55401-2520
http://www.upress.umn.edu

Library of Congress Cataloging-in-Publication Data

Noble, David W.
Death of a nation : American culture and the end of exceptionalism / David W. Noble.
p. cm. — (Critical American studies series)
Includes bibliographical references and index.
ISBN 0-8166-4080-7 (acid-free paper) — ISBN 0-8166-4081-5 (pbk. : acid-free paper)
1. Criticism—United States—History—20th century. 2. Nationalism and literature—United States—History—20th century. 3. Literature and history—United States—History—20th century. 4. American literature—History and criticism—Theory, etc. 5. United States—Civilization—20th century. 6. United States—Historiography. I. Title. II. Series.
PS78 .N63 2002
801'.95'09730904—dc21 2002009538

Printed in the United States of America on acid-free paper

12 11 10 09 08 07 06 05 04 03 02 10 9 8 7 6 5 4 3 2 1

To the memories of my grandmothers, Lucinda and Willahmina,
and my mothers, Estelle and Agnes

To my wife Gail and our two youngest grandchildren, Ella and Zach

Contents

FOREWORD

The Unpredictable Creativity of David Noble

George Lipsitz

> The temporal distance separating us from the past is not a dead interval but a transmission that is generative of meaning.
>
> —Paul Ricoeur, *Time and Narrative*

David Noble is an original and generative thinker. For more than five decades, his writings have offered us unparalleled insights into the U.S. nation and its collective imagination. Like most historians, he concerns himself with change over time, with what can be learned once we realize that part of "what things are" lies in "how they came to be." But Noble is not just interested in *what* we know, he also wants us to think about *how* we know. His analyses probe beneath surface appearances to reveal unexamined assumptions and uninterrogated ideologies embedded in the seemingly neutral terms and concepts that we use when we think about national history, national culture, and national belonging.

Noble shows how the dominant intellectual traditions of the United States have produced distinctly nationalist ways of knowing and thinking that have most often served the selfish interests of elites. He asks us to examine the forms of cognitive mapping that lead us to think of ourselves primarily as national citizens and national subjects, to understand the origins and implications of the enduring belief that our nation remains uniquely innocent and pure in a corrupt and degraded world, and to contemplate the contradictions that emerge when a bounded nation believes itself entitled to boundless markets. Although Noble's many and varied writings over the years have encompassed a dazzling range of subjects, his research coheres around a clear and consistent set of questions about the nation and knowledge.

Among his students and colleagues, Noble's remarkable life history and compelling personality sometimes overshadow the specificity of his ideas. He is a decent, kind, caring, and courageous person, someone deeply loved and respected by those who know him best. His admirers often marvel at the contradictions that make him so memorable. Noble is a World War II veteran who has spent more than fifty years courageously and consistently criticizing U.S. nationalism and military adventurism. He is a person of Irish and German ancestry who insists on recognizing the enduring role of anti-Catholic and anti-Semitic attitudes, actions, and ideas in national life. He is a heterosexual white male who has done as much as any other individual to call attention to the valuable ways of knowing that have emerged from feminist, critical race, and queer theory. He has been a university teacher since 1951, has published ten books and scores of articles, has delivered thousands of lectures, and has served as primary adviser on an astounding total of more than one hundred Ph.D. dissertations. Yet many of those who know him and his work best today are the most junior members of the profession, young scholars who view Noble as one of the few people in his generational cohort to remain intellectually and politically alert to the new possibilities emerging from contemporary contradictions and conflicts.

Although his unusual personal history and memorable qualities make David Noble interesting, they are not why he is important. His importance comes from his intellectual work, from the originality and power of his ideas. David Noble interrogates what others take for granted. He encourages us to question why we study history (and literature and politics) one nation at a time when we know full well that transnational networks across national boundaries play a huge role in determining the history that happens inside any one country. He asks us to think creatively about time, to understand that the conception of history as a linear developmental narrative of progress is itself a historical creation, a construct developed for particular purposes at a particular place by people with particular interests. The title of his popular history textbook, *The Free and the Unfree* (coauthored with Peter Carroll), reveals another central component of his method: the ability to see relationships where others see merely paradox. *The Free and the Unfree* not only reminds us that some Americans were not free but explains that their confinement was what made "freedom" possible for their oppressors. While many historians worry about the price we pay as a society for not knowing enough about the past, Noble is one of the few members of his profession who warn us about the dangers of basing too many of our hopes on an idealized view of the past, of forfeiting the fight for freedom to the mechanisms of memory.

Noble refuses to retreat intellectually or politically from his commitment to asking and answering hard questions about the nature of nationalism and its effects on people in the United States and around the world. He insists on seeing the nation as only one of many frameworks capable of providing a focus for social life and scholarly inquiry. Perhaps most important, his intellectual significance comes from his search for patterns in history, from his insistence on seeing the "big picture" that is obscured by narrow and specialized studies. By breaking with the standard conventions of professional historians (whose studies generally focus on limited time periods and carefully circumscribed spaces), Noble prods us to imagine what we might know if we could only free ourselves from our unreflective allegiance to traditional temporalities and spatialities.

Questioning core assumptions, as Noble's perspective demands from us, can be a difficult and daunting task. It is always easier to "add on" new evidence to familiar paradigms than to challenge the paradigms themselves. Moreover, as hard as it is to learn new ideas, it can be even harder to "unlearn" taken-for-granted assumptions, methods, and categories. Yet the serious circumstances we face today compel us to follow another path, to generate what Noble describes as "unpredictable creativity."

We can see everywhere in the world today where the old ways of thinking and being have led us. Every day, some thirty thousand children under the age of five die from malnutrition or from completely curable diseases. This adds up to nearly ten million a year, one every three seconds. The wealthiest 20 percent of the world's population controls 85 percent of the globe's wealth, leaving little more than 1 percent for the poorest fifth of the global population. More than one billion people around the world subsist on incomes of less than one dollar per day, and more than 125 million migrants and refugees now reside outside their countries of birth or citizenship.[1] In the United States, the poorest 60 percent of the population has experienced no gain in wealth over the past twenty years, while the richest 20 percent has experienced a 21 percent jump in income. The wealthiest tenth of U.S. families shared 85 percent of the three-trillion-dollar increase in the valuation of stocks between 1989 and 1997; the bottom 80 percent of households control less than 2 percent of the total value of equity holdings.

We now need new kinds of knowledge capable of preparing us for the national, subnational, transnational, and postnational circuits and networks that shape our shared social existence. Everything from the past is worth knowing; nothing from the past ever disappears completely. But past truths and truisms are never adequate for facing the foreboding future.

Noble's writings call our attention to the significance in U.S. history of "the metaphor of two worlds"—the idea of a radical contrast between an innocent and virtuous "America" and a corrupt and degraded outside world. Drawing on research by Sacvan Bercovitch and J. G. A. Pocock, Noble identifies the intellectual origins of the metaphor of two worlds in Europe, in Renaissance political theorist Machiavelli's distinction between the corruptions of time and the virtues of space. Early theorists of republicanism in Europe longed for a "timeless" and free space that might liberate them from the vices and corruptions of society that had built up over time. Noble shows how British settler colonialists and their descendants hoped that virtuous American space would provide them with an escape from European time. Noble thus proves that the idea of "American Exceptionalism"—of the United States as foundationally and fundamentally different from other nations—originated in Europe, not in the New World. But he then shows how this idea came to have a life of its own, how an ideological fiction became a "social fact" because it was the lens through which Euro-Americans viewed Native Americans and nature, capitalism and community, immigration and expansion.

The ideological and political desire to see "America" as a timeless space filled with virtue conflicted with the realities of conquest, settlement, and expansion. American land was not empty: it was populated by indigenous peoples whose relationships with the land went back thousands of years. Settlers did not really escape the corruptions of European time by moving to North America; instead, they brought those corruptions with them. Every time settlers moved westward and opened up new lands, they enacted the hope of living in a "timeless" space, but their very success ensured continued settlement and the eventual encroachment of European society on the new land. Westward (and later global) expansion thus served important ideological as well as economic and political purposes, but each advance of the frontier seemed to also offer evidence of a victory by corrupt time over virtuous space.

In *Death of a Nation,* Noble shows that European settlers viewed their battles with Native Americans not just as a conflict over land and natural resources, but as a clash of worldviews and epistemologies. America could not be a timeless space unless its natural environment was unspoiled; it could not offer an escape from European time if it was inhabited by people with history. The Europeans saw virtue in their decision to leave their homes and seek out the benefits of new spaces, while viewing Native Americans with contempt because they stayed at home and drew nourishment from familiar spaces. Europeans prided themselves on breaking with the world of their ancestors, on the ways in which the Renaissance, the Reformation, and the Age of Discovery enacted a fundamental rupture with feudal society in order to find the sacred in the future. They felt that this mapping of the past and future, this progressive and teleological trajectory, made them superior to Native Americans, who found the sacred by living in harmony with their ancestors. European Americans defined freedom as a release from the reciprocal relations and responsibilities they identified with feudalism. Native Americans, on the other hand, found fulfillment inside communities, not outside them.

European settlers in North America could not afford to view these differences as simple contrasts between two equally valid ways of knowing. They had to explain why the natural landscape of America that they hoped would free them had not given freedom to indigenous peoples. They solved their problem with yet more ideology, by describing Native Americans as underdeveloped, not fully human, and incapable of living in freedom. Anthropologist Eric Wolf describes this way of thinking as a distinction between "Europe and the People without History." This ideology not only explained why Native Americans had not derived freedom from the American landscape, it provided an ideological rationale for their extinction because a free society could only be created by people with history.

Noble is not the first scholar to notice the importance of the designation of non-Europeans as "people without history." But he makes an original and generative contribution in explaining how this concept continued to shape U.S. nationalism in subsequent centuries. He shows, for example, that to many nineteenth-century nationalists, southern and eastern European Catholics and Jews were also people without history and therefore subversive to freedom. The hierarchical structure of the Catholic church and the corporatism in its teachings, the persistence of collective Jewish life in the shtetls of Europe, and the prevailing structures of collective self-help and radical solidarity within the "new immigrant" communities reminded elite Anglo-Saxon Protestants of feudalism and enabled them to dress up their visceral anti-Semitism and anti-Catholicism in the more respectable cloak of ideological fidelity to national freedom.

In helping us see the ideological underpinnings of nineteenth-century nativism, Noble also enables us to understand Frederick Jackson Turner's famous 1893 frontier thesis (warning that the impending closing of the frontier threatened the future of freedom) to be at least as much a response to immigration on the East Coast as it was a reaction against the decline of new spaces for homesteading in the West. The increase in new immigrants and the decline in new homesteads both signaled to Turner that European time and its corruptions were encroaching on free American space. By imagining America as a bounded sacred space, the metaphor of two worlds gave ideological impetus and affective appeal to policies professing to protect the nation from alien outside forces.

Noble's understanding of the depth, reach, and scope of the metaphor of two worlds enables us to see beyond surface appearances. His analysis shows us, for example, how political positions that might seem diametrically opposed often share ideological and epistemological assumptions. Nineteenth-century imperialists wanted to expand America's sacred space overseas; anti-imperialists opposed them. But part of the anti-imperialist position stemmed from the fear that overseas expansion would bring even more "people without history" into the U.S. polity, while part of the imperialist position originated in despair that too many "people without history" were already on the North American continent and that American space could be saved only by making the whole world like the United States. Battles over making citizenship more or less restrictive, over increasing or decreasing the numbers of allowable legal immigrants, all still serve to maintain and strengthen the citizen/alien distinction. Abolitionist opposition to slavery designated slaves and slave owners as people without history, as products of feudal social relations. This position depended on denying the modern nature of slavery—its role in creating surpluses vital to the industrialization of

Europe and North America, its rebirth after the invention of the cotton gin. Abolitionists could thus oppose slavery, but absolve northern capital of its complicity with the slave system. They could argue for the abolition of slavery, but on terms that made black citizenship after slavery seem impossible—because they identified African Americans as people without history.

The very terms of political and intellectual debates become transformed because of Noble's refusal to confuse surface appearances with deeper truths. In *The End of American History*, he drew upon the writings of William Appleman Williams to identify and critique assumptions held in common during the cold war by the United States and the Soviet Union, by capitalists and anticapitalists. Whatever else divided these antagonists, they shared a joint epistemology, and in Noble's view an erroneous one. Marxists and capitalists could fight over the world because both believed that the spaces in which they were entitled to act embraced the entire globe. Russians and Americans could counter their national interests against each other, because both believed that allegiance to particular places proceeded at the level of the nation-state. Thinkers on the left and the right could battle over the trajectory of history because both defined time as the present as it would look to the future. Noble's question for us is not *which* of these two sides we support, but *why* we are faced with such a limited, uncreative, and unimaginative choice in the first place. Instead of replacing one national narrative with another, Noble argues that all nations employ some variant of exceptionalism, that nationalism is a transnational project, and that elites in most nations have more in common with each other than they have with the majority of their national populations.

In *Death of a Nation*, Noble shows how the national ideological project shaped the national aesthetic project, how the protection of the sacred and bounded space of America from outside influences permeates cultural production in the United States through persistent searching for idealized images of the national landscape. Through a dazzlingly erudite overview of diverse forms of American expressive culture over the centuries, Noble shows how the nation's cultural workers return again and again to the metaphor of two worlds. Yet he does not imbue this search with any "essence," does not give it any metaphysical priority in defining "what is an American." Instead, Noble insists that the search for a redemptive national landscape was a situated historical project, one that was always fraught with contradictions. The United States grounded its ideology in ideas about liberty, yet practiced slavery. National myths, symbols, and ideologies portrayed the United States as a bounded, sacred, and timeless space, yet actual social practice revolved around territorial expansion and the search for boundless markets.

By the 1940s, Noble argues, the nation could no longer contain the contradictions inherent in a bounded nation committed to boundless markets. Once the market became more sacred than the landscape, artists and intellectuals could no longer envision the nation as a space filled with virtue and free of corruption. The death of the national landscape undercut the political and aesthetic authority of those who had profited most from the metaphor of two worlds over the centuries. Conservatives and liberals alike tried to keep the paradigm alive; they tried to preserve through memory and elegiac nostalgia cultural artifacts from previous eras, when imagining America as a timeless space could be done without reference to the marketplace as sacred space. Academic American studies owes much of its early history and enduring curriculum to that effort. At the same time, liberals and conservatives joined forces from the onset of the cold war to the present to fashion a "countersubversive" political culture that deploys anticommunism, moral panic about deviancy, and religious and cultural chauvinism to create surrogate "people without history" and to obscure the fragmentation of social life engendered by the supremacy of market relations within U.S. society.

But Noble also points out that the collapse of the cultural authority of the national landscape has brought the experiences and ideas of suppressed and marginalized groups into greater visibility. What Immanuel Wallerstein calls the "forgotten people of modernity" have thrown forth a seemingly endless stream of artists, intellectuals, and cultural workers armed with rich cultural and intellectual resources uniquely suited for transcending the limits of the metaphor of two worlds.

The exclusionary mentality at the heart of the metaphor of two worlds never allowed for the full inclusion of people of color, women, sexual minorities, and other aggrieved and nonnormative groups into the ranks of national subjects. Constant barriers to citizenship rights, impediments to opportunities for asset accumulation, obstacles to the freedom to bargain over wages and working conditions, and limits on the exercise of cultural self-determination forced members of these groups to develop alternative epistemologies, archives, and imaginings with extraordinary utility for postnationalist ways of knowing and being.

David Noble knows there is important work to be done and that we have to do it. He knows that in asking for "unpredictable creativity" from historians he demands much of us. Perhaps it is the World War II veteran in him that knows that the hard way is the right way, that the ambush is always on the path of least resistance. But I think it is the intellectual in him, the careful reader, the calm and reflective thinker, who concluded that we cannot come to new and useful conclusions if we continue to use the same old inadequate and outworn methods.

Noble's kind of critical thinking resonates in my mind with the words of Buck O'Neill, a great player and manager in the Negro baseball leagues during the 1930s and 1940s. When St. Louis Cardinal outfielder Enos Slaughter was inducted into the Baseball Hall of Fame in Cooperstown, a St. Louis reporter wondered if O'Neill had a response. Slaughter was an above-average player, but also a confirmed white supremacist: he fought the entry of Jackie Robinson into major league baseball and once dug his spikes into Robinson's leg during a play at second base—what most observers believed was a clear intent to injure the first black player in the major leagues in the modern era. But O'Neill did not seem particularly agitated by Hall of Fame status for Slaughter. Grinning coyly, O'Neill said slowly to the reporter, "It's not like he was the *only* one."

O'Neill realized that it was pointless to criticize Slaughter as an individual when a much larger structure of racist exclusion kept O'Neill, Satchel Paige, Josh Gibson, and other greats out of the major leagues. Like Buck O'Neill, David Noble sees the big picture. He knows that it does not matter so much if we like this writer or that writer, this president or that president: first we have to ask questions about the larger intellectual, ideological, and social structures that guarantee that their actions and ideas are not simply the strengths or failings of one individual.

Death of a Nation is the culmination of a long and distinguished career, a senior scholar's effort to summarize the most important things he has learned. It registers with extraordinary and exact sensitivity the ways in which ideas about time, space, and history have shaped our understandings of—and our relationships to—the nation-state. Yet while it takes us back to the past, it does so primarily out of concern for the present and the future. It warns us about the dangers of confining the fight for freedom to matters of memory. It invites us to look beyond the categories of modernity, to become aware of the many different ways of knowing and being that would be available to us if we knew how to look for them. Most important, it requires us to look carefully at the things that are already being done and said (and painted and danced and sung) in the world right now, the things that contain seeds of the unpredictable creativity we are certain to need as we face the future.

Acknowledgments

Because I don't believe that the academic world is a new world of purity and objectivity segregated from an old world of society, one of corruption and subjectivity, I see this book, like all my others, as an outgrowth of my experience before and after I received my Ph.D. I want to express my gratitude to the many people who have participated in the construction of my intellectual identity. My grandmothers planted seeds of doubt in my mind about the metaphor of a European Old World and an American New World. My mothers, as they struggled to hold the family together in the 1930s, taught me that there were no self-made individuals. My Italian American friends from school and the African American friends with whom I worked in farming and in construction helped me change my social values. In the army, a friend, Sam Notkin, introduced me to socialist theory. My deceased wife, Lois, helped me sustain hope during 1943 and 1944. A sophomore in college when I started Princeton University, she taught me how to focus and clarify my writing. She was an invaluable adviser for my senior thesis and doctoral dissertation; she was an intellectual companion and a skillful editor. Her generosity in these areas continued through the writing of my books in the 1950s, 1960s, and 1970s.

At Princeton University two young professors, Jeter Isely and Tom Pressley, offered me friendship and helped me with my writing. I was also inspired there by the teaching of E. Harris Harbison. At the University of Wisconsin, my fellow graduate student, William Appleman Williams, kept reminding me that the narratives we historians write always are informed by our values. Along with Carl Becker, he has been the greatest influence on my life as a historian.

During the 1950s at the University of Minnesota, I was influenced by the dissertation of an American studies graduate student, Roland Van Zandt. He criticized the symbol-myth scholars for their belief that individuals can step outside of culture. This was a belief that, for him, structured their narratives about the separation of an America, although populated by European Americans, from Europe. His dissertation was not accepted by the faculty, but he had it privately published in 1959 as *The Metaphysical Foundations of American History.* Many other American studies graduate students in the 1950s also helped me to identify the paradigmatic boundaries that had been established in American civilization programs during the 1930s.

In the history department of the University of Minnesota, Hy Berman and I discussed the underlying assumptions of the consensus historians who were our contemporaries. Hy made a major contribution to my analysis and critique of those assumptions. Our conversations have continued to the present. Peter Carroll pushed me in the direction of multiculturalism in the late 1960s, and we have remained intellectual companions, friends, and coauthors since then. As I became interested in modern nationalism, I was fortunate to find a number of graduate students in history and American studies who shared that interest, and I have learned much from their research. Those who have worked with me during the past ten years are, in history, Richard Nelson, Nan Enstad, Jon Davidann, Paul Barclay, and Mark Soderstrom; and, in American studies, Esther Romeyn, Erik Peterson, Tony Smith, Carla Bates, Mark Hulsether, Frieda Knobloch, Karen Murphy, Robert Schultz, April Schultz, Polly Fry, Elizabeth Anderson, David Pulsipher, Randy Hanson, Andy Walzer, Randy Rodriguez, Bill Anthes, Brett Mizelle, Deirdre Murphy, Adam Pagan, Gaye Johnson, Adrian Gaskins, and Carter Meland. These students, who are also colleagues, help me understand how much I am part of a paradigmatic community. This also is the major gift of two colleagues who have left Minnesota, George Lipsitz and Dave Roediger.

In the American Studies Program, which has been my institutional home since 1984, my friend Lary May has shared my belief that the 1940s were a revolutionary decade, and his conversations and writing have been crucial to the development of my views about the paradigmatic changes in that decade. Another colleague, Elaine May, has written about the dramatic cultural changes that characterized the 1950s. Beyond her academic contributions, her friendship gave me invaluable support during the terminal illness of my wife Lois. This support also was true of another colleague, Riv-Ellen Prell, whose important scholarship focuses on the problems of cultural nationalism for Jews in the United States. The American Studies Program at Minnesota has changed from one that had only adjunct faculty to one with both adjunct and core faculty. Our core represents a rich cultural diversity, and these colleagues have contributed a wonderful environment for me as I began to imagine this book. These new colleagues—Brenda Child, Carol Miller, Kathy Choy, Jennifer Pierce, and Rod Ferguson—also provide links to the confederation of American studies with American Indian studies, Afro-American studies, Chicano studies, and women's studies. I have cotaught with the chair of American studies, Jean O'Brien, who studies the history of Native Americans. This has been a wonderful learning experience for me.

In the 1980s as Lois's health failed, our daughter, Patricia Noble-Olson, took over editorial responsibility for my writing. Sharing a house with her family has helped me understand the culture of global capitalism. She and her husband, Michael, and their children, Matthew, Joshua, and Ella, hold a strong ecological critique of the vision of a boundless marketplace, and all have a strong sense of social justice. Matt has done important editorial work for this book.

My wife Gail has been a participant in American studies at Minnesota since 1966. At the University of Minnesota she has taught courses on the literatures of the United States. I cannot express how much I have learned from our conversations about the paradigmatic crises in American studies, particularly in literary studies. Her dissertation focused on the revolution in theories of general education that found educational theorists in the 1950s rejecting the educational theories of the 1930s. We have been able, therefore, to share our understandings of what the larger intellectual and political ramifications of that paradigm revolution were. She has been both a contributor to and a critic of this book, and she has done indispensable editorial work throughout the entire length of this project.

INTRODUCTION
Space Travels

In 2000, a collection of essays titled *Post-Nationalist American Studies* was published. The contributors understood themselves to be participants in a scholarly revolution that, for them, had begun in the 1960s. At that point, American studies as an academic discipline was only thirty years old. The 1960s revolutionists, as the contributors saw them in 2000, were rejecting elders who "justified American exceptionalism" and "rarely challenged the assumption that the nation-state was the proper unit of analysis for understanding American experience."[1] This unusable past, for the current writers about the field, was built on the erroneous tradition begun by the men who led the American Revolution in 1776. The intellectual legacy from the political founders of the nation in 1789 to the men who founded American studies in the 1930s was "their conviction that the United States marked a break from the history of Europe, specifically the history of feudalism, class stratification, imperialism, and war."[2]

But this metaphor of two worlds, an American New World and a European Old World, had lost much of its persuasiveness by the 1960s, and American studies scholars could, then, see that class stratification was a major characteristic of the new nation. Postnationalist scholars also argued that class inequities had been obscured by the gender and racial prejudices of Washington's generation. For the political leaders of the 1790s, the inherent intellectual weakness of women required that men accept patriarchal leadership of their childlike wives and daughters. The inherent intellectual weakness of African Americans and Native Americans also required that white men accept patriarchal leadership of these inferior and childlike peoples. For Washington, Jefferson, and Madison, therefore, citizenship needed to be the exclusive privilege of white males, who alone were capable of rational maturity.[3]

And when scholars such as Ralph Gabriel, Perry Miller, and F. O. Matthiessen created the new academic discipline of American studies in the 1930s, they continued to share the vision of an American New World free from the class hierarchy of the European Old World. These founding fathers, like those of the 1790s, continued to define American citizens, those who had meaningful agency, as white males. Their story of American exceptionalism would not examine the history of women or Native Americans or African Americans because such an analysis would reveal that power, imperialism, and war had not been left behind in the Old World.[4]

The younger scholars of the 1960s who were rejecting their elders—the historians and literary critics who created American studies in the 1930s and 1940s—could no longer ignore the warfare that the European invaders of North America had used to establish beachheads along the Atlantic coast. They could not ignore the constant warfare that the descendants of those invaders, Euro-Americans, had used to expand those beachheads until by 1880, they had conquered all of the homelands of the American Indians from the Atlantic to the Pacific. Nor could they continue to ignore the imperialism that forcibly moved millions of Africans to the New World to work as slaves and enrich their white masters. This was not the history of liberty as the exodus from the oppressive Old World of Europe to the freedom of the New World of America.[5]

I see my book *Death of a Nation: American Culture and the End of Exceptionalism* as part of the ongoing development of postnationalist American studies. I believe I can add to the conversation by focusing on the definitions of spaces—geographic and cultural—that were used by the nationalist American studies scholars from the 1930s to the 1960s. I will then contrast these definitions with those used by the members of the postnationalist American studies movement. It is my argument that the nationalist scholars were not self-conscious of their definitions of geographic and cultural space because they believed that their culture was created by nature. It is also my argument that many postnationalist scholars are not self-conscious of how their alternative definitions of space represent what Thomas Kuhn, in his book *The Structure of Scientific Revolutions* (1961), called a paradigm revolution. Kuhn argued that scientific communities cluster around paradigms—hypotheses—about the nature of reality. Members of these communities, accepting the reality of these paradigms, then proceed to solve problems defined by their shared hypotheses. Kuhn calls this process of problem solving normal science. But since, for him, no hypotheses can exhaust reality, researchers experience anomalies that contradict their paradigms. As these anomalies accumulate, members of a community begin to have a crisis of faith in their fundamental hypotheses. When doubt becomes widespread, members of these paradigmatic communities, especially younger people, are willing to listen to prophetic voices that offer alternative hypotheses about the nature of reality. If enough people convert to a new vision, a new community forms. This, according to Kuhn, is a moment of revolutionary science. That moment, however, will be followed by a period of normal science as members, acting as if their new hypotheses were reality, begin to solve puzzles defined by their shared hypotheses.[6]

As a participant in the postnationalist American studies community, I am concerned that my younger colleagues—and almost all my colleagues are younger because I was born in 1925—continue to define the dramatic differences in attitudes toward space that separate them from the founders of American studies in the 1930s in national terms. They see the tradition of American exceptionalism that stretches from Washington and Jefferson to Perry Miller and F. O. Matthiessen as a nationalist tradition, now bankrupt, particular to the United States. I will argue, however, that the tradition of American exceptionalism is a variation on a transatlantic bourgeois definition of modern nations as the embodiments of a state of nature.

International

Let us, therefore, examine the implicit attitudes toward space contained in the tradition of nationalism that stretched from George Washington to Perry Miller. From my perspective, when the creators of the United States in the 1780s saw their nation as the opposite of "feudalism, class stratification, imperialism, and war," they were working within the tradition of the Enlightenment developed first by the middle classes in Europe. The metaphor of two worlds for European middle classes about 1750 was the medieval Old World and a modern New World. In this metaphor of two worlds the medieval world represented a pattern of complex traditions created by human imagination. But the New World represented the simple laws of nature to be discovered by human reason. And reason was the attribute of individuals, while imagination was the attribute of groups. Between 1770 and 1830, as Benedict Anderson has argued in his *Imagined Communities* (1983), middle classes on both sides of the Atlantic were defining themselves as citizens rather than subjects. Subjects were aristocrats and peasants who were trapped within the irrational cultural boundaries of their classes. But citizens were individuals who used their reason.[7]

When middle-class Anglo-Americans in 1776 rejected the English king, they rejected their identities as subjects. Now citizens, they could escape the artificial worlds of the aristocratic and peasant classes and achieve a classless and artless relationship with nature. But this, of course, was also the vision of the French middle classes in their revolution of the 1790s. And it would be the vision of the English middle classes as they made a gradual and peaceful revolution toward self-definition as citizens. This transition was true of all middle classes in all the emerging modern nations.

Paradoxically the middle classes in each modern nation saw their individual and rational relationship with nature as exceptional. Every other nation was characterized by an artful group mentality. The universal state of nature imagined by the philosophers of the Enlightenment had contracted to become the foundation of each modern nation, a particular state of nature protected by the political boundaries of every modern nation. All the modern nations, therefore, saw themselves as isolated and autonomous states of nature. Their cultures had grown out of their national landscapes, those virgin lands whose naturalness and purity were protected by national political boundaries.

Benedict Anderson contradicted this bourgeois paradigm in his *Imagined Communities* by denying that it represented a timeless reality. Instead he defined it as a human creation, comparable to the traditions of the medieval world that the bourgeoisie had rejected in the eighteenth century because they were merely human creations. Bourgeois historians had played a major role in creating a modern isolated England, or France, or Argentina, or Brazil, or United States. History writing from the late nineteenth century until after the 1940s was primarily nationalist. Bourgeois historians who controlled academic history in all the modern nations focused on what was exceptional about their nations or about other nations. Guarding the boundaries of their paradigmatic communities, they defined the history of Karl Marx as an irresponsible and foolish heresy. Marx was arguing by 1840 that a transnational bourgeois culture existed and that historians should explore the cultural, political, and economic commonalties that linked bourgeois nations.

In the next chapter I will focus on the historians George Bancroft, Frederick Jackson Turner, and Charles and Mary Beard. I will argue that from the 1830s to the 1940s these historians, the most influential theorists of their particular generations, defined the United States as a unique state of nature whose cultural virginity needed to be kept isolated from the rest of the world, which because it was not in harmony with nature, dwelled in darkness. I believe that Anderson's book, like that of Thomas Kuhn, attracted great scholarly attention because Anderson, although only implicitly, was expressing a paradigm revolution. He and his readers could no longer believe that modern nations represented the end of history. They could no longer accept a normal science whose puzzle solving explored the timeless exceptionalism of each nation. In my book I will argue that the events of World War II broke what I call the aesthetic authority of bourgeois nationalism. The bourgeois elites in the United States and in the other major industrial nations converted during the 1940s from a self-conscious isolation to a self-conscious internationalism. They converted from seeing their nations as expressions of the state of nature to seeing the international marketplace as the state of nature.

I will analyze in subsequent chapters the U.S. historians, literary critics, artists and art critics, musicians and music critics, architects and architectural critics, and the philosophers who had the authority to define the national culture of the United States in the 1930s. They, like the men who constructed American studies in that decade, were certain that their national culture had grown out of the national landscape. They were employing, therefore, the state-of-nature anthropology developed by the European middle classes between the Renaissance and the Enlightenment. Because only bourgeois citizens had the rationality to achieve harmony with nature, it was the responsibility of bourgeois intellectuals to guard the purity of the natural, national culture from unnatural cultures. Any culture coming from outside the nation was unnatural because it was the product of human imagination rather than of reason. It had not grown out of a state of nature. This was also true of the cultures of the American Indians. Their cultures were not American because they were products of group imagination rather than of individual reason. Irrational group cultures had always kept Indians from being in harmony with nature. This was why Native Americans were not part of the American people discussed by Gabriel, Miller, and Matthiessen in the 1930s.

I will also argue that this paradigmatic definition of reality disintegrated so rapidly in the 1940s and 1950s because the bourgeois paradigm in the United States and other modern nations had been unstable from the moment that bourgeois nations succeeded traditional cultures in Europe and the Americas. The bourgeoisie were imagining bounded nations built on the foundation of static nature, on the foundation of a timeless space. But the bourgeoisie were also committed to the constant expansion of a boundless marketplace. From the 1830s to the 1930s bourgeois intellectuals and artists in all the modern nations had to fit the crucial importance of international trade for their countries within the paradigm that asked them to do a normal science, to solve problems, which demonstrated how their nations were autonomous and isolated from international influences.

Anomalies, contradictions to the paradigm of national autonomy, had been accumulating for the century that stretched from the 1830s to the 1930s. As I will point out, bourgeois elites in many countries, including the United States, had tried to deal with these anomalies by experimenting with international paradigms from the 1880s to World War I. But the two decades from 1920 to 1940 saw renewed efforts on both sides of the Atlantic to repress these experiments and return to the fundamentalism of the 1830s, the absolute autonomy of the timeless nation. Then, in the 1940s, not only did political, economic, and military elites reject this fundamentalism and return to the pre-1920 experiments in internationalism, but so did many of the artistic and intellectual elites.

I believe, therefore, that it is this dramatic rejection of the definition of modern nations as expressions of a state of nature that caused the disintegration of the nationalist school of American studies. I believe that Anderson's book found a wide audience in the 1980s because so many scholars shared his thesis that the modern nation was a cultural creation rather than a timeless space.

During the 1940s and 1950s many students of the men who defined American studies in the 1930s did not search for an alternative paradigm but, instead, developed a nostalgic, even elegiac scholarship committed to preserving the memory of the period 1830–1850, when, for them, there had briefly existed an autonomous and natural, national culture. As a colleague of two of these men, Henry Nash Smith and Leo Marx, at the

University of Minnesota in the 1950s and 1960s, I witnessed their sadness, even their pain, when they were confronted by graduate students who did not want to worship at Emerson's tomb. These students were the heirs of the paradigm revolution of the 1940s. Isolation no longer seemed normal to them. They were in the process of replacing state-of-nature anthropology with the cultural anthropology that began to be constructed during the period of international experimentation at the end of the nineteenth century. This meant that they could no longer define traditional cultures as unnatural. Culture was seen as a necessary and natural space for human beings. And culture as a dynamic space-time continuum could not be contained within a nation's borders; it could not be kept from flowing across national boundaries. Postnationalist American studies scholars, then, can no longer imagine that national political boundaries coincide with national cultural boundaries. They also cannot make a distinction between an "authentic rational" national culture and "inauthentic, irrational cultures" that exist within a nation's political boundaries. The American studies leaders of the 1930s were necessarily monoculturists because they believed in that distinction between authentic and inauthentic cultures. Postnationalist American studies scholars are necessarily multiculturists because they see all cultures as authentic. This acceptance of all cultures as authentic was the major cause for the tension between Smith and Marx and a number of graduate students. Nationalist American studies scholars had no interest in the popular culture that developed in the cities of the Northeast and Midwest at the end of the nineteenth century. African American music and the vaudeville and movies created by Catholics and Jews represented cultures that had not sprung from the national landscape. Instead, they represented "inauthentic" cultures created by imagination in Africa and Europe—cultures that had no roots in the nature revealed to rational citizens. But graduate students in the 1960s wanted to write dissertations about what they saw as American urban cultures that had given meaning to their lives.

In the remainder of this introduction I will engage in a series of guesses about why, when I became an undergraduate at Princeton University in February 1945 and a graduate student at the University of Wisconsin in February 1948, I doubted the authority of the major literary critics and historians of the 1930s. These doubts later caused me to distance myself from my colleagues in American studies at the University of Minnesota, whom I joined in 1952. I could not write elegies for Emerson and his generation of male Anglo-American artists and intellectuals.

I start with a brief autobiography because I have rejected the state-of-nature anthropology that says an individual can stand apart from that which he observes, that a rational male can be a neutral observer. In contrast, embracing cultural anthropology, I understand myself as a participant-observer who is concerned not only with the true, but also with the good and beautiful. As a child I had been confused by the metaphor of two worlds—a timeful Europe, where conventions and traditions entrapped the individual, and an America, where the individual could be free from those oppressive conventions. I was born in 1925 on a dairy farm just outside of Princeton, New Jersey. My father identified his name, "Noble," with ancestors who came from England before the American Revolution. It was the racial heritage of Northern European Protestants, I learned, which made me an "American."

When I reached college and graduate school, I would find American history textbooks that reassured me that I was part of a uniform and classless white Protestant American people. But this had not been my childhood experience. I was becoming aware that it was so much easier to guard the boundaries of an isolated America and its homogeneous people in the abstractions of print than it was in daily experience. When I was five I began kindergarten in Princeton Township School. The school was situated on the northern edge of the town to make it possible for the majority of students to walk to class. The streets containing Italian Americans were zoned as part of the township. My family informed me that I had the responsibility of sustaining the boundaries that defined me as an authentic American and that defined the majority of my fellow students as, for my family, eternal foreigners. Italian Americans were about 75 percent of my school population, and I felt the need to become friends with boys such as Frank Schiavone, Angelo Cinereno, and Nick Diaforli. And my best friend was Antonio Luccarelli, who immigrated from Italy when we were nine.

As I came to have some perspective on the whole town, the task given me by my father to imagine myself as part of the authentic uniform and classless national culture began to seem impossible. Princeton, a town of eight thousand in the 1930s, had one grade school, Princeton Country Day, for rich boys and another grade school, Miss Fine's, for rich girls. My father taught me that the rich, even if they were Anglo-Protestants, were not really American. But the rich were visible in the town and in the estates that surrounded our farm. In the town there also was a Catholic grade school, a white public school, and a black public school because New Jersey had legal segregation until after World War II.

My problem with borders intensified when my mother began, about 1935, to allow me to go to the movies in Trenton with our black farm workers. I was aware of the extralegal patterns of racial segregation, such as those that separated whites on the ground floor of movie theaters from blacks in the balconies. I understood the risks that our workers were taking when they entered the theater with me and smuggled me up to the balcony. Ironically, much of my questioning of my father's boundaries was inspired by his mother and my mother's mother. My father's mother lived with us on the farm. She wanted to be called Armagh for the Irish county her parents had fled in the 1840s. Born in the United States in 1850, she made me feel that the landscape of the Old World was more enchanting than that of the New World. She wanted to teach me Celtic songs and to admire the Celtic heroes who had fought the English. My mother's parents came from Germany in 1880, and her mother lived in the United States for half a century, refusing to learn a word of English. I was told that in 1914 she had sold her few jewels and sent the money to Germany to support the war effort there. She, too, found it more fulfilling to live in the memories of the Old World.

But the masculine story was that of the American New World as an environment of peace and plenty in contrast to Europe as a world of war and poverty. I was informed that my German grandfather had fled Germany to avoid conscription and that he had prospered in the United States. By 1935, however, I was also aware that our farm was in economic trouble. After 1937 we could no longer afford to heat the house. In 1940 the farm was foreclosed. My father was now terminally ill with stomach cancer. In poverty, however, we could not afford morphine to ease his pain.

I escaped poverty in 1943, when, after graduating from high school in June, I entered the Army on July 2. When I arrived in my first Army camp in Texas, I had another lesson in cultural complexity. A high fence separated white soldiers from black soldiers, and we were told that we were not to fraternize with black American soldiers. But in our white section there were German prisoners of war, and we were encouraged to fraternize with them. My infantry division went to Europe in the fall of 1944 to fight the German army. I was discharged at the end of 1944, and, with national economic resources, I was able to start Princeton University in February 1945. I decided to major in history with a focus on the United States because so many of the truths about the nation that I was taught as a child had turned out to be untruths.

But many of the paradigmatic patterns I found in my history texts were very similar to those I had learned from my father. The American people were male Anglo-Protestants or Northern European Protestants. One could see this was true because all our presidents were descendants of such people. Fortunately I found a way to organize my doubts about this story when I took a course on the Enlightenment. There I read Carl Becker's *The Heavenly City of the Eighteenth-Century Philosophers* (1932). I think I embraced Becker so enthusiastically because his argument that the eighteenth-century philosophers were men of faith spoke to my youthful experience. My father had given me a set of hypotheses about the nature of reality. One of those hypotheses was that the United States was a promised land of perpetual peace and prosperity. The failure of that prophecy was more painful for him than it was for me. He was bewildered by the Great Depression. I started college, therefore, as someone who had experienced a paradigm crisis, and I was searching for new hypotheses.[8]

Implicitly Becker was rejecting the state-of-nature anthropology held by the eighteenth-century bourgeois intellectuals. Implicitly he was arguing from the position of cultural anthropology that we always perceive from within a pattern of cultural assumptions about the nature of reality. Implicitly he was arguing the inevitable existence of the kind of patterns Kuhn suggested thirty years later in his *The Structure of Scientific Revolutions.*

The adviser for my senior thesis was Eric Goldman, a specialist on what was called the Progressive Era in American history. I knew that Goldman was a Jew who had not been able to find an academic job before World War II. Toward the end of the war he had been hired by Princeton University to help obscure its long institutional history of anti-Semitism. Coming to the Progressive Era with Becker's interpretation of the Enlightenment in mind, I found that the most powerful paradigm being used by historians was that the late nineteenth century was characterized by a revolution in higher education in which the authority of Protestantism was replaced by the authority of science. The principles of the Enlightenment had triumphed. An age of religion had been replaced by an age of reason.

Goldman had suggested that I do my senior thesis on the *New Republic* magazine, founded in 1914. I analyzed the editorial policy of the magazine between 1914 and 1920. The patterns that emerged for me were a set of millennial expectations. The United States was moving from a history of chaos and confusion to one of harmony and order. And the editors were willing to expand this marvelous exodus to the whole world because they saw World War I as a revolutionary moment that was purging a corrupt and complex Old World and establishing a virtuous and simple New World. All of these expectations had crashed by 1920, and the editors had no meaningful paradigm to provide a coherent editorial policy in the 1920s.

I started graduate school, therefore, at Wisconsin in February 1948 as a nonbeliever in the view of the Progressive Era as a period characterized by a transition from faith to reason. I decided to do my dissertation on a number of the major male Anglo-American intellectuals who were leaders during the Progressive Era in a variety of fields—psychology, sociology, economics, philosophy, and history. My puzzle solving was based on my hypothesis that they, like the editors of the *New Republic,* were men of faith who created a set of expectations between the 1890s and World War I, expectations that crashed in 1919. My senior thesis was published in article form in 1951 as "The New Republic and the Idea of Progress, 1914–1920." My dissertation was published in 1958 as *The Paradox of Progressive Thought.* The paradox I saw was that these American intellectuals imagined that they were moving forward in order to return to a state of nature.[9]

I was now very interested in the persuasiveness of a vision of timeless space for the male Anglo-Americans who had dominated the definition of American national culture. This interest led me to my second book, *Historians against History* (1965). Here I analyzed the paradigm employed by a series of major historians from George Bancroft in 1830 to Daniel Boorstin in the 1960s to describe America (the United States) as unique and natural space separated from the complexity of the artificial patterns of culture that existed in Europe. In 1968 I published *The Eternal Adam and the New World Garden.* Comparing the narratives of the major historians with those of the major male Anglo-American novelists, I found that a number of Bancroft's contemporaries—James Fenimore Cooper,

Nathaniel Hawthorne, Herman Melville, and Henry James—were self-consciously rejecting the hypothesis that the American nation was nature's nation. They were rejecting the two-world metaphor of a European culture based on time and an American culture based on space.[10]

As I taught American studies and was in conversation with graduate students who were interested in many aspects of various American cultures, I gained the confidence to discuss how men and women from the dominant Anglo-American culture were responding to a crisis of space at the end of the nineteenth century. In *The Progressive Mind* (1970) I argued that intellectuals and artists in the dominant culture could, by 1880, no longer believe that the United States was simply nature's nation. They looked instead at a new urban-industrial space as one that provided a way to escape artful and complex cultural patterns and achieve an artless, rational, and virtuous relationship with the laws of nature. I looked at both a variety of social scientists and a variety of painters, musicians, and architects. I was aware that this paradigm of an urban-industrial space that embodied the rationality of the Enlightenment transcended national boundaries.[11]

While I had been deconstructing the paradigm of hegemonic male Anglo-American culture in the 1950s and 1960s, the voices of other American cultures began to be heard in the academic world. In the late 1960s, Peter Carroll was hired by the history department of the University of Minnesota to teach colonial history. A generation younger than I am, Peter, as a graduate student in the 1960s, had felt the disintegration of the male Anglo-American ability to monopolize national identity. In 1970 he asked me if I was interested in writing a multicultural American history textbook. Our first effort, *The Restless Centuries,* was published in 1973. Our second effort, *The Free and the Unfree,* was first published in 1977. We were implicitly working with the paradigm that all cultures that existed within the political boundaries of the United States were authentic American cultures whose voices must be heard in the conversations about national identity. Implicitly we had separated cultural identity from the bourgeois concept of a state of nature. We, therefore, could not make a distinction between rational and irrational cultures.[12]

While working in the 1970s to uncover the histories of American peoples that had been repressed for so long by the dominant male Anglo-Protestant culture, Peter and I became aware that the revolution of the 1940s was transnational. Middle-class elites in European countries had lost their ability to repress the histories of the peoples they had colonized in Asia, Africa, Australia, and New Zealand. They had also lost the ability to repress the variety of local cultures that existed within their national boundaries. Reading J. G. A. Pocock's *The Machiavellian Moment* (1975) now gave me a language to relate the crisis of American national space with the crises of national spaces in a Canada, England, or France. Those crises of national spaces in the 1940s had dissolved the sacredness of the homogeneous peoples who were supposed to have emerged from national landscapes as particular expressions of the state of nature.[13]

Pocock argued that the republicanism that appeared in Renaissance Italy related republican virtue to timeless space and monarchical corruption to time as the environment of ephemeral tradition. He described the spread of this dualism to England and the English colonies. He concluded his book with a discussion of my colleague Henry Nash Smith. For Pocock, Smith's analysis of an American myth of exceptional national virtue rooted in a virgin land was a latter-day expression of Machiavelli's distinction between virtuous space and corrupt time.

I had studied all of Carl Becker's writing when I did my doctoral dissertation. I learned that he had explicitly identified the Progressive movement with the Enlightenment and he had identified World War I as a moment when Enlightenment rationality would triumph over irrational traditions. When he tried to understand why his prophecy and that of so many of his colleagues had failed, he, like many of them, looked at the role of capitalism. For Becker, capitalism was irrational. He had looked, at first, at medieval Europe as the major source of irrationality, but now, in 1919, he had to take a new, modern force, capitalism, into account as the major source of irrationality in human affairs.

capitalism.

Now Pocock was telling me that English republicans in the eighteenth century had identified capitalism with timeful chaos. They had made a distinction between virtuous private property, which was rooted in land, in the realm of immutable natural law, and the corrupt private property of capitalism, which freely floated across the expanse of nature and scorned rootedness. Committed to a boundless marketplace, capitalism would not be disciplined by the bounded laws of nature.

I believed I now could explain what happened to the writers of American history during the 1940s. A colleague, Gene Wise, had discussed with me the possibility of using Kuhn's model of paradigm revolution to clarify the destruction of the reputations of "Progressive" historians such as Charles Beard and Vernon Louis Parrington in the 1940s. His analysis, *American Historical Explanations,* was published in 1973 and described the way counterprogressive historians had gained cultural leadership by the 1950s. But Pocock's book made clear what Wise and I had not been clear about in 1970. Progressive historians, as isolationists, had used republican theory to criticize capitalism. Counterprogressive historians embraced capitalism when they embraced internationalism, and they renounced the vision of the United States as a particular expression of timeless natural laws.[14]

I wanted to use Pocock, therefore, to make explicit what had somehow remained only implicit for most historians who taught the history of the United States—that the acceptance of a new paradigm describing the United States as a nation with a capitalist culture contradicted the paradigm of American exceptionalism. I hoped to accomplish this with my 1985 book, *The End of American History.* I had just finished writing this book when Benedict Anderson's *Imagined Communities* (1983) was published. It was very exciting for me to speculate about the relationship between Pocock and Anderson. Pocock had focused on English and Anglo-American republicans and how they were employing themes of space to distinguish themselves from their enemies and to justify their political positions. Anderson, however, spoke about a middle class that originated in Europe but whose culture had spread across the Atlantic. He was interested in the construction of a model of bourgeois nationalism, roughly 1770–1830, that imagined modern nations as spaces in which each citizen would be in harmony with every other citizen. Anderson emphasized that it was technological developments that made possible an economy of print capitalism. And it was this print capitalism that made it possible for bourgeois elites to imagine that every citizen was reading the same words in newspapers and books, that every citizen was a participant in a homogeneous and rational culture.[15]

But Anderson did not emphasize the deep relationship of this homogeneous cultural space to the state-of-nature philosophy that the bourgeoisie had been developing since the Renaissance. Nor did he speculate about the motives, the passions, that were driving the bourgeoisie to want to use print capitalism as the foundation for a culture of uniform citizens. Anderson saw his bourgeois nationalists rejecting the authority of universal religions and diverse local cultures. He did not, however, focus on how state-of-nature philosophy could be used to destroy the legitimacy of those cultures. In contrast, Pocock was aware of why republicans would want to use state-of-nature philosophy to destroy the tradition of generational continuity that gave legitimacy to monarchy. I wanted to use Anderson to go beyond Pocock's Anglo-American focus and discuss the tradition of American exceptionalism as a particular expression of transnational bourgeois culture. But I wanted to use Pocock to give richness and depth to Anderson's relatively flat hypothesis about the origins of bourgeois nationalism.

I was beginning in the late 1980s to think about what has become this book. But it has taken me a long time to complete the project. First I experienced two major family tragedies, and then I had a joyful experience. Writing was, for some time, out of the question. But as I connected the revolution of the 1940s with the growing discussion of globalization in the 1990s, I felt confident that I could construct a powerful argument that linked the aesthetic authority of the international marketplace to the collapse of the aesthetic authority of the national landscape during World War II. Modern nations as sacred spaces had been replaced by the sacred space of a universal marketplace. The bourgeois culture that began to imagine a state of nature during the Renaissance and Reformation as a utopia beyond time had not died when the modern nation no longer seemed to represent the end of history. Instead, bourgeois elites since the 1940s have transformed that hope of transcending history as an unpredictable flow of time to the global marketplace. For the middle classes, that marketplace now represents the end of history.

From the Renaissance to the present, then, much of the cultural creativity of the middle classes has gone into constructing timeless spaces. To desacralize the medieval world in which the bourgeoisie felt trapped, they invented a state of nature. In the middle-class state-of-nature anthropology, rational male individuals had once lived in harmony with immutable laws of nature. The middle classes could escape from the profane societies of Western Europe by returning to a state of nature, and suddenly they were presented with a New World. Imaginatively leaving the cultural complexity of home, the bourgeoisie had discovered the Americas as a symbolic expression of the state of nature.

When the English began their invasions of North America, they found the anomaly of the indigenous peoples, who, in their eyes, were trapped like medieval Catholics and Jews within traditions and conventions that were the product of the human imagination. The indigenous peoples of North America imagined themselves living at home. Exile was the ultimate punishment. But the English settlers had fled from home. They feared that they might be forced to stay within existing boundaries. For Native Americans, one gained physical and spiritual nourishment from living in a particular place. For those who had chosen to flee England, physical and spiritual nourishment had not been available in the particular places they had inhabited in England. Indians believed that their ancestors were in harmony with a sacred. This sacred was passed down from generation to generation. In contrast to this sense of generational continuity, the English Protestants had redefined the sacreds passed down from generation to generation in the medieval world by Catholics and Jews as profane. Escaping the elders, the young adults would find the sacred in the future. Native peoples in North America believed the individual was fulfilled by his or her reciprocal relations with the extended family, which was the foundation of community. The English wanted to liberate the individual from the medieval web of reciprocal relationships and from those relationships in Indian cultures.

The Indians believed their communities, based on generational cycles of birth, death, and rebirth, were interrelated with a physical nature that was also characterized by such generational cycles. For them, society and nature were not in opposition, as they were for the modern English. The individual received the good, true, and beautiful by participating within the circle of the community and within the circle of nature. But the Protestants and republicans of early modern Europe were condemning the generational patterns of Judaism, of the Roman Catholic church, of the aristocracy, of the peasants as unnatural. The alternative to the generational patterns of medieval society was a physical nature that was not generational. And this, of course, was the basis for the modern European dismissal of American Indian "superstitions." Any history Indians had in North America was, like the medieval past in Europe, unusable.

Property in the medieval world was placed within the context of families who lived in particular places from generation to generation. But a new form of agriculture was being established in England. A farmer imagined that his land was private property. Individuals could buy and sell private property without considering any impact on a web of reciprocal relationships with relatives or the local community. This vision of private property already characterized the imagination of urban merchants. It was impossible within medieval values to sacralize this new concept of private property, in which an individual could ignore the generational continuity of families and dissociate property from a particular community and a particular place. This also was a definition of property that contradicted the sacred communal relationships that American Indians had to the land. It was the intention of this small agricultural and urban middle class, then, to define the sacreds of traditional societies in Europe and in North America as profane.[16]

From the Renaissance and Reformation until the end of the eighteenth century, however, middle classes in Western Europe were unable to move rapidly to purge traditional political, economic, and cultural patterns from the landscape. In the English colonies, Indians fiercely resisted the expansion of English beachheads. Until the American Revolution, there was a balance of military power between the invaders and the defenders. The purging of traditional cultural patterns was so slow that bourgeois elites had not yet developed the art form of modern historical writing—the art form that would celebrate the physical exodus from an Old to a New World. But men of the middle class had already constructed a physics and a landscape painting that made possible a psychic exodus to a New World. As individuals they had escaped medieval "superstition." They could be rational and objective in their private lives. Using that rationality, they saw beyond the artful patterns of the human imagination. Using telescopes and microscopes, they saw the state of nature. Men like Isaac Newton, physicist and Protestant theologian, provided scientific proof that the universe God had created was timeless. This space, free of time, was immutable. Middle classes could be confident that if they purged the landscape of ephemeral traditions, if they destroyed old sacreds, this wonderful environment of perpetual harmony would become their home. One could not doubt the success of their exodus from an unstable Old to a stable New World.

This abstract New World of science and theology, which promised that a natural landscape did exist beneath the clutter of human conventions, was reinforced by the style of painting created by artists during the Renaissance. Middle-class science and theology had an ally in middle class painting. These artists were antigenerational in the personas they presented. They were self-made artists, as modern scientists and

Protestant theologians were also self made. They were heroic individuals whose art could liberate the people from medieval superstitions. Painters joined Protestant theologians and scientists as an avant-garde.[17]

Medieval people, like other traditional peoples, assumed religious and economic equilibrium. The religious sacred passed down from generation to generation was the same gift for each generation. This also was true for the economic resources in the particular place in which the community lived. But early modern scientists had seen a physical nature that embodied so much plenitude that it did not experience the transition from the surpluses of summer to the scarcity of winter. This nature was so abundant that it did not need the miracle of rebirth in the spring to overcome the hunger of winter. This nature was so bountiful that one did not need group cooperation to survive. An individual, unaided, could acquire resources from this unbounded source of wealth and energy. This was a parallel to Protestant theology, which insisted that the sacred was so bountiful that one did not need to receive it as a member of a community. An independent individual could achieve harmony with the divine.[18]

Renaissance painting offered such a vision of plenitude. Medieval art presented a web of symbols. It taught the individual to find spiritual fulfillment within the community. Its symbols expressed the traditions of the community. Like the art of American Indians, it initiated the individual into an understanding of the sacred stories that needed to be passed down from generation to generation. This art evoked a sense of an eternal present. Renaissance painters offered an alternative vision. Symbolically breaking windows in the medieval circle, they announced the existence of a world of meaning outside that circle. Renaissance art embodied geometric techniques that provided the illusion of depth. Within this spatial box, the painters evoked human and natural figures that had three dimensions. The artist, seeing and representing reality for the first time, had no need for symbols. These techniques also provided the illusion that the depth of the painting was infinite. The viewer's eye was drawn to a vanishing point that seemed to exist at the back of the picture. If one went beyond the limits of the medieval circle, one was reassured that there was a bountiful, even boundless, world. One also was encouraged to imagine an exodus from the medieval past because this New World of boundless space was so beautiful in its simplicity. In such an environment perhaps it was possible to escape the human experience of birth, death, and rebirth. Perhaps in this natural world that did not age, humans would also not grow old. The focus in this ritual of rebirth, as one participated in an exodus from an Old World to a New World, was on that brief moment in the life cycle when sons left fathers behind. Perhaps the generations celebrated by the symbols of traditional art could not survive the exodus from the unreality of the Old World to the reality of the New World. This, then, was an art that shared the logic of Protestant millennialism. This was a promised land where one escaped the tragic consequences of Adam's fall. Armed with a science, art, and theology that proved the intellectual bankruptcy of the old political order, bourgeois elites began to create the new political order of the modern nation. Bloody revolutions and peaceful revolutions were taking place by the end of the eighteenth century. Subjects were being reborn as citizens on both sides of the Atlantic. Now the bourgeoisie had both the political power and the cultural authority to clear the landscape of the presence of aristocrats and peasants in Europe and of indigenous peoples in the Americas. At last the middle class would have a home.

In the Old World of subjects, the political sovereignty of a monarch was often exercised over a variety of cultures. In 1776 the English monarch had political authority over Wales, Scotland, and Ireland. In the English colonies the monarch assumed he had authority over white and red subjects. But inspired by the visions of uniformity and simplicity in Newtonian physics, Renaissance landscapes, and Protestant theology, the nation builders imagined that in the new nations political boundaries and cultural boundaries would be one and the same. A nation's citizens, stepping out of the Old World of cultural diversity, were the children of the nation's landscape. Since this landscape was imagined as a universal national, all citizens would be participants in this universal national culture. This was one of the great contradictions in the culture of bourgeois nationalism. The new nationalists believed that a state of nature existed only within their particular nation's political boundaries. From a French perspective, the people in all other nations continued to be trapped within artificial conventions. And this perspective was, of course, repeated by bourgeois elites in other nations.

The invention of the modern nation embodied, therefore, the Renaissance-Reformation concept of negative revolution. A national landscape, a national state of nature, appeared when all of the artificial international and local cultural patterns were removed from within the nation's political boundaries. It followed that each group of bourgeois elites believed their particular nation was eternal because it was a particular expression of Newton's immutable universe. The nation had not been constructed in time by humans. One discovered one's nation through a ritual of purification that restored the original landscape, this particular expression of the universal state of nature.[19]

The style of Renaissance painting was useful to the bourgeoisie as they imagined that the existing diversity of international and local cultures would disappear. The painters of national landscapes, who appeared in all bourgeois cultures on both sides of the Atlantic, evoked a national universal. These artists suggested that there was not a variety of landscapes within a nation's political boundaries. These landscape painters also minimized the significance of the variety of local cultures within those boundaries. Their painting dramatized the strength of bourgeois citizens and the weakness of those groups, who, because of their irrationality, could not become part of the fraternity of rational people.

Another bourgeois art form, modern historical writing, created during this revolutionary period, 1770–1830, now became of crucial importance in evoking the vision of history as progress, of history as a ritual of purification. Modern historians told the story of the movement from artful international and local diversity to artless, national uniformity. These historians were celebrating the liberation of their nations from the suffocating complexity of the medieval world. A modern historian was a historian of France or England or the United States or Brazil. Modern historians might write about vestiges of the past that did not fit the model of the modern nation. But the lesson to be learned from such histories was the inadequacy of cultures that were not like those of the modern nation. Cut off from the independence granted the individual by his home in the national landscape, this particular state of nature, such peoples were outside of history as progress. Bourgeois historians could see the circulation of cultural patterns throughout Europe during the medieval period. But they denied that their liberated and independent nations participated in the circulation of transnational bourgeois cultural patterns.

The paradox, then, was that the writing of national history was a transnational cultural pattern. It joined other transnational bourgeois cultural patterns such as Protestant theologies, landscape painting, and

quest for an American
writh/novel

the celebration of Newtonian physics. Bourgeois cultural historians could not imagine that the novel was a transnational bourgeois art form or that similar styles of music, architecture, furniture, clothing, of manhood, womanhood, childrearing and education circulated among the bourgeoisie in Boston, New York, Berlin, London, Paris, and Stockholm. In turn this isolationist belief that a nation's artless culture emerged from the nation's state of nature, its landscape, led to the development of the transnational bourgeois pattern of racism.[20]

If a citizen was a child of his national landscape and he was different from people outside his national boundary or from those within the national boundaries who did not belong to the deep fraternity of the nation's people, these differences must be caused by nature, not culture. One of the contradictions in the transnational pattern of bourgeois national isolation, then, was the belief that there was a superior Anglo-Saxon race to be found throughout northern Europe and those colonies peopled by the English. Bourgeois histories in England dealt with that contradiction by arguing that English Anglo-Saxons were superior to those in Germany; or American historians argued that American Anglo-Saxons were superior to those in England or Germany. Anglo-Saxons not only participated in New World spiritual, intellectual, and economic plenitude, but they also participated in biological plenitude.

When the exodus of a people with history, history as progress, had culminated in a modern nation as a particular state of nature, then the great problem for bourgeois historians became that of explaining change away. Change was celebrated when it had a forward direction away from the meaningless flux of traditional societies and their generational cycles. But from the moment a middle class believed that it had become dominant within its home, a national landscape, it experienced a crisis of cultural identity. Each nation's middle class had symbolically replaced the homes of peasants and aristocrats and the homes of indigenous peoples with its own home. But bourgeois citizens shared the logic of Protestantism. Their children could not be initiated into a sacred tradition. Protestant children had to find the timeless truths of the Bible for themselves. And children of citizens had to find the timeless truths of the national landscape for themselves. But it was likely that bourgeois children would recognize that their parents had not really engaged in a successful negative revolution. Instead children could see their parents as positive revolutionists who had replaced conventions with conventions.

For Protestants this meant a continual succession of religious revivals to once again liberate the individual. For citizens it meant a constant succession of political, economic, and artistic revivals. Imagined as perfectly stable, bourgeois homes ironically became arenas of generational conflict.[21]

But there was an even more fundamental contradiction existing within every bourgeois citizen. The nation's landscape was a sacred space. The national culture that grew out of that landscape was sacred. The public religion of the nation was more important than any private religion that might exist within the nation's political boundaries. This eternal landscape was so full of plenitude that it could provide perpetual inspiration for the nation's civil religion. It could provide inspiration for painters, architects, composers, novelists, poets, and historians forever. In politics and the arts the constant problem, then, would be the protection of that bounded sacred from the infiltration of alien and profane influences from the outside or from the development of heresy within the nation's boundaries. The essence of the bourgeois nation was the spiritual nature of its national landscape. But the bourgeois citizen also was a capitalist who imagined economic plenitude in an ever expanding and boundless marketplace. It was necessary to imagine such a marketplace if one was to imagine bourgeois children becoming free from generational continuity. To leave home and become an independent individual demanded expanding space. The bourgeois citizen could not be at home in his national landscape. Each was a heretic, a traitor who chose boundless materialism over the bounded spirituality of his nation. Bourgeois citizens, however, did not see themselves as heretics or traitors. Instead they created scapegoats. They insisted that they were nationalists, not capitalists. They always chose to use their private property within the national interest. They were loyal to the nation's civil religion. They were different from the small number of capitalists who existed within each modern nation. These men were materialists. They mocked the nation's spiritual identity. They were committed only to self-interest. Overwhelmed by greed they would break down the nation's boundaries and drown its spirituality in the sea of materialism that was the international marketplace. Some capitalists were Jews, but Jews were always capitalists. These wanderers had not been born from a nation's landscape. They had received no spirituality from that landscape. Their pre-national traditions were bankrupt and could provide no authentic spirituality. Jews and other capitalists were always engaged in a materialistic attack on the nation's spirituality. It was legitimate to be anticapitalist and anti-Semitic in all bourgeois nations until World War II. It was then that bourgeois elites found it impossible to sustain the contradiction between their commitment to a bounded spiritual nation and a boundless marketplace, between a fixed state of nature and the constant flux of the marketplace.[22]

For bourgeois nationalists who saw the modern nation as the end of history, it was the spiritual nation that was the engine of progress, pushing and pulling humanity out of savagery and barbarism upward to civilization. When the nation symbolically lost its spiritual essence in the 1940s, it became very difficult to continue to see a modern civilization that was the end of history and the beacon of enlightenment for all backward people. Since that revolution, language about progress can only talk in terms of the modern contribution to economic plenty. The idea of progress in the arts has collapsed in the bourgeois nations on both sides of the Atlantic. While many intellectuals and most political leaders deny that there is a profound crisis of meaning when the nation no longer has the aesthetic authority of being the symbolic climax of modern civilization, there is a growing number of postmodern theorists who insist that we must rethink all our assumptions about progress and history.[23]

Postmodernists are found on both sides of the Atlantic because the history of the modern nation, as Benedict Anderson insisted, is transnational. When the aesthetic authority of the national landscape and its children, a national people, lost persuasiveness in the 1940s, previously repressed groups immediately became visible. Women scholars in Europe and the Americas could make the experience of women part of the public record because the cultural hegemony of an exclusive male citizenship no longer existed. This collapse of the aesthetic authority of a universal national also allowed the identities of class, ethnicity, race, and region to be seen as part of a nation's history. And one was no longer dismissed as an illegitimate scholar if one talked about a transnational, modern middle-class culture.

When, in the next chapter, I discuss the narratives of George Bancroft, Frederick Jackson Turner, and Charles and Mary Beard, I will suggest that these "American" historians were writing within the conventions of modern bourgeois nationalism. Their writings span the century from the 1840s to the 1940s. I hope to illuminate how unstable their narratives were because of their participation in the bourgeois contradiction between a bounded, spiritual national landscape and an unbounded, materialistic marketplace. I hope to show how difficult it was for them to sustain a vision of an autonomous nation. I hope to demonstrate how difficult it was for them to sustain a belief in a universal national in the face of complex international and local patterns. I suggest that it was the century-long instability of the narrative of the modern nation that made possible the dramatic rejection of this narrative in the 1940s, both in the United States and elsewhere in the modern world. But in subsequent chapters, I will also discuss how difficult it has been for historians, literary critics, painters, musicians, and architects to imagine an alternative narrative. Perhaps this is why some postmodern theorists argue that we will never see another metanarrative that hopes to enclose all human experience within a single framework.

CHAPTER ONE

The Birth and Death of American History

I had argued in *Historians against History* (1965) that George Bancroft, Frederick Jackson Turner, and Charles Beard wrote their histories from the paradigmatic assumption that Europe represented time and America (the United States) represented timeless space. I was able to place this metaphor of two worlds in an international context in *The End of American History* (1985) by relating the vision of timeless space to a republican tradition that moved from Renaissance Italy into the English colonies. Now, in this book, I am placing this theory that time and space are dichotomies within the transatlantic bourgeois culture, which, by 1800, imagined that modern nations would be rooted in timeless space. I see these three books as expressions of the paradigmatic shift from nationalist to postnationalist American studies.[1]

I am arguing, then, that in the bourgeois synthesis of the Enlightenment and romanticism, of nature and nation, of rationality and a national people, a generation of Anglo-Protestant men born about 1800 in the United States shared the vision of the Prussian G. W. F. Hegel that only a particular nation could lead the exodus from a lower to a higher civilization. Like Hegel they believed that such an exemplary nation would be Protestant. They shared Hegel's view that Catholics refused to abandon their memories of their now superseded world. They also shared Hegel's theory that there was a coincidence between Protestantism and the Germanic peoples. It was the Germanic peoples alone who had rejected the Catholic past and opted for the Protestant future. As Protestants, for Hegel, the Germanic peoples alone were capable of moving from the complex and overlapping political allegiances of Old World subjects to the unified and rational allegiance of citizens to the nation-state. Protestants could do this because they had rejected the corporate outlook of Catholicism. To be a Protestant was to be the autonomous individual who was capable of giving total loyalty to the nation-state.[2]

William A. Prescott, John L. Motley, Francis Parkman, and George Bancroft were the most important historians whose narratives helped construct the aesthetic outlines of an American nation that would share the characteristics of the model of the modern nation described by Benedict Anderson. It was this group who defined the United States as the only American nation with a progressive history. It was this group who drew the boundaries between a progressive "American" people and the unprogressive and, therefore, non-American peoples who lived within the boundaries of the United States.

The two major histories by Prescott (1796–1859) were *History of the Conquest of Mexico* and *History of the Conquest of Peru.* In them he compared these two great indigenous civilizations to the civilizations of the Orient. Like those of the Orient, the politics of the Aztecs and Incas were, for him, those of despotism. For Prescott the Catholic Spanish were also despots, but their patterns of tyranny were less oppressive than those of the Aztecs and Incas: they were higher in the story of history as progress. The evils of the Oriental despotism of the Aztecs, Prescott wrote, "were the best apology for their conquest."[3]

For these Anglo-Protestant historians, as for Hegel, the most influential spokesman for these transatlantic paradigms of bourgeois nationalism, history as progress, always linked time and space. Progress as the history of liberty was a movement from the space of the despotic Oriental civilizations westward. According to this story, a great battle between tyranny and liberty began in western Europe when the Germanic peoples of Scandinavia, the Netherlands, England, and the German states chose Protestant liberty over Catholic tyranny. Motley (1814–77) celebrated one of the major victories of Protestantism over Catholicism in his *The Rise of the Dutch Republic.* In this perspective, southern and eastern Europe were not part of that sacred space, the West, in which the history of liberty would reach its final destination. But, of course, for these men the North America occupied by the English colonies was part of that sacred space. For them, just as Spain and Portugal symbolized a profane space in which liberty could not fulfill its destiny, so that space from Mexico to the southern tip of South America was not part of the West. When Catholicism displaced the Oriental civilization of the Aztecs and Incas, one could not expect that Protestant liberty would supersede Catholic tyranny. Central and South America were a hopelessly profane space.[4]

But this was not true of the space north of the English colonies. It was the manifest destiny of that space to be the home of Protestant liberty. This was the theme of *France and England in North America* by Parkman (1823–93). In contrast to Prescott, who portrayed Spanish despotism as preferable to the despotism of the Aztecs and Incas, Parkman purposely had described the presence of the Catholic French in North America as equal in antiprogressive tyranny to that of the Native Americans. For Parkman, "Lord and vassal and black-robed priest, mingled with the wild forms of savage warriors, knit in close fellowship." Both of these lower stages of human history, French and Indian, were to be cleared from the Canadian landscape, as well as from the landscape of the Ohio and Mississippi valleys. All of North America above Mexico would become the West, the space in which history as progress would culminate in Protestant liberty.[5]

Bancroft (1800–1891), whose writings concentrated on the United States, agreed with Hegel that particular nations played a crucial role in the unfolding of history as progress. He also agreed with Hegel that one nation superseded another as the leader of progress. For Bancroft, then, England had played its role in the exodus from tyranny to liberty. England had driven Catholic France from North America. But England, in Bancroft's history, was not destined to achieve the highest stage of liberty and neither was Hegel's Prussia. Prussia had played a necessary role in driving Catholicism out of northwestern Europe. But, according to Bancroft, neither England nor Prussia was able to abandon the institutions of organized power that they had been forced to use in their victories over Catholicism. The United States of America was the beneficiary of the use of English and Prussian power. These Protestant nation-states had sacrificed their possibility of moving completely from an Old World of power to a New World of liberty. They ensured that progress would culminate in the United States.

When English leaders looked at the liberty enjoyed by the English colonists in the space of the New World, they moved to use their institutional power to limit the liberty of the colonists. In the march of spirit in history, this was an inevitable event that forced the colonists to engage in a revolution that would bring into being their nation-state. This nation was destined to bring into being the final stage of history as progress, when liberty would completely transcend power. The United States would represent the perfect separation of liberty from power. Protestant England and Prussia, although they embodied a great deal of liberty within the spaces that were their national landscapes, had become an Old World. The space of the nations of northwestern Europe was not destined to be the final home of liberty as it had moved from the east to the west. The promised land, the West, where liberty would find her final home, was that space in North America populated by the descendants of English Protestants—the space destined to be the national landscape of the United States.

Bancroft felt, therefore, that he had an advantage over Hegel when it came to imagining the national landscape in which the histories of the local states would not be present. The national landscape that would provide a spatial home for the nation was already present in spirit in colonial Massachusetts. For Hegel, the German national landscape and the German national people, that New World, could appear only as a Bavaria, Saxony, or Schleswig-Holstein disappeared into the dustbin of history. But this Prussian vision of a German nation needed to use power to displace those local peoples and those local landscapes. Bancroft, however, could imagine one more exodus from east to west. West of the thirteen colonies and their long local histories, intertwined with European power, across the Appalachians, was a "Virgin Land." The special role of the United States as a nation was to achieve democracy. This role was fulfilled when men from South Carolina, Maryland, New Jersey, or Connecticut crossed those mountains and became "Americans." They had left their local histories and local landscapes tainted by European power. West of the mountains they became a people born of that national landscape. This was the valley of democracy because "Here, and here only, was a people prepared to act as the depository and carrier of all [democratic] political power."[6]

Bruce Greenfield has written about the aesthetic authority used by Lewis and Clark to remove from the accounts of their expedition to the Pacific the many local Native American peoples and their long local histories. Like Myra Jehlen in her *American Incarnation*, however, Greenfield does not relate that aesthetic authority to the transatlantic patterns of nationalism discussed by Benedict Anderson. But for Bancroft, as for Hegel, peoples and geographic areas had no meaning unless they were part of the nation-state. Bancroft had no problem not seeing the Native Americans. To him they were peoples without history and without meaningful space. His problem was to supersede the colonial past. And so he celebrated the birth of a national people and a national landscape where no one should remember the colonial peoples. "Everywhere," he rejoiced, "an intrepid, hardy, and industrious population was moving westward through all the gates of the Alleghenies . . . accepting from nature their title deeds to the unoccupied wilderness." The ideal of a German nation held by Prussians would need the power of the Prussian army to persuade Bavarians and Hessians to forget their local histories. But, for Bancroft, the ideal of a national people first appearing in colonial Massachusetts would achieve reality within the framework of innocence and not power when Americans discovered their national landscape in the last West.[7]

But when Bancroft died in 1891 his narrative was in crisis. He had assumed that history as progress had culminated in the space, the virgin land, west of the Appalachian Mountains. He had assumed that a classless democracy of a homogeneous American people had grown out of that national landscape. He had assumed that the peoples without history who lived within the United States would vanish from that landscape. He believed that "Indians" and "Negroes" were dying races. But he was faced with evidence that in the supposedly entropic world of Europe, an unexpected new landscape—urban and industrial—had been born and was crossing the Atlantic. Here it was becoming the dominant landscape in New England and was threatening to spread westward.

Bancroft associated this new landscape with the chaos of capitalism. There was, for him, a sharp distinction between a system of virtuous private property associated with the democratic people and the corrupt private property of capitalists. Capitalist private property expressed self-interest, in contrast to the public interest of virtuous private property. Capitalists threatened to replace the equality and fraternity of the democratic people with class divisions and class conflict. Capitalists were ready to subvert the harmony of homogeneous people because their true environment was that international chaos that existed outside of national boundaries.

Benedict Anderson has argued in *Imagined Communities* that it was bourgeois elites in the English, Spanish, and Portuguese colonies in North and South America who began the invention of the modern nation. They envisioned the revolutionary replacement of subjects with citizens. They saw a future in which peoples rather than monarchs would be sovereign. But articulating the vision of a classless people, bourgeois elites were living contradictions to their nationalist ideology. Bancroft recognized that the Founding Fathers expected what current political scientists and political historians call the "politics of deference." They expected that average citizens, the people, would recognize the necessity of leadership from a "natural" aristocracy. Bourgeois elites had rejected hereditary aristocracy but believed that the best educated citizens and those who could afford the time for public service needed to lead less qualified and less privileged citizens.

This was why Bancroft had linked the cultural independence of the nation with Anglo-Saxon settlement of the trans-Appalachian West. The colonial world had been part of a profane European past, one that was profoundly undemocratic. In Bancroft's narrative, then, it was not surprising that many of the Founding Fathers, born and raised in the colonial world, embraced hierarchy. But, for Bancroft, there were a few, such as George Washington and Thomas Jefferson, whose identities were formed by their vision of a nation that was to come. Feeling the strength of the trans-Appalachian West, they could imagine an America without class hierarchy. Their prophecy was fulfilled, according to Bancroft, when Andrew Jackson was elected in 1828. Jackson symbolized a United States in which all colonial memories of local and hierarchical cultures were forgotten.

But now, at the end of Bancroft's life, the United States was dominated by powerful capitalist elites who threatened to replace the classless democracy of 1828 with class hierarchy and class conflict. The chaos of the international world had penetrated the boundaries of the nation. Perhaps because this capitalist vitality could not be interpreted as meaningful history as progress toward a harmonious space, it coincided with the first significant migration of Catholics and Jews to the United States. These were peoples without history. They were committed to ancient, irrational traditions. They were not prepared to make an exodus from those traditions to be reborn from the national landscape. They could not participate in the universal national.

This was the crisis of Anglo-Protestant historical understanding in which Frederick Jackson Turner (1861–1929) became the most famous historian in the United States from the 1890s to the 1920s. Turner achieved instant notoriety in 1893 when he delivered his paper, "The Significance of the Frontier in American History" at the Chicago Columbian Exposition. The paper brought to consciousness the fears that the autonomy of the nation, achieved between the 1770s and 1830s, was being lost. Indeed, this was Turner's explicit message. The America of 1830 was dead because the frontier had ceased to exist. For several generations, historians have argued about what Turner meant by the term "frontier." I agree that Turner used the term ambiguously, but it is my position that the most powerful meaning of "frontier," for him, is what I am calling the "national landscape."[8]

Like Bancroft and all subsequent historians who have been committed to the paradigm of bourgeois nationalism, Turner had to explain why Anglo-Americans, whose social pattern of the nuclear family, whose Protestant religious patterns, whose political pattern of representative government, whose economic pattern of private property, whose language was an English language, were not participants in a culture brought with them from England. Like Bancroft and like these subsequent historians, Turner did this by having Europeans experience a conversion from their timeful European cultures to the American national landscape. Turner deliberately rejected Bancroft's explicit linking of Anglo-Saxons to national citizenship. Turner wrote about the ability of the frontier, the West, to free Europeans from their ancestral cultures. To become Americans, adult Europeans crossing the Atlantic forgot their pasts and became as little children. Then they were able to be born again. They were given new identities by the sacred national landscape. This is why Turner, like Bancroft, participated in an aesthetic authority that separated Native Americans from the national landscape. This landscape stood as the destination, the promised land, for those peoples who were within history as progress. Indians, as people without history, had no meaningful relationship to a nation that represented the culmination of progressive history. Their presence was accidental and irrelevant. As metaphysical aberrations they needed to vanish.

Turner spent most of his scholarly energy describing the transplanting of English culture to the New World and explaining how, as a set of traditions produced by the English landscape, English culture needed to wither and die within the environment of the American landscape. His emphasis was in contrast to Prescott, Motley, Parkman, and Bancroft, who used much of their aesthetic authority as historians to remove the Spanish, French, and Indians from the American landscape and to explain why the United States needed to supersede Protestant Prussia and England as the West in which liberty would find her final home. But Turner accepted their artistic erasure of everyone but English Protestants from the American landscape and concentrated on the conflict from 1600 and 1828 that would result in the victory over English tradition of an American culture that sprang from the American landscape.

Perhaps Turner focused on the victory of the New World plenitude of the national landscape over the entropy of Old World English tradition because he had grown up in what Mark Twain had named "The Gilded Age." Twain had seen the years from 1865 to 1890 as the victory of the self-interest of capitalism over virtuous private property committed to the public interest of the nation. In the rhetoric of Jacksonian politics, Thomas Jefferson represented the virtuous property identified with the national landscape. His opponent, Alexander Hamilton, represented the chaos of the international marketplace because he wanted to expand the power of English capitalism in the United States. Twain's Gilded Age could be interpreted as the defeat of the classless democracy of Jefferson and Jackson by English capitalism and its apologist, Hamilton. That capitalism was introducing class hierarchy as it shattered the homogeneity of the people and dissolved the sacred boundaries of the nation.

Turner found the origins of the conflict between English hierarchy and American equality in the first English colonies in North America. Early in the seventeenth century, he reported, the English belief in class structure and class interest was challenged by the frontier, the unsettled land (of the "vanishing" Indians). Here Englishmen could walk away from the hierarchy constructed in the colonies hugging the edge of the Atlantic. Inland they could establish an egalitarian society. They could become Americans. But these frontiersmen were pushed out of their democratic relationship with the virgin land as Massachusetts, Virginia, and the other English colonies expanded westward. He described a sequence of such episodes. In these conflicts between English tradition and American nature, first nature won and then tradition. The American Revolution, for him, was an especially important episode. Like Bancroft before him, Turner had no interest in the revolutions that swept through the Spanish colonies. Turner implicitly shared Bancroft's explicit belief that real nations could not be created from within Catholic cultures, as real nations also could not be created from within Indian cultures. Only south of French Catholic Canada and north of Spanish, Indian, Catholic Mexico was it possible for there to be a national landscape, the West, where progress would culminate and fulfill itself in political liberty. Only here could there be that universal national in which individuals were free from chaotic tradition.

But the American Revolution, for Turner, did not mark the culmination of history as progress. The creation of the political boundaries of the nation in 1789 was an empty triumph. The men who wrote the Constitution continued to participate in an English political culture that was hierarchical and in an English economic culture that placed self-interest above public interest. Turner, like Bancroft, was correct in his understanding of the Founding Fathers as an elite. As Benedict Anderson argued in his *Imagined Communities*, the revolutions for national independence throughout South and North America were led by colonial elites. They appealed to the sovereignty of national peoples to justify their rejection of the sovereignty of an English or Spanish monarch. But they were not prepared to believe that their social, political, and economic privileges should be dissolved in order to achieve that vision of a deep fraternity of a homogeneous, middle-class people, which Anderson sees as one of the essential characteristics of bourgeois nationalism. Turner agreed, therefore, with Bancroft that it was necessary for the aristocratic republic of the Founding Fathers to be replaced by the democracy symbolized by the election of Andrew Jackson to the presidency in 1828. Only then was there an American people whose nation was the final embodiment of that march of history as progress toward the West. Sons of liberty had once again escaped the authority of fathers. On the national landscape, perhaps one could transcend generational experience.

Again, like Bancroft, Turner explained that the new democratic nation of the 1830s was the child of the national landscape. It was only, Turner declared, "from the time the [Appalachian] mountains rose between the pioneer and the seaboard" that "a new order of Americanism arose." The colonies were particular cultures accepting the sovereignty of the English monarch. But going into the virgin land of the valley of democracy, colonists became Americans. They became a sovereign national people. This was the West that was more powerful than English culture. This was the sacred moment, for Turner, when "Into this vast shaggy continent of ours poured the first feeble tide of European settlement. European men, institutions, and ideas were lodged in the American wilderness, and the great American West took them to her bosom, taught them a new way of looking upon the destiny of 'the common man.'" Moreover, Turner insisted, "American democracy was born of no theorist's dream. . . . It came stark and strong and full of life out of the American forest."[9]

Turner's language was consistently that of a civil religion when he described the birth of the national people from the national landscape. "Jefferson," he wrote, "was the first prophet of American democracy, and when we analyze the essential features of his gospel, it is clear that the Western influence was the dominant element." But Jefferson, he continued, was but "the John the Baptist of democracy, not its Moses. Only with the slow settling of the tide of settlement farther and farther toward the interior did the democratic influence grow strong enough to take actual possession of the government." Andrew Jackson, then, was that Moses figure who led the people into the promised land of the West. Jackson was a self-made man inviting all sons to be self-made.[10]

Turner wrote only two books of narrative history, *The Rise of the New West, 1819–1828* and *The United States, 1830–1850*. Both focused on the sacred moment of the birth of a nation whose citizens were a deep and homogeneous fraternity. Turner, like Bancroft, felt no need to explain the exclusion of Anglo-American women, African Americans, Native Americans, Mexican Americans, or Irish and German Catholic immigrants from the American people. And, like Bancroft, he assumed that Anglo-American elites and Anglo-Americans living in poverty were not present on the national landscape. For bourgeois historians in all the new nations, upper and lower classes were anomalies who were expected to disappear in time or could simply be ignored.[11]

not American so narrow!

But, like Bancroft, Turner had to explain the Civil War. What irony or paradox could explain how the homogeneous democracy achieved under Jackson in the 1830s broke into warring sections only thirty years later? Once again Turner made only slight variations on Bancroft's explanation. Bancroft, as an active participant in the Democratic Party of the 1830s, had largely ignored slavery. It was not immediately clear to him that a slaveholding democracy was a contradiction in terms. By the 1840s, however, it was becoming difficult for northerners like Bancroft to ignore or apologize for slavery. David Brion Davis, in his book *Slavery and Human Progress*, has demonstrated that until the end of the eighteenth century, bourgeois elites in the Atlantic world included slavery within history as progress. This was why republican theorists in England and France could identify an American Revolution led by slaveholders with liberty. This was why the slaveholder, Thomas Jefferson, when he traveled in England and France, could be called an apostle of liberty. This was why both Bancroft and Turner could designate Jefferson, the slaveholder, as a prophet of American democracy. And this was why both Bancroft and Turner could identify the slaveholder, Andrew Jackson, as the symbolic father of democracy in the United States.[12]

Davis has argued that between the 1770s and 1830s, the bourgeois elites of Western Europe and North and South America gradually changed their view of slavery. By the 1830s they were defining slavery as a vestige of the medieval past. It was no longer an engine of progress; rather, it was an impediment to progress. But the slaveholders of the southern states did not share in this conversion. Instead, by the 1830s they were insisting on the virtue of slavery. It was, they argued, more than an economic institution. Uncompromising apologists for slavery, they were now outside the consensus of the cultural leaders of the Atlantic community.

First Bancroft and then Turner discovered this South, this "peculiar" region that existed for them from roughly 1840 to the abolition of slavery in 1865. Both Bancroft and Turner disassociated the Virginia slaveholders—George Washington, Thomas Jefferson, James Madison, and John Marshall—from this peculiar region. They also disassociated Andrew Jackson, a slaveholder and the father of American democracy, from the South. They were creators of the nation, not sectionalists outside the boundaries of a homogeneous American people. And so Jackson, for them, was a nationalist, the Moses who led the people out of their fragmented colonial past. Giving structure to the stories told by Bancroft and Turner was the implicit assumption that the sons and grandsons of Washington and Jefferson became a sectional minority when they rejected the new transatlantic consensus that slavery was the antithesis of history as progress.

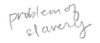

When he discussed the Civil War, Bancroft wrote those sons and grandsons of the Founding Fathers out of the nation. When he reluctantly accepted the need for the abolition of slavery, he began defining white Southerners as participants in a medieval society as alien to North America as French Catholicism had been. Motley, Prescott, and Parkman always defined Spanish or French Catholics as aggressive conspirators against Protestant liberty who always forced Protestants to fight defensive wars. Now Bancroft described the Civil War as a defense of the liberty enshrined in the West against the effort of the Cavaliers of the South to force slavery and the medieval past into this virgin land.

But for Bancroft, Andrew Jackson, the people's president, had a symbolic son, "one whose wisdom was like the wisdom of little children . . . the choice of America fell on a man born west of the Alleghenies, Abraham Lincoln." Lincoln, Bancroft concluded, pledged himself to preserve the nation that represented God's goal for all humanity. He realized that the progress of mankind might suffer a mortal setback if the nation were destroyed. Lincoln then set himself on the course of preserving the Union against the rebellion of the slaveocracy and looked to the people and to God for strength to win. He did not look in vain. "When it came home to the consciousness of the Americans that the war which they were waging was a war for the liberty of all the nations of the world, for freedom itself, they thanked God for giving them strength to endure the severity of the trial to which He put their sincerity, and nerved themselves for the duty with an inexorable will. The President was led along by the greatness of their self-sacrificing example."[13]

When Bancroft began to write history in the 1830s, the link he made between colonial New England and the nation that was the child of the trans-Appalachian West was tenuous. More fully than Bancroft, however, Turner was able to explain the unity between the West of Andrew Jackson and Abraham Lincoln and the New England of Ralph Waldo Emerson. Turner had shared Bancroft's rejection of local colonial memories and the colonial politics of deference. Both men had rejoiced in the uniform national culture that supposedly began west of the Appalachian Mountains. But the Mississippi valley was not fully the valley of democracy because an un-American slaveocracy controlled the states from Missouri to Louisiana. As the redemptive power of the trans-Appalachian virgin land shrank, Turner, like Bancroft, moved New England out of an irrelevant colonial past to become the source of the intellectual and artistic vitality of Lincoln's nation. Turner no longer associated the un-American policies of Alexander Hamilton with New England.

The aesthetic pattern Turner used to transform New England from a threat to the democratic fraternity of national citizens to a cultural center of artists celebrating the national landscape and its unique people is very similar to what Marlon Ross calls a "national romance." Ross finds Englishmen around 1800 identifying national identity with a pastoral national landscape. He sees English poets, novelists, and historians defining that landscape as a timeless space—the foundation for the eternal life of the nation. The dramatic development of an urban-industrial England threatened to displace the pastoral landscape with a new landscape of cities and factories. It threatened to force the English nation back into time. But, for Ross, English cultural leaders solved the problem by offering the vision of organic development as an alternative to a vision of disruptive change. English nationalists declared that the urban-industrial landscape was an organic development out of the pastoral landscape. The "new" England was rooted in the "old" England.[14]

Now Turner disassociated the colonial New England that had been the antithesis of the national landscape discovered west of the Appalachians from the New England of the 1830s. The most urban and industrial part of the United States in the 1830s, a "new" New England had organically developed out of the valley of democracy. Henry David Thoreau and Ralph Waldo Emerson and other New England writers were not the children of Alexander Hamilton, but rather the children of Thomas Jefferson and the brothers of Andrew Jackson.

This was a major argument in Turner's book, *The United States, 1830–1850*. Industrialism in New England, Turner declared, destroyed the undemocratic colonial past that survived in the Federalist Party, which, in 1808, discussed the possible secession of New England from the nation. Industrialism "broke the crust of custom" and allowed her people to share "more fully in the temper of the nation." Now no longer part of the colonial past, New England could become the literary center of the nationalism born in the Midwest. "Beyond any other New Englander," Turner reported, "Emerson caught the spirit of the New West . . . the belief in the perfectibility of the common man, the connection of wagon and star, the appeal to the imagination made by vast spaces, affording opportunity for a newer and finer society." But Turner in his 1893 address had announced that "the vast spaces, affording opportunity of a newer and finer society" no longer existed. The tragedy, for Turner, was that "the free lands are gone. The material forces that gave vitality to Western democracy are passing away." When Turner looked at the United States after 1865, therefore, he saw Mark Twain's Gilded Age. Turner had written a national romance in which a democratic urban-industrial New England was an organic development out of the bountiful, pastoral national landscape of the upper Mississippi valley. Turner, however, agreed with Twain that this national landscape had lost its plenitude and had become entropic. As it withered and lost its redemptive power, it could not make the urban-industrial landscape advancing from New England into the Midwest into a democratic environment. And so Turner lamented, "under the forms of American democracy there is in reality evolving such a concentration of economic and social power in the hands of a comparatively few men as may make political democracy an appearance rather than a reality."[15]

Turner, then, was back to his vision of a chronological sequence of English settlements based on hierarchical tradition being challenged, for a time, by egalitarian frontier communities; authoritarian fathers, for a time, were defeated by sons of liberty. Always, however, he reported that in this sequence from 1600 to 1790, European hierarchy moved westward and displaced American equality. He had written his two books about that moment in the early nineteenth century when it appeared possible that the egalitarian American society born of a national landscape west of the Appalachians would bring the permanent triumph of harmonious American space over the chaos of European time. In 1890, however, he agreed with Twain that the chaos of European time had defeated the last harmonious American space; fathers would dominate sons. European class hierarchy would replace "American" equality. The cultural independence of the United States was over. The autonomy of the nation and its homogeneous people was at an end. Twain's Gilded Age symbolized the victory of chaotic English capitalism, the victory of Hamilton over that American system of responsible private property best symbolized by Jefferson. The deferential society of the Founding Fathers would be restored.

Twain lived the twenty years from 1890 until his death in 1910 in despair. His sacred nation was dead. He lived on in a profane world where the passage of time only meant that humanity was sinking deeper into the Dark Ages. In his novels, sons no longer defeated fathers. For Twain the exodus from medieval darkness to enlightenment had been reversed. But Turner refused to accept this loss of history as progress. He developed two contradictory narratives to help him sustain hope. One of these admitted that the reality of the national landscape no longer existed, but insisted that the memory of that landscape could be kept alive. This memory, he believed, could help sustain democracy after an economy of many small producers, after a democratic economy, had disappeared when the national landscape vanished. "It is to the realm of the spirit, to the domain of ideals and legislation," he wrote, "that we must look for Western influence upon democracy in our days." The strongest refuge for these democratic ideals, he insisted, was to be in the public universities of the midwestern states. Here, presumably, historians like himself and literary critics would keep alive the democratic visions of Andrew Jackson and Ralph Waldo Emerson.[16]

This narrative is to be found scattered in his essays. His only two books had been celebrations of the age of Jackson and Emerson. The other, and contradictory, narrative is also found in his essays. Here he, like so many of his generation, expressed his conversion to an idea of evolution. This idea allowed him to imagine a complete escape from the horror of Twain's Gilded Age. As Turner understood evolution it meant that history as progress had not culminated in pastoral national landscapes. Bancroft was right in seeing a distinction between the meaningless time of tradition and the meaningful time of progress from tradition to nature, but this nature was now to be found in the urban-industrial landscape.

Progressive history existed because it was an expression of a dynamic nature. Nature was an unfolding process carrying humanity ever upward on a progressive course. This was a universal nature that transcended particular national landscapes. One should not assert the possibility of a universal national because the universal was transnational. A nation was provincial. It was an expression of an ephemeral state.

In this narrative Turner associated the pastoralism of the national landscape with a particular stage of human economic activity. From this perspective the Populists of 1890 did not represent the tragic last stand of the autonomous and virtuous nation of Jefferson and Jackson. Rather the agricultural nation of 1800 had been in harmony with the evolutionary process, but by 1890 evolution had passed it by and the Populists were provincial conservatives who represented a cultural lag. The Italian economist, Achille Loria, was quoted by Turner to illuminate how the American national landscape was only a temporary provincial frontier. "Loria," Turner wrote, "has urged the study of colonial life as an aid to understanding the stages of European development. . . . There is much truth in this. The United States lies like a huge page in the history of society. Line by line as we read this continental page from West to East we find the record of social evolution." In this particular reading of Charles Darwin's theory of evolution, Turner made the corporate capitalists of a transatlantic urban-industrial landscape the avant-garde of his generation. They were the leaders of a progressive exodus from an ephemeral Old World of tradition to the substantial natural laws of a New World. To the many peoples in the United States whom Turner saw as without history—Anglo-Protestant women, Native Americans, African Americans, Mexican Americans, Chinese Americans, Catholic and Jewish new immigrants from Europe—he had added those who clung to Jefferson and Jackson as spokesmen for a usable past. But, of course, Turner in his alternative, nostalgic narrative was one of those who refused to kill Jefferson and Jackson.[17]

Turner tried to participate in the modern narrative that taught him that avant-gardes, as discoverers, were setting people free. One did not focus on the power they used to destroy the traditions of the people without history. One focused on the liberty that individuals from those traditional societies would enjoy when they were free from suffocating traditions. The Populists talked about losing their liberty to the power of the corporate elites. But Turner could argue that they were being set free from the irrational traditions of the provincial agricultural society. Twain had feared that an American state of nature was being replaced by an artificial world brought from Europe. But, at times, Turner reassured himself that corporate capitalism did not represent the chaos of human imagination. It was not, as Twain believed, a human creation comparable to that of the medieval society. Corporate capitalism was a higher stage of history than the society of small farmers. Corporate capitalists had not created this stage of history as progress. They were the children of evolutionary nature. Still Turner could not celebrate corporate capitalism even if he defined it as natural. He did not see the international urban-industrial landscape as an organic unity of the true, good, and beautiful.[18]

It did represent the current expression of the evolutionary laws of nature. It did represent truth. But Turner continued to define the good as the deep fraternity of equal citizens. Corporate capitalism, however, had introduced class hierarchy. There no longer was the democracy of a classless people. It was the memory of such a people that Turner wanted to preserve in the midwestern universities, and he could not associate beauty with factories and cities. Beauty was an expression of a pastoral landscape embodied in the poetry of an Emerson. The terrible irony, for Turner, was that history as progress was destroying all that he held good and beautiful. It is not surprising that he spent most of his life repressing this narrative. He wanted to think about history as progress when it had led to the national landscape; or he chose to consider how the memory of that landscape could be preserved in the ivory tower of universities, segregated from the uninspiring reality of corporate capitalism.

By World War I, Charles Beard (1874–1948) was replacing Turner as the most influential historian in the United States. Beard achieved this reputation because he was able to shed Turner's nostalgia for the national landscape. If Turner was right that corporate capitalism was a higher stage of history as progress than the society of small farmers that seemed to dominate the United States when it achieved its identity as a nation, why be nostalgic for that provincial society and its irrational traditions? And if history as progress was leading to a democratic world whose citizens would share liberty, equality, and fraternity, why imagine that progressive history had culminated in the undemocratic world of corporate capitalism? The Gilded Age was not the end of history!

Beard, a fellow midwesterner of Turner's, went, as an undergraduate, to England. Mark Twain had just published his *A Connecticut Yankee in King Arthur's Court.* In this novel Twain shared Turner's view that the economy of industrialism would be the foundation for social and political hierarchy. For both Twain and Turner an American future coming from England meant the end of the classless democracy of the people. Twain did not share Turner's faith that the Gilded Age with all its faults was the creation of the natural laws of evolution. Believing industrialism to be as artificial as medieval culture, Twain visualized this artful, ephemeral modern disappearing in a violent catastrophe. But what Beard saw in England contradicted the dark visions of Turner and Twain.[19]

The story of English history, as Beard understood it, was a variation of the progressive narrative developed by Karl Marx. Medieval aristocracy, in this story, was replaced by a capitalist aristocracy. But industrialism, for Beard as for Marx, was an extrahuman event. It was a force of nature. It destroyed the cultures of the peoples without history and liberated them to participate in progressive history. They became members of the exodus from irrationality and power toward rationality and liberty. The England of the nineteenth century was dominated by the frontier force of an urban-industrial landscape. This force was obliterating the capitalist aristocracy that had become dominant by 1800.

Twain, for Beard, was right to see that aristocracy as both irrational and committed to arbitrary power. Twain had used his novel to write a parable about his America. Yankee industrialists had destroyed the artificial, corrupt, provincial, slaveholding aristocracy of Twain's native South. But just as the Yankee, Hank Morgan, replaced the medieval aristocracy of England with a new aristocracy that also lusted after power, Beard saw the victorious Yankees of 1865 substituting their corrupt industrial aristocracy for that of Twain's South. The southern slaveocracy of 1860 was like the medieval aristocracy. It was a human construction. But Yankee industrialists, for Twain, were also undemocratic and irrational.

Beard agreed that capitalists represented the stage of history that followed the medieval era. But capitalists had not created industrialism, as Twain believed, and they were not the products of industrialism, as Turner believed. Instead, industrialism in England was destroying the irrational, corrupt, provincial society of capitalism. It was liberating the people of England. It was rapidly making England into an economic, social, and political democracy. In the oscillation between hierarchical English capitalism and American frontier democracy, capitalism did not, as Turner feared, have the last word. It was not that end of history that Twain feared would be so catastrophic. Capitalists were also on the verge of becoming a people without history.

For the youthful, precocious Beard in the 1890s, the crucial weakness of his elders, Twain and Turner, was that they had not fully escaped their commitment to the aesthetic vision of an autonomous American nation. Both visualized democracy as the product of an American national landscape. Both believed, therefore, that American democracy was unique and could not be shared. Both, looking at the United States at the end of the Civil War, saw the dominant economy as industrial and that industrialism had originated in England. Both believed that the United States had lost its national autonomy and had become part of international patterns. But, for Beard, it was possible for his younger generation to consider that national autonomy was a myth. Turner said that he believed in universal laws of evolution, but he was unable to write history based on that hypothesis. Beard, however, was ready to write the history of the United States within an international context. Twain and Turner imagined that the national landscape had produced democracy, a classless people. But, as Beard saw it, it was an international urban-industrial landscape that was producing democracy. It was producing democracy in England in 1890. Twain and Turner were wrong about democracy being lost in the United States during the Gilded Age. The transnational pattern of undemocratic capitalism had dominated the United States since the beginning in 1789. As industrialism came to the United States it was going to make a democracy of liberty, equality, and fraternity possible for the first time. The year 1890 was not when democracy died in the United States; it was the moment when democracy was born.

This was the jubilant message Beard brought back from England. Before he began his graduate education at Columbia University he published his first book, *The Industrial Revolution* (1901). When Beard began his graduate studies he chose to get a Ph.D. in political science. Implicitly he now associated the writing of history with what had become for him the myth of autonomous nations. Historians such as Bancroft and Turner wrote histories that were artful expressions of an irrational and provincial culture. They were men without a progressive history. Beard believed the intellectual avant-garde of 1900, those who could distinguish between meaningless tradition and meaningful natural law, would be social scientists. Like natural scientists they discovered reality. Seeing that reality they could show the people the difference between their ephemeral current environment and that reality that could be their home once they rejected their unusable past. Social scientists would demonstrate that there was no universal national. They would reveal that the rational and universal existed only in the transnational urban-industrial landscape.[20]

Self-consciously Beard and his friends at Columbia, James Harvey Robinson as well as Carl Becker, looked back to the eighteenth-century Enlightenment for their usable past. They believed that the Enlightenment vision was of the rationality of the universal laws of nature that could not be contained within national political boundaries, boundaries that were always artful and time bound. Beard joined with Robinson to write *The Development of Modern Europe.* They announced that they were putting emphasis on the eighteenth rather than the nineteenth century because the nationalism and capitalism of the nineteenth century were not a usable past. The nineteenth century, for them, was a dark age whose chaos needed to be transcended. The industrial revolution of the eighteenth century held forth the promise of a world of rational order that could replace the irrationality of both capitalism and nationalism. And the Enlightenment had created a way of intellectually understanding that promise and of bringing about its fulfillment through the use of the scientific method.[21]

Robinson and Beard promised that the transition from the destructive self-interest of capitalism and the fragmentation caused by nationalism would be peaceful. They admitted that there were parallels between their vision and that of Karl Marx. But they rejected Marx's belief in the necessity of violent revolution to destroy the existing chaos. Their optimism was based on their ability to distinguish between capitalism and the middle classes found in modern nations. This situation was not that seen by Marx. There was not a contrast between a proletariat made rational by interrelationships with the productive forces of industrialism and the irrational self-interest of capitalists. Rather, as bourgeois nationalists insisted, most of the middle class was committed to the use of private property for the purposes of rational production. Capitalists, for Robinson and Beard, were only a small minority in each nation.

But capitalists had disproportionate power because they could escape from national public interest in the wilderness outside of national boundaries. This refuge for these outlaws, however, could be destroyed if the middle classes in each nation recognized that the industrial revolution was making the world outside of national boundaries an environment of rational production. Capitalists were using the outdated national belief system of the responsible middle class to sustain their capitalist rejection of a harmonious world. Robinson and Beard hoped to teach the responsible middle class in the United States that they could only ensure the victory of rational public interest over irrational self-interest by committing themselves to the inherent rationality of the international urban-industrial landscape.

As he participated in the growing enthusiasm of a Progressive movement, Beard saw President Theodore Roosevelt as a possible Moses figure. Beard had rejected Thomas Jefferson and Andrew Jackson as Moses figures because they were part of an unusable past. But Roosevelt had a vision of the urban-industrial landscape in which the chaos of capitalist self-interest could be overcome and in which a cooperative democracy could emerge. Feeling that he could help this new world be born, Beard began to publish at a furious rate. These books were designed to be an antihistory of the United States as it existed from 1789 to 1890. Beard would demonstrate that behind the appearance of agrarian democracy there was the reality of capitalist hierarchy. Behind the appearance of national interest, he would reveal the self-interest of capitalism.

He published *American Government and Politics* in 1910; *The Supreme Court and the Constitution* in 1912; *An Economic Interpretation of the Constitution* in 1913; *Contemporary American History* in 1914; and *The Economic Origins of Jeffersonian Democracy* in 1915. Together they formed a massive rejection of the metaphor of a European Old World and an American New World. For Beard the medieval world and its organic metaphor of a hierarchical social body had been replaced by the chaos of capitalist self-interest. Bancroft had been wrong in believing that Europeans crossing the Atlantic escaped that chaos. Bancroft was wrong in believing that an organic metaphor of an egalitarian social body had emerged from the virgin land of the American landscape. In these books Beard described how capitalists wrote their commitment to hierarchy into the Constitution. Their emphasis on checks and balances in the Constitution revealed their fear of a democracy in which the will of the people would be expressed.[22]

Turner had written in 1890 that "we are witnessing the birth of a new nation in America." By that, he meant that an agricultural democracy was being displaced by industrial capitalism. For Beard, however, the new nation being born in the 1890s represented the defeat of capitalism and the triumph of industrial democracy. Jefferson, for Bancroft and Turner, was the great symbol of the virtuous nation that embodied an agricultural democracy. Jefferson, for Bancroft and Turner, was committed to the defense of the new, autonomous nation against the attempt of un-American men like Alexander Hamilton to pull the nation back into Old World corruption. But in *The Economic Origins of Jeffersonian Democracy* Beard desacralized Jefferson and the supposed democracy of his time. Jefferson, Beard announced, represented "an aristocracy of slave-owning planters." Jefferson, he continued, did not provide a usable past for a democracy that represented an urban-industrial landscape. He wrote, "Today nearly half of us belong to what Jefferson labeled 'the mobs of the great cities—sores on the body politic.'" Beard bitterly remarked, "What message has the sage of Monticello for us?"[23]

So certain was Beard that the culture lag of nostalgia for a mythic past was ending that he also found the energy to publish *American City Government* in 1912 and *American Citizenship* in 1914. They provided guidelines for his generation on how to use government in the coming industrial democracy. "The purpose of government," he wrote, "is to do those things which cannot be done well or justly by individuals working alone, and to regulate doings of private persons in such a manner as to improve the general standard of life, labor, and education. The very essence of government, according to the democratic ideal, is cooperation or union of effort for the common good." A major theme in all these books was that courts in general and the Supreme Court in particular protected the self-interest of the capitalist aristocracy. The courts frustrated the will of the people. They kept society in a state of conflict. But, for Beard, the people were moving to destroy the power of the courts. They were moving to establish a deep fraternity of equal citizens. Soon there would exist for the first time in the United States a homogeneous culture.[24]

The uniform culture imagined by Beard in 1914 was different from that of Bancroft and Turner because he saw it as the expression of an urban-industrial rather than a pastoral landscape. He imagined, therefore, that the democratic people in the United States were in harmony with the productive forces of industrialism. The rationality of these "natural processes" was transnational. It was possible, then, for the democratic people in the United States to share this universal international with democratic peoples in other industrialized nations. But Beard's vision of an urban-industrial democracy was as exclusive as that of the agricultural democracy of Bancroft and Turner. The vanguard of history as progress was made up of middle-class white people. It was they, for Beard, who were in harmony with the rationality of industrial productivity. Looking at the world, he imagined Asians, Africans, and South Americans as people without history. Within the United States he excluded capitalists and industrial workers from the vanguard of the rational. He ignored the existence of those peoples whom Bancroft and Turner had defined as without history. Native Americans, African Americans, Mexican Americans, Asian Americans, Catholic and Jewish immigrants from Europe were not part of the democratic people defined by Beard. Implicitly the rational vanguard was, for Beard, Anglo-Protestant. But Anglo-Protestants in the South, which, in 1914, was still overwhelmingly rural, were also a people without history. The new nation of the urban-industrial landscape was that of the Northeast and Midwest. Beard, however, did include middle-class Anglo-Protestant women from these regions as part of the rational vanguard.

This meant that Beard felt closer to the bourgeois elites of England and France than he did to most of the peoples who lived in the United States. Ironically he also identified with the bourgeois elites of Germany, the most industrialized nation of Europe. Beard, like his contemporaries, the philosopher John Dewey and the economist Thorstein Veblen, believed that the inherent rationality of industrial production had created a rational middle class in Germany. The Americans felt sympathy for the German vanguard of history as progress, which, in their interpretation, was frustrated by the political power of an irrational medieval aristocracy and the presence of capitalist irrationality. World War I was caused, according to Beard, Dewey, Veblen, and many of their academic colleagues, by both of these chaotic forces.[25]

For Beard, Dewey, and Veblen, the unwanted war now presented a moment of revolutionary opportunity. They wanted the United States to enter the war. In this situation violence was legitimate because it would destroy the vestiges of medieval irrationality in Russia, the Austro-Hungarian Empire, and Germany. And the need for planning in the wartime economies of England, France, and the United States would speed the triumph of the rational ethic of middle-class productivity over the irrationality of capitalist self-interest.

Having abandoned Jefferson, Jackson, and Lincoln as democratic heroes, Beard replaced them with Woodrow Wilson and Theodore Roosevelt, who were leading the country into the promised land of industrial democracy. He joined Frederic Ogg in publishing *National Government and the World War* in 1919. Wilson, they wrote, had become the spokesman for a worldwide transformation. His views reflected "the slowly maturing opinion of the masses of the people everywhere in the earth . . . those who have faith will believe that a real change has come in the long course of history and that the years, 1917–1918, will mark the opening in the rise of government by the people and in the growth of a concert among the nations."[26]

But even as this book was being published, Beard had lost his faith that an international urban-industrial landscape representing the natural laws of evolution was giving birth to a worldwide industrial democracy

WWI

WWI failure

led by the middle class. Like many of his academic generation, he was suddenly left without any sense of reality. If everything he had believed in for thirty years had no substance, what was the meaning of history? What was truth? From 1941 into the 1950s the dominant leadership in the history profession worked to destroy the scholarly reputations of Charles Beard and Carl Becker. One of the charges hurled against them was that they were relativists who had abandoned the search for truth. But what Beard and Becker were doing in the 1920s was rejecting their association of truth with the transnational universals of the Enlightenment. They were rejecting the truth of history as the progressive succession of transnational stages of civilization. Beard, however, unlike Becker, once again knew by the end of the 1920s what truth was: it was truth as Bancroft had known it in 1830. It was the truth of bourgeois nationalism. The only reality was the nation. The killing of Beard's reputation in the 1940s was evidence that once again a younger generation would try to find meaning outside the nation's borders. These academic parricides would return to one of Turner's narratives—the one that linked industrialism and capitalism. After 1945 both of Beard's narratives, his early internationalism and later nationalism, would be defined as un-American because of their hostility to capitalism.

During the 1920s Beard formed a writing partnership with his wife, Mary Ritter Beard (1876–1958). They became the authors of a four-volume history of the United States entitled *The Rise of American Civilization*, published between 1927 and 1942. This was the most powerful and popular synthesis of American history since that of Bancroft. The first two volumes were distributed by the Book of the Month Club. At the same time many young graduate students in the 1930s such as Richard Hofstadter and Arthur Schlesinger Jr. found ideas for dissertations in the Beards' overview. One of the crucial aspects of the series that made it both popular and powerful was the apparent ease with which the Beards reconstructed a national romance. In the 1890s Charles Beard, like Turner, could not imagine a way to blend the national landscape with the urban-industrial landscape. But for the Beards' bourgeois readers in the United States, who had turned their backs on the adventure of World War I in internationalism and returned to isolation, the Beards suggested that it was inevitable and natural that an urban-industrial landscape coming from England should be absorbed within the preexisting context of the national landscape.[27]

This was natural, according to the Beards in 1927, because the only permanent reality that existed in the world was the nation. Outside of national boundaries there was chaos. This was the lesson Charles Beard had learned in 1919. Blinded by the false categories of universal history—feudalism, capitalism, and industrial democracy—he had failed to see that conflict was not caused by the movement from one transnational stage to another stage. Instead conflict was between the order within nations and the disorder beyond national boundaries. Capitalism was the major disruptive factor that existed in this unstable international realm. Capitalists, who existed in all nations, were always trying to subvert the commitment to public interest that characterized national peoples. In the 1920s, therefore, Charles Beard had become part of a group of "revisionist" historians. These men were refuting the argument, supported by many of them in 1917–18, that World War I was caused by the aggressiveness of the feudal aristocracies of Germany and Austro-Hungary. Instead their research in various national archives now demonstrated, for them, that it was the self-interest of capitalists, particularly munitions makers and bankers, that destabilized the relationships between the nations of Europe and threw that continent into chaos. It was also the covert political pressure of such selfish men that had helped push the United States into the war.[28]

The tragedy of World War I, in the Beards' synthesis, was that a vigorous national movement to revitalize democracy in the United States, Progressivism, was thwarted, for a moment, by the revitalization of the enemy of democracy, capitalism. Everywhere in the world capitalists had profited both financially and politically from the irrationality of civil war between the nations. Never again, for the Beards, should Americans deceive themselves that they were part of a meaningful international community. The choice was between national order and international disorder.

This was the meaning of their title, *The Rise of American Civilization.* There was no truth in a vision of a transnational civilization. Like Bancroft and like Turner's first narrative, the Beards began their epic history with the conflict between the European cultures brought across the Atlantic and the American landscape. Like Turner, the Beards did not feel the need to explain, as Bancroft had, why the spaces in North and South America settled by French, Spanish, or Portuguese Catholics could never be a virgin land, could never be American. But the Beards, like Turner, implicitly assumed that the Englishmen who became Americans were Protestants. Again, like Turner, they did not feel Bancroft's need to clear the land of Indians. Their aesthetic authority simply removed Indians from the virgin land that was the national landscape. The Beards wrote as if Indians had never existed. In imagining that, as Englishmen abandoned their culture, they were reborn as the children of the landscape, the Beards also used their aesthetic authority to remove African Americans from the landscape. There was an unbroken continuity from Bancroft to Turner to the Beards in which the American people born of the national landscape were to be white, Anglo-Saxon Protestants.

English colonists, for the Beards, were transformed into Americans as they became independent agricultural producers. By 1776 these yeomen farmers were a democratic people, a deep fraternity free from the hierarchical patterns of English society. It was the people who formed a "mass movement in which producers, pamphleteers, committees, lawyers, and state governments advanced the revolutionary cause." But, then, the capitalist aristocracies in the colonies created a counterrevolution that, in the Constitution, "reestablished in effect the old British system of politics, economics, and judicial control."[29] The Founding Fathers, for the Beards, frustrated any expression of the will of the people in a constitution that embodied a complex pattern of checks and balances. For the Beards in 1930, as for Bancroft and for Turner's first narrative, the national landscape did not become all-powerful until American pioneers went over the Appalachians into the valley of democracy. The Beards shared the sense of the triumph of a sacred future over a profane past that Bancroft and Turner had felt when they contrasted the fragmented colonial past with the wholeness born of this virgin land. The Beards' prose became ecstatic as they invited their readers to recall this miraculous moment:

> It was a marvelous empire of virgin country that awaited the next great wave of migration. As the waters of the Tigris, the Euphrates, and the Nile had invited mankind to build its civilization along their banks... so the valley of the Mississippi now summoned the peoples of the earth to make a new experiment in social economy in the full light of modern times....
>
> The rolling tide of migration that swept across the mountains and down the valleys, spreading out through the forests and over the prairies,

> advanced in successive waves. In the vanguard was the man with the rifle—grim, silent, fearless. He loved the pathless forest, dense and solitary, carpeted by the fallen leaves of a thousand years and fretted by the sunlight that poured through the Gothic arches of the trees . . . and where the campfire at night flared up in the darkness of knitted boughs as the flaming candles on the altar of a cathedral cast their rays high into the traceries of the vaulted roof. . . .
>
> In this immense domain sprang up a social or a social order without marked class or caste, a society of people substantially equal in worldly goods, deriving their livelihood from one prime source—labor with their own hands on the soil. . . .
>
> In its folkways and mores there was a rugged freedom—the freedom of hardy men and women, taut of muscle and bronzed by sun and rain and wind, working with their hands in abundant materials, shaping oak from their own forests and flax from their own fields to the plain uses of a plain life, content with little and rejoicing in it, rearing in unaffected naturalness many children to face also a career of hard labor, offering no goal in great riches or happiness in a multitude of things. . . . all satisfied by the unadorned epic of Christianity inherited from their fathers.[30]

In the narrative of this civil religion of the American nation, history as progress had culminated in a sacred landscape around 1830 and produced a virtuous people whose destiny was to live in peace and prosperity forever. The drama in the narrative as it dealt with the years from 1600 to 1830 was the series of struggles between the power of the national landscape and the power of European culture. By the 1830s this drama was concluded. But Bancroft, Turner, and the Beards all found a new dramatic pattern after the 1830s. There would be a series of challenges to the virtuous people and their national landscape. For Bancroft and in Turner's first narrative, the threat that developed between 1830 and 1860 came from the neomedieval slaveocracy of the South. But the West, for them, this all-powerful national landscape, brought forth a representative hero of the people, Abraham Lincoln, who purged the land of this alien culture.

Turner, in his first narrative, had written a national romance in which industrial New England had become democratic because of the power of the West. It was the West and New England that became the North that defeated the South. Then when his narrative reached the years after the Civil War, Turner lost his ability to write a national romance. Instead of blending with the national landscape, the urban-industrial landscape now, for him, represented an alternative and more powerful nature, that of universal evolution. And, unhappily for Turner, capitalism was part of the final stage of society called into existence by the laws of evolution.

The Beards, in *The Rise of American Civilization,* by rejecting the idea that there were transnational stages of human history, were able to write a national romance in which an urban-industrial landscape coming from Europe did blend with the national landscape. This, however, did not occur in their story until after the Civil War. That war, for them, grew out of the colonial past. The capitalist aristocracy that had written the undemocratic Constitution had been defeated by the democratic people of the Mississippi valley. But the lesson that Charles Beard had learned from World War I was that capitalism thrives on the chaos of war. The Civil War, for the Beards, was a second counterrevolution. Again, as in the 1780s, capitalists seized control. The war did not save the national landscape; instead it gave capitalists power over it. "While the planting class was being trampled in the dirt—stripped of its wealth and political power," they wrote, "the capitalist class was marching onward in seven league boots."[31]

The Beards' language had emphasized the beauty and sacredness of the triumph of the national landscape and its virtuous people in the early nineteenth century. Now their language was equally powerful in evoking the ugliness and profanity of the years 1865–90, Twain's Gilded Age, when the reality was that corrupt capitalists with no sense of national interest temporarily held power. This control meant that the capital of the nation was no longer Washington, D.C. "Roads from four continents," they lamented, "now ran to the new Appian Way—Wall Street—and the pro-consuls of distant provinces paid homage to a new sovereign." But Wall Street was more than a center of the nation; it was the capital of an international empire.[32]

The Beards, like Bancroft, explicitly linked Protestantism to the civil religion of the nation. Now, again like Bancroft, they also explicitly linked the Anglo-Saxon race to the civil religion. When Charles Beard, during the years 1890 to 1920, had seen history as a series of universal stages, he had denied Bancroft and Turner's sanctification of Thomas Jefferson. He had dismissed Jefferson as a slaveholding aristocrat. But when Charles and Mary Beard, after 1920, reimagined the national landscape as the basis of an absolutely exceptional American nation, they made Jefferson the greatest political saint in their civil religion. The Jefferson they praised "was a nationalist in a narrow and racial sense, and looked to the development, on this continent, of a homogeneous people . . . a society of people speaking a common language, knit together by ties of blood."[33]

This was the sacred world of Anglo-Saxon Protestants that the internationalists of Wall Street profaned by bringing in Catholic immigrants to work in their mines and factories. These were peoples whose identities had been created by alien national landscapes. The position of the Beards was that only the American national landscape had produced a people with a democratic and rational tradition. All other national landscapes had produced irrational and hierarchical traditions. The Beards, like Bancroft and Turner, had exercised an aesthetic authority that removed Native Americans, African Americans, and Mexican Americans from the national landscape. But now their aesthetic authority recorded the ugliness of the invasion of the national landscape by the irrational cultures of European peoples: "vaudeville shows, prize fights, circuses, dime museums, and cheap theaters, like the spectacles of ancient Rome, kept countless millions happy in penury." For the Beards, the United States' international plutocracy chose Catholic workers because they knew that the Catholic Church encouraged their political passivity. "The Catholic Church, with its gorgeous ceremonials and its sublime consolations for suffering and wretchedness, followed the poor everywhere." These international bankers, whose chosen environment was the chaos that existed outside of national boundaries, were, according to the Beards, out to destroy the order born of the national landscape. "Not since the patricians and capitalists of Rome scoured the known world for slaves," the Beards warned, "had the world witnessed such deliberate overturn of a social order by masters of ceremonies."[34]

In *The Rise of American Civilization,* the Beards rejoiced that legislation in the 1920s cut off immigration from southern and eastern Europe. That legislation, the Beards explained, had passed because the American people began to regain control of the nation in the 1890s. "Between the urban masses with their circuses and prize fights," the Beards rejoiced, "and the plutocracy with its political mansions . . . stretched a wide and active middle class engaged in professional, mercantile, and clerical pursuits. It was within this group that the early Puritan characteristics of thrift, sobriety, and self-denial appeared to survive and unfold in the most natural fashion." The parents and grandparents of this middle class had learned the lesson of responsible productivity from the national landscape. Although that agricultural world was giving way to an urban-industrial world, this new world inherited the democratic tradition of rational private property that was used in the public interest. When industrialism came to all other nations, it inherited the undemocratic and irrational traditions born of their national landscapes. But in the United States the productive logic of industrialism was absorbed by the productive and democratic logic of the pastoral national landscape.[35]

To an extent, then, the Beards attributed the Progressive Era to the energy released by the fusion of agricultural and industrial productivity. But the battle of a middle-class people against an alien capitalism also was the result of a spiritual revival. American Protestants constructed a social gospel that refuted the acquisitive capitalism whose philosophical justification had been worked out primarily by Englishmen. In some ways, however, the Beards reported, the social gospel was a return to the anti-English and democratic Protestantism of Jefferson's era. In the Progressive Era, 1890–1914, the people enacted legislation to force capitalists to work within the framework of national interest. The people also enacted taxes to halt the growing gap between the wealth of capitalists and the people. Thus, for the Beards, "by a gradual and peaceful operation was effected a transfer of economic goods greater in value than the rights shifted from the French nobility to the peasants by the national assembly. . . . historians now recorded in their books that the theory of the public interest was being substituted for the older doctrine of laissez-faire."[36]

As the trans-Appalachian West had defeated the European capitalism of the Founding Fathers and brought about true national independence, so, for the Beards, the fusion of that West with the urban-industrial landscape had defeated the capitalists of Wall Street, who had seized control in 1865, and national independence had been restored. This is why the Beards' prose again expressed a sense of religious ecstasy. The fusion of the two landscapes provided the mysterious and beautiful power to recreate democracy. "Presidents came and went, governors and legislatures came and went," read the Beards' litany, "but the movement of social forces that produced this legislation was continuous. It was confined to no party, directed by no single organization, inspired by no overpowering leadership. Such were the processes and products of American democracy."[37]

Is this the tradition true of the romantic in literature?

The national romance, as Marlon Ross had defined it, is a drama of constant conflict between good sons, who are committed to preserving the pastoral time of origins, and bad sons, who want to replace their heritage with an alien world. Good sons see the possibility of development that grows out of the national landscape. Bad sons want change that is not organic, but revolutionary. The Beards used the term *people* for the virtuous sons and the term *capitalists* for the evil sons. Tragically, just as people regained national independence and restored continuity with the national landscape around 1914, they were challenged once again by capitalists. The Civil War had given the evil sons the opportunity to threaten the organic nation. Now World War I gave corrupt family members the opportunity to destroy the order and unity of the virtuous national family. International competition by the capitalists who existed in every country seduced the people of those nations out of the order and harmony that existed within their boundaries and into the chaos of the nonrational universe of capitalism and war.

Writing at the end of the 1920s, the Beards reluctantly admitted that capitalists had been in control of the nation since 1917, but they reassured readers that this was only temporary. Capitalism, they emphasized, was irrational and parasitical. It was contradicted by the logic of industrialism, which, like the prior agricultural world, was rational and productive. Soon, they promised, that constructive, democratic, and American reality would defeat the unreality of an un-American capitalism. They could only rejoice, then, when the collapse of Wall Street seemed to confirm how insubstantial capitalism was. In 1933 the Beards were ready *Depression* to place the new president, Franklin Delano Roosevelt, at the same level of sainthood in their civil religion as Thomas Jefferson. Roosevelt was the hero who symbolized the final victory of the urban-industrial landscape that had organically developed out of the national landscape over the alien influence of capitalism.

In a 1933 book, *The Future Comes,* written with George H. E. Smith, Charles Beard rejoiced that Roosevelt's New Deal of early 1933 envisioned an organic nation. "The Recovery Program," Beard and Smith wrote, "accepts the inexorable development of combination in industry, abandons all faith in the healing power of dissolution and prosecution, and makes use of combination in planning." The "Recovery Program," they continued, "calls upon millions of individuals in industry and agriculture, who have hitherto been pursuing their own interests at pleasure, to cooperate in adjusting production, setting prices and maintaining standards." They concluded that "[t]hrough its banking, credit, public-corporation, process-taxing, and railroad measures, the Recovery Program is moving in the direction of a new economic situation that subjects private interests to a broad nationalization. . . . The New Deal signalizes the coming of a future collectivist in character."[38]

But Charles and Mary Beard again stressed the spiritual nature of this organic politics; again they returned to Thomas Jefferson as the spiritual father of the nation. Jefferson, for them, in contrast to the English classical economists and Karl Marx, was not a materialist. Jefferson's civil religion, as it was revived in the 1930s, "will be simple at bottom, as simple as the Sermon on the Mount. . . . It will take the good life as its centre, for the plain reason that there is no immovable benchmark in the universal flux. It will be peaceful, because the good life cannot be lived without scheme and control, and the supreme instrumentality of our age, engineering, is peaceful in operation. . . . It must be valid whatever varieties of religious faith may prevail, and must command the assent of multitudes, who differ in religious belief. It must find its sanctions in society itself." This is the vision of a religion of the organic nation that Beard tried to convey in "Written History as an Act of Faith," his presidential address to the American Historical Association in 1933.[39]

He asserted that the only meaningful definition of historical writing is to be found in historiography, the study of the premises on which historians build their narratives. Historians should use empirical data "authenticated by criticism and ordered by the help of the scientific method." But narratives do not emerge from the facts, from criticism, or from the scientific method. Rather, he argued, our narratives express our philosophy of history. We are philosophers rather than scientists. We are not caught, however, in meaningless relativity. There is, first, the philosophy that history has no meaning, but no one can possibly write history who holds to this view of history as chaos. Second, he asserted, one can believe that history is marked by cycles and man is doomed to the endless repetition of the past. And, finally, he declared, one can believe in history as progress.[40]

From 1890 to 1920 Charles Beard had tried to escape Turner's sense of the decay of the national landscape by committing himself to what he saw as a scientific understanding of the universal laws of history as evolutionary progress. When his social science turned into a failed faith after 1920 he had turned, with his wife Mary, to the narrative form of the national romance. According to this formula, there could be endless organic development out of a national landscape. As Beard was using "progress" in his address, it meant for him just such endless organic development that never lost its roots in the national landscape. Having rejected the authority of science after 1920, he gave legitimacy to his narrative through an expression of faith in the religion of the nation. His faith was that progress would bring about a "collectivist democracy." His collectivist democracy was a fulfillment of the promise of bourgeois nationalism that there was a homogeneous people who were a deep fraternity.

In 1935 the Beards had a millennial vision of the nation, led by President Roosevelt, fulfilling its promise as an organic people from whom the conflict of competing interests would be banished. But then the Beards faced the possibility that growing tensions in Europe might precipitate another world war. This meant the possibility of a rebirth of capitalist power in an environment of international chaos. To head off this possibility, Charles Beard again joined with Smith to publish two books in 1934, *The Idea of National Interest* and *The Open Door at Home*. Both books focused on the conflict that began between the good son of the republic, Jefferson, and the bad son, Hamilton. Hamilton and his descendants had no loyalty to the nation. They were willing to destroy its organic harmony by plunging the country into the chaos of international competition and by "bring[ing] in immigrants still less adapted to the national heritage than many races later excluded by law, thus adding to the confusion of peoples, the Babel of tongues." The disloyal men of the Hamilton tradition from the 1790s to the 1930s tried to seduce the people out of their commitment to the nation's boundaries by arguing that national prosperity depended on international commerce. In contrast, Jefferson and the loyal men who sustained his tradition understood that Americans were chosen people who had the responsibility of sustaining their experiment in democracy in isolation from a world that could never become democratic. Jefferson and his followers were correct, according to Beard and Smith, that the continental dimensions of American civilization were vast enough to provide the raw materials and markets necessary for prosperity. The United States could be economically, as well as politically and culturally, isolated from the rest of the world because of its natural plenitude.[41]

Meanwhile, Charles and Mary Beard were writing the third volume of *The Rise of American Civilization,* published in 1939 as *America in Midpassage.* President Roosevelt was the heroic figure in the book, as he used the government to support the arts that would help complete the organic unity of the people as a deep fraternity. It appeared that the 1930s would be a particularly sacred decade, comparable to the epiphany of the 1830s. But when the book appeared, the Beards had completely changed their mind about the president. What they saw in 1939 was an evil son masquerading as a good son, a Hamiltonian pretending to be a Jeffersonian. The Beards had reluctantly come to believe that Roosevelt did not mean what he said in 1933 about the need to solve the economic depression within a national context. He did not mean it when he said prosperity did not depend on foreign trade. He did not mean it when he lamented American participation in World War I and promised that the United States would avoid the economic policies that had led it toward participation in that terrible tragedy. By 1937 the Beards were certain that Roosevelt was pursuing a devious foreign policy. He was fooling the electorate by saying one thing and doing another. And the actions were designed to end the Jeffersonian policy of preserving the political, economic, and cultural autonomy of the nation.[42]

Charles Beard quickly wrote two books, *Giddy Minds and Foreign Quarrels* and *A Foreign Policy for America,* published in 1939 and 1940. Here Beard tried to rip the mask of deception from the president and reveal Roosevelt's conspiracy to act against the will of the people and lead the nation step-by-step into the war that had begun in Europe in 1939. Confronted by the success of this evil son, Charles and Mary Beard now wrote the fourth volume of *The Rise of American Civilization.* This volume, *The American Spirit,* was published in 1942. In their national romance, evil sons who were not committed to preserving their family inheritance had momentarily defeated the good sons. Those loyal to the democratic tradition that was a gift from the national landscape had experienced defeat in the 1780s, the 1870s, and the 1920s. But always the good sons, strengthened by the mysterious plenitude of the national landscape, had reclaimed their legitimate leadership of the country. The Beards' message was simple and clear. In looking at American participation in World War II, they could say, "This too shall pass." The Revolution, the Civil War, World War I, and now World War II were moments when international chaos penetrated the boundaries of the nation and the self-interest of capitalists became more powerful than the public interest of the people.[43]

The Beards, however, reassured their readers that the nation and its democratic traditions were eternal. There was no reality in the chaos of the international void that existed outside of national boundaries. Capitalists did not represent a true, or a good, or a beautiful. To see the future when the nation would again restore its boundaries and again achieve synthesis of the true, the good, and the beautiful, the Beards asked their readers to imaginatively return to the 1830s, when there had been an organic unity of a democratic politics, economy, and art—all the gift of the national landscape. Since the national landscape was the source of unbounded energy, the people could once more make a spiritual pilgrimage to this eternal and mysterious plenitude when World War II ended and find the inspiration to restore their exceptional national democracy.

This, the Beards recounted, was the meaning of their title, *The Rise of American Civilization.* They were using the term "civilization" to symbolize a society that achieved a synthesis of the true, the good, and the beautiful. They again presented Jefferson as the great spokesman for this vision. Jefferson assumed that because man was a social animal, the community needed to be democratic and cooperative; that progress was not automatic, but depended on human will; that this will needed to be inspired by an ethical faith. Jefferson believed that the idea of civilization could serve as a national faith only in America because of the uniqueness of American social harmony. Built upon the foundation of the national landscape, America's origins, "unlike those of European societies, were not lost in prehistoric darkness, in mythological time, in the dim twilight of barbarian and pagan gods, superstitions, and fears." By the 1830s this idea of a democratic civilization was producing a great renaissance of American culture. Ralph Waldo Emerson, Walt Whitman, and George Bancroft all gave artistic expression to the unique American destiny. In economics, Henry C. Carey criticized English classical economics for forgetting the Jeffersonian principle that man is an ethical animal. These English economists had abstracted man from society, made him a prisoner of economic law, and argued that he was motivated only by selfishness.[44]

No longer able to celebrate the second renaissance of the 1930s that they had predicted in *America in Midpassage,* the Beards had turned back to the first American renaissance. Because of the power of alien English capitalist ideology in the 1930s, young Americans were not aware that there was a native democratic and spiritual alternative represented by the New England renaissance of the 1830s. Instead young people listened to Catholics, who asked them to look to medieval Europe to find spirituality. Or they listened to Marxists to find an alternative to capitalism. Sometimes they forgot their nationalism completely and listened to doctrines of internationalism propounded by men like "Louis Finkelstein under the title 'American Ideals and the Survival of Western Civilization' in the *Contemporary Jewish Record* of June, 1941."[45]

But in *The American Spirit* the Beards reassured their readers that the redemptive power of the national landscape could not be lost and the international influences of capitalism, Marxism, Catholicism, and Judaism would soon disappear. The Beards found the strongest evidence for continued loyalty to Jeffersonian nativism in the efforts to preserve the purity of the people. "Expressing in many respect this revulsion and this determination to protect American civilization against European and Oriental invasions," they declared, "immigration legislation, especially the Acts of 1921 and 1924, stood out in public discussions and in law as positive testimony to renewed concentration on the reinforcement of civilization in the United States."[46]

In the next chapter I will analyze the writings of three historians—Richard Hofstadter, Arthur Schlesinger Jr., and William Appleman Williams—who, in 1940, were loyal intellectual sons of the Beards. But during World War II, they, like most Americans of their generation, were asked to convert from isolationism to internationalism. They were asked to give up the home, the national landscape, that the Beards had promised was eternal. They were faced in the 1940s with the possibility that confronted Turner and Beard in the 1890s—that the autonomous nation was not the end of history; that it was an ephemeral style, a provincial entity, destined to be displaced by a more cosmopolitan world.

But Hofstadter, Schlesinger, and Williams in the 1940s did not share Turner's and Beard's commitment in the 1890s to the laws of evolution. And, like Turner and unlike the early Beard, they would disassociate an international future from the belief of bourgeois nationalism in a people as a deep fraternity. They, therefore, would have difficulty reassuring themselves and their readers that internationalism did not mean what bourgeois nationalists had believed for a century and a half—that it was an environment of constant flux where one could not sustain the modern dichotomies of objective/subjective, rational/irrational, individual/society; that it was an environment where one could not establish criteria to measure the progress of civilization; that the arts would lose their spirituality and become expressions of the materialism of the marketplace. I began to read these older academic brothers of mine in the late 1940s. As they rejected the Beards' isolationism, they were also implicitly rejecting the state-of-nature anthropology that informed the Beards' *The Rise of American Civilization.* I was beginning to learn that space and time are not dichotomies, but rather a continuum.

CHAPTER TWO

Historians Leaving Home, Killing Fathers

Richard Hofstadter (1916–70)

When Richard Hofstadter published his book *The Progressive Historians* in 1968, he described it as an act of parricide. He believed that he had cut himself off from the historians who were most important to him in the 1930s, the literary historian Vernon Lewis Parrington as well as Turner and Beard. It was the Beards' *The Rise of American Civilization,* however, that had been the most important text influencing the narratives of Hofstadter, William Appleman Williams, and Arthur Schlesinger Jr. at the beginning of the 1940s. In 1965 I had published *Historians against History,* which criticized Turner, Parrington, and Beard. There, like Hofstadter in 1968, I ignored the role Mary Beard had played in the writing of *The Rise.* No matter how dramatic our break was from the narrative of *The Rise,* Hofstadter, Williams, Schlesinger, and I continued in the 1960s to see a public world of men and a private world of women. We had abandoned much of the narrative of bourgeois nationalism to embrace reluctantly the international marketplace, but we continued to give a monopoly of agency to white middle-class males. The only debates, the only conflicts that we could see, were between loyal and disloyal sons who were white. These white males, however, no longer had to be Anglo-Protestants. Male Jews and Catholics from Europe could be included in our definition of an American people who were no longer guarding the national boundaries against the threat of international capitalism.[1]

Coming of age in New York in the 1930s with a Lutheran mother and a Jewish father, Hofstadter had friends who were Marxists, and he considered himself a Marxist. But when he began graduate studies at Columbia University in 1938, he remembered that "I took up American history under the inspiration that came from Charles and Mary Beards' *The Rise of American Civilization.*" Merle Curti, a longtime admirer of Charles Beard and a pioneer in the new field of intellectual history, became his adviser. Hofstadter's dissertation was published in 1944 as *Social Darwinism in American Thought* and was awarded a prize by the American Historical Association. This is powerful evidence, as was the prize awarded to Arthur Schlesinger Jr.'s *The Age of Jackson,* published in 1945, that the Beards' national romance was still the narrative that provided meaning to many, if not most, of the men teaching the history of the United States in the early 1940s.[2]

Social Darwinism in American Thought can be read as an extended footnote to the perception of the Gilded Age the Beards had presented in *The Rise.* Hofstadter's book documented in great detail that evil capitalist sons had captured control of the nation after 1865. Like all evil sons in all national romances, they had no loyalty to their national family and its traditions. These were men who, in pursuing their self-interest, would so blur the boundaries of the national family that it would lose its unity and dissolve into chaos. Working within the Beards' national romance, Hofstadter assumed that the national family and its traditions so endangered by selfish capitalists were the fraternal democracy, the homogeneous people of the era 1830–60. This people, these virtuous sons of Jefferson and Jackson, placed public above private interest.

Following the Beards' distinction between the Jeffersonian spirituality of the religion of the nation and the valueless materialism of the English economists who had developed the soulless philosophy of capitalism, Hofstadter described the way the disloyal American sons imported this alien English philosophy to give legitimacy to their rejection of the national tradition of fraternal democracy. "American social thought had been optimistic, confident of the special destiny of the country, humanitarian, democratic," Hofstadter wrote, but that national heritage was challenged by evil sons, such as William Graham Sumner, who "tried to show his contemporaries that their 'natural rights' were nowhere to be found in nature, that their humanitarianism, democracy, and equality were not eternal verities, but the passing mores of a stage of social evolution." The social Darwinism that Sumner and other antidemocratic academics were borrowing from the Englishman Herbert Spencer, was an argument that the chaos of capitalism was unavoidable. It was a message that capitalists in the United States wanted to hear because it fitted their experience. "With its rapid expansion, its exploitive methods, its desperate competition," Hofstadter lamented, "post-bellum America was like a vast human caricature of the Darwinian struggle for existence."[3]

Following closely the outline of the Beards' *The Rise,* Hofstadter examined in depth the writings of Lester Frank Ward who, for the Beards and Hofstadter, was a social scientist who had remained loyal to the pre-1865 democratic tradition. For Ward, evolution was not driven by competition, as English and American capitalists believed; rather, it was characterized by cooperation. This was the kind of cooperation that Ward saw embodied in the fraternal democracy of 1830. Continuing to follow closely the national romance of *The Rise,* Hofstadter argued that the American people were, by the 1890s, throwing off the influence of English ideology and were placing the chaos of capitalism under political control. "The transition to solidarism, which was part of a larger reconstruction in American thought, became apparent in the nineties," he declared. "The change in the political outlook of the common man," he continued, "was responsible for a change in the fundamental mechanisms of thought in the social sciences." As Turner and the Beards had seen the artists of the New England renaissance giving aesthetic form to a vision born of the people, Hofstadter was arguing that the social scientists who were loyal sons in the Progressive Era were giving scholarly form to a vision born of the people.[4]

The democratic revitalization of the Progressive Era, for Hofstadter as for the Beards, was energized by the fusion of the industrial landscape with the national landscape. And, like the isolationist Beards of the 1930s, he made it clear that only in the United States could there be a fusion of democracy and industrialism. He specifically rejected the position of Karl Marx that an industrial democracy must be international. It was the democratic heritage of the national landscape, he argued, that made it possible in America and only in America for a peaceful transition to take place from capitalism to industrial democracy.

Hofstadter had called the position of William Graham Sumner, the defense of capitalist chaos, "conservative Darwinism," and he called the position of Lester Frank Ward, the affirmation of democratic unity, "reform Darwinism." Again, following the narrative of *The Rise,* he had to delay temporarily the full victory of the industrial democracy of reform

Darwinism because of the entry of the United States into World War I. This was an environment of capitalist chaos and so conservative Darwinism was revitalized because "it was made to fit the mold of international conflict just when its inapplicability to domestic economics was becoming apparent." But, continuing to echo the Beards, he concluded his first book with the promise that "[d]espite the interruption of the 'twenties' the trend toward social cohesion kept growing."[5]

The terrible irony for Hofstadter and those older historians who awarded him a prize for this book was that the promise of the fulfillment of democratic solidarity in the 1930s had again been interrupted by the resurgence of the chaotic environment of World War II, in which capitalism flourished. And Hofstadter was aware when the war ended in 1945 that the Roosevelt administration had managed to make internationalism legitimate and isolation illegitimate. This political revolution shattered the aesthetic authority that Hofstadter had inherited directly from the Beards, but also indirectly from the whole tradition of bourgeois nationalism, which had become dominant in the United States between 1789 and the 1830s. As Hofstadter prepared to write his second book, *The American Political Tradition,* published in 1948, he no longer saw an American people born of a national landscape. Having lost that vision, he had lost the narrative of the national romance. He no longer saw good sons attempting to preserve the unity, the goodness, truth, and beauty of the people as a national family. He no longer saw evil sons whose selfishness put them in conflict with the national family. He could no longer identify such evil sons with the chaos of the capitalism that existed outside national boundaries. He no longer could make the distinction so central to his *Social Darwinism in America* that there was a responsible, productive, private property that celebrated the public interest in contrast to the irresponsible, parasitical, private property of capitalism that ignored the national interest. His second book, *The American Political Tradition,* therefore, was written in anger. He had become a professional historian believing in the lie that there were good sons committed to one kind of private property and bad sons committed to another kind of private property. The Beards had misled him. Merle Curti had misled him. He should have listened to his Marxist friends, who said that the fundamental conflict was between international capitalism and international socialism. His purpose, then, in this second book was to rip the mask of public virtue from the faces of the heroes of the Beards' *The Rise.* He would reveal that these good sons, starting with Jefferson, were as committed to self-interest as were the bad sons descended from Alexander Hamilton. He did not seem aware that he was repeating the desacralization of Jefferson and Jackson that had characterized the writing of Charles Beard from 1890 to 1920. He was not aware that he, like Beard a half century earlier, was denying the autonomy of the American nation by placing it within the framework of international capitalism.[6]

Working within the American variation of bourgeois nationalism in 1944, Hofstadter had written a consensus history in *Social Darwinism in American Thought.* There was a homogeneous people who, within the story of the national romance, had a seamless history, one that was an organic development out of the past. There was conflict in the national romance because of disloyal sons, un-Americans, who wanted to disrupt this organic development that had kept contact with the pastoral past, the national landscape. Such cultural traitors wanted change that would break the continuity of national history. Historians writing a national romance described the consensus of the national people and their conflict with those outsiders who would destroy the national boundaries and introduce class conflict.

But by the 1950s historians of Hofstadter's generation were being designated as "consensus historians" because they rejected the conflict central to the Beards' national romance, the conflict between a democratic people rooted in a national landscape and capitalists committed to the chaos of the international marketplace. The Beards' generation, from the perspective of this new consensus generation, were "conflict historians." But they were writing about a false conflict. The orthodoxy of the consensus school of the 1950s was that capitalism and democracy were synonymous. Hofstadter argued, however, that "my own assertion of consensus history in 1948 had its sources in the Marxism of the 1930s." The consensus he presented in this book was that of an antidemocratic capitalism. From 1789 onward, the dominant culture in the United States was one that placed self-interest above public interest and the chaos of competition above fraternal democracy.[7]

When capitalism collapsed in 1929, Hofstadter explained, the New Deal of Franklin Roosevelt did not move to restore a fraternal democracy because no such tradition existed in the United States. The established historians of the 1930s had engaged in a "quest for the American past" that was "carried on in a spirit of sentimental appreciation rather than critical analysis." "The fierceness of the political struggle has often been misleading," he continued, "for the range of vision embraced by the primary contestants in the major parties has always been bounded by the horizons of property and enterprise." Ours, he concluded, has been "a democracy in cupidity rather than a democracy of fraternity." He then proceeded to analyze Jefferson, Jackson, Lincoln, Theodore Roosevelt, Woodrow Wilson, and Franklin Roosevelt as men who were committed to cupidity rather than fraternity. For Hofstadter in 1948 there was no usable American past on which to build a fraternal democracy. Only by turning to Karl Marx could one find a vision for such a democracy. Hofstadter knew that in the 1930s he had friends who saw themselves as Marxists and patriotic Americans. He also knew in 1948 that the rapid development of a cold war culture in the United States denied that a Marxist could be a loyal citizen. By 1948 cultural orthodoxy defined any kind of Marxist as un-American. Between 1948 and the publication of his next book, *The Age of Reform*, in 1955, he abandoned his Marxist analysis. He would replace class analysis with cultural analysis. In *The Age of Reform* he continued his angry deconstruction of *The Rise*. But his focus was now explicitly on the Anglo-Protestant culture that informed so much of the Beards' narrative.[8]

His major rhetorical strategy was to identify and then trivialize the Anglo-Protestant myth of national origins. He depended on Henry Nash Smith's *Virgin Land: The American West as Symbol and Myth* for much of his analysis. But Smith in 1950 had written an elegy for a beautiful myth. Hofstadter, however, emphasized that the myth was not true, beautiful, or good. As in *The American Political Tradition*, he insisted that the economy of nineteenth-century America was capitalist. This, however, no longer outraged him. Implicitly he had returned to one of Turner's narratives, the one in which he stoically accepted the truth of capitalism without finding it good or beautiful. Hofstadter repressed the existence of a New England American renaissance in which major Anglo-Protestant artists had celebrated the pastoral national landscape. Instead he chose to locate the pastoral in the Populist political movement of the late nineteenth century.

Hofstadter was implicitly locating a new cultural center for the nation of 1890 in the cities of the Northeast. The Populists of the South and West, therefore, were a provincial movement. He agreed with the second Turner narrative that those farmers were now a people without history. Like the Turner of the second narrative, Hofstadter was rejecting the narrative of the national romance. There was, for him, no continuity between the old, rural, Anglo-Protestant America and the new, urban America as the Beards had claimed. For Hofstadter the Populists were clinging to the myth of America as the garden of the world. They believed they were living in harmony with the natural landscape. But they were practicing capitalist agriculture; they were producing for a world market. They embraced new machines and new marketing techniques. They were cutting their ties with the subsistence agriculture of the colonial past. But the Populists refused to believe that they were creators of historical discontinuity. They saw themselves keeping an organic connection to the past. Unwilling to admit their contradictory position, Populists created scapegoats, especially Jewish financiers, to explain why they could not sustain continuity with their Edenic myth.[9]

Anti-Semitism had suddenly and dramatically lost its legitimacy in the United States by 1945 as it became associated with the Nazis and the Holocaust. Hofstadter, however, did not choose to discuss the anti-Semitism of the Anglo-Protestant elites in the Northeast, an anti-Semitism that found expression in the public admission policies of many of the Ivy League universities. Instead he implied that anti-Semitism was not part of the new urban America of the Northeast.

The second section of *The Age of Reform* dealt with the Progressive Era that Hofstadter had celebrated in *Social Darwinism in American Thought.* Now he described the Progressives as an Anglo-Protestant urban elite who entered the twentieth century participating in the same culture lag as the Populists. Clinging to their vision of an essential America that was pastoral, they hated the capitalist corporation they, themselves, were creating and feared the cities in which they lived. Hofstadter now praised capitalism for creating discontinuity in the nation's history. He presented capitalism as a system of ceaseless change. This was the reality to which humans must adjust. All efforts to stop history and imagine a timeless landscape as the Populists and Progressives had tried to do were doomed to failure. Within this narrative pattern, Hofstadter celebrated World War I for helping to bring about the collapse of the Progressive outlook. The war helped Americans reject their erroneous vision of living in a static space.

With the end of these backward-looking reform movements, Populism and Progressivism, both products of Anglo-Protestant culture, Hofstadter could end his book by pointing to the success of the New Deal as a new kind of reform movement. "What seems outstanding about the New Deal," he declared, "is the drastic new departure that it marks in the history of American reformism." In *The American Political Tradition* he had been angry at President Roosevelt for not trying to replace capitalism with socialism. Now he praised Roosevelt for his rejection of the moral absolutes of the Anglo-Protestant Populists and Progressives. Roosevelt rejected their idea of a homogeneous people and embraced the cultural pluralism of an urban America created by the "new" immigrants from Europe, the Catholics and Jews. Reform was no longer related to the hope of restoring an ideal democracy; rather, it was a continuing pragmatic process made possible by new Americans who were not participants in the Anglo-Protestant myth that a perfect nation was established by 1830. The cultural villains of the Beards' *The Rise,* the Catholics and Jews, had become Hofstadter's heroes.[10]

In many ways he was echoing in 1955 Turner's pronouncement in 1893 that American exceptionalism had ended. He agreed with Turner that a twentieth-century America, dominated by corporations, labor unions, and government bureaucracies, would be more like Europe than like the America of 1830. But unlike Turner, Hofstadter was not nostalgic for that early republic. After his first book he had vehemently rejected any aesthetic appreciation of that "old" republic. There was no beauty or goodness to be found there. The vision of a homogeneous people rooted in a national landscape was too similar to fascist ideologies. Such dichotomies of virtue and corruption had led to the Holocaust. In his first book, *Social Darwinism in American Thought,* Hofstadter thought it was tragic that World War I had disrupted the recovery of a fraternal democracy. In *The Age of Reform,* however, he had rejoiced that the war of 1917 had shattered the moral absolutes of the Progressives. Now he expressed his hope that the entry of the United States into World War II would complete the erosion of the dichotomies that had been so central to Anglo-Protestant culture. Now he celebrated what he had feared in his first book, that capitalist internationalism would disrupt the domestic politics of an exceptional and homogeneous national people. Because of World War II, he wrote, Americans were thrust "into a situation in which their domestic life was largely determined by the demands of foreign policy and national defense. With this change came the final involvement of the nation in all the realities it had sought to avoid; for now, it was not only modernized and urbanized and bureacratized but internationalized as well."[11]

But in his book of 1963, *Anti-Intellectualism in American Life,* Hofstadter lamented that the dichotomies of good and evil, American and un-American, continued to find powerful expression in the United States, especially in the anticommunist witch-hunts of Senator Joseph McCarthy. Hofstadter, however, had also discovered a more powerful rhetorical position from which to criticize the absolutes of the Anglo-Protestant culture he had come to despise. He no longer had to say that the usable American past had begun with the "new" immigration of Catholics and Jews to the cities of the Northeast. Now he claimed that the culture of the Founding Fathers was a pluralist one in which they posited a human nature that was both good and evil. Like the administration of Franklin Roosevelt, the politics of the Founding Fathers was one of necessary compromise because, for them, one could never achieve a political community of saints. Once again the villains of Charles Beard had become Hofstadter's heroes.

There is a significant parallel between the development of Hofstadter's analysis of American history and the analysis of bourgeois nationalism made by Benedict Anderson in 1983. Like Anderson, he suggested that the colonial elites who supported the Revolution did not imagine that there really was a homogeneous people, a fraternal democracy. Like Anderson, he would find such an imagination developing a generation after the colonial revolutions. But, unlike Anderson, Hofstadter did not see this pattern encompassing all of the new American nations, nor did he see parallels with the bourgeois nationalism emerging in Western Europe. Although he had pronounced the United States to be part of an international world in 1945, he believed in 1963 that the United States had had an isolated national history from the 1830s until World War II.

He described, then, an unfortunate fall from the European realism of the Founding Fathers, from their real world of perpetually competing interests and perpetual compromise. Evangelical Protestantism and the ideology of a fraternal democracy had persuaded most Americans that they could achieve heaven on earth and they began to think in terms of purging religious and political sinners. "Just as the evangelicals repudiated a learned religion and a formally constituted clergy in favor of the wisdom of the heart and direct access to God," he declared, "so did advocates of egalitarian politics prepare to dispense with trained leadership in favor of the native practical sense of the ordinary man with its direct access to truth." The great academic hero of Hofstadter's first book was John Dewey because his philosophy embraced the wisdom of the common man. Twenty years later Dewey became, for Hofstadter, the villain who made the tenets of evangelicalism and egalitarianism academically respectable from 1900 to the 1940s.[12]

Hofstadter continued his effort to reveal the fall from the usable past of the Founding Fathers and the hope of its recovery in the New Deal in his book of 1968, *The Progressive Historians.* He described Turner, Vernon Louis Parrington, and Beard as spokesmen for the early nineteenth-century world of evangelical Protestantism and egalitarian democracy. These men, for him, were historians against history because "time is the basic dimension of history, but the basic dimension of the American imagination is space." It was, he continued, Turner who most fully incorporated "the awareness of space, this yearning for rebirth under natural conditions, into our historical thought." The Progressive historians, then, were fighting to save a timeless spatial democracy from the ravages of time as symbolized by capitalism. "Beard thought of democracy," Hofstadter concluded, "not as a relative matter or as an unfolding historical reality that must be understood at each point in its temporal context but as an eternal absolute."[13]

In his next book, however, *The Idea of a Party System in America* (1970), Hofstadter again dramatically changed his narrative. Now he denied that the Founding Fathers provided a usable past but said that Jacksonian America did. Aware of the recent scholarship about the republican tradition in England and the English colonies upon which Bernard Bailyn had based his book, *The Ideological Origins of the American Revolution* (1967), Hofstadter now placed the Founding Fathers explicitly within the tradition of republican virtue. It was this tradition, developed by the country party in England, that demanded a unified public interest. And because the revolutionary generation was loyal to republicanism, a major crisis erupted in the new nation during the 1790s when it became apparent that there were competing theories of the public interest. Republican ideology taught the leaders of 1789 that their opposition represented a conspiracy of evil men. But the Founding Fathers were able to temper their political theory with their experience. They knew that diversity existed and that it must be accepted. Whatever their fears and misgivings, the Federalists accepted their defeat by the Jeffersonian Republicans in 1800, and the United States "gave the world its first example of the peaceful transition of a government from the control of one party to another." For Hofstadter, the United States in 1800 provided a political model of a pluralist democracy because its leaders had chosen to live not by the European ideology of the republican tradition, which declared the possibility of harmony with the universal, but by the encounter with a dynamic flow of particulars. "I do believe," Hofstadter affirmed, "that the full development of the liberal democratic state in the West required that political criticism and opposition be incarnated in one or more opposition parties, free not only to express themselves within parliamentary bodies but also to agitate and organize outside them among the electorate, and to form permanent, free, recognized oppositional structures." This, he affirmed, "was something new in the history of the world; it required a bold new act of understanding on the part of its contemporaries."[14]

The political pluralism of the New Deal, therefore, was, after all, not new. The full acceptance of competing parties had come in the 1830s with the organization of the Democrats and Whigs. Whatever Americans had imagined about the possibility of a homogeneous people, they had always accepted the reality of a pluralism of competing interests. The vision of egalitarian democracy was not a dangerous tradition in the United States. It no longer needed redemption by Catholics and Jews.

In 1970, when his life was cut short by leukemia, Hofstadter had begun work on a multivolume history of America. The fragment that he completed before his death, *America in 1750*, dismissed his earlier fears that Protestantism was a potential source for a totalitarian definition of an American people. Colonial Americans lived with the experience of competing Protestantisms. "Religious tolerance, and after it, religious liberty," he concluded, "were the creations of a jumble of faiths too complex to force into any mold. Puritanism, after all, was not America's gift to the world but England's; what America brought was the separation of church and state."[15]

In his first book Hofstadter had hoped to keep the fraternal democracy born of the national landscape isolated from the chaos of capitalism. He wanted to separate American space from European time. Twenty-five years later he saw Europeans trapped in an ideology of timeless space. Europeans crossing the Atlantic had brought the ideology of timeless homogeneity with them. But American conditions encouraged economic, religious, and political marketplaces. Europeans became Americans when they accepted the continual pluralism produced by the flow of time. In 1940 Hofstadter identified capitalism as the enemy of liberty, equality, and fraternity. In 1970 he saw capitalism as the necessary foundation for liberty. He no longer valued fraternity and equality. This was a liberty that the United States could share with the rest of the world. Capitalism could break down all attempts to defend local cultures as islands of homogeneity, of fraternity and equality. This was a world of power that capitalism could defeat.

In 1940 Hofstadter saw no power involved in the three hundred years of warfare as Euro-Americans displaced the Native Americans. Nor did he see that exercise of power in 1970. In 1940 and again in 1970 he saw no power involved in the Euro-American enslavement of African Americans. At the beginning and the end of his academic career he saw no power involved in the conquest of the northern half of Mexico by Anglo-Americans in 1846. Continuing in 1970 as in 1940 to assume that historians dealt only with the public world of men, he saw no patriarchal power in the patterns of family life brought from Europe. In 1940 Hofstadter did see patterns of class hierarchy and power caused by capitalism. In 1970, however, he described capitalism as creating a pluralistic society in which there were no clear-cut class divisions. Under capitalism, history as unmanageable conflict had ended; history as chaos would cease when people no longer tried to escape history. The future, for Hofstadter in 1970, was a capitalistic one in which a spirit of pragmatic compromise would sustain a harmonious human experience within the inevitable flow of time.

Between 1945 and 1970 Hofstadter had great difficulty in locating a usable past. But Turner and Beard also had changed their definitions of a usable past. For the older historians, however, a usable past was always associated with a landscape, national or international. Meaningful history, for them, was an exodus from meaningless history, time as flux. Meaningless history was an environment of irrational tradition. Meaningful history took humans from irrational time to rational space. By the end of his life, however, Hofstadter was defining this quest for rational space, for a universal national or universal international, as an irrational myth. The end of history meant the rejection of all boundaries. Only the capitalist marketplace offered such a boundless environment. The vision of a classless society, a fraternity of equal citizens, was both a nationalist and a Marxist vision. This vision was responsible for conflict and war. Only when individuals celebrated the liberty made possible by the marketplace could humanity escape the experience of internal and external conflict. For Hofstadter, then, the marketplace could fulfill the failed promises of the national and international landscapes; it could provide a world without power. It would mark the end of history.

William Appleman Williams (1921–90)

But for William Appleman Williams, who emerged with Hofstadter as an acknowledged leader in the history profession of the 1950s, Hofstadter's affirmation of a capitalist world without power was a lie. When Williams became a graduate student at the University of Wisconsin after his years as a naval officer during World War II, he was determined to remain loyal to the narrative of the Beards. He would continue to find a conflict between the American sons of Thomas Jefferson and the un-American sons of Alexander Hamilton. The good sons wanted to preserve the boundaries of their nation and keep it safe from the chaos that lay outside those boundaries. The evil sons wanted to destroy those boundaries and force the nation into the chaos of the international marketplace.[16]

Williams was presented with a story that told him that Japanese and German aggression forced the United States to enter World War II. To preserve the nation's boundaries and its sacred national traditions, the United States reluctantly responded to these foreign threats. Even more reluctantly national leaders believed that the nation needed to become an international power to limit future threats to the national heritage. Immediately after 1945 the leaders of the United States saw the Soviet Union replacing Japan and Germany as such a threat. Again with great reluctance, President Truman and his advisers decided that the United States needed to enter into a cold war to contain Soviet aggression.

For Williams, however, working from the perspective of the Beards, this story was not true. He knew that capitalists in the United States accepted Hamilton's position that prosperity depended on foreign raw materials and foreign markets. He knew that capitalists had played a major role in involving the United States in World War I. He knew that

President Roosevelt's foreign policy after 1936 was based on the Hamiltonian argument for foreign raw materials and markets. What Roosevelt and his advisers, these evil sons, wanted in the late 1930s was a revolution that would destroy the legitimacy of Jeffersonian continentalism and establish the legitimacy of Hamiltonian international capitalism. Williams saw the men in the Roosevelt administration and then in the administration of President Truman disguising their intended revolution by presenting the story that internationalism was forced on the country by external aggressors. They hid the aggressiveness of their Hamiltonian tradition.

In his dissertation published in 1952 as *American-Russian Relations, 1781–1947*, he argued that until 1917 those relations were based on pragmatic balance-of-power policies. But after the Russian Revolution, the political leaders of the United States were in a rage against the new Russia, the Soviet Union. The only explanation for this rage, according to Williams, was that President Wilson envisioned the United States as the center of worldwide capitalist internationalism and was shocked by the potential rivalry of a communist internationalism. The new Marxist Russia was economically and militarily weak throughout the 1920s and 1930s. Certainly it did not share with Japan and Germany the energy or the will to alter drastically the world order. And yet, Wilson had joined his wartime allies in sending troops into Russia in a vain attempt to suppress the revolution. And this absolute hatred of the Soviet Union kept the United States from cooperating with it in the 1930s to contain Japanese and German aggression. Only this kind of rigid ideology could explain "the failure of the United States to collaborate with the Soviet Union against Japanese expansion from 1920 to 1922, during Tokyo's invasion of Manchuria in 1931, and later, when Japan began to wage hostilities against China in 1937."[17]

Williams related this specific declension from a policy of balance of power toward Russia to the decision by political and economic leaders in the 1890s that the United States needed an overseas frontier because "the financial and industrial powers of the United States soon came to dominate their domestic market and looked abroad for new opportunities." Implicit in his argument was the desire of American leaders to define and control this overseas market. Assuming that the world's future would be one of corporate capitalism, they were prepared to repress revolutions that did not conform to that ideal and threatened to create alternative futures. This was their policy toward the Mexican Revolution, which began in 1910. Their continued hostility toward the Russian Revolution in the 1920s and 1930s stemmed from the fact that the existence of the Soviet Union compelled American leaders to be aware of their inability to control totally the development of an international marketplace.

Williams, therefore, had nothing but contempt for those who believed the United States returned to an isolationist policy in 1919. "The policy of the United States toward the Soviets," he argued, "exemplified the victory of those domestic forces that, though generally labeled isolationist, in fact desired the further and unrestricted overseas expansion of American economic and political powers." He concluded, "Far from isolation, the American policy of these inter-war years was one characterized by decisions and actions taken with sole reference to unilaterally determined goals—decisions and actions for the consequences of which Washington disclaimed all responsibility."[18]

Much of what Williams had said about the revolution in American foreign policy in the 1890s was implicit rather than explicit. But in an article published in 1955, "The Frontier Thesis and American Foreign Policy," he believed he was offering a new hypothesis. Almost simultaneously Hofstadter had written an article on the 1890s that explained the Spanish-American War as the explosive result of a sense of cultural defeat by both rural and urban Anglo-Protestants. For Hofstadter, these groups were prisoners of a tradition of static national virtue and had not yet abandoned what he labeled as their ideological "soft" side and accepted their pragmatic "hard" side. He suggested that once that conversion took place, further foreign adventures were no longer needed to escape the cultural contradiction between space and time.

Williams confronted this assumption that American imperialism in the Spanish-American War was an aberration. "One of the central themes of American historiography is that there is no American Empire," he said, but he also asserted that "the United States has been a consciously and steadily expanding nation since 1890." He turned to the writings of Frederick Jackson Turner to provide a way of understanding why the 1890s marked the beginning of systematic overseas expansion by economic and political leaders. "Turner's frontier thesis," Williams declared, "made democracy a function of an expanding frontier." At the very moment when Hofstadter was attacking Turner because he was a spokesman for a mythical, anticapitalist agrarian democracy, Williams was attacking Turner for providing the justification for American capitalism to become expansive and imperialistic. "Turner," Williams continued, "gave Americans a national world view that eased their doubts, settled their confusions, and justified their aggressiveness." Like the Spanish-American War, World Wars I and II were not aberrations from an established anti-imperialist isolation; they were, for Williams, the inevitable price that the shapers of foreign policy were willing to pay for their commitment to the necessity of an overseas marketplace.[19]

At a time when many younger members of the historical profession were destroying Charles Beard's reputation, Williams defied his peers in the new consensus school by praising Beard. "Beard," he declared, "was a brilliant student of history keenly aware of the consequences of imperial expansion." Beard recognized that the New Dealers' commitment to an overseas frontier "would lead to war and tyranny" and "that democracy would be negated." Williams's warning about the grim future of the United States was more powerful than that of the Beards because Williams saw the possibility that atomic weapons might be used by American leaders in an attempt to control history. These leaders, he hoped, were "dimly aware that the United States had finally caught up with History, Americans were no longer unique. Henceforward they, too, would share the fate of all mankind. For the frontier was now on the rim of hell, and the inferno was radioactive."[20]

In his second book, *The Tragedy of American Diplomacy,* published in 1959, he argued that democracy and capitalism had been intertwined in the nineteenth century. Hofstadter had made this same claim in *The Age of Reform.* Hofstadter had argued that what he called the "soft" side of the agrarian majority, their belief in a virtuous, participatory democracy, gave way to a "hard" side after the 1890s: farmers were on their way to accepting a compromising, pragmatic, pluralist democracy that embraced the capitalism that always had been central to American experience. But Williams envisioned a dialectical relationship between democracy and capitalism that continued after the 1890s. The result of that relationship, however, once Americans became committed to spreading democratic institutions to the rest of the world, was to destroy the balance of democracy and capitalism. The hegemony of a centralized and arrogant corporate capitalism was the unintended result of attempting to export American democracy.[21]

Visualizing their new overseas frontier as identical with their western frontier, Williams wrote, the generation of the 1890s found the embodiment of their expansionist philosophy in the Open Door notes, in which American foreign policy leaders had urged that China should not be broken up, as Africa and much of Asia had been, into parts of European empires. The westward expansion of the United States had always increased the size of the marketplace as an environment for the free flow of trade. Stopping the momentum of European imperialism in China, American leaders hoped they had begun a movement to disestablish the existing empires. Associating war with imperial competition, these leaders contended that if their Open Door policy for China were accepted as universal policy, wars would cease. Business leaders from the various American states competed as individuals within the national marketplace and not as representatives of their state governments. Their competition, therefore, did not escalate into wars between the states. A similar world marketplace embodying Open Door principles would also limit competition to the level of individuals. "In a truly perceptive and even noble sense," he declared, "the makers of the Open Door policy understood that war represented the failure of policy." But the policy also "derived from the proposition that America's overwhelming economic power would cast the economics and politics of the poorer, weaker, underdeveloped countries in a pro-American mold." Designed to end the continual warfare caused by the imperial ambitions of the great powers, this policy ironically increased world tension because American corporations, in their search for markets and raw materials, aborted the prosperous development of the poorer nations and then enlisted the United States government to coerce those nations when they rebelled against this pattern of exploitation.[22]

This contradiction in the Open Door policy, according to Williams, did not become clear until World War I. "Given entry into the war on the grounds that 'the world must be made safe for democracy,'" he stated, "the crucial questions became those about the definition of democracy and the means to secure its security." Wilson, however, represented the consensus of American leaders in believing that democracy must include a synthesis of the nineteenth-century marketplace of natural harmonies with the large corporation. Wilson, therefore, had opposed the Mexican Revolution as subsequent American leaders opposed all revolutions that did not identify democracy with the nineteenth-century marketplace and the corporation. By now Williams had joined Hofstadter in seeing history as a flow of time that had not culminated in the spatial landscapes of modern nations. For Hofstadter that flow of time was moving humanity toward the harmony of a universal marketplace. But for Williams, the marketplace was a human construction. All human creations appeared in time and disappeared in time. It would take human power to try to make the marketplace universal and that effort would fail because humans could not overcome the particulars of experience.[23]

This was the tragedy of American diplomacy. Increasingly American leaders would use the power of war to achieve an impossible universal where, they hoped, there would be no more war. Williams evoked the figure of Herbert Hoover to clarify the inevitable tragedy of the Open Door policy. Hoover, according to Williams, understood that overseas military competition would create a government of unchecked power. But Hoover could not see an alternative to the Open Door policy and watched stoically as President Roosevelt led the nation inexorably toward a warfare state. "Men who began by defining the United States and the world in economic terms, and explaining its operation by the principles of capitalism and a frontier of historical development," Williams lamented, "come finally to define the United States in military terms as an embattled outpost in a hostile world. When a majority of the leaders of America's corporate society reached that conclusion, the nation went to war." Roosevelt and his advisors had set the nation on a course of inevitable tragedy. "Beginning in 1938 and 1939," he declared, "the evolving corporate coalition called in the military to execute a policy that they—the civilians—were formulating and adopting."[24]

After Roosevelt's death in 1945, the new president, Harry Truman, and his advisors continued to look on war as a successful tool for the Open Door policy. The United States had eliminated Japan and Germany as rivals for world leadership. This left only the Soviet Union as a possible competitor. And they decided on an immediate showdown with Stalin, which would force him to acknowledge that the international future was to be defined in Open Door terms. "This decision," Williams declared, "represented the final stage in the transformation of the policy of the Open Door from a utopian idea to an ideology, from an intellectual outlook for changing the world into one concerned with preserving it in the traditional mold." By 1960 Williams, then, like Hofstadter, had shifted his narrative from that of a conflict between a national democracy and an international capitalism to one in which capitalism was the dominant aspect of the culture of the United States. Hofstadter in the 1960s had begun to imagine a history of the English colonies in North America and the nation that had grown out of that colonial past in which the capitalist marketplace, joined by a religious and political marketplace, had provided an environment of liberty free from the ancient patterns of European power. For him capitalism and liberty had become synonymous. But for Williams, capitalism was synonymous with power. Had he been mistaken, therefore, in sharing with the Beards the belief that there had been a tradition of Jeffersonian democracy that offered an alternative to the aggressiveness of capitalism?[25]

In his third book, *The Contours of American History*, published in 1961, Williams joined Hofstadter in slaying their academic father, Charles Beard. Williams had joined the consensus school in redefining the relationship between capitalism and democracy. Capitalism was no longer something alien to the national democracy of 1830. The new nation was not that bounded entity imagined by bourgeois nationalism; it was not autonomous, economically, politically, or culturally. The colonies and the nation that emerged from them were part of the capitalist world system that marked the shift from medieval to modern Europe. The need for constant frontiers was not an idea that should be attributed to Frederick Jackson Turner. The institutionalization of Turner's idea by a group of political and economic leaders in the United States should not be analyzed within the framework of an exceptional national history. Turner, Theodore Roosevelt, and Woodrow Wilson represented only minor variations on the culture of capitalist expansion that had motivated the development of European colonies in North and South America.[26]

The cultural commitment to ceaseless expansion was dominant in Spain, Portugal, France, England, and the Netherlands by 1500. Where Hofstadter in the 1960s insisted that capitalist history was the history of liberty, Williams saw only power. From the beginning of colonial expansion, capitalists had used military power to force people to participate in the marketplace. The tragic coupling of the marketplace and military power had not begun with Franklin Roosevelt in World War II. The English colonists, as they became Americans, always had used military power to displace the American Indians. From this perspective the use of American military power against the indigenous peoples of the Philippines during the Spanish-American War was only a continuation of three hundred years of warfare against the native peoples who populated the "empty" American continent.

Williams had now lost the last vestiges of the aesthetic authority of bourgeois nationalism. There was no national landscape; there was no people born of that landscape. Euro-Americans were invaders who had retained their capitalist culture, which taught them they must engage in constant expansion. When Hofstadter had placed the United States within the international history of capitalism, he argued that the United States had proceeded further than the countries of Europe in refusing to be nostalgic for a world of boundaries. In this way the United States, for him, was an example of liberty for the rest of the world. For Williams, however, if the United States stood out from the other capitalist nations, it was because it had more power to destroy the boundaries of communities around the world and force them to participate in the international marketplace.

Williams' next book was *The Great Evasion* (1964). Here he confronted the implications of his thesis that there was no usable American past to which one could appeal as an alternative to the expansionist, capitalist nation-states that had grown out of the Reformation and the Renaissance. Academic Progressives, such as John Dewey and Charles Beard, Williams wrote, had criticized big business and had warned that capitalism was incompatible with democracy. But they were only "socialists of the heart" who tried "to take for their own purposes Marxian socialism's magnificent reassertion of the ideal of a Christian commonwealth without taking its commitment to social property." Can American liberals, Williams asked, explain the failure of the prophecies of men like Dewey and Beard, who had insisted that there was enough strength in the American democratic tradition to make Marx irrelevant as a critic of the American present and as a prophet for an American future? Dewey and Beard, Williams continued, were prisoners of Turner's belief in the two worlds of Europe and America with two distinct histories. But as he had tried to demonstrate in *The Contours of American History*, American history was a national variation of the capitalist history that characterized the development of early modern Europe. Men like Dewey and Beard had refused to confront "Marx's central thesis about the assumptions, the costs, and the nature of capitalist society. We have never confronted his central insight that capitalism is predicated upon an over-emphasis and exaltation of the individualistic, egoistic half of man functioning in a marketplace system that overrides and crushes the social, humanitarian half of man." Dewey and Beard could not be prophets of fraternity and equality.[27]

Specifically, Williams continued, Marx predicted that a capitalist society would have an imperialist foreign policy, something Williams had tried to demonstrate in his first three books. He now expanded his argument about continental imperialism. The constant succession of wars between Euro-Americans and the nations of the American Indians from 1600 to 1880 should become the major content of textbooks in American diplomatic history; so also should the colonial slave trade; so also should the conquest of the northern half of Mexico.

Marx also had predicted increasing economic misery under capitalism. But liberal colleagues in the 1960s, such as Hofstadter and Arthur Schlesinger Jr., insisted that current national prosperity proved Marx wrong. But, Williams argued, there was significant poverty in the United States and the postwar economic boom rested on immense deficit spending. Liberals also did not recognize that the qualified national prosperity depended on the exploitation of an external proletariat; these were the people of the underdeveloped world whose resources and labor were siphoned off as profits for the developed world.

Finally, Marx had predicted increasing alienation within the capitalist nations. The two major examples of such alienation in the United States, for Williams, were the confusion, anger, and resentment being expressed by the present generation of adolescents and the decline of voter participation. Marx had argued that capitalism needed to betray its utopian promise to make every individual a productive participant in the economy. The history of corporate capitalism in the United States had fulfilled his prediction of "the loss of any participatory role in the principal decisions of the capitalist marketplace" by dependent wage earners. It was inevitable, Williams concluded, that the loss of meaningful participation in the productive economic system would lead these wage earners to feel alienated from the political system. The average citizen, he said, was "becoming a mere consumer of politics as well as a mere consumer of goods." But these workers could not imagine an alternative system in which they would be vital participants in the economy and politics because they were ensnared in a culture in which "the sharing of profits is mistaken for sharing of direction and control of the enterprise itself, just as the sharing of the leaders' charisma is mistaken for the sharing of power."[28]

In the early 1960s, then, Williams saw a usable past in the teachings of Karl Marx, but, by the late 1960s, he had rejected Marx. In *The Great Evasion* he had accepted Marx's position that industrial capitalism was a necessary stage in history as progress. It was industrial capitalism that created the engines of productivity that made affluence possible for all the people, rather than a privileged few. But Williams had criticized the growth of an American empire, first across the continent and then overseas, that promised increasing wealth. And the bureaucracies necessary for that expansion and that accumulation of wealth destroyed the possibility of true community. Did Marx's advocacy of unlimited wealth also lead to huge bureaucracies in socialist and communist countries? Were Marxists also frontiersmen unable to stop and define spiritual community as they pursued a future of more material goods? In *The Great Evasion,* Williams had explicitly separated Marx's teachings from the political practice of the Soviet Union. But now he suggested that he was mistaken. The Soviet Union, with its vast bureaucracy, had become the mirror image of the United States because Marx, in the manner of capitalist theorists, believed that democracy was only possible in an environment of increasing wealth.

As he entered the 1970s Williams was certain that the good, the true, and the beautiful could be found only in communities smaller than the modern nation. And he pointed to the world of many small Native American communities that existed in 1600 before the arrival of European frontiersmen, with their commitment to centralization, as such a synthesis of the good, the beautiful, and the true. But he also believed that he could not reach modern readers with an appeal to the goodness and beauty of the decentralized world of early Christianity or the decentralized world of American Indians. His only hope was to persuade modern readers that what they believed was true was really false. Then, perhaps, they could imagine another truth and another goodness and another beauty.

This was his purpose in his books *Some Presidents: Wilson to Nixon* (1972) and *America Confronts a Revolutionary World* (1976). It was not true that history as progress had culminated in the modern nation, as he and Hofstadter had believed in 1940 when they were loyal sons of

Charles and Mary Beard. Nor was it true, as Hofstadter believed in 1970, that history as progress was the liberation of humanity from all local boundaries. For Hofstadter the marketplace had become the universal landscape in which people could escape from power to liberty. But Williams believed in 1970 that reality, the true, was one of particulars. It took power to replace small-scale human communities with larger ones. And once larger communities replaced smaller ones, it took energy to sustain the larger units. Power had been used by Euro-Americans to force the hundreds of Native American communities into the national marketplace of the United States. It had taken power to force the thirteen states of 1783 into a national marketplace. It had taken power to force the eleven states of the Confederacy back into the national marketplace in 1865.[29]

Williams, in his book on the presidents, argued that because the United States was not the inevitable conclusion of a mysterious national destiny, it was held together by power. And since this huge nation defied the reality of a large number of particular landscapes and communities that existed within its borders, all the presidents in Williams's lifetime, from Wilson to Nixon, had failed to fulfill their domestic policies. They had to deal with a politics of complex coalitions, regional and cultural. There was no national landscape, and there was no national people. But all presidents pretended that there was such unity. They all, therefore, failed. This also was the argument of *America Confronts a Revolutionary World.* All the presidents pretended that history as progress was moving toward a universal marketplace. All based their foreign policies on this pretension. But since they had to use power to force the many varieties of human experience into the model of the marketplace, they all failed. Even the United States, the most powerful nation in the world, did not have enough power to force uniformity on the natural diversity of human experience.

In his 1978 textbook, *Americans in a Changing World,* and in *Empire as a Way of Life* (1980), Williams kept telling Americans that their pursuit of a false understanding of history was leading them to personal and public destruction. He again asked them to understand that the frustration of their personal lives came from the fact that they were uprooted from their families, neighborhoods, and geographic localities and forced to be abstract units who fitted the demands of the marketplace. But asking Americans in 1980 to define their present situation as a declension from the Native American world of decentralized communities was an almost impossible task. In *Empire as a Way of Life,* he lamented that "once people begin to acquire and take for granted and waste surplus resources and space as a routine part of their lives, and to view them as a sign of God's favor," it is difficult for them to give up a philosophy that more is better. But, he affirmed, we must nevertheless try to "create a culture on the basis of agreement upon limits." He made it clear how far he had moved from 1964, when he had momentarily joined Marx in promising a cooperative commonwealth with great affluence. Now he declared that the promise of a decentralized America meant that everyone must make tremendous economic sacrifices. But what was the choice? The pursuit of rising standards of living had led to an empire and to an arms race with Soviet Russia. "Empire as a way of life," he insisted, "will lead to nuclear death." The alternative to this declension into internal and external chaos caused by national and international centralization was decentralized community. And "community as a way of life will lead for a time to less than is necessary. Some of us will die. But how one dies is terribly important. It speaks to the truth of how we have lived."[30]

With the simultaneous collapse of the narratives of bourgeois nationalism and Marxism since the 1940s, academic voices, with increasing frequency, speak of the transition from a modern to a postmodern world. One of the definitions of the postmodern is that it, unlike the modern, has rejected metanarratives. This, for example, is the argument of Jean-François Lyotard in his *The Postmodern Condition* (1984). Both Hofstadter and Williams, after losing their narrative of bourgeois nationalism, were briefly attracted to a Marxist international narrative. Rejecting that narrative, they both embraced a narrative of international capitalism. This is a metanarrative often ignored by postmodernists. Both Hofstadter and Williams, at the end of their lives, believed that the history of the English colonies and the United States was always within the larger context of a transnational capitalism. For Hofstadter the narrative was one of the triumph of liberty. The end of history as chaos would occur when all individuals were free from boundaries. But for Williams, the pursuit of such a goal would necessarily end in ecological catastrophe. Only by embracing spatial boundaries smaller than the nation would it be possible for humanity to survive. Only by rejecting the lure of a boundless marketplace could individuals experience limits.

Only by rejecting the metanarrative of capitalism as well as Marxism could humans find the good, the true, the beautiful in particular places.

Arthur Schlesinger Jr. (b. 1917)

The contemporary of Hofstadter and Williams, Arthur M. Schlesinger Jr., who has outlived them, was in 1940 also a loyal son of Charles and Mary Beard. His book, *The Age of Jackson,* published in 1945, won a Pulitzer Prize. His academic readers, like those of Hofstadter's *Social Darwinism in American Thought,* were still committed to that American variety of bourgeois nationalism that gave narrative form to *The Age of Jackson.* Like Hofstadter, however, Schlesinger had rejected Beard by 1948 and was struggling to find a story that could synthesize bourgeois nationalism and international capitalism. To a great extent Schlesinger was, throughout his subsequent career, content to stay with this unstable synthesis of 1948. Unlike Hofstadter and Williams he felt no need to develop a narrative that clearly placed the nation within the context of the international marketplace. From 1948 until the late 1980s, Schlesinger saw no need to reexamine his cold war vision of American history. By the 1980s, however, the increasing aesthetic authority of cultural pluralism within the United States forced him to reconsider the implications of his rejection in 1948 of his 1945 vision of a national landscape and a homogeneous people. Hofstadter and Williams died before the meaning of that revolutionary change in aesthetic authority became clear. Schlesinger did not ask in 1950 how he would define America if America did not mean an autonomous landscape and a unified people born from that landscape. He did not participate in those groups outside and inside the university during the 1960s who were insisting that the concept of a single people be demystified and analyzed in terms of differences in gender, race, ethnicity, region, and class. From this perspective there were American peoples, not an American people. Williams was initiated, like Hofstadter, Schlesinger, and myself, into an academic world that was white and male. Committing himself to the reality of decentralization, Williams imagined, unlike the rest of us, the breakdown of the public world of those white males, the nation, into a number of regional public worlds. Like us, however, he did not imagine decentralization by gender, race, ethnicity, or class. This, however, was the decentralization Schlesinger faced and recoiled from at the end of the 1980s. And he could not imagine that he had helped give aesthetic authority to this vision of a variety of American peoples when he had worked, after 1945, to undermine the aesthetic authority of the bourgeois nationalism represented by Charles and Mary Beard, the aesthetic authority of a fraternal, national people in conflict with an antidemocratic, international capitalism.[31]

Schlesinger was twenty-eight when *The Age of Jackson* won the Pulitzer Prize in 1945 and it went through thirty printings in the next three years. A large and appreciative audience applauded his vigorous affirmation that the New Deal policies of President Franklin D. Roosevelt and the Democratic Party in the 1930s were the embodiment of a usable past that had been constructed by Jacksonian Democrats in the 1830s. Schlesinger insisted that the writings of historians were always political and built on myths that were necessary for the victory of their cause. He affirmed that the Jacksonians had invented the tradition of a farmer-labor democracy that became the ideological foundation of the New Deal in its conflict with the Republican Party.

When the nation began in 1789, according to Schlesinger, its politics were characterized by a conflict between the Jeffersonian vision of a democratic society of independent and equal farmers and the Hamiltonian vision of a society dominated by an elite of capitalists who pushed men of small property or no property to the fringes of political life. In Schlesinger's story, the Jeffersonian ideal of a virtuous republic based on the widespread ownership of productive private property, a society of many small freeholding farmers, had no chance of defeating the Hamiltonian elite. This was because the industrial revolution had crossed the Atlantic. Under this European system, a few capitalists owned the means of industrial production, and their factories employed an economically and politically dependent workforce.

Sounding like the Charles Beard of 1900, Schlesinger declared that the political philosophy of the Jeffersonians had nothing to offer this growing group of factory workers. The Jeffersonians were trying to conserve a vanishing world in which small farmers could be autonomous individuals. Such a celebration of economic independence had nothing to say to the collective dependence shared by the men working the machines owned by capitalists. But these workers, Schlesinger insisted, were agents of change. "Shut off from the rest of society," these workers "began to develop a consciousness of class which helped them recover a sense of human function in a social order that baffled them by its growing impersonality."[32]

Instead of seeing themselves in Jeffersonian terms as independent individuals who had lost their freedom, they began to define themselves as a people, an organic whole, who together would create the future of America. Andrew Jackson, Schlesinger admitted, had been influenced by both the Jeffersonian and Hamiltonian positions. Nevertheless, when he was elected president in 1828, Jackson embraced this new vision of a democratic people. Continuing the rhetoric of civil religion used by Bancroft, Turner, and Beard, Schlesinger wrote that "Jackson grew visibly from the day of his inauguration. The people called him, and he came, like the great folk heroes, to lead them out of captivity and bondage." Under Jackson a revolution in the roles of Congress and president took place. "The great party leader," Schlesinger wrote, "was no longer the eloquent parliamentary orator, but this popular hero, capable of bidding directly for the confidence of the masses."[33]

As "the Jacksonians grew much more insistent about theories of capitalist alienation," Schlesinger continued, they "had to be supported by the full mobilization of the noncapitalist groups." His definition of capitalism, like that of the Beards, included only those who owned the means of industrial production, were bankers, or lived on investments. This meant, for Schlesinger, that artists, intellectuals, and small property owners were not capitalists, and he described how most of them joined the newly formed working class in their battle against capitalism.[34]

"Historians of revolution," he said, "describe a phenomenon they have named the 'desertion of the intellectuals.' This is the stage in society when the artists, the writers, the intellectuals in general, no longer find enough sustenance in the established order to feel much loyalty to it." This applied to writers such as George Bancroft and Walt Whitman. "Every great social movement," Schlesinger declared, "generates its 'social myth.' The myths are 'not descriptive of things, but expressions of a determination to act.' It is thus idle to refute a myth, since it exists as an emotional entirety whose essential function is to mobilize men for action." The artists and intellectuals of the 1830s, then, in his estimation, especially Whitman, were constructing the social myth of a democratic people led by a strong president who could assert the primacy of public interest against the destructive self-interest of the capitalists. "Moved typically by personal class, rarely by public considerations," Schlesinger insisted, "the business community has invariably brought national affairs to a state of crisis."[35]

As Schlesinger's story unfolded, he followed the Beards' narrative, in which the Civil War marked the declension of the national democracy into the chaos of capitalism. Like Hofstadter, he had to report with regret that the Jacksonian politicians and intellectuals had not been able to establish firmly the new social myth of the democratic people as an organic body before the sectional crisis leading to the Civil War confused the American political imagination for the next half century. The crisis had shattered the unity of the Democratic Party. When the Civil War was over, the Republican Party kept itself in power by wrapping itself in the mantle of Jeffersonian individualism. Controlled by capitalists, the Republican Party obscured the conflict between capitalism and democracy. Like the Whig Party from which it had descended, the Republican Party preached "the identity of interests between the classes, the unimportance of class, the nonexistence of class."[36]

Although such political deception by the Republican Party prevailed from the end of the Civil War to the coming of the Great Depression in 1929, Schlesinger, like the Beards, reassured his readers that the "traditions of Jefferson and Jackson might recede but could never disappear." The social myth of Jacksonian democracy was available, therefore, to President Roosevelt when he was elected in 1932 and to the artists and intellectuals of the 1930s. Speaking as one of those intellectuals, Schlesinger affirmed that "we have seen how the growth of impersonality in economic relations enhanced the need for the intervention of government. As the private conscience grew increasingly powerless to impose effective restraint in the methods of business, the public conscience, in the form of the democratic government, had to step in to prevent the business community from tearing society apart in pursuit of profit."[37]

The message for Schlesinger's readers was that the capitalist pursuit of self-interest had brought about the economic and social catastrophe of 1929 and that Roosevelt, like Jackson, had to reassert the public interest. Roosevelt, then, like Jackson, was overcoming alienation and class conflict. He was recreating the body politic first imagined by the Jacksonians; he was reestablishing democratic equality and fraternity.

Because he was concerned only with the political health of a particular nation, Schlesinger had no interest in 1945 in the universals of the

Enlightenment. Affirming the centrality of myth in the construction of a fraternal nation, he had no concern for the Enlightenment ideal of the rational individual capable of achieving harmony with transnational universals.

His book, therefore, was a vigorous reassertion of the national romance that gave narrative structure to the Beards' *The Rise.* The New Deal was an organic development out of Jacksonian democracy. The national landscape and the industrial landscape represented a powerful and fruitful synthesis. They were the foundation for the farmer-labor democracy that was the authentic American tradition. The sons of Hamilton, disloyal to American national identity, had tried to hide this democratic tradition from the people. But the people could always be led out of their false consciousness by the sons who remained loyal to Jefferson and Jackson. The narrative of the Beards' *The Rise* expressed this cyclical pattern in which the sons of Hamilton, the spokesmen for self-interest, for a moment gained power. But then the sons of Jefferson and Jackson, the spokesmen for public interest, regained power because the people could never be truly separated from their tradition of public interest, from their identity as members of a commonwealth.

In the age of Jackson the only major threat to the American nation, in Schlesinger's analysis, came from capitalists within the national boundaries. The conflict, for Schlesinger as for the Beards, therefore, was implicitly between two groups of Anglo-American men. When he described the individuals who made up the people of Jacksonian democracy, they were Anglo-American males. When he described the Federalists, Whigs, and Republicans, who were the opponents of the people and the apologists for aristocracy and self-interest, they were Anglo-American males. Capitalists, for Schlesinger in 1945, lived within the nation but were not loyal to it. The conflict that had raged from the time of Jefferson and Hamilton to the 1930s was between democrats, who embodied loyalty to the nation as an organic whole, and capitalists, who had no commitment to the nation as a deep fraternity.

In 1945 the boundaries that Schlesinger drew so explicitly to exclude capitalists from the body politic also implicitly excluded Anglo-American women, Catholics, and Jews, as well as all Americans of color. When Schlesinger celebrated Jefferson and Jackson as heroes who fought against the Hamiltonian attempt to import European patterns of hierarchy, his political imagination did not see Jefferson and Jackson as slaveholders who exploited their slaves. Slavery and white racism were not part of the dramatic difference he portrayed between a Europe of class distinction and an America of equality. Nor in 1945 did he see Jefferson and Jackson as participants in the ongoing war of European Americans against the Native Americans. He did not see them as envisioning a continent in which all red people would be replaced by white people. He did not see that this vision of the conquest of the continent was leading the Jacksonians toward a war with Mexico that would force the northern half of that country within the expanding boundaries of the United States.

By 1949, however, when Schlesinger published his next major book, *The Vital Center,* many of the aesthetic boundaries of his narrative in *The Age of Jackson* were shattered. In 1945 he had expressed his gratitude to Charles Beard, the most influential historian in the United States from 1910 to 1945. Schlesinger had understood himself to be a participant in a democratic tradition that stretched from President Jackson to President Roosevelt and from the Jacksonian historian, George Bancroft, to Charles Beard, who had celebrated the election of Franklin D. Roosevelt in 1932 as a sign that the democratic people were reclaiming political power from the capitalists. But in 1949 Schlesinger defined himself as part of "a new and distinct political generation."[38]

Schlesinger felt he had the responsibility as a participant in this revolutionary generation to help construct a new set of aesthetic boundaries for the narrative that would provide meaning for Americans. He expressed his sense of participation in this radical restructuring of historical narrative by beginning his book with a quotation from the Irish poet, William Butler Yeats: "Things fall apart, the centre cannot hold; / mere anarchy is loosed upon the world." For Schlesinger, then, there was a desperate need to construct a new center.

His center in *The Age of Jackson* was the American nation characterized by a fraternal democracy. The threat to the center came from capitalists dwelling within the national boundaries but disloyal to the national interest. An American landscape had made possible the Jeffersonian world of free and equal farmers. An aristocratic culture that had originated in the European landscape had been brought into the New World. That culture had diminished in significance as the American landscape produced the society of rural freeholders. Then, however, industrialism had come across the Atlantic from Europe and had revitalized hierarchy through the pattern of capitalist ownership of the factories. But the new class of industrial workers had rejected their dependent role and joined with farmers to construct a democratic politics. Led by a strong president, the people could keep capitalists from creating social chaos. The most recent triumph of the people had come in the 1930s.

But in 1949, for Schlesinger, the vital center for Americans was Western civilization, and the major threats to its social harmony came from fascism and communism. He wrote about this crisis as if he had never celebrated a myth-informed fraternal America. The middle classes of Western civilization, he argued, were responsible for this crisis because they had developed a historical narrative of perpetual progress and had argued that rapid technological change was liberating the individual from a series of irrational old worlds to become independent and rational. For Schlesinger, however, "the eighteenth century had exaggerated man's capacity to live by logic alone." Men, he affirmed, needed a sense of the good and beautiful as well as the true. The middle classes had neglected their responsibility to construct a society that met the emotional needs of the average person. The pervasive sense of alienation among the masses had led the people to try to find fulfillment in either fascism or communism.[39]

The fascist and communist alternatives to the social fragmentation and alienation of capitalism were evil because they both demanded that the individual sacrifice himself to the state. Instead of twentieth-century history being the triumph of middle-class capitalism, then, it had become the century in which fascism and communism were the dynamic developments. In contrast to the false optimism of their academic fathers, such as Charles Beard, Schlesinger's academic generation had "discovered a new dimension of experience—the dimensions of anxiety, guilt and corruption," and "the consequence of this historical re-education has been an unconditional rejection of totalitarianism and a reassertion of the ultimate integrity of the individual."[40]

The vital center of the future, for Schlesinger, should have been one in which there was a balance between the independence of the individual and social responsibility. In *The Age of Jackson,* he had defined a clear distinction and conflict between capitalism and democracy. But in *The Vital Center,* he always used the term "capitalist democracy." A capitalist democracy was the vital center, affirming both individual independence and social responsibility. He joined Hofstadter in celebrating the New Deal as such a synthesis. In contrast to his position in *The Age of Jackson,* Schlesinger now wrote, "liberals have values in common with most members of the business community—in particular a belief in a free society." This new theme of consensus between capitalist and liberal was one that he kept repeating throughout the book. "The modern American capitalist," he affirmed, "has come to share many values with the American liberal" and "the differences among classes in a capitalist democracy are often wide and bitter; but they are much less impossible than the differences between capitalist democracy and authoritarianism." In *The Age of Jackson,* Schlesinger had celebrated the achievement of a democracy that spoke through a strong president. In *The Vital Center,* however, he had begun to identify the concept of the people speaking through a strong leader with totalitarianism. The voice of the majority should not be allowed to silence the voice of any individual. A people could never become a virtuous society. Humanity would forever be characterized by imperfection and sin.[41]

Since Schlesinger in 1949 criticized the Enlightenment ideal of a rational individual as part of the destructiveness of modern utopianism, his hope for a vital center rested on the development of a faith in the balance of good and evil, of society and the individual. We must have, Schlesinger declared, a fighting faith in our capitalist democracies. "Free society will survive, in the last resort, only if enough people believe in it deeply enough to die for it," and, he added, "Today democracy is paying the price for its systematic cultivation of the peaceful and rational virtues." His conclusion was that "we desperately need a rich emotional life, an enduring social order must base itself upon the emotional energies and needs of man."[42]

Schlesinger, by 1949, had turned against Charles Beard on the issue of foreign policy. Fascism and communism were more dangerous to the American people than was the materialism and self-interest of capitalism. The boundaries of the nation were not secure against these agents of chaos without the mobilization and use of military power. In 1949 he also was willing to engage in a cold war against the Soviet Union as long as it was necessary to contain that new threat to world stability. But Schlesinger was never able to imagine a "fighting faith" for Western civilization in its long-term battle against Soviet aggression. His analysis in *The Vital Center* was that the capitalist classes in the European nations had failed to give the peoples in those nations any sense of public identity so that they could resist the political seductions of fascism and communism and the tyrannical public identity they offered. Only the United States had a tradition that blended the individualism of capitalism with a sense of public responsibility.

Schlesinger, therefore, went into the 1950s unable to imagine a transnational history in which the United States participated. He did not share Hofstadter's celebration of the capitalist marketplace as the potential source of worldwide liberty. Nor did he share Williams's view that the dominant capitalist culture in the United States participated in the general history of chaos caused by the capitalist world system. In the 1950s, therefore, he had a very unstable narrative about how an exceptional American community existed that transcended the fragmentation caused by the self-interest and materialism of capitalism. But the American community also embraced capitalism and had the international responsibility to contain totalitarianism.

In *The Vital Center*, then, he rejected the story of the conflict between the public interest of the people and the self-interest of capitalists, between the spiritual nationalism of the people and the materialism of capitalists that had informed his *Age of Jackson*. For the next forty years he argued that the people were made up of a variety of interest groups. Conflict was not between the people and capitalists, but within the people. There was always conflict in the shifting coalitions of particular interest groups. Sounding like the Hofstadter of the 1950s, Schlesinger was pleased to report that the American tradition was "empirical, pragmatic, ironic, pluralistic, competitive." And, he continued, this constant competition was the source of progress. "The choice is between conflict and stagnation." He was celebrating those capitalist values, which, he had argued earlier, caused the alienation leading to fascism and communism.[43]

It is not surprising, then, that when he wrote a trilogy about the New Deal—*The Crisis of the Old Order* (1957), *The Coming of the New Deal* (1959), and *The Politics of Upheaval* (1960)—Schlesinger found it necessary to smuggle some of his 1945 political vision back into his narrative. He found it necessary to imagine a nation that was more than the materialistic self-interest of individuals. He did this by making variations on a theory of the cycles of American history proposed by his father, Arthur Schlesinger Sr. The older Schlesinger, a professor of history at Harvard and an admirer of Charles Beard, had taken the cycles of conflict in Charles and Mary Beard's story and, before them, in Turner's first narrative, and made them explicit. Schlesinger Sr. suggested that

cycles of conflict

progress in the United States was something of a spiral. A period of democratic public interest was always followed by a period of capitalist self-interest. But then the capitalist moment was succeeded by a democratic moment. And this democratic moment was a fuller expression of public interest than the earlier democratic expression. The older Schlesinger had the faith of the Beards that any capitalist victory was temporary because democracy was the true national identity. The history of the United States was an exodus from an irrational Old World, in this case a chaotic capitalism, toward the universal national of democracy. But the exodus was one of a slow spiral upward. It was an exodus interrupted periodically by a temporary victory of capitalist fragmentation.[44]

Since Schlesinger Jr. had rejected the commitment to a universal national held by his father and the Beards, he reworked the theory of cycles in the 1950s. He substituted a variety of interest groups for a fraternal people. The democratic moment, he argued, was when all the groups in the nation found a voice in a particular presidential administration. The undemocratic moment was when a single interest group, business, dominated a presidential administration and silenced all the other interest groups. The 1920s were such an undemocratic moment; Roosevelt's New Deal was a democratic moment.

In the 1950s, therefore, Schlesinger Jr. continued to cling to the faith of his father and the Beards that history as progress was inevitable. The victory of the Republicans in 1952 was a return to an era of business self-interest and a silencing of other voices. But, for Schlesinger Jr., the Eisenhower administration was much more committed to the public interest than Harding, Coolidge, and Hoover had been in the 1920s. The New Deal had brought the country to a high level of democracy and the next democratic moment that inevitably would replace the business control in the 1950s would lead the nation still further up the spiral of progress.

John F. Kennedy was aware of the cyclical theory of progress propounded by both Schlesingers. When he was elected president in 1960, he invited the younger Schlesinger to become an intellectual in residence in his administration. But Kennedy's assassination revealed how much more fragile Schlesinger's theory of democratic progress was than that of his father. In *The Age of Jackson* he had defined Jackson as a representative hero of the people. The people had called Jackson to be their leader. But by 1949, Schlesinger had replaced the vision of an organic people with the vision of a variety of interest groups. How could these groups perform the mythical act of calling a hero to represent them?

For Schlesinger Jr. in 1960, they could not. In 1940 he had seen Franklin Roosevelt as a hero called by the people. By 1950, however, Schlesinger Jr. saw Roosevelt as a master politician who had created a powerful coalition from a variety of interest groups that could end the business domination of the 1920s. Now he saw Kennedy as such a coalition builder. The defeat of the business domination of the 1950s depended on the triumph of Kennedy's skill and will. Kennedy had constructed a vision of public interest out of a variety of interest groups. Schlesinger Jr. said he believed in the inevitability of an upward spiral of cycles as his father had. But how could Schlesinger Jr. prophesy there would be a democratic moment if there was not a strong hero available? Unlike Bancroft and his father, he could not count on the mythical body of the people to produce such a hero.

This, then, was the tragedy of Kennedy's death. When he memorialized Kennedy in his book of 1965, *A Thousand Days* (another Pulitzer Prize winner), he had to report that the democratic cycle could not survive the death of its creator. When Schlesinger Jr. described Roosevelt and Kennedy, they were for the people, but not of the people. They were, he wrote, "patrician, urbane, cultivated, inquisitive, gallant; both were detached from business ethos." But, for Schlesinger, Lyndon Johnson, Kennedy's successor, did not have the heroic strength and skill to hold together the democratic, antibusiness coalition constructed by Kennedy.[45]

Schlesinger Jr. had announced in 1949 that the United States had rejected isolation and embraced internationalism. But he never tried to clarify what internationalism meant. He poured his energy, therefore, into writing histories of the New Deal and the Kennedy administration. Now a significant part of his biting criticism of President Johnson pointed to Johnson's tragic choice to make foreign policy more important than domestic policy. Focusing on Vietnam, Johnson lost sight of Kennedy's project of expanding welfare and civil rights. Johnson hoped to be remembered as a hero in foreign policy. For Schlesinger, President Nixon followed Johnson's emphasis. This meant that the nation had slipped back into rule by the single interest of business.

In spite of Schlesinger's outward optimism that this period of chaos would be replaced by an upward spiral of progress, he seemed to be aware that according to his own story this could not occur without the chance appearance of a heroic figure. As he went into the 1970s, then, he seemed to be overwhelmed by the vision of the nation falling deeper and deeper into chaos. He expressed this dark view in *The Crisis of Confidence: Ideas, Power, and Violence in America* (1969). For the first time he talked about a dark side to national identity that was permanent. Responding to the assassinations of Martin Luther King Jr. and Robert Kennedy, he wrote that Americans had always been "a violent people with a violent history," that our "national instincts for aggressiveness and destruction" were a constant contradiction to our "national capacity for civility and idealism."[46]

Implicit in Schlesinger's position in 1970 was that the permanent dark half of the American psyche was encouraged during that part of the historical cycle when the country was dominated by the self-interest of business. "The urgent problem of our politics," he wrote, "is to give the presently alienated groups a feeling of membership in the national process." When business was in control, "the liberal remaking of America," he concluded, "was rooted in the understanding, firmly grounded in our history, that the rich always rule in their own interest."[47]

The liberal cycle that began in 1960 and should have lasted, according to the calculations of his father, for sixteen years had been unnaturally replaced by business control. Johnson had abdicated his domestic leadership to focus on Vietnam. Schlesinger lamented in his book of 1973, *The Imperial Presidency,* that voters had come to identify presidential leadership with foreign policy. It seemed as if they only imagined heroic leadership within the context of the cold war. And potential heroic leaders of domestic reform such as Robert Kennedy had been killed. Trapped in a cycle of business selfishness that should not have been occurring, Schlesinger wrote a eulogy, *Robert F. Kennedy and His Times* (1978). He focused on what might have been if Kennedy had lived. He did not want to write at length about the weak presidencies of Nixon, Ford, and Carter, which allowed aberration and violence to intensify. As the selfishness of the rich became respectable in the administrations of Ronald Reagan and as Reagan continued to identify presidential leadership with the cold war, Schlesinger felt the need to explain why the social fragmentation of the business-dominated political cycle had lasted for more than twenty years. In a collection of essays, *The Cycles of American History* (1980), he suggested that the alternating cycles of public and private interest might have the length of a generation, of thirty years, rather than the sixteen years his father had suggested. He hoped, then, that the election of Clinton to the presidency marked the end of the long period of social chaos under the politics of business self-interest. This unnatural era was ending and the normal pattern of the democratic representation of all interest groups was reappearing. But again the mysterious inevitability of this constructive era depended on Clinton's capacity for heroic leadership. There was no people to speak as his father, and the Beards, had believed. The public interest could only be constructed by a strong president who brought together a coalition of many interest groups.[48]

By the 1980s Schlesinger also was confronted by another major problem caused by his rejection of the bourgeois nationalist vision of a homogeneous people whose citizens formed a deep fraternity, that vision that had informed his *Age of Jackson.* The task of a heroic president, Schlesinger now believed, had become much more difficult. In addition to creating a coalition of economic interest groups that could drive the self-interest and social irresponsibility of business from political control, a potentially heroic president was now faced with the possible cultural fragmentation of the nation. How could a president with the character of a John or Robert Kennedy lead the nation on its upward spiral of progress if there was no homogeneous people? How could a progressive president construct a politics of public interest out of groups that believed they each had a unique cultural destiny?

But when Schlesinger lamented the multicultural threat to his vision of the cycles of American history in his book of 1991, *The Disuniting of America,* he could not openly denounce African American, Mexican American, or Native American nationalisms as threats to an American nationalism that demanded an organically unified people. After all, he had destroyed the aesthetic authority of the universal national in 1949 in *The Vital Center.* Instead, his explicit criticism of these nationalisms evoked an aesthetic authority that celebrated the cosmopolitanism of the Enlightenment of the eighteenth century. He linked African American, Mexican American, and Native American nationalism to the ugliness of nineteenth-century European romantic nationalism. This terrible declension from the Enlightenment was, for Schlesinger, a return to the tribalism of an uncivilized past. In 1991, as in 1949, Schlesinger made no effort to explain how the history of the United States was both that of a particular nation and also that of the Enlightenment universals of

Western civilization. But, as in 1949, he linked nationalism to the irrational, the world of myth he had celebrated in *The Age of Jackson*.[49]

There, in 1945, he had praised the artists and historians of the 1830s who created the myth of a democratic people. That was necessary, for the young Schlesinger, if humans were to escape the alienation and materialism that were the legacy of the Enlightenment. But in 1991 he insisted that the real America was committed to the Enlightenment ideal of rational individuals free from the artful boundaries of all particular cultures. And he saw no need to explain how the cycles of a national history in the United States were related to those timeless truths of the Enlightenment.

Schlesinger's narrative in *The Disuniting of America,* which contrasted the promise of Enlightenment universalism with the declension into the particulars of romantic nationalism, was one he shared with other major critics of a multicultural America. Allan Bloom's *The Closing of the American Mind* (1987), Roger Kimball's *Tenured Radicals* (1990), and Dinesh D'Souza's *Illiberal Education* (1991) had all argued the superiority of the rational universals of Western civilization over the irrationality of particular cultures. Specifically, Schlesinger argued that men had been able to leave a European world of particular and irrational cultures to fulfill the Enlightenment ideal of the autonomous and rational individual in an American landscape free from the chaos of the many Old World cultures that repressed the rationality of individuals. Schlesinger celebrated the European men "who, in repudiating their homelands and joining to make new lives, melted away ancient ethnic differences."[50]

In 1945 Schlesinger had imagined a people as a deep fraternity. In 1991 he continued to exclude women from his narrative. For him individual men had stepped out of European cultures to become autonomous and rational. Families had not migrated across the Atlantic. Men were not in a position of patriarchal power over their wives and children. Families were not particular cultures that placed boundaries around their members. He imagined that family members were autonomous and rational, free from nonrational loyalties. To focus on families also meant a focus on life cycles. How could one distinguish the history of generations from the history that was not characterized by progress, that meaningless history of time-bound particular cultures?

Schlesinger's Enlightenment America, like the capitalist America Hofstadter imagined in 1950, was a nation that did not have the colonial legacy of two centuries of warfare against Native Americans and two centuries of enslaving African Americans. But, then as he told a story that echoed Hofstadter's critique of nineteenth-century Anglo-Protestant culture, this Enlightenment America of the Founding Fathers experienced declension into an unreal America of romantic nationalism. Anglo-Americans in the nineteenth century defined themselves as a particular and biologically superior culture. Drawing boundaries around themselves, they defined Native Americans, African Americans, and Mexican Americans as racially and culturally inferior.

These excluded groups, according to Schlesinger, were not strong enough to challenge the ability of Anglo-Americans to write American history in a way that justified their domination. But the millions of Catholic and Jewish immigrants who had poured into the United States did begin to write alternative histories to the Anglo-American story. Anglo-Americans, however, were able to keep what Schlesinger labeled "compensatory" histories out of the major universities. "American history," Schlesinger declared, "was written in the interests of white Anglo-Saxon Protestant males" until the 1940s. Then during the crisis of World War II, Anglo-Americans suddenly recognized "[t]he corruption of history by nationalism." Returning to the ideals of the Enlightenment, to the real America, they now understood that "the purpose of history is not to promote self-esteem, but understanding of the world and the past, dispassionate analysis, judgment and perspective."[51]

The terrible irony for Schlesinger was that while Anglo-American historians after 1945 were willing to give up the "exculpatory" history that had justified their domination, the formerly dominated cultures refused to give up "compensatory" history, history that romanticized their experience as victims of Anglo-American power. "Instead of a nation composed of individuals making their own free choice," he lamented, "America increasingly sees itself as composed of groups more or less indelible in their ethnic character." He blamed the Catholic and Jewish Americans whose ancestors had come from southern and eastern Europe for initiating this post-1945 emphasis on the identity of Americans as members of particular groups rather than as rational and independent individuals. In 1974, he reported, "after testimony from ethnic spokesmen denouncing the melting pot as a conspiracy to homogenize America, Congress passed the Ethnic Heritage Studies Program Act." This emphasis on ethnic identity, he continued, "began as a gesture of protest against the Anglocentric culture. It became a cult, and today it threatens to become a counter revolution against the original theory of America as a single nation."[52]

The great danger of this cult of ethnicity, he declared, is that "as an individual deprived of memory becomes disoriented and lost, so a nation denied a conception of its past will be disabled in dealing with its present and its future." The most dramatic example, for him, of the danger of losing an accurate memory of the past was the insistence at that time of some African American leaders that African Americans had a separate culture from that of European Americans. Such "self-Africanization after 300 years in America" was, in his estimation, mere "playacting." He concluded, "American Afrocentrism is really a case of what the English historian Eric Hobsbawm calls 'the invention of tradition.'"[53]

Schlesinger poured out his anger as he contrasted what he saw as an invented Afrocentrism with what he called "the facts of history: that Europe was the birthplace of the United States of America, that European ideas and culture formed the republic, that the United States is an extension of European Civilization, and that nearly eighty percent of Americans are of European descent." The concept of history as progress toward liberty for the individual came, he affirmed, from "European ideas, not Asian, nor African, nor Middle Eastern ideas, except by adoption."[54]

In *The Disuniting of America* Schlesinger did not make an explicit connection between what he described as the end of Anglo-American "exculpatory" history and the increased power and vigor of the "compensatory" history written by groups so long dominated by Anglo-Americans. Instead he celebrated the return of Anglo-Americans to the principles of the Enlightenment. "The American synthesis has an inevitable Anglo-Saxon coloration," he affirmed, "but it is no longer an exercise in Anglo-Saxon domination. The republic embodies ideals that transcend ethnic, religious and political lives." His language indicates, however, that he realized that a vital center of abstract, universal principles might not have the persuasive power that had been exercised by those myths of Anglo-American nationalism that in 1945 he had once embraced. Several times he remarked on "the brittle bonds of national identity that hold this diverse and fractious society together." He had begun this book by celebrating the United States as the embodiment of the Enlightenment search for a space that would allow the individual to escape history as nonrational tradition. And he damned the members of what he called the new "cult of ethnicity" for rejecting this ideal of "the escape from origins" in order "to search for roots." But he concluded the book by informing all those Americans who were not male Anglo-Americans that their search for roots was precluded by the power of Anglo-American roots. In the 1990s Americans could not begin the world anew because they could not escape the nonrational traditions that surrounded them. Ironically Schlesinger now seemed to be rejoining the Anglo-American historians who were his teachers in the 1930s as he insisted that collective art was more powerful than individual reason. "For our values are not matters of whim and happenstance," was his final pronouncement. "History has given them to us. They are anchored in our national experience, in our great national documents, in our national heroes, in our folkways, traditions and standards." Schlesinger had declared in 1949 that he had killed his academic father, Charles Beard, and replaced national with international history. But in 1991 it seemed impossible for him to make a coherent narrative out of his commitment to both the rootless universalism of the Enlightenment and the rooted particularism of an American nation. In 1949 he had rejected the form of the national romance in order to justify the shift from isolation to internationalism. Now he seemed to re-embrace the narrative of the national romance. In his seven decades of writing history, he had not become self-conscious of his ambiguous use of both state-of-nature anthropology and cultural anthropology.[55]

CHAPTER THREE

The Crisis of American Literary Criticism from World War I to World War II

Vernon Louis Parrington (1871–1929)

Going into World War II, historians who specialized in the study of the history of the United States called their professional organization "The Mississippi Valley Historical Association." But soon after the end of the war, they discarded this designation and renamed themselves "The Organization of American Historians." This change symbolized the generational discontinuity experienced by men such as Hofstadter, Schlesinger Jr., and Williams. They had lost their ability to believe in the Anglo-American myth of national origins, which had been such a powerful reality for Bancroft, Turner, and the Beards. They no longer saw a people born from that national landscape that was imagined to exist west of the Appalachian Mountains. The suddenness of this change in the aesthetic foundations of national identity is symbolically dramatized by whom the members of the Mississippi Valley Historical Association chose in 1946 as the author of the most influential book by a historian during the previous decade. They voted for *Main Currents in American Thought* by a deceased professor of American literature, Vernon Louis Parrington. The importance of this masterpiece was something I had been taught by my teachers at Princeton when they learned of my desire to become a professional historian. They had informed me that *The Rise of American Civilization* by the Beards, Parrington's *Main Currents,* and F. O. Matthiessen's *American Renaissance* were special books to which I should look for inspiration and guidance when I began to write history.[1]

Parrington, a contemporary of the Beards, had died just as his three-volume study was beginning to be published in 1927. Perhaps historians chose his book, rather than the Beards' *The Rise of American Civilization,* because, in contrast to the Beards' many books, this was both Parrington's first and last book. Or perhaps they chose it in 1946 because, unlike the Beards' *The Rise of American Civilization,* it was very much an elegy for the national landscape. Parrington's masterpiece did not have the narrative of the national romance so central to *The Rise of American Civilization.* Writing in the 1920s, Parrington did not imagine a synthesis of the national and urban-industrial landscapes. He saw only the defeat of the pastoral democracy of the 1830s by an alien capitalism during the Gilded Age. But in contrast to Turner, Parrington, in his book written in the 1920s, continued to denounce capitalism as un-American. He continued to hope for a miracle that somehow, someday, American democracy would be reborn.

It was Parrington's hatred of capitalism and his refusal to accept the death of a democratic people, a fraternity of equal citizens, that made his book so popular among younger historians and teachers of literature during the 1930s. For this younger generation, Parrington's death had coincided with the miracle of the collapse of capitalism in 1929. With the death of capitalism, Jacksonian democracy had become, as Arthur Schlesinger Jr. had written, a usable past for Franklin Roosevelt's New Deal. Associating capitalism and class hierarchy with England, Parrington's book spoke to young literary critics who shared that upsurge of isolationism and nationalism that followed World War I. Now was the time in American English departments to end the monopoly of literature written in England. Now was the time to achieve fully the independence of American literature from English literature. The Beards' *The Rise of American Civilization* continued the tradition of Bancroft's multivolume history of the United States, but Parrington's *Main Currents in American Thought* was the first major history of American literature. Here, for young literary critics, was a usable past. Parrington reminded them that by the beginning of the eighteenth century a democratic American language was emerging from the virgin land of the American continent and was superseding the aristocratic English language of the European continent. One of the young founders of the Harvard Program in American Civilization, Howard Mumford Jones, remembered how his generation was intellectually invigorated when they found Parrington.

"Who can forget," he wrote, "the tingling sense of discovery with which we first read those lucid pages?"[2]

The men who developed the Harvard American Civilization Program had no difficulty, then, in imagining that their program would combine literary criticism and the history of ideas. Literary criticism would reveal how the reality expressed by American literature was different from the reality expressed by English literature. It would reveal, following the authority of the Beards' *The Rise of American Civilization* and Parrington's *Main Currents in American Thought,* that English literature and American literature were the artistic expressions of two different landscapes. The development of American civilization programs in a number of Ivy League universities in the 1930s provided a way of immediately segregating American literature from English departments and their continuing commitment to the literature of the Old World. Like Bancroft, Turner, and the Beards, Parrington built his three-volume history on the metaphor of two worlds. His trilogy assumed progress from an Old World of irrational tradition to a New World in harmony with nature. He, too, believed meaningful history was an exodus that would culminate in the sacred space of the national landscape.

Parrington's aesthetic authority in giving boundaries to this chosen people was that of Turner and the Beards. He did not feel the need to explain, as Bancroft had, why a virgin land existed only between French Catholic Canada and Spanish Catholic Mexico. He did not feel the need to explain why he saw no Native Americans, African Americans, or Mexican Americans profaning the virgin land. Parrington's story focused only on one conflict, that between English hierarchical tradition and American democratic nature. As in history departments, the conflict was between the good sons who honored their American identity given them by the virgin land and bad sons who rejected the land, their mother, from whom they were born and chose Old World tradition as the father of their identity.

A tone of anger was much stronger in Parrington's writing than in the Beards' work. Because their national romance linked this pastoral, national landscape to the urban-industrial landscape, the Beards had a way of explaining how good sons since the 1890s gained vitality from an urban-industrial landscape in their conflict with the bad sons. But Turner had seen a cycle in those conflicts from 1600 to 1830 in which the good sons had grown stronger because the pastoral landscape had become more powerful. Parrington worked within this story of cyclical conflicts until the exodus into the trans-Appalachian West, the valley of democracy, had apparently made it possible for the good sons to eliminate the corrupting presence of English tradition once and for all. Without this tradition to sustain them, the bad sons would wither away and disappear. But, then, Parrington agreed with Turner that English capitalism had captured the nation after the Civil War. If the marketplace was more powerful than the national landscape, the situation was reversed. There no longer was a fountain of strength pouring forth from the national landscape to sustain the good sons. The pattern of Parrington's trilogy, therefore, is much closer to Turner's than to the Beards'. But with this great exception, Parrington, unlike Turner, was not stoic about the victory of capitalist hierarchy and inequality. Unlike Turner he did not link the victory of capitalism to the evolutionary laws of nature. In contrast to Turner, he saw only one nature, that of the national landscape. Here, he was closer to the Beards' position in *The Rise of American Civilization* because Charles Beard by 1920 had renounced his earlier commitment to universal laws of evolution. Parrington especially expressed his anger at the young intellectuals, writers, and artists in the 1920s, who seemed to be so stoic in their acceptance of the victory of international capitalism over national democracy. This was an anger that could become a usable past for the intellectuals and writers of the 1930s, who were certain that the collapse of capitalism meant the recovery of the national democratic heritage. They could share Parrington's contempt for the "Lost Generation" writers of the 1920s, for whom there was no hope that virtue could defeat corruption.[3]

Most of the literature that Parrington analyzed in the first two volumes of his trilogy was explicitly religious and political. Like Bancroft, Parrington saw New England as the region in which the first signs of national identity appeared. In the tradition of bourgeois nationalism, Parrington assumed that history as progress would culminate when the modern nation was totally free from international influence. He assumed that this nation would be a classless, middle-class democracy characterized by the fraternity and equality of its citizens. He assumed that the democratic nation had a mortal enemy in capitalism. Capitalists imagined the boundless world of the market, not the bounded world of the nation. They gave priority to self-interest over national interest. Capitalists expected class hierarchy. Capitalists celebrated materialism; they had no respect for the soul of the nation.

Parrington portrayed seventeenth-century New England Puritans as having brought the hierarchical traditions of England with them across the Atlantic. By 1700, however, he could contrast Cotton Mather, who clung to the ways of the generation of 1630, with John Wise, who "understood the plain people whom he served, and [he] sympathized heartily with the democratic ideals then taking form in the New England villages." Here Parrington was invoking the creative power of the natural landscape. It liberated the individual from the boundaries of European culture and was making him part of a new democratic culture.[4]

He shared the belief of the Beards that such a democratic culture was widespread by 1776. "A popular will to self-rule had long been developing in America, and when the outbreak of hostilities clarified its latent objective, it speeded a conscious republican purpose." And, he continued, "An American mind had been created by the silent pressure of the environment." But in the pattern of the Anglo-American myth of national origins expressed by Bancroft, Turner, and the Beards, the final independence of the nation from European traditions was completed by the exodus from the colonial past across the Appalachians into the Mississippi Valley. And Parrington fully participated in this narrative. The Revolution of 1776 did not achieve a classless, middle-class democracy because, as Turner and the Beards argued, the Founding Fathers were inheritors of English tradition, rather than children of the natural landscape.[5]

For Parrington, as for Turner and Charles and Mary Beard, Jefferson was the great saint of the religion of the nation. The democratic people of 1776 had been frustrated by the undemocratic republic of checks and balances constructed by the Founding Fathers. Now the people found a heroic leader in Jefferson. He, according to Parrington, was "the product of the first West in American history. . . . Jefferson loved his backwoods neighbors, and he, in turn, was loved by them." When the people were inspired by Jefferson's prophecy that they would find redemption in the valley of democracy, they renewed their exodus. And they found the prophecy fulfilled in this virgin land. "The age of theology was gone, the age of political speculation was passing, the age of constitution building was over." Parrington could rejoice that "[d]isintegration had come upon every system of caste brought over from the old world."[6]

In reporting the conflict of the 1790s between Jefferson, the good son of nature, and Hamilton, the bad son who chose Old World tradition, Parrington knew his readers could easily recognize the villain. He described Hamilton as "hard, almost brutal," and a man "utterly devoid of sentiment and without a shred of idealism." Hamilton was a man of "intellectual arrogance" with "cynical contempt" for the people. Repressing the existence of African Americans in the United States, Parrington could identify Jefferson, the slaveholder, with liberty. The essential conflict, for Parrington, was between the democratic sons of nature, all Anglo-Protestants, and the undemocratic sons of European tradition, all Anglo-Protestants. When he carried his story of this conflict forward to the Civil War, he expressed his concern that a new group of bad sons, a generation younger than Hamilton, were learning to disguise their evil intentions. This was possible, he declared, because a culture of romanticism came to characterize the United States between 1830 and 1860. This culture was divided between a good and an evil romanticism. The good romanticism expressed the spirituality of the democracy born of the national landscape. The evil romanticism was that of a generation of un-American capitalists, committed to self-interest, materialism, and hierarchy, who disguised themselves as romantics and pretended to be part of the national democracy.

Like Turner and the Beards, Parrington argued that the New England renaissance, led by men such as Emerson and Thoreau, was a national renaissance. "In the vast territory drained by the Mississippi—the 'Valley of Democracy'—was conceived the most romantic dream that ever visited the mature mind of America." Inspired by this West, the New England transcendentalists, Parrington declared, "were impatient of any falling short of the ideal, and their lives in consequence became an open indictment of a Yankee world given over to materialism." They pointed out "how economic forces were in league against the ideal republic. There could be no true democracy till this matter of economics was put in subordination to higher values."[7]

But the tragedy, for Parrington, was that most New England writers such as James Russell Lowell, Henry Wadsworth Longfellow, and Nathaniel Hawthorne were creating a "genteel tradition." In contrast to the transcendentalists, the genteel romantics refused to focus on the conflict between the beauty, goodness, and truth of the national landscape and the ugliness, corruption, and deception of capitalism. These false romantics replaced the masculine vigor of the national landscape with an effeminate world of convention. They tried to persuade their readers that the only reality was to be found in the genteel tradition. It was here that one could find beauty, truth, and goodness. One could be sheltered within the genteel tradition from the harsh realities of capitalism. For the angry Parrington this false romanticism obscured, therefore, the victory of international capitalism over the national democracy that was taking place during the Gilded Age. The academic implications, for Parrington, were clear. Too many professors of English in the 1920s defined their roles as spokesmen for the philosophy of art for art's sake. Continuing the genteel tradition, they focused on the beauty of particular pieces of literature. These effeminate men were afraid to use art to confront the powerful men of the marketplace who produced so much ugliness.

The irony of Parrington's critique was that, for him, after the victory of capitalism in 1865, the language of democracy produced by the national landscape was lost to most of the people. The common speech of the common people had been expressed in sermons, in political pamphlets, in essays on economics. The first two volumes of Parrington's trilogy, in looking at the years from 1600 to the Civil War, had discussed such everyday and democratic language. But the final volume, which described the years from 1865 to the 1920s, looked primarily at writing by literary figures. Parrington saw the cultural victory of capitalism after the Civil War. For most of the people, reality was no longer the spirituality of democracy, but capitalist materialism. For most of the people, reality was no longer public interest, but self-interest. Reality was no longer equality and fraternity; it was the liberty to compete in the marketplace and destroy one's friends and neighbors. But the universities taught students to avert their eyes from this bloody battlefield. Literature professors taught their students to dwell in the false romance of an effete art.

The good romanticism of the transcendentalists, the democratic literature sprung from the national landscape that confronted the evils of capitalism, was kept alive after the Civil War, then, only by a handful of writers such as Walt Whitman, Theodore Dreiser, and Sinclair Lewis. These heroes wanted to remind Americans that there was an alternative to the chaos of capitalism—that there was another America. Parrington was joining this group of heroes when he wrote his book. Americans needed to be reminded that once there had been a successful exodus out of the chaos of a European Old World into the harmony of an American New World. Once there had been a universal national. It was not inevitable, it was not necessary that the universal national be replaced by the fragmentation of capitalism. The writers that Parrington admired, and who were now his political companions, he called "realists." The writers of the genteel tradition obscured the reality that was the horror of capitalism. They did not have the courage to confront the social disorder caused by capitalism because they did not have a strong faith in the democratic America of the 1830s. The realists had such a faith. They were idealists, the true romantics, who would not allow the memory of the lost America to die.

As such an idealist and realist, Parrington was prepared to reveal the ugliness of capitalism. This new America, he wrote, "was an anarchistic world of strong, capable men, selfish, unenlightened, amoral. In the Gilded Age freedom was the freedom of buccaneers." Parrington's civil religion expressed a belief in an America that had become sacred about 1830. Like Mark Twain, he dated the life span of this sacred world at about a generation. Then the nation had slipped back into the profane world of unstable and meaningless change. With painful nostalgia he expressed his envy of Thoreau, who "was fortunate in dying before the age of exploitation had choked his river with weeds." Writing in the 1920s, with capitalism still triumphant, Parrington could only cling to the memory of Thoreau's world, when the national landscape had produced an organic unity of the good, true, and beautiful.[8]

But Parrington was ready to preach the gospel of a democratic America until he had no more breath. For him, most Americans from the 1860s to the 1920s believed they were democrats and their nation was a democracy. Popular culture was so corrupted by capitalism that citizens no longer knew the language of equality and fraternity. They no longer understood that there could be no meaningful democracy unless there was a classless society. To regain this understanding, he preached, Americans needed to listen to those martyrs of the civil religion such as Walt Whitman. Whitman, for Parrington, "accepted the twin duties laid upon him: to make clear to America her present failure in the great adventure . . . and to mark out afresh the path to the Canaan of democratic hopes." But this "poet and prophet of a democracy that the America of the Gilded Age was daily betraying" had not accomplished in the 1870s what Parrington had not achieved in the 1920s. Neither man had a persuasive story that envisioned how post–Civil War capitalist corruption could be defeated.[9]

But for Parrington, the only artists after Whitman who should be called "American" were those who continued to denounce vehemently the post–Civil War declension into soulless money making. This was why Parrington was especially angry at Mark Twain. Emerson, Thoreau, and Whitman were artists from the Northeast who were inspired by the democratic promise of the Mississippi Valley. But Twain was the first major writer from the valley of democracy. Here, wrote Parrington, "at last was an authentic American—a native writer, thinking his own thoughts, using his own eyes, speaking his own dialect—everything European fallen away, the last shred of feudal culture gone." Twain, however, betrayed this heritage. In Parrington's eyes Twain had sold his soul to the materialistic values of capitalism.[10]

Parrington did find a number of writers who continued Whitman's tradition of condemning capitalism as the antithesis of democracy. He named Harold Frederic, Hamlin Garland, Frank Norris, Theodore Dreiser, Sherwood Anderson, Carl Sandburg, and Vachel Lindsay as writers who dramatized the difference between fraternal democracy and the heartless competition of the marketplace. For the decade in which he was writing, the 1920s, Parrington gave his greatest praise to Sinclair Lewis for being "an incorruptible idealist." In contrast to Lewis's idealism, there were "[t]he younger liberals who love to tweak the nose of democracy" and "are too much enamored of what they find in their own mirrors."[11]

Parrington concluded his epic history with a plea to young writers to participate in the Whitman tradition, as Parrington himself had tried to do. We must demonstrate, he affirmed, that "democratic aspirations have been thwarted by the uncontrolled play of the acquisitive instinct." We must work for "the control of that instinct in the common interest." We "must trace the rise of political power in America in order to understand how that power has fallen into the unsocial hands of economics."[12]

F. O. Matthiessen (1902–50)

It is probable, then, that Parrington's *Main Currents* rivaled the Beards' *The Rise of American Civilization* in popularity during the 1930s because young radicals found a usable past in Parrington's invocation of the ideal of a classless democracy whose citizens shared equality and fraternity.

For Parrington, the clear link between capitalism and social fragmentation had been obscured by the success of capitalism in capturing popular culture. The people no longer spoke the language of the national landscape, but rather the language of the marketplace. But for those who hoped for the restoration of the democratic past, the Great Crash of 1929 was indeed a miracle. The Great Depression proved to the common man that capitalism was not a path toward reality. Capitalism could provide no essentials, no timeless truths, no social stability. All capitalism offered was meaningless flux. But now in the 1930s, the nation would escape the chaos of the international marketplace. It would return to the stability of the national landscape. Once again there would be an organic unity of the good, the true, and the beautiful. The 1930s would be characterized by a second American renaissance.

But that renaissance did not occur. When the political leadership of the nation declared in 1945 that isolation was an ephemeral myth and internationalism was reality, it was clear to many young radicals that capitalism had regained control of popular culture. The imaginative world of most citizens would not envision a homogeneous people committed to national interest. They would not envision that equality and fraternity were of greater value than individual self-interest. When Hofstadter, Williams, and Schlesinger Jr. discovered that capitalism had defeated democracy, they responded by denouncing Charles Beard as a false prophet. And young literary critics, such as Lionel Trilling, made their reputations by attacking Parrington as a false prophet. Many of these literary critics replaced Parrington's book with F. O. Matthiessen's *American Renaissance*, published in 1941, as the single text that most powerfully revealed a usable literary past.[13]

Those who expressed their preference for *American Renaissance* contrasted Matthiessen's sophistication as a literary critic to Parrington's crudeness. Parrington, for them, achieved no depth in his analyses of any particular literary text. Matthiessen, however, in their view, engaged in close reading that revealed the complexity present in all literature. Parrington might devote a single page to a novel by Hawthorne; Matthiessen, in comparison, would use fifty pages to analyze a Hawthorne novel. Because of his superficiality, Parrington could not recognize whether an author explored the psychological complexities of his characters. But Matthiessen used his deep and patient reading to analyze how an author revealed the many layers of a character's personality. Parrington was not concerned about a novel as a work of art, but only for its political position. Matthiessen, however, was concerned with whether all the elements of a novel came together. There needed to be a unity of style and content.

I believe that the political purpose of this post–1945 focus on how a literary critic should discuss the artistic merits of a text was to destroy the authority of Parrington's contrast of a true and false romanticism. Parrington had seen a true romanticism, 1830–60, which celebrated the spiritual democracy born of the national landscape. This true romanticism also denounced the soulless materialism of capitalism that threatened the integrity of the people. And he had seen this conflict between good and evil obscured by the false romanticism of the writers of the genteel tradition, writers who chose to see art as autonomous, existing in a realm apart from politics and economics. This was an art that obscured the victory of capitalism over democracy in the Gilded Age.[14]

If one uses Parrington's analytic framework, one might suggest that Parrington's critics were reacting to this second victory of capitalism in the 1940s over the potential democracy, the possible second American renaissance of the 1930s, by recreating a second genteel tradition. They would focus on the intrinsic aspects of a literary text; they would insist that a literary critic was irresponsible if he did not focus on the question of whether a text was a success or a failure only as a work of art. From a Parringtonian perspective, these literary critics were obscuring the crucial distinction between a sacred national democracy and the profanity of international capitalism.

I believe, then, that a major reason Matthiessen's *American Renaissance* was so admired after 1945 was that, in contrast to *Main Currents,* it was not a call to political action. Matthiessen shared Parrington's belief that the most sacred moment in the history of the United States was the period 1830–60. He agreed that the national landscape had produced a literature free from European influence. Like Parrington he saw this literature as a symbolic expression of the democratic language of the people. This was a democratic language because it expressed the reality of the people as a deep fraternity. But when Matthiessen looked at the writers of the American renaissance, he saw men who recognized that harmony with the sacredness of the national landscape was a fleeting moment. It came, and then it was gone. And it could never be recovered. For Matthiessen, to cherish their memory meant that he, like Turner, would be a stoic. Like these heroic novelists before the Civil War, he would note the ugly, sordid materialism of capitalism. He would recognize the appalling difference between the universal national that was the gift of the national landscape and the terrible fragmentation of a society dominated by capitalism. But like the men he most admired, Hawthorne and Melville, he knew the enemy could not be defeated.

If Parrington wrote a book of literary criticism that he intended to be like the novels of Dreiser and Sinclair Lewis, Matthiessen wrote a book of literary criticism that was to embody the outlook of the novels of Hawthorne and Melville. As Matthiessen read these men, they tried to segregate the memory of the sacred, that wonderful moment when a chosen people achieved harmony with the universal, from the almost instant fall into the chaos of time. Matthiessen, like the Hawthorne and Melville he imagined, would not go into the streets and try to call his fellow citizens out of their lives of public sin. His book, unlike Parrington's, was marked by sadness rather than rage. The triumph of capitalism was so complete that it would be embarrassing to write as Parrington had written about Mark Twain. How foolish it was of Parrington to think that he could convince Americans that the wages of participation in capitalism were spiritual death. Why had Parrington exposed himself to ridicule when he built a literary sermon on the tragic life of Twain? "And when in the end," Parrington had ranted, "the fool's gold turned to ashes in his mouth, still [Twain] pursued his way alone, a solitary pioneer exploring the universe, seeking a homestead in an ironical cosmos, until overwhelmed by the intolerable solitude he made mock at all the gods."[15]

Matthiessen would not write like Parrington because even though he participated in the creation of the Harvard Program in American Civilization in the 1930s, he no longer believed, as he wrote *American Renaissance,* that there was a living American civilization that was separate from European civilization. He did believe that for a brief moment, no longer than a generation, an American civilization had existed. His book, then, like Parrington's, was an expression of the Anglo-Protestant myth of national origins. He, too, shared the narrative of Bancroft, Turner, and the Beards. He, too, saw an exodus from the meaningless time of the Old World, which culminated in the sacred space of the American landscape. For him, as for them, that magic moment when this exodus had reached this miraculous New World was given expression in the arts, especially literature. In the 1920s Parrington believed this literature could be a usable past that might redeem the American people. In the 1930s the Beards believed it was a usable past and was inspiring a second American renaissance. For the Beards there was a living American civilization. But for Matthiessen there could be no second American renaissance. The first and only American renaissance was, for him, a usable past but only on a personal, not a public level; the art of the renaissance could save his soul, but not the soul of the nation.

The memory of the American renaissance provided Matthiessen a private space that was a refuge from the ugly and corrupt capitalist marketplace. In their novels, Hawthorne and Melville provided such spaces for themselves and their readers. Now, as the hope of a second American renaissance faded at the end of the 1930s, Matthiessen could remind his readers of the existence of such an alternative space. They could remember that beautiful New World that was, for a generation, an alternative to the Old World of meaningless flux into which American society had sunk since the Civil War. When Matthiessen committed suicide in 1950, his admirers hoped to keep the memory of his book alive. At this second epic moment of the victory of capitalism, Matthiessen's message was that the organic unity of the true, good, and beautiful that existed in the 1830s could be preserved in books. The literary critic, as a public figure writing for an audience outside the academy, was no longer possible. Corrupted by capitalism, a public did not exist that could understand organic unity. Matthiessen's legacy was to be an apology for the role of literature departments as monasteries where the light of 1830 could be preserved in the new dark ages that had come to America with the Gilded Age and had become all-powerful in the 1940s.

Matthiessen's *American Renaissance* provided these literary critics with criteria, very different from those of Parrington, for distinguishing between good novelists, who provided a usable past, and bad novelists, who did not. The good novelists, those with artistic integrity, recognized the tragic fragility of the American renaissance. They bravely accepted that its organic unity was fleeting. They were resigned to the permanence of the new capitalist dark ages. But the good novelist, this realist and idealist, was not paralyzed by his sense of tragic declension. If the physical existence of the American renaissance, that spectacular epiphany in human history, could not be sustained, the spirit of the renaissance could be preserved by novelists. The good novelist taught his readers to find consolation in that memory. Parrington and the novelists he admired were the false idealists because they did not teach their readers how, trapped in the capitalist dark ages, they could sustain themselves by cherishing the memory of that moment when there was an America that embodied the true, good, and beautiful. They led individuals toward despair because they encouraged them to engage capitalism in hopeless political conflict.

Matthiessen studied literature as an undergraduate at Yale and as a graduate student at Harvard. For him, the participation of the United States in World War I challenged the metaphor of two worlds, European and American. Many universities created courses on the history of Western civilization. But this effort to establish the authority of a metaphor of one world was vigorously rejected in the 1920s. And Matthiessen came of age in the academic community of literary studies when there was a renewed attempt to bring American literature out from under the shadow of English literature. It was this revitalization of the Anglo-Protestant myth of national origins that had found expression in the creation of American civilization programs at a number of Ivy League universities during the 1930s. And *American Renaissance* was a powerful manifesto for the study of an exceptional American literature.[16]

Matthiessen's graduate career illustrated the dominance of English literature in the 1920s. In his dissertation he analyzed literature of the English renaissance. The dominant scholarly paradigm about Shakespeare's England was structured by the conventions of bourgeois nationalism. From that perspective the medieval world was one of meaningless fragmentation. It was a world of many cultures without clear boundaries. There was no England, only a variety of local cultures that had similarities to cultures on the European continent. But the revolution of Protestantism had severed ties with Europe, and a unified England had emerged. The English people were not a part of a European civilization; they were the children of their national landscape. They had an organic relationship to that land that had given the people their language. Until this magical moment of liberation from a chaotic past, literature in England had been a variation on transnational medieval patterns. But now the homogeneous English people spoke a language that expressed the organic unity of the true, good, and beautiful, and Shakespeare participated in this national epiphany.

For the academic participants in this paradigm, however, this exodus from the flux of time to the harmony of a national landscape was quickly replaced by a declension back into the flux of time. Escaping medieval internationalism, England was overwhelmed by capitalist internationalism. For Matthiessen the most powerful analysis of this tragic demise of the English renaissance was being written by T. S. Eliot. An American who had gone into voluntary exile in England, Eliot, in the 1920s, was recognized as a great poet, perhaps the greatest of his generation. He also was an influential literary critic. Eliot defined England, after the tragic fall into the soulless materialism of the marketplace, as a "Wasteland." Matthiessen did not seem aware that his vision of the tragic history of an American renaissance was influenced by the scholarship on the English renaissance that he was reading in the 1920s. He was not aware that he had accepted the central contradiction of bourgeois nationalism. He was not aware that bourgeois nationalists were overtly committed to a bounded national landscape, but covertly committed to an unbounded marketplace. He was not aware that, in his lifetime, the bourgeoisie were going to bring their commitment to such a marketplace to self-consciousness. And when they did, they would renounce the national landscape and its organic metaphor as an irrelevant myth.

Matthiessen's dissertation was published as *Translation: An Elizabethan Art.* His second book was on Sarah Orne Jewett. He approached her from his vision of the tragedy of the English renaissance. He also was thinking of the parallel tragedy of the American renaissance. In his book on the English renaissance, he had expressed a vicarious exuberance at that New World that was England after the nation had achieved cultural independence from the medieval past. "Knowledge was fresh," he wrote, "language could be bent to one's will, thoughts swarmed so eagerly they could not be separated from emotions. The language was more fully alive than it had ever been which means that the people were also."[17]

Now, in his first study of an American author, Sarah Orne Jewett, he made it clear that the national landscape, which had made it possible for an organic American nation to escape the fragmentation of the Old World, had been quickly overrun and destroyed by an industrial capitalism coming from Europe. The pastoral world of Jewett, he wrote, had been "grappled by bands of steel and wire to Lawrence and Lynn.

Throughout New England the invigorating air that Emerson and Thoreau had breathed was clogged with smoke." But why, then, was Matthiessen using the writings of a woman to illuminate the quick and terrible death of the national landscape?[18]

The public world of Emerson and Thoreau was one of male citizens. Democracy was a deep fraternity of these men. In the 1920s Matthiessen, like the men of the 1830s, imagined an exclusive male democracy. It not only contained no women, but for him, as for Bancroft, Turner, the Beards, and Parrington, it included no Native Americans, African Americans, or Mexican Americans. Matthiessen used the same aesthetic authority as these other Anglo-Protestant men to imagine the national landscape as a virgin land waiting to turn English men into American men. Meaningful conflict in America again was between the good Anglo-Protestant sons, who were loyal to the national landscape, and the bad Anglo-Protestant sons, who abandoned their bounded natural landscape and gave their loyalty to the boundless marketplace. For Matthiessen, as for Parrington, it was a tragic defeat for the good sons when the bad sons replaced the organic language of the nation's landscape with the fragmented language of capitalist self-interest.

Matthiessen argued, therefore, that Jewett, as a woman, could not comprehend the profound horror of the defeat of the national landscape by the marketplace. Women were not part of the universal national. Their imagined world was local; it was provincial. Women were people without history, without a story of progress. Jewett's sense of the loss of the local was insignificant compared to Hawthorne's or Melville's sense of the loss of the universal national. Jewett, for Matthiessen, could only be nostalgic for the loss of her private relationship to a pastoral landscape. No woman could know the agony of losing one's nation to an alien culture. This was why he also dismissed the writing of Emily Dickinson. Her drama, he declared, "however intense, remained personal and lyric."[19]

He called attention to the insignificance of the women writers' sense of loss of a pastoral America by comparing it to the magnitude of Hawthorne's despair. In a book review of 1931, Matthiessen wrote that Hawthorne "realized in his imagination that he had failed to meet life squarely, that this was the great failure of America. There seemed to be no alternative to a ruthless individualism which preyed upon itself until the individual was destroyed." But for Matthiessen, Hawthorne had the strength not to accept "what he knew to be false, and to embody in his quiet prose a searing criticism of what was, then as now, the dominant direction of American life."[20]

As Matthiessen entered the 1930s, then, his hero was Hawthorne, who expressed his hatred of capitalism in his art, but who would not engage in a hopeless politics in a vain effort to defeat capitalism. It is not surprising, therefore, that Matthiessen now wrote a book on T. S. Eliot. In Matthiessen's reading, Eliot's position on capitalism was similar to that of Hawthorne. Eliot believed it was impossible to restore the organic language of the English renaissance, and it was clear from Matthiessen's image of Hawthorne that he could not imagine such a restoration of the organic unity of the American renaissance. He affirmed that he had learned from Eliot to see that in moments such as the English and American renaissances, the internal unity of literary form and content had been part of a larger organic unity of art, people, and national landscape. But he agreed with Eliot that in both cases, the people had fallen into the wasteland of capitalist fragmentation. They had lost their ability to speak a language that expressed the organic unity of truth, goodness, and beauty.

By 1930 Eliot, therefore, was a salvation figure for Matthiessen because he seemed to offer an alternative narrative to that of the cycles of virtue and corruption that informed the writings of Turner, the Beards, and Parrington. Their definition of those cycles was very similar to that put forward by Machiavelli. For that Renaissance political philosopher, corruption was related to the particulars of time, while virtue was related to the universals of space, of nature. Machiavelli argued that a republic could be virtuous when it was in harmony with natural law. But he insisted that such a situation could not be sustained and it was inevitable that republics would sink back into the particulars of time. Given the significance of the national landscape for bourgeois nationalism as an alternative to the flux of traditions experienced by the peoples without history, it is probable that the sense of declension held by Eliot and Matthiessen was also present in other modern nations.

For the young Matthiessen, then, Eliot, who had been grappling with the problem of the fall from virtuous space into corrupt time for at least twenty years, seemed to offer a story that was an alternative to that of inevitable cycles—that awful story that had left Twain in bleak despair for the last twenty years of his life. Choosing Eliot as his model for doing literary criticism meant that Matthiessen would not try to use his art to help construct a second American renaissance. To escape despair one had to shun the inevitable cycles of political life. He sympathized with his contemporaries, such as Granville Hicks, who saw in Marxism a way of teaching the public a different language from that of capitalist self-interest. Hicks's book of 1934, *The Great Tradition,* shared Parrington's criteria for separating authentic American novelists from those who were not truly American. For Hicks, as for Parrington, the authentic novelists were those who dramatized the conflict between democracy and capitalism, between public and private interest. Writing after the Great Crash, Hicks believed he was participating in the recovery of American democracy. But while Matthiessen shared Hicks's hatred of capitalism and would act as an individual to support particular social justice causes, he rejected Hicks's vision of a public role for literary criticism. For Hicks, Matthiessen wrote, "literature is inevitably a form of action; and it has been one of the great services of Marxian criticism that it has brought to the fore the principle that art not only expresses something, but also does something."[21]

But Matthiessen agreed with Eliot that art cannot restore the virtuous moment of renaissance space once the nation has receded back into the darkness of history. It followed, therefore, that "the greatest art performs its most characteristic action in more subtle ways . . . by bringing its reader a new understanding or a fresh insight into the fullness of existing." What Matthiessen was reaching for in this definition of the active element in art was a narrative where, in contrast to public life, good was not inevitably defeated by evil. A lifelong communicant in the Episcopal church, Matthiessen publicly identified himself as a Christian. He found his hopeful artistic narrative in the writings of a fellow Anglican, T. S. Eliot. According to Matthiessen, Eliot recognized "that there can be no significance to life, and hence no tragedy in the account of man's conflicts and his inevitable final defeat by death, unless it is fully realized that there is no such thing as good unless there is also evil—that until the double nature of life is understood by a man, he is doomed to waver between a groundless optimistic hopefulness and an equally chaotic, pointless despair." The prophecy of the victory of democratic good over capitalist evil found in Parrington's *Main Currents* and in Hicks's *The Great Tradition* necessarily led to hopelessness when the prophecy inevitably failed.[22]

There was no doubt, however, of Matthiessen's hatred of capitalism. And he would use the memory of the democracy of 1830 to remind the readers of his *American Renaissance* just how ugly capitalism was. Indeed reading only the preface of the book, one might assume that Matthiessen was in total agreement with Parrington and Hicks. One might assume that Matthiessen was writing to inspire revolutionary political action. He began with the metaphor of two worlds, the old European world of time, power, and tragedy and the new American world of space, innocence, and optimism. He wrote as if after Shakespeare's renaissance England had disappeared, it was only in the American landscape that men could find an alternative to the meaningless ebb and flow of time.

Scholars who have analyzed *American Renaissance* have commented on how Matthiessen's description of the perfect democracy of the 1830s was extremely vague. But that was true of the descriptions of this sacred democracy by Bancroft, Turner, the Beards, Parrington, and Schlesinger Jr. When Benedict Anderson suggested that the homogeneous national people imagined by bourgeois nationalists repressed the many differences of class, region, ethnicity, race, and gender that existed within the political boundaries of each nation, his model, of course, applied to the United States. David Simpson, in his *The Politics of American English*, argues that Emerson's generation of artists and intellectuals was the first one in the United States that was able to deny the variety of languages that existed in the country. Simpson contrasts the imagined communities of the older James Fenimore Cooper and the younger Ralph Waldo Emerson. Cooper, for Simpson, heard varieties of American English in the different regions from New England to the deep South. He heard class differences among Anglo-Protestant speakers. He heard the languages of German immigrants. He heard African American dialects. He heard the languages of the Native Americans.[23]

But Emerson heard only the voice of a single American people. He indeed was a transcendentalist, as he imagined a universal national language that existed above all those particular languages that Cooper heard. Bancroft, Turner, the Beards, Parrington, and Schlesinger Jr. shared Emerson's transcendental vision of the voice of a single American people. Matthiessen, like these predecessors, had to be vague about the democracy of 1830, whose existence was central to his belief system. One did not arrive at a knowledge of an organic whole by building it out of many particulars. One either saw the people as a whole, as Emerson did, or saw particulars, as Cooper had. When Matthiessen in 1940 looked at 1830, he saw one people, and he heard their single voice. In 1940 he was Emerson's transcendental son. Matthiessen still felt the meaning of being a child of the national landscape.

For Matthiessen, however, that parental national landscape was gone, conquered by the marketplace. And the people who spoke an organic language that embodied the true, good, and beautiful were gone. Their descendants spoke the fragmented, debased language of capitalist self-interest. The democratic economics and politics of the 1830s were gone. All that was left from that enchanted moment was its literature. Like Turner, the Beards, and Parrington, Matthiessen had no doubt that the literature of the national landscape came from the Northeast. In the politics of his American English, the Anglo-Protestant South was not part of the nation. When Matthiessen wrote about the American renaissance, he saw only five writers from the Northeast whose art expressed the language of the people. Through the writings of Emerson, Thoreau, Hawthorne, Melville, and Whitman, the voice of the people was given expression.

Now readers of these men in 1940, loyal sons like Matthiessen who no longer had contact with their mother, the virgin land, could transcend the materialism and fragmentation of capitalism and draw strength from the vicarious experience of the 1830s world of wholeness. But this reader would also learn from these writers how to cope with the pain of knowing this was not a world in which one could live one's daily life. So, when Matthiessen declared, "The one common denominator of my five writers was their devotion to the possibilities of democracy," he did not mean the possibility of political, economic, or social democracy.[24]

Nevertheless he praised them for their belief "that there should be no split between art and the other functions of the community, that there should be an organic union between labor and culture." But, because his authors understood that capitalism was destroying this organic union, in economics and politics, they would concentrate on evoking and preserving the organic in their literature. Matthiessen, however, created a hierarchy among his heroes. For him, Emerson, Thoreau, and Whitman were slow to recognize the inevitable defeat of the national landscape by the marketplace. Hawthorne and Melville, in Matthiessen's analysis, were quicker to recognize this cruel fact and to develop an art that would save them and their readers from feeling that life had lost its meaning. Indeed he became angry at Emerson, Thoreau, and Whitman for imagining that the renaissance generation could reproduce itself. Hawthorne and Melville were the essential usable past, as they had anticipated Eliot in seeing the need to find hope amidst a permanent darkness.

In *American Renaissance* Matthiessen presented two narratives that were similar to those of Turner. In his first narrative, Turner celebrated the completion of the exodus out of the flux of history into the promised land, the West, the national landscape. In his second narrative he acknowledged that the plenitude of the virgin land of the national landscape was overwhelmed by the more powerful energy of a capitalist future coming from Europe. In the opening sections of *American Renaissance,* Matthiessen focused on how the completion of the exodus was celebrated by his writers.

He quoted the exuberant Melville, who wrote, "It is for the nation's sake, and not for her authors' sake, that I would have America be heedful of the increasing greatness of her writers," and so "Let us away with this leaven of literary flunkeyism toward England." America, for Matthiessen's chosen five, was nature's nation. But Matthiessen prepared himself and his readers for the defeat of nature by time when he stressed the significance of symbol and myth for his group of writers. Symbols could evoke and sustain a sense of unity as capitalism fragmented the culture. And myth expressed a level of experience that transcended time. The greatest gift Matthiessen could give his readers was that the art of the renaissance, understood as symbol and myth, would be a timeless legacy for every generation who chose to read these works. "Where the age of Emerson may be most like our own," Matthiessen declared, "is in its discovery of the value of myth." Emerson, he continued, understood that "when we come to the quality of the moment we drop duration altogether," and so did Thoreau, who believed that "a fact truly and absolutely stated acquires a mythologic or universal significance." Emerson and Thoreau were "celebrating life whereby the moment becomes infinitely larger than itself, and the individual existence escapes from its narrow bonds and finds sanction and consecration."[25]

But Matthiessen now began to criticize Emerson, Thoreau, and especially Whitman for believing that the political and economic life of the democracy could, like its art, achieve the timelessness of myth. Only Hawthorne and Melville were able to surrender their optimism about economic and political democracy and focus on art as the realm in which "existence escapes from its narrow bonds and finds sanction and consecration." Emerson, Thoreau, and especially Whitman, according to Matthiessen, unfortunately participated in a "cult of the future." Whitman, for Matthiessen, did fit into that group of writers admired by Parrington who engaged in a political jeremiad to call the people back to political and economic virtue. Perhaps Whitman did not realize that the sacred moment of a perfect nation had come and gone. Perhaps he hoped that the moment of rebirth and organic unity was still to come. But, for Matthiessen, that was a false hope. "The strength of Whitman's democratic faith made the strength of his poetry," Matthiessen wrote, "but his inability to discern the meaning of [Matthew] Arnold's analysis of the age is one sign of how different a level from Melville's Whitman's mind habitually moved on. Melville found many passages in Arnold to support his own discrimination between good and evil."[26]

Melville, then, became the hero of *American Renaissance* because he, unlike Whitman, understood that the renaissance moment had gone into irreversible declension. Melville accepted the necessity of living in an Old World in which there was both good and evil and in which there could be no organic unity in political and economic life. Melville, Matthiessen concluded, had given "full expression" to the "energetic desire" of men of the renaissance "to master history by repossessing all of the resources of the hidden past in a timeless heroic present. But he did not avoid the darkness in that past, the perpetual suffering in the heart of man. He thus fulfilled what Coleridge held to be the major function of the artist: he brought the whole soul of man into activity." To follow Whitman, for Matthiessen, was to be led inevitably into the hopelessness of Machiavelli's political cycles. But to follow Melville was to be led into the Christian perspective that there is always hope. "After all he had suffered," Matthiessen insisted, "Melville could endure to the end in the belief that though good goes to defeat and death, its radiance can redeem life." Perhaps Matthiessen was writing to instruct himself when he declared that Melville's "endurance is a challenge to a later America."[27]

According to Matthiessen it was "the successive generations of common readers, who make the decisions, that would seem finally to have agreed that the authors of the pre–Civil War era who bulk largest in stature are the five who are my subject." In claiming to be a participant in a democratic tradition of "common readers," Matthiessen did not seem to be aware that he was excluding the majority of readers in the United States. Most readers in the nineteenth century were Anglo-Protestant women and the best-selling novelists were women. Matthiessen's commitment to two spheres, the public sphere of men and the private sphere of women, made it possible for him to ignore women readers. He focused, then, on the white males, who ironically also were not reading Melville. This was so, for Matthiessen, because most of those readers were no longer culturally American. Their culture had become that of international capitalism. After the Civil War the only "common reader" was, like Matthiessen himself, part of a saving remnant who preserved the language of democracy by segregating it from the popular culture dominated by capitalism.[28]

Committing himself to the socialism of Eugene Debs during the 1920s, Matthiessen voted for the Socialist Party candidate, Norman Thomas, in 1932. He then was pleasantly surprised by President Roosevelt's domestic policies. "In '32, with the depression at its worst, I thought that here at last was a chance for the Socialists to regain the broad base that had developed under Debs, and I joined the party," Matthiessen wrote, but "Roosevelt in office was something quite other than I had foreseen, and after he began to effect even some of the things for which Thomas had stood, I voted for him enthusiastically though always from the left until his death."[29]

Matthiessen believed that as a private citizen he should be an active opponent of capitalism. During the 1930s, he was president of the Harvard Teachers' Union and a member of the Massachusetts Civil Liberties Union. Then in 1941 the entry of the United States into World War II threatened both his personal political position and his philosophy of literary criticism. Both of those positions demanded the integrity of national boundaries. Politically he wanted the government to plan the national economy. In literary criticism he wanted to celebrate the literature that remembered the democracy of the national landscape. He wanted "common readers" to remember how Hawthorne and Melville faced the victory of capitalism without giving up hope. They could show successive generations of authentic Americans how to be inspired by the radiance of that moment of organic wholeness.

When Matthiessen had spoken of the victory of capitalism in the United States of 1865, he had imagined the corruption of language within the boundaries of the nation. Imagining the continuing power of those boundaries, he had seen the possibility of national planning during the 1930s. But what if the revolutionary shift from isolation to internationalism meant dissolving national boundaries so that national space was absorbed into the space of the international marketplace? If that space achieved aesthetic authority, there could be no authority for the art of national planning. There also would be no authority for a literary criticism committed to the memory of the national landscape.

Matthiessen personally felt this revolutionary shift of aesthetic authority. Immediately after the end of World War II he was warned, along with other American critics of capitalism, that he was helping an enemy of his country, the Soviet Union. If he continued his criticism he would be a traitor. He responded by writing two books that continued his criticism of capitalism. In a book on Henry James he reasserted the model of literary criticism that informed *American Renaissance.* James had responded to the Gilded Age by becoming an expatriate a generation before T. S. Eliot moved to England. For Matthiessen, James was a bridge between Hawthorne, Melville, and Eliot. Like them, James developed a concept of tragedy that made it possible for the individual to sustain hope in the midst of the materialism and fragmentation of the marketplace. James also felt that hope was strengthened by the inspiration of literature that, through its unity of form and content, evoked a vision of wholeness. Redemptive art acted positively to sustain the soul. Perhaps because of the frightening power of the aesthetic authority of the imagined space of the international marketplace, Matthiessen, in discussing James, affirmed that there were similarities between a literature and a literary criticism in England that was trying to protect a vision of organic unity from the fragmenting power of the marketplace and the American literature of Hawthorne and Melville and now the literary criticism of Matthiessen.[30]

But Matthiessen also felt the need to link his identity as a democratic citizen in conflict with capitalism to an international context. It was becoming increasingly difficult for him to separate his two anticapitalist identities. He had suffered from clinical depression in the 1930s. He lost his lover of twenty years, Russell Cheney, in 1945. Now he was confronted with a cold war that might end in a worldwide nuclear catastrophe. His colleague, Perry Miller, who played a major role in constructing the Harvard American Civilization Program, had responded to his loss of the metaphor of two worlds during World War II by filling his last writing with terrifying images of an atomic holocaust. The haunted Matthiessen wrote, "How much the state of the world has to do with my state of mind I do not know." Then, he confessed, "as a Christian and a socialist and believing in international peace, I find myself terribly oppressed by the present tension."[31]

Many of Matthiessen's generation responded to this sense of personal crisis by having conversion experiences. They had lived in a world of political sin and error when they believed that international capitalism was the enemy of national democracy. But now they saw the light. Democracy was threatened by international enemies. First fascism and then communism demonstrated that the emphasis on fraternity and equality was incompatible with liberty. If the essence of democracy needed to be liberty, that liberty was the gift of the marketplace. Capitalism and democracy were synonymous. Matthiessen recoiled from this disassociation of democracy from fraternity and equality. Thrust into an environment of international capitalism, he argued that defenders of democracy in the United States needed to seek allies among Marxists everywhere in the world. He wrote that if he lived in England, he would be a member of the Labor Party and if he lived in France he would be a member of the Communist Party. He asserted that the Marxist revolution in Russia in 1917 was, like the American and French Revolutions, an effort to create a democratic society.

But if democracy was to be understood as an international phenomenon, how could Matthiessen continue to argue for a literary criticism whose purpose was to keep alive the memory of the American democracy born of the national landscape in 1830? How could he continue to argue that the crucial action of the literary critic was to help the reader see the redeeming radiance of the literature that expressed that sacred moment? How could he continue to ask readers to imitate Hawthorne and Melville and find solace in the vision of the lost national organic wholeness in the midst of the capitalist wasteland? Perhaps Parrington, Hicks, and the Marxist literary critics of the 1930s were right. The literary critic should direct the reader to those novels that exposed all the ugliness of a society dominated by capitalism. He should focus on the novelists who wanted a political revolution that would replace capitalism with democracy.

Matthiessen now wrote, therefore, a book in praise of Theodore Dreiser. For the desperate Matthiessen, Dreiser had recognized "that in the fierce competitive jungle of the big city there are no equals, only those moving up or down." Dreiser also saw that international capitalism could not be defeated by appealing to the lost American democracy of 1830. And Matthiessen agreed with him that "we are faced with the grave question of how long positive values can endure as the aftershow of something that had been lost." Matthiessen now applauded Dreiser's decision to join the Communist Party and fight international capitalism as part of an international coalition of Marxists. Matthiessen threw all his political energy into the presidential campaign of Henry Wallace in 1948. He hoped that a Wallace victory would stop capitalists in the United States from escalating the cold war.[32]

By 1948 Matthiessen had synthesized his personal commitment as a citizen to engage in political combat with capitalism and his role as a literary critic. He had abandoned the literary criticism of *American Renaissance.* He could no longer urge Americans to save themselves from capitalism by remembering, through the literature of that renaissance, the beauty and goodness of that moment of organic unity. Now he demanded that they save themselves by reading authors like Dreiser, who urged them to save their souls by revolutionary political action. "Literary critics," he warned, "have come to the unnatural point when textual analysis seems to be an end in itself."[33]

In 1948 Matthiessen seemed to have joined Whitman's "cult of the future," which he had mocked in 1940. He had rejected the narratives of Hawthorne, Melville, James, and Eliot that enabled the individual to retain hope after the fall into the capitalist wasteland. He could no longer find solace in an art where form and content were an organic whole. He had made the narrative of Parrington, the narrative that seemed trapped in the Machiavellian political cycles of hope and despair, his own in 1948.

And what happened in 1948? Wallace was crushed. The cold war intensified. Artists and writers who continued to criticize capitalism were blacklisted. Academics who continued to criticize capitalism, if they did not have tenure, were fired. In some cases even tenured professors were fired. A new definition of American identity was clearly dominant. If you criticized capitalism, you were un-American. If Matthiessen continued his public denunciation of capitalism and his public praise for international Marxism after 1948, he would, at best, be ostracized. He also was threatened by the cold war consensus that identified all homosexuals as major enemies of the nation. These were terrible burdens to add to his history of clinical depression. The Machiavellian cycle in which virtue must be defeated by corruption gave him no hope. In 1950 he committed suicide.[34]

CHAPTER FOUR

Elegies for the National Landscape

In 1943 a graduate program in American studies was begun at the University of Minnesota. Tremaine McDowell and several other professors in the English department who taught American literature played major roles in its creation. Until the end of the 1960s the program's doctoral seminar was taught by a member of the English department. The chairs of the program were also from English. McDowell persuaded three of the early graduates of the Harvard Program in American Civilization—Henry Nash Smith, Bernard Bowron, and Leo Marx—to join the Minnesota English department and give intellectual substance to the new American Studies Program. But perhaps because the United States, once again, was committed to war in Europe in 1941, McDowell did not imagine a Minnesota program in "American Civilization."[1]

Soon after the end of the war, scholars from American literature, American history, and other related disciplines formed a new professional organization named the "American Studies Association," and not the "American Civilization Association." Looking back at the decades from 1945 to 1965, one finds agreement that a symbol-myth school provided the dominant paradigm for American studies during those years. Two of the leaders of this school were Henry Nash Smith and Leo Marx. R. W. B. Lewis, another student in the Harvard Program in American Civilization, was also a leader. Lewis joined the English department at Yale and was a member of the program in American studies there. The most influential works by these men were Smith's *Virgin Land: The American West as Symbol and Myth* (1950), Lewis's *The American Adam:*

Myth and Innocence in the American Novel (1955), and Marx's *The Machine in the Garden* (1964).[2]

The narratives in all three books were directly dependent on Matthiessen's *American Renaissance.* Smith, Lewis, and Marx had quietly rejected what Matthiessen was saying in his book on Dreiser, a work still incomplete at his death. Instead they focused on what he had said about symbol and myth. In their writings they followed the advice he had gained from Hawthorne, Melville, Henry James, and T. S. Eliot. Smith, Lewis, and Marx did not present themselves as men whose hope in 1940 that national democracy would defeat international capitalism had vanished by 1948. They did not reveal themselves in their writings as having been vanquished on the political battlefields of the 1940s. They now took Matthiessen's message of 1940 very seriously: national democracy had been defeated long ago by international capitalism in the Gilded Age.

Like Matthiessen, they constructed elegies for the national landscape. But their books—*Virgin Land, The American Adam,* and *The Machine in the Garden*—unlike *American Renaissance* did not try to evoke the ugliness, the corruption, the falsity of capitalism. Smith, Lewis, and Marx emphasized the beauty, the goodness, and the truth of the national landscape. They wanted their readers to experience vicariously that sacred moment that lasted no more than a generation. But they only implied, they were not explicit, as Matthiessen had been, that such a memory might save the souls of a saving remnant in the capitalist wasteland.

A major characteristic of these men of the symbol-myth school, therefore, was that they wanted only to study the American renaissance. Much has been written about the belief of these men that American studies, unlike American literature or American history, had a method that approached culture holistically. Other disciplines looked at parts of a culture. But American studies, they claimed, looked at a culture as a whole. American studies could see how the various arts were interrelated with political, economic, and social patterns. But the Anglo-Protestant variation on bourgeois nationalism that stretched from Bancroft to Matthiessen described a unified culture only after 1830, one that did not survive the Civil War. For Bancroft the different histories of the thirteen colonies did not become a national history until those disparate parts were left behind in the exodus across the Appalachians into the virgin land of the Mississippi Valley. There the pioneers found a national landscape where, for Emerson, they began to speak a common language.[3]

Smith, Lewis, and Marx, therefore, could not apply a holistic method of culture study to the different American cultures that existed before the transcendental moment of the 1830s. And they could not apply it to the fragmentation that occurred after the Civil War. The symbol-myth school had a methodology that applied only to the American renaissance. When graduate students expressed their discontent about spending their academic lives remembering the American renaissance, Smith stopped teaching the American studies doctoral seminar at Minnesota. He took a position elsewhere, where he would not have such an intense relationship with graduate students. Leo Marx took over the doctoral seminar at Minnesota, but he left to teach undergraduates at Amherst. At Yale, R. W. B. Lewis followed his *American Adam* with books that were closer to conventional literary criticism. Writing elegies for the American renaissance, Smith, Lewis, and Marx did not want to think about what the relationship of American studies would be to the new world of 1945, when one could no longer imagine an isolated national culture.

Implicitly Smith, Lewis, and Marx were escaping the dramatic collapse of the vision of an autonomous American civilization that was so powerful in the 1930s by returning to Turner's presentation of two narratives. They participated in Turner's first narrative, which said that the exodus from Europe and the colonial past into the national landscape had concluded in the cultural miracle of the American renaissance. But they repressed the pain of participating in the collapse of the 1930s vision of an American civilization that had been given symbolic expression in the Harvard Program in American Civilization. That vision had been built on the narrative of a national romance. Expressed in music, painting, architecture, and in literary works such as the Beards' *The Rise of American Civilization,* the national romance pictured the national landscape as a usable past, a necessary foundation for the urban-industrial landscape of the 1930s. The rational truth, as well as the beauty and goodness, of these landscapes was an alternative to the chaos of capitalism.

Turner, however, in the 1890s had announced that the national landscape had been succeeded by an international urban-industrial landscape and that capitalism was an intrinsic part of that new world. If Turner was right, there could be no tragic defeat of American civilization by capitalism in the 1940s. This, of course, was what Matthiessen had said in *American Renaissance.* But then he publicly revealed that he felt the victory of capitalism in the 1940s was not merely a continuation of the victory of capitalism in the Gilded Age. The 1940s, for Matthiessen, marked a new and terrifying period. All hope for a democratic America was being lost. There would be a new era in which capitalist control would be overwhelming.

A reader of Henry Nash Smith's *Virgin Land* in 1950 would not have known from the book's narrative that Smith had seen an American civilization in the 1930s and that this had brought him to the Harvard program. The reader would not know that a believer in an American civilization in 1940 used the narrative of the national romance that blended an industrial landscape with the pastoral of the national landscape. The reader would not have known that adherents of the vision of an American civilization in the 1930s had expected that the combination of the national landscape and the industrial landscape would give the fraternal democracy of the people the strength to defeat the soulless materialism of international capitalism. They would not have known that two of Smith's teachers, Matthiessen and Perry Miller, had become suicidal in the 1940s in part because they saw the spiritual core of the nation, its civil religion, being destroyed by capitalism. All the readers would have known from the pages of *Virgin Land* was that Frederick Jackson Turner had expressed anguish in the 1890s when he became aware that the democracy born of the national landscape had been replaced by the hierarchical society of the international marketplace. A reader might infer that the history of the United States as a culture independent from Europe had ended a half century before the intense debate about whether isolation should be replaced by internationalism in 1940. A reader would never guess that the cultural logic of the Harvard Program in American Civilization, so vigorous in the 1930s, had been destroyed in the 1940s. A reader would have known, however, that Smith found the national landscape of 1830 to be beautiful and good and true in a way that the triumphant capitalism of 1865 could never be. In 1944 and 1945 academic readers of Hofstadter's *Social Darwinism in American Thought* and Schlesinger's *The Age of Jackson* awarded those books prizes for the persuasiveness of their arguments that the 1830s were a usable past for the 1930s. Now, in 1950, academic readers awarded Smith's *Virgin Land* a prize for the persuasiveness of its argument that the 1830s had not been a usable past since the 1890s, but that elegies for the beauty and goodness of Jacksonian society should continue to be the major responsibility of American studies scholarship. These academic readers continued to cling to the aesthetic authority of bourgeois nationalism, which found no beauty in the landscape of the marketplace.

And like Smith, his admiring academic readers continued to participate in the bourgeois aesthetic authority that saw only a homogeneous fraternal democracy emerging from the national landscape. It did not seem odd to those readers, therefore, that Smith shared Turner's belief that the national landscape was a vacant land, a virgin land. Smith saw no history of cultural pluralism among the European colonists. He saw no history of the many American Indian tribes. He saw no history of the variety of cultures brought by the African slaves. He saw no variety of Mexican cultures brought into the expanding United States by the successful war against Mexico in 1846. In other words in 1950 he defined Americans as Bancroft had in 1830: Americans were Anglo-American men. Again, like Bancroft, he did see the national culture born from the landscape of the Mississippi Valley as one linking the Midwest and the Northeast. The culture of southern Anglo-American men, for Smith, was outside of national culture and in conflict with it.

Smith asked his readers to be self-conscious of his relationship to Turner. He did not invite comparisons with Parrington, the Beards, or Matthiessen. Smith pointed to Turner when he wrote, "The present study traces the impact of the West, the vacant continent beyond the frontier, on the consciousness of Americans." And he stressed his agreement with Turner when he declared, "Whatever the merits of the Turner thesis, the doctrine that the United States is a continental nation rather than a member with Europe of an Atlantic community has had a formative influence on the American mind." Smith, like Turner, insisted, therefore, that "the belief in a continental destiny quickly became a principal ingredient in the developing American nationalism."[4]

Turner had seen the period between 1600 and 1789 as one in which European culture, brought to the English colonies, had entered into conflict with American nature. For Turner, American nature finally had defeated European culture when the pioneers had crossed the Appalachians into the Mississippi Valley. It was here that a nation of equal citizens, a political fraternity, could emerge free from the class hierarchy of the European cultural heritage. Smith in 1950 repeated the position held by Turner in 1890 almost word for word. "The political ideology of the

1830s and 1840s," Smith declared, "assumed that the common man had risen to dominate, or at least share control of the government, without ceasing to be the common man; it was a process whereby power in the state passed from one class to another." Political democracy, for Smith, therefore, as for Turner, had emerged out of the social and economic experience of an agrarian world of many small and essentially equal producers.[5]

But if European class hierarchy had disappeared west of the Appalachians and a political good, the virtue of fraternal democracy, was in relationship to the economic truth of a society of small and equal farmers, there was, for Smith, no aesthetic expression of the beauty of this new American nation. He chose, then, to obscure his relationship to Matthiessen's *American Renaissance.*

James Fenimore Cooper

Smith used James Fenimore Cooper as an example of the way in which American novelists in 1830 remained dependent on conventions of the English novel. Since Smith accepted the metaphor of two worlds, European hierarchy and American democracy, as the foundation of American cultural independence, he was angry that Cooper's generation could only imagine the American farmer as a member of a lower class. Cooper, according to Smith, was representative of the American novelists who continued to believe that they needed to write about heroes and heroines who embodied upper-class values. This, for Smith, was why Cooper could never imagine a marriage for the lower-class Leatherstocking. Cooper, Smith insisted, did believe there was beauty and goodness in the national landscape. He presented Leatherstocking, therefore, as a person of innate goodness and beauty who, as a natural aristocrat, could not marry a lower-class woman. But Cooper, in Smith's analysis, was not able to imagine that the American landscape could dissolve the class hierarchy brought from Europe. This was why Cooper would not let Leatherstocking marry an upper-class woman. The conflict between European culture and American nature became the dramatic tension in Cooper's novels. But, for Cooper, as beautiful and good as American nature was, it could not defeat the truth of the class structure brought from Europe. Leatherstocking could not, in Cooper's imagination, become the model for a classless American society.[6]

Perhaps Cooper was such a central figure in Smith's book because the painful confrontation between European society and American nature in Cooper's writing in the 1830s pointed to the painful confrontation between European society and American nature in Turner's writing in the 1890s. And that confrontation was to be played out again in 1950 in Smith's *Virgin Land* as he was confronted by the collapse in the 1940s of the aesthetic authority of a fraternal democracy. Cooper had been able to imagine that a figure like Leatherstocking, free from European conventions, could emerge in the American West. But Cooper had argued that it was inevitable that the conventions and class hierarchy characterizing the English colonies would follow the pioneers into the Mississippi Valley.

Turner in the 1890s had built a powerful narrative around the emergence of the yeoman farmer in the Mississippi Valley as a figure finally free from European conventions and therefore the ideal type of the American citizen. It was such a citizen who symbolized the cultural independence of the nation from Europe. Smith was now repeating that narrative in 1950. But Turner had written a second narrative to describe the United States after the Civil War. There he had described the power of an industrial landscape coming from Europe to replace the national landscape. In this narrative the United States had lost its cultural independence and became, once again, part of the Atlantic community.

Now, in 1950, Smith reluctantly repeated the narratives of Cooper and Turner. Like Turner he had described the achievement of a political democracy based on a society of freehold farmers. But, like Turner, Smith, in *Virgin Land*, had a second narrative. The reality of a fraternal democracy was replaced by the reality of class hierarchy and class exploitation as industrialism came from Europe. Cooper had been right. The power of the national landscape was limited and fleeting.

When Smith looked at the development of narratives about Western heroes and heroines after Cooper, he did not celebrate these stories as evidence of an indigenous American art free from European influences. For him they did not embody the beauty and goodness of the national landscape. "The wild Western hero has been secularized," Smith lamented. "He no longer looks to God through nature, for nature is no longer benign." Smith, therefore, found nothing but mindless violence in these novels. This, for him, was the pattern that was to characterize the endless stream of novels and movies about the West that continued to dominate popular culture into the twentieth century.[7]

The meaningless sound and fury of these aspects of popular culture from 1850 to 1950 was, for Smith, evidence that much of the population had been corrupted by materialism. There was no longer a virtuous people, a fraternal democracy, when the majority of individuals opted for material wealth. "The spiritual meaning which a former generation had believed it found in nature became more and more inaccessible after the middle of the century," Smith lamented, adding that the beauty and goodness of this national landscape "proved quite irrelevant for a society committed to the ideas of civilization and progress, and to an industrial revolution."[8]

Truth after 1850, for Smith, was to be found in the industrial landscape that came from Europe and was the antithesis of the national landscape. Now, for Smith, the vision of the beauty and goodness of a society of equal and fraternal citizen-farmers became a myth contradicted by a reality "wholly foreign to Agrarian assumptions. The greatest of the new forces was the technological revolution." He presented the Homestead Act as an example of this contradiction between myth and reality. The purpose of this act was to make possible the spread of the society of small farmers into the Great Plains. But "the Homestead Act failed," Smith asserted, "because it was incongruous with the Industrial Revolution." For Smith the industrial revolution meant control of the economy by corporations that were able to buy the support of Congress for their monopoly of economic power. As in Europe, economic, social, and political power was now in the hands of a privileged elite. The worst of this situation, for Smith, was that much of the public continued to believe that agrarian democracy was reality rather than myth. "So long as it survived in its increasing irrelevance to the facts," Smith bitterly commented, the myth of a perpetual agricultural democracy "could be manipulated by cynical men for selfish purposes." A major example of this manipulation was the doctrine of the West as a safety valve in which unemployed and impoverished people in the eastern states could find independence and prosperity as owners of farms. "The doctrine of the safety valve was an imaginative construction," Smith asserted, "which masked poverty and industrial strife with the pleasing suggestion that a beneficent nature stronger than any human agency... would solve the new problems of industrialism."[9]

Smith in 1950, therefore, like Turner in 1890, was writing an elegy for that moment in time between 1830 and 1850 when he believed that the new American nation embodied the good, the beautiful, and the true. Out of the goodness of the natural landscape had sprung a virtuous and beautiful society of free and equal farmers. But, contradicting

Matthiessen, he argued that the beauty of that society had never found expression in the novel. One can feel the power and pain of Smith's elegy for that magic moment in 1830 when one reads his celebration of Hamlin Garland. Just when European class hierarchy embodied in industrialism had replaced the egalitarian society of Jacksonian America, a novelist in 1880 found a way to celebrate the farmer in literature. From Cooper's day to that of Hamlin Garland, Smith said, authors writing about the West had to struggle against "the notion that their characters had no claim upon the attention of sophisticated readers. But by 1890, Smith wrote, the farmer "could be presented as a human being, unfortunate perhaps, but possessed of dignity, even in his tribulations." In Smith's narrative, however, as in Turner's, the farmers of the Midwest had become politically and economically powerless because a small group of corporate capitalists controlled the nation's economic and political life. Garland's artistic presentation of the farmer as a figure of dignity who should not be judged by the class bias of the European novel was, by the logic of Smith's narrative, a cruel irony. Smith in 1950 believed that the goodness and beauty of the natural landscape had become impotent by 1880 as the truth of the natural landscape expressed in a society of yeoman farmers was overwhelmed by the truth of the industrial landscape, where elites had power over the majority.[10]

But Smith in 1950, like Garland and Turner, did not want to forget the America of 1830, which had died by 1890. There was a beauty and goodness in that national landscape that could not be found in the industrial landscape. In the literary art, therefore, of Garland, Turner, and Smith, the memory of the lost landscape was to be presented to future generations so they could remember what was now dead. Smith's elegy was most eloquent, therefore, when he declared that "[i]t had at last become possible to deal with the Western farmer in literature as a human being instead of seeing him through a veil of literary convention, class prejudice, or social theory."[11]

But Smith was speaking at a funeral. Indeed he was a member of the generation that killed the artistic nationalism of the 1930s. Smith's generation now denied that the corruption of the people by materialism in the late nineteenth century had been reversed after 1929 by the New Deal. They rejected their faith that the virtue of the people in the 1930s was possible because there was an organic relationship between the pastoral national landscape of 1830 and the industrial landscape of 1930.

They no longer believed that democracy could be the product of an industrial landscape that embodied the characteristics of the national landscape. *Virgin Land* was one of the many blows that helped kill the vision of an isolated American civilization in order to replace it with the vision of the United States as a nation within an Atlantic civilization. Perhaps just as Cooper was reluctant to bring Leatherstocking, the child of nature, back into a culture characterized by time and death, Smith was reluctant to bring the American nation, the child of nature, back into the cultural realm of time and death. Nevertheless he was a slayer of the timeless pastoral whose virtues he continued to extol in the elegy that was *Virgin Land*.

For Smith, as for so many intellectuals of his generation, World War II marked the end of the quest for an American innocence, a world of nature and space. The war meant the necessary acceptance by adolescent Americans of their European parents, who represented the world of society and time. By embracing their place in an Atlantic civilization, Americans needed to reject innocence in favor of experience. Smith joined others of his generation in making a confession that the quest for innocence had destructive consequences. Speaking implicitly of the antiwar position of so many Americans in 1940, he confronted the nineteenth-century belief in American exceptionalism. "Since evil could not conceivably originate within the walls of the garden," he declared, "it must by logical necessity come from without, and the normal strategy of defense was to build the walls higher and stop the cracks in them." He continued, "These inferences from the myth of the garden will be recognized as the core of what we call isolationism. . . . Indeed, since the myth affirmed the impossibility of disaster or suffering within the garden, it was unable to deal with any of the dark or tragic outcomes of human experiences." He concluded that "[t]he agrarian myth has made it difficult for Americans to think of themselves as members of a world community because it has affirmed that the destiny of the country leads her away from Europe toward the agricultural interior of the continent."[12]

It is possible, however, that Smith, in 1950, was angry at himself for his rejection of the 1930s vision of a unique American civilization. It is possible that he displaced that anger onto Frederick Jackson Turner. Repressing the powerful romantic synthesis of nature and culture, space and time, pastoral perfection and industrial progress that had informed painting, music, architecture, history writing, and literary criticism in the 1930s, Smith focused on the discontinuity of Turner's two narratives. It was not Smith's generation in the 1940s that had surrendered the vision of an organic tradition. It was Turner in the 1890s who had given subsequent generations a legacy of discontinuity. By 1890 the story of an exceptional nation based on nature was replaced by the story of the United States as one of many nations sharing an international industrial landscape.

It is possible, too, that Smith tried to displace his pain by presenting himself as an objective scholar, while describing Turner as a poet. It was Turner, according to Smith, who believed that nature was sacred. Smith, the reader was to infer, had not participated in this belief, which supposedly had died by 1900. Smith, a half century later, was only a detached observer. Turner had actually believed that American nature made it possible for European men to be reborn. Turner, Smith insisted, had written poetry, not history, when he declared that American democracy had come "stark and strong and full of life out of the American forest, and it gained new strength each time it touched a new frontier." Turner, who had built his first narrative around the emergence of a sacred national landscape, had felt pain when he had constructed his second narrative, in which the superior power of a complex international industrial civilization had replaced the simplicity of American nature. But Smith, as an objective scholar, should not have felt pain as he reported that Turner was representative of the way that most Americans at the end of the nineteenth century agreed that the narrative of the birth of a nation made sacred by its natural environment had been superseded by the narrative of an international civilization whose law was constant progress.

But Smith could not use this persona as a scientific historian to hide completely the pain he felt in the 1940s when he reluctantly surrendered his belief in an American civilization made sacred by its emergence out of the pastoral national landscape. In reality *Virgin Land* was an elegy for what Smith had believed in 1940, as well as for what Turner had believed in 1890. And so Smith's supposedly neutral observations ended with a lament about the consequences of seeing the United States as part of an Atlantic civilization. Such a narrative, Smith concluded, "prevented any recognition that the American adventure of settling the Continent had brought about an irruption of novelty into history." It meant, Smith wrote, that the United States was "only an extension of Europe."[13]

The common use of the term "myth" in 1950 was as the opposite of "the real." This was one meaning of Smith's title. But another use of myth identified it with a timeless realm outside the timeful circumstances of history. This was the second meaning of Smith's title. The West as myth could transcend time. It would be a living memory for all subsequent generations of Americans. This was the artistic power of Smith's elegy and his way of easing his guilt and pain. It was his way of remembering Matthiessen's affirmation that the American renaissance killed in time could live forever as a sacred and redemptive myth.

Four years after the publication of *Virgin Land*, R. W. B. Lewis, a professor of English and American studies at Yale, published *The American Adam: Innocence, Tragedy, and Tradition in the Nineteenth Century*. It, too, was an elegy for an American civilization that had sprung from the national landscape. But Lewis, unlike Smith, sometimes wrote as if an American culture distinct from Europe was only critically wounded and not dead. Lewis was able to sustain this ambiguity because, in contrast to Smith, his discussion of literature did not confront issues of class, industrialism, and capitalism. Lewis was going to focus only on the literature of the American renaissance. But unlike Matthiessen he would not discuss a capitalist wasteland.

Lewis, like Smith, was writing out of the revolutionary impact of World War II on the scholarly orthodoxy of the 1930s. Working within the conventions of bourgeois nationalism, Lewis believed that American culture had a spatial foundation in the national landscape, while European culture expressed the timeful flux of tradition. Only in the United States had history as progress culminated in a timeless national space. For literary critics this meant that American culture had escaped the history of irony and tragedy that was the European heritage. But when it became politically necessary by 1945 to consider the United States as part of the Atlantic community, intellectuals who had converted from "isolationism" to "internationalism" often followed the leadership of the Protestant theologian, Reinhold Niebuhr, in denouncing an American tradition of "innocence" and praising a European tradition of "experience." Thus for the "internationalists" the foreign-policy revolution demanded that Americans leave their identity as perpetual adolescents in rebellion against their European fathers and become adults who would share the European tradition. They needed to accept irony and tragedy as inevitable aspects of human experience. This, of course, had been the message of Schlesinger's *The Vital Center.* Participating in the imaginative world of this new America, Lewis felt the need to accept the reality of irony and tragedy. But, like Smith, he believed that if he gave up innocence, American literature and American studies as expressions of American culture would lose their meaning. His book can be read, therefore, as an attempt to salvage American exceptionalism while accepting the "European" truths of irony and tragedy. Here Matthiessen's embrace in *American Renaissance* of irony and tragedy as the legacy of Hawthorne and Melville powerfully informed Lewis's argument.

In 1955 Lewis continued to embrace the Anglo-Protestant myth of national origins as historical truth. "This book," Lewis wrote, "has to do with the beginnings and the first tentative outlines of a Native American mythology. The period I cover runs from about 1820 to 1860; the scene for the most part is New England and the Atlantic seaboard." Lewis, like Smith, therefore, was continuing to use the aesthetic authority of Anglo-American nationalism to monopolize the term "American" for male Anglo-Americans of the Northeast and Midwest. This aesthetic authority removed Anglo-American women, southern Anglo-Americans, Native Americans, African Americans, and Mexican Americans from the national landscape, and, for Lewis, it also removed all traces of European culture from that landscape. "The American myth," he continued, "saw life as just beginning. It described the world as starting up again under fresh initiative, in a divinely granted second chance for the human race, after the first chance had been so disastrously fumbled in the darkening Old World. It introduced a new kind of hero, emancipated from history, happily bereft of ancestry, untouched and undefiled by the usual inheritances of family and race." That new man, the American, Lewis declared, was "Adam before the fall."[14]

We should remember that the aesthetic authority of the Anglo-American nationalism of 1830 with which Smith and Lewis continued to work in 1950 not only excluded the majority of the peoples of the United States from the national landscape, but also identified the national landscape of the United States as the only American national landscape that had escaped the European past. Lewis, like Smith and Turner, could not imagine the reality of the other nations of North and South America. And so, for Lewis, "The evolution of the hero as Adam in the fiction of the new world rightly begins with Natty Bumppo. I call such a figure the hero in space. The hero seems to take his start outside of time and his initial habitat in space as spaciousness, as the unbounded, the area of total possibility."[15]

Lewis identified this vision of an America as space free from time with what he called the literary party of Hope. Along with Cooper the major proponents of this position, for Lewis, were Emerson, Thoreau, and Whitman. Here he agreed with Matthiessen, who had implicitly defined Emerson, Thoreau, and Whitman as a literary party of hope in *American Renaissance.* Lewis then argued that all cultures are characterized by a debate and that throughout American history the party of Hope had been challenged by the party of Memory and the party of Irony. He was primarily concerned with what he saw as the dialogue between the party of Hope and the party of Irony, whose chief spokesmen were Hawthorne and Melville. Again his identification of Hawthorne and Melville followed the pattern of *American Renaissance.* The party of Memory would return us to Europe, but the party of Irony was able to criticize and to qualify the simple optimism of the party of Hope without rejecting the Adamic hero. "The characteristic situation" in Hawthorne's fiction, according to Lewis, was "that of the Emersonian figure, the man of hope, who by some frightful mischance has stumbled into the time-burdened world." But, for Hawthorne, this time-burdened world is not that of European tragedy. Hawthorne's heroes experience "a 'fall' which can be claimed as fortunate because of the growth in perception and moral intelligence granted the hero as a result of it." Again Lewis was making an argument explicit that had been implicit in *American Renaissance.* For Matthiessen the "fall" of the nation from the organic unity of 1830 might be read as fortunate in these terms.[16]

party of Hope

1830's

Hawthorn

This also, for Lewis, was the pattern in Melville's writings where "It is not, as with the European characters, that the realities of social experience and action catch up with them, but it is they who approach and enter into those realities." Lewis saw Melville's Billy Budd as the greatest literary expression of the party of Irony in its qualified acceptance of the Adamic hero. Billy Budd, like Melville himself, "began with the hopeful dawn—but a dawn transfigured. Melville salvaged the legend of hope both for life and for literature by repudiating it in order to restore it in an apotheosis of its hero."[17]

Melville

Billy Budd

In *American Adam,* as a parable of the experience of the 1940s, Lewis wanted his readers to understand the participation of the United States in World War II as such a fortunate fall. One might see the experience of the United States in the war as similar to that of the heroes of the party of Irony: "It is not, as with the European characters, that the realities of social experience and action catch up with them; but it is they who approach and enter into those realities." The American nation, like the American Adam, did not begin in an environment of tragedy. Americans in the 1950s, like Hawthorne and Melville a century earlier, needed to understand that they could participate in a tragedy like World War II without losing their innocence. "The American writer," Lewis insisted, "has never (if he is honest and American) been able to pretend to an authentic initial communion with the European past." The logic of Lewis's argument, then, was that Americans could involve themselves in the tragedy of European history while knowing they were not part of that history.[18]

Committed to American exceptionalism, Lewis was angry when he reported that "only recently has the dialogue between the party of Hope and the party of Irony tended to die away. For only recently has the old conviction of the new historical beginning seemed to vanish altogether." He was angry when he continued that "recent literature has applauded itself for passing beyond the childlike cheerfulness of Emerson and Whitman; but, in doing so, it has lost the profound tragic understanding—paradoxically bred out of cheerfulness—of a Hawthorne or a Melville."[19]

Lewis, in his determination to preserve a unique American cultural identity within the context of the revolutionary commitment to internationalism in the 1940s, had dropped Matthiessen's suggestion that Hawthorne's and Melville's artistic synthesis of tragedy and hope was a secular parallel to Anglo-Catholic theology. Matthiessen's self-conscious identity as a Christian had led him to empathize with T. S. Eliot and Henry James. But Lewis expressed no interest in exploring parallels between the Adamic myth, an American fortunate fall, and Christian mythology.

After Melville, however, Lewis could find no major representatives of the party of Irony. Instead, in the twentieth century the simple optimism of the party of Hope was being defeated by the party of Memory. This, for Lewis, was not a dialogue but a confrontation. In his analysis, the disappearance of the party of Irony meant the disappearance of the party of Hope and the victory of the party of Memory, whose members in 1950 congratulated themselves "for having settled, like adults or Europeans, upon a course of prolonged but tolerable hopelessness." Again he did not refer to Matthiessen's implicit argument in *American Renaissance* that as there could only be one generation of artistic genius related to the English renaissance, there could be only one generation of artistic genius born of the American renaissance. Unlike Matthiessen and Eliot, he did not describe the post-renaissance world as one in which the moment of organic unity was replaced by the fragmentation of capitalist materialism.[20]

Smith's elegy for the national landscape of the early nineteenth century, that unique American space free from European time, held out no hope for the resurrection of that landscape, which had been overwhelmed by the landscape of a transnational marketplace. For Smith the national landscape could only be preserved in memory as timeless myth. Having found the origin of American (Northern, male, Anglo-Protestant) literature in the national landscape, Lewis, however, did not confront the Adamic tradition with urban-industrial or capitalist landscapes coming from Europe. He did not confront the Adamic tradition with the experiences of World War I and World War II. He complained that "ours is an age of containment . . . both our literature and our public conduct suggest that exposure to experience is certain to be fatal." But in presenting his readers with the growing power of a party of Memory, he made no effort to ground that party in any experience outside that of the world of literary critics.

We may find an explanation for this containment of his story to the realm of ideas when we read his expression of hope that the dialogue between the party of Hope and the party of Irony might be brought back to life by a new generation of novelists—Ralph Ellison, J. D. Salinger, and Saul Bellow. Lewis, like Smith, had believed in the 1930s in the real and living presence of the national landscape. There was a vital American civilization distinct from Europe drawing strength from that landscape. Then during the 1940s this living presence, this reality, had become, for them, a myth and a memory. But the myth and the memory, like the reality of the living presence, continued to be sacred. Lewis, however, revealed his inability to believe that the myth of the national landscape was a real presence in 1950 when he described the spiritual difficulties faced by Ellison, Salinger, and Bellow. "It is their aim to test

Lewis
Smith
authors

the Adamic tradition," he declared, "by irony and drama; but they must create it from within, since they can scarcely find it any longer in the historic world about them."[21]

Leo Marx, another graduate of the Harvard Program in American Civilization, had come to the Program in American Studies at the University of Minnesota with Henry Nash Smith. As Smith's *Virgin Land* is considered the first major document of the symbol-myth school, Marx's *The Machine in the Garden,* appearing in 1964, is considered the last major document of that school. Like Smith, who left Minnesota for the University of California, Berkeley, to work with the Mark Twain papers, Marx also abandoned the teaching of American studies graduate students, going first to Amherst College and then to the Massachusetts Institute of Technology.

R. W. B. Lewis continued his career at Yale, but his writing after *The American Adam* was within more traditional patterns of literary criticism. I believe that this pattern of withdrawal from active American studies scholarship by Smith, Lewis, and Marx is related to the fact that each of their famous books—*Virgin Land, The American Adam,* and *The Machine in the Garden*—was an elegy for an American civilization that, for them, no longer existed. Having written their elegies, they no longer had anything significant to say about American culture.

Marx in *The Machine in the Garden* was much more explicit than Smith or Lewis that the boundaries of the national landscape, the boundaries that separated the United States from Europe, had been shattered by the force of industrialism coming from Europe. Working within the tradition that stretched from Bancroft to Matthiessen, Marx was not interested in the boundaries that separated the United States from other American nations. For Marx, as for Bancroft, those nations had no real existence. He, like Henry Nash Smith, was repeating Turner's two narratives—the first in which the landscape of the early nineteenth century had provided the spatial environment for Europeans to step out of Old World cultures, to step out of the flux of time, and became Americans. Then he repeated the second narrative, in which an industrial landscape ironically, tragically arrived from Europe just when a sacred national identity had been achieved. And Marx in 1964 saw no national romance that blended the two landscapes. Like Smith and Lewis, then, Marx was repressing his vision of a vital American civilization in the 1930s, a vision he had lost after 1945.

Again like Smith and Lewis, Marx was unable to confront directly this attack on that American civilization by international capitalism in the 1940s. In *The Machine in the Garden* he disguised his political criticism within the language of literary aesthetics. In this book the political conflict between Jefferson, as the advocate of an isolated pastoral democracy, and Hamilton, as the advocate of a transnational capitalist oligarchy, became a conflict between the literary symbols of the garden and the machine. Like his contemporaries, Smith and Lewis, Marx was returning to the example of Frederick Jackson Turner, who, in the 1890s, had tried to depersonalize the defeat of democracy by capitalism by invoking the impersonal forces of evolution.

When Marx wrote that "[t]he pastoral ideal has been used to define the meaning of America ever since the age of discovery, and it has not yet lost its hold upon the native imagination," he was using the aesthetic authority with which Bancroft, Turner, and the Beards had removed the Native Americans from the landscape. For him it was this "virgin land" that had taken Europeans and made them American. Jefferson and Emerson, for Marx, were native Americans because they were the children of the "Garden." Pastoral America, for Marx, as for Smith and Lewis, was not a European cultural invention that displaced the cultural values of the Indians when Europeans invaded the homelands of these American peoples.[22]

But Marx in 1964 did believe that the homeland of these native (male, Anglo-Protestant) Americans was invaded by European industrialism. He was so committed to the aesthetic authority of bourgeois nationalism, which envisioned autonomous nations as the necessary containers of reality, that he could not imagine that nationalism as well as industrialism was a transnational phenomenon. Marx, in 1964, therefore, was still mourning the loss of a national landscape and the cultural independence of the United States. He still imagined that there had been a homogeneous American people. Like Matthiessen he shared the aesthetic authority of the transcendentalists, who repressed the cultural diversity of the 1830s to imagine that there was one American language.

Marx began his elegy by distinguishing between "two kinds of pastoralism—one that is popular and sentimental, the other imaginative and complex." These categories were very similar to the party of Hope and the party of Irony presented by R. W. B. Lewis in *The American Adam*. And both Marx's sentimental and complex pastoral and Lewis's party of Hope and party of Irony were derivative of Matthiessen's distinction between the shallow optimism of Emerson and the profound sense of tragedy held by Melville. Henry Nash Smith in *Virgin Land* had argued that stories about the West had lost their spiritual relationship with the national landscape by the 1860s. Now Marx joined in this denunciation of naive optimism. There were many people in the United States, Marx declared, who still believed the pastoral was alive and well. These were the sentimental Americans who devoured the celebration of the pastoral in popular novels, movies, and television. Their motive was a "desire to withdraw from civilization's growing power and complexity." Such sentimental celebrations of the pastoral had characterized popular poetry, drama, and novels throughout the nineteenth century. But Marx made it clear that he was going to celebrate such unpopular writers of the nineteenth century as Hawthorne and Melville, who wrote "imaginative and complex pastorals." Writing an elegy for the complex pastoral in 1960, Marx was going to celebrate the men who wrote elegies for the complex pastoral in 1850.[23]

Before he reached Hawthorne and Melville, however, Marx found a hero in Jefferson. "By 1785," he declared, "when Jefferson first printed his *Notes on Virginia,* the pastoral idea of America had developed into something like an all-embracing ideology." The pastoral, as Marx described it, assumed a middle landscape as its ideal. This middle landscape existed between an overly complex civilization and an overly primitive wilderness. Explicitly appealing to the authority of Smith's discussion in *Virgin Land,* Marx identified the yeoman farmer as the ideal inhabitant of the middle landscape, who stood between the decadence of a European aristocracy and the savagery of the Indians. Smith, according to Marx, had identified this pastoral as a destructive myth that denied the experience of time in the realm of politics and economics. Once constructed, the middle landscape, according to this delusion, would last forever. This was the message of the popular and sentimental pastorals that stretched from the nineteenth century down to the present. America would always be an agrarian democracy.[24]

But, for Marx, such a mythic pastoral should not be identified with Jefferson. Jefferson, Marx insisted, could not believe that the space of the pastoral was free from the influence of time. "Like certain great poets who have written in the pastoral mode," Marx continued, "Jefferson's genius lay in his capacity to respond to the dream yet to disengage himself from it." This is the essential aspect of Marx's elegy, as it was for Lewis and, before them, Matthiessen. Identifying industrialism with time, Marx believed that the space of the national landscape—the pastoral—had ceased to be a lived experience. But the purpose of Marx's elegy was to keep the memory of the dream alive after its death. And so Marx concluded, "Jefferson anticipates the tragic ambivalence that is the hallmark of our most resonant pastoral fables."[25]

In Marx's elegiac nationalism there was no place for the Jefferson described in the national romances of Bancroft, in Turner's first narrative, in Parrington, and in the Beards' *The Rise of American Civilization.* Marx's Jefferson was not the good son locked in combat with the bad son, Hamilton. The elegiac nationalism of Marx, Lewis, and Smith imitated Turner's second narrative in stoically accepting the victory of the industrialism that came from England. Marx then agreed with the pattern of elegiac nationalism expressed in *American Renaissance:* industrialism was not an organic development out of the pastoral national landscape. The coming of industrialism from Europe was a revolutionary disruption. But, as in the case of Lewis, Marx's elegiac nationalism was more bounded than that of Matthiessen. Like Lewis, Marx did not discuss Matthiessen's suggestion that there was a parallel between the Christian synthesis of tragedy and hope and the secular synthesis of tragedy and hope expressed by Hawthorne and Melville. Marx and Lewis did not associate themselves with T. S. Eliot.

Unable to confront the vision of an American civilization holding the pastoral and industrialism together that was the context for his undergraduate education at the end of the 1930s, Marx displaced his rejection of the Beards' national romance on Emerson. Emerson refused to embrace Jefferson's tragic understanding of the inevitable replacement of the American pastoral landscape by a European industrial landscape. Emerson, according to Marx, insisted that industry could be fitted into the middle landscape. Emerson, Marx wrote, argued that "[i]f technology is the creation of man, who is a product of nature, then how can the machine in the landscape be thought to represent an unresolvable conflict?" The relationship of Jefferson and Emerson, then, was a preview of the relationship between Turner and the Beards.[26]

Marx in the 1940s, therefore, had rejected the Beards' synthesis of the landscape of nature and the landscape of industrialism; he had rejected the narrative of a national romance and had chosen to live in the memory of the pastoral. He now celebrated Thoreau's rejection of Emerson's national romance in the 1840s. "*Walden,*" Marx reported, "belongs among the first of a long series of American books which, taken together, have had the effect of circumscribing the pastoral hope." Thoreau and, after him, Hawthorne, Melville, and Twain were writing what Marx labeled the complex pastoral. "Taken together they exemplify a view of life which dominates much of our literature. It is a complex distinctive American form of romantic pastoralism." This complex pastoralism, in Marx's story, accepted the defeat of space by time. "For Thoreau, like Melville's Ahab," Marx continued, "this machine is the type and agent of an irreversible process . . . the implacable advance of history." In contrast, Emerson, like so many other Americans, was the prisoner of a simple pastoral, who was "reaffirming the Jeffersonian hope of embodying the pastoral dream in social institutions." But, for Thoreau, "the pastoral way of life is being whirled past and away."[27]

If Marx, like his fellow students Smith and Lewis and their teacher Matthiessen, believed that the isolated space of American civilization was being dissolved into the flux of a transnational history, then the realm of myth offered the only refuge for an exceptional American nation from a modern civilization whose changing patterns contained no ultimate meaning. Always implicit, occasionally explicit in the narratives of Smith and Lewis was that the memory of the national landscape, defeated by the realm of history, could be sustained in the timeless realm of art. The elegies of Marx, Smith, and Lewis were themselves works of art in which memory was enshrined in the timeless realm of myth. Matthiessen had convinced them of the power of myth to transcend time. This myth, for them, was redemptive. It used art to provide the vision of the organic unity of the good, true, and beautiful that had once existed. Art could sustain the memory that would give strength to successive generations who would have to live in the fragmentation of the capitalist wasteland. This "good" myth of the pastoral America of 1830 stood in contrast to the "bad" myth of the pastoral, which insisted that the social, political, and economic democracy of 1830 still existed.

Marx, in *The Machine in the Garden,* was always explicit about his commitment to the realm of this "good" myth. In writing an elegy for the loss of the middle landscape as an economic, political, and social way of life, he continued, like Matthiessen, to have a usable past. The great American writers—Thoreau, Hawthorne, Melville, and Twain—

had witnessed the loss of the middle landscape as a way of life. Unlike Emerson and so many other Americans, they had not tried to obscure the contradictions between the machine and the garden with a myth of an eternal social and economic democracy. Facing that reality, they had then argued that the pastoral could remain alive in their minds, their imagination, their art. "In *Walden,*" Marx rejoiced, "Thoreau is clear, as Emerson seldom was, about the location of meaning and value. He is saying that it does not reside in the natural facts or in social institutions. It is a product of imaginative perception. For Thoreau, the realization of the golden age is, finally, a matter of private and, in fact, literary experience."[28]

Like Turner, the leaders of the symbol-myth school, whose major texts were *Virgin Land, The American Adam,* and *The Machine in the Garden,* did not write about the history of the United States after 1890. Having lost their commitment in the 1940s to the synthesis of the pastoral and industrial myth with which they had kept the United States imaginatively isolated from European history until World War II, they had chosen to invest their artistic energy in recreating that magical time between 1776 and 1850, when their nation had achieved cultural independence from Europe. While political, social, and economic independence was gone, they, as scholars of American literature and American studies, could sustain a canon that enshrined the complex pastoral of the male, northern, Anglo-American artists from Thoreau to Twain. The memory of that sacred moment, therefore, would not disappear. Within the walls of the academy the spirituality of that heritage would not be corrupted by the surrounding sea of capitalist materialism.

The generation of students in the discipline of American studies who were coming of age in the 1960s, however, had only known a world in which the aesthetic authority of bourgeois nationalism had been shattered. They saw American peoples and American cultures where Smith, Lewis, and Marx wanted to remember a people and a culture. They saw various American spaces where the men of the symbol-myth school had wanted to remember a single space. Hoping to preserve the enchanted world of 1830, Smith, Lewis, and Marx, nevertheless, had worked in their scholarship to disenchant the aesthetic authority of the national landscape and its fraternal democracy as a current reality. They did not directly dismiss nineteenth-century cultural mythology as had their contemporaries, the historians Hofstadter, Williams, and Schlesinger. For the historians one must choose reality over myth. But Smith, Lewis, and Marx had also drawn a dramatic distinction between nineteenth-century myth and twentieth-century reality. For the men of the symbol-myth school, as for the historians of their generation, the idea of an American civilization in the 1930s was a myth, not a reality. And that vision dissolved before their eyes in the 1940s. But, having known the aesthetic power of that synthesis, they were trying to preserve the beauty of the myth against the ugliness of the capitalist reality that became triumphant in the 1940s. The students of Smith, Lewis, and Marx, however, did not have the experience of their teachers. They had not known the living presence of the aesthetic authority of 1830. For them the scholarship of the symbol-myth school focused only on a dead past that seemed irrelevant to a largely urban and industrial America. They would focus American studies scholarship on the twentieth century. They could not define their century as profane because they no longer had a sacred to compare it to. They would embrace the study of twentieth-century popular culture, which, for them, was not as Smith and Marx had claimed, a tragic declension from the virtuous popular culture that existed before the Civil War. No wonder, then, that Smith and Marx turned their backs on this generation of graduate students.

CHAPTER FIVE

The New Literary Criticism: The Death of the Nation Born in New England

When modern nations were imagined as sacred spaces, it became the duty of all artists—historians, novelists, poets, musicians, painters, and architects—to express the beauty, the goodness, and the truth of national landscapes. These landscapes were given substance as the variety of artists gave them representation. The orthodoxy of modern nationalism insisted that the purpose of art was to represent the recently discovered and marvelous realities. A nation's people, its male citizens, had emerged from this landscape. The arts needed to share the organic relationship of the people to the landscape. They, too, needed to emerge organically from the soil of the nation. Then the arts, like the people, would express the soul of the nation.

Because a nation's art was sacred, the productions of artists who could represent the soil and soul of the nation were canonized. The boundaries between the national sacred and the alien profanities needed to be drawn and defined. In the United States this meant that there needed to be a clear distinction between American and European art. The custodians of the national culture did not feel threatened by Canadian or Mexican art. But, of course, their definition of what was American also excluded most of the people within the political boundaries of the United States. The boundaries of the national arts, therefore, needed to be defended against these internal aliens. In the Anglo-Protestant myth of origins, it was English colonists who had been liberated from their Old World culture; these men had become like little children, and they were endowed with their American identity by the virgin land. When artists represented the American people, they would represent the presence of Anglo-Protestant men on the landscape.

Understanding that politics is an art form, we can see the canonical character of the presidency. All of our presidents have been white men. All but John F. Kennedy have been Protestants. Elected in 1960 and assassinated in 1963, Kennedy, a Catholic, now seems to have been an aberration. Clearly it is the role of the president to be the symbolic representative of the people. And as the canonical presidency guards the purity of the people, so the canons of literature, history, painting, music, and architecture guard the purity of the people as male, Anglo-Protestant citizens. Until the collapse of the aesthetic authority of the national landscape, the art by Anglo-Protestant women as well as the art of American Indians, African Americans, Mexican Americans, Asian Americans, Catholics, and Jews was excluded from being considered as American art. American art represented the universal national. Only art by male Anglo-Protestants could express that universal national as only a male Anglo-Protestant president could express the universal national.

No arts by other Americans could be canonized because they represented only a particular class, a particular section, a particular gender, a particular race or ethnicity. But, when it became impossible for me to imagine a universal national, I came to see the keepers of the canons as representing a particular class, section, gender, race, and ethnicity. The members of the literary canon presented by Matthiessen, whose passing was mourned by his students, Leo Marx and R. W. B. Lewis, was made up of Anglo-Protestant men from the Northeast—men seen by the canonizers as members of a classless, middle-class democracy.

In the myth of Anglo-American origins, cultural independence was not achieved at the moment of political independence, but waited until the 1830s and 1840s. These decades, for Matthiessen, were the context for the American renaissance. There is, therefore, a time discrepancy between the literary canon and the presidential canon, which began with Washington in 1789. We must notice that until 1852, the presidential canon was dominated by Anglo-Protestant slaveholders. During the years between 1789 and 1852, eight southerners and three northerners were selected to represent the American people. Many of the southerners held the presidency for two terms; the northerners, however, each had only one term.

It is clear, then, that during the 1850s white southerners lost their authority to symbolize the universal national. After the southern defeat in the Civil War, northern Anglo-Protestants claimed that they alone represented the universal national. White southerners were now part of a particular section. As permanent provincials they could not provide presidential leadership. This pattern did not disappear until 1976, when Jimmy Carter from Georgia was elected president. Carter, unlike Kennedy, was not an aberration. Since 1960 it has been impossible for a Republican from the Northeast or Midwest to be nominated as the party's presidential candidate. And Kennedy was the last Democratic Party candidate from the Northeast or Midwest to be elected President.

The ability of Anglo-Protestants from the South and West to control the boundaries of the presidential canon since the 1960s followed the capture of the literary canon by southern, Anglo-Protestant literary critics in the 1940s. During the 1940s and 1950s, after the American Studies Program at the University of Minnesota had been established by men from the English department, Robert Penn Warren and Allen Tate, both from the South, became members of that department. From the perspective of Warren and Tate, the work of Tremaine McDowell, Henry Nash Smith, and Leo Marx to construct a holistic method for the study of an American national culture was a provincial effort in futility. Warren and Tate were leaders of a revolutionary change in the way literature was taught in English departments throughout the entire United States. Between 1935 and 1945 this "New Criticism" became more persuasive for younger teachers of literature than the commonly accepted approach to the study of American literature in the mid-1930s—the historical.[1]

The historical method of studying American literature assumed the reality of a homogeneous national culture. It encouraged young scholars to analyze the ways in which particular authors reflected the national culture in their writings. There was, of course, an intense debate about national identity that began in the early twentieth century. During these years of the Progressive Era, Parrington had developed his vision of the conflict between the real national identity—a democracy born of the national landscape—and the false national identity introduced by an international and undemocratic capitalism. A similar perspective was expressed in John Macy's *The Spirit of American Literature* (1913) and in Van Wyck Brooks's *America's Coming-of-Age* (1915).[2]

After the Great Crash of 1929, this vision of the ways literature expressed the conflict between democracy and capitalism was taken up by literary critics who explicitly defined themselves as Marxists. Some identified with the Socialist Party, but others identified with the Communist Party. The formation of a People's Front by 1935 encouraged radicals to minimize their differences and cooperate in purging undemocratic capitalism from the nation. Representative of the People's Front was the League of American Writers, begun in 1935. It included, among others, Lewis Mumford, Van Wyck Brooks, John Steinbeck, William Carlos Williams, and Richard Wright. Most of them saw Marxist analysis as a tool that would help restore the national democracy that existed before the Civil War. Their socialism imagined that social and economic reality was contained within national boundaries.

V. F. Calverton's *The Liberation of American Literature* (1932) and Granville Hicks's *The Great Tradition* (1935) were the first major works of Marxist literary criticism that continued Parrington's thesis of a conflict between the two Americas. Both, like Parrington, were primarily interested in the political outlook of the authors they analyzed. Calverton declared that "I have intentionally avoided the problem of aesthetic analyses and evaluation. In short . . . I have taken the aesthetic element for granted, and in almost all cases have immediately proceeded to an analysis of the philosophy, or ideology if you will, that underlay the individual author's work." And, for Hicks: "Believing that criticism is always a weapon, I see no reason to disguise, either from others or from myself, the nature of the conflict in which I am engaged, or the side I have chosen."[3]

Robert Penn Warren and Allen Tate had been part of a group of southerners who contributed essays to *I'll Take My Stand* (1930). In the face of the devastating crisis of corporate capitalism, they advised northerners to abandon their cities and factories and look to the tradition of southern agrarianism for a usable past on which to build their future. For northern Marxists, like Hicks, this message was certainly an essay in futility. He wrote, "The proclamation of Mssrs. Davidson, Ransom, Tate, and others, who have taken their stand for agriculture as opposed to industry and for southern ideals as opposed to northern, may deserve whatever admiration one can accord such a quixotic gesture, but it is peculiarly futile."[4]

But, by the end of the 1930s, Hicks had abandoned the People's Front and with it the hope for any immediate defeat of capitalism. His loss of faith in the victory of democracy over capitalism was representative of his colleagues in the League of American Writers. By 1945 only an insignificant remnant of the literary radicals of the 1930s still saw in Marxism usable theories for the critique of literature. More importantly they no longer believed that there was a usable past that had sprung from the national landscape. No American civilization had really existed in the 1930s that was a synthesis of the democratic impulses of the national landscape and the urban-industrial landscape. The aesthetic authority for a literary criticism that analyzed literary art as an expression of a clearly defined national identity was gone. The national landscape and the urban-industrial landscape were no longer spaces that had transcendent meaning. The space of the international marketplace now seemed to have achieved omnipotent aesthetic authority. Could there now be any alternative to discussing literature as an expression of this space, which most literary critics found to be an environment that was physically ugly and socially destructive?

The alternative offered by Tremaine McDowell, Henry Nash Smith, Leo Marx, and other participants in the symbol-myth school was to have literary criticism evoke the memory of the national landscape. Literary criticism should focus on the literature that celebrated the moment when national autonomy had been achieved. It should focus on the literature that both celebrated and mourned the birth and death of a national culture, that fleeting miracle that had come and gone within the limits of a single generation. Putting the memory of that space, which had been true, good, and beautiful, into the realm of myth would provide a refuge for those who could not bear to live in the capitalist wasteland. This was a way of salvaging the national romance. The victory of capitalism in the 1940s had meant that the organic development of the nation was at an end and that the American future was one of discontinuity rather than continuity. But at the level of myth one could preserve the national romance and keep the future in organic contact with the past.

For most young literary critics, however, the New Criticism, for which Warren, Tate, and other "Southern Agrarians" were spokesmen, offered a more powerful and vital alternative to the cash-nexus of capitalism than did the symbol-myth school. Tate has been described as a man whose public persona was one of arrogance. And the New Criticism was presented by him and his allies as an arrogant, self-confident alternative to capitalism. The New Critics would demonstrate that a literature that embodied the good, true, and beautiful was alive and vital in 1940. It provided a high moral ground from which one could look down on capitalism with disdain. They would show that this organic literature could survive the cultural fragmentation caused by the victory of the marketplace. For them the decade of the 1940s was not a turning point in history. Tate and the other New Critics shared the view of T. S. Eliot that capitalism had become triumphant after the renaissance. In that international world of fragmented materialism in which the false, ugly, and evil prevailed, writers throughout the Western world had continued to construct organic unity in their poetry and prose. Such literature sustained the living presence of a unity of the good, true, and beautiful. The New Critics taught a way of analyzing and explicating the redemptive literature that embodied this organic unity.

Tate had written that "[t]he literary artist is seldom successful as a colonial; he should be able to enjoy the belief that he is the center of the world." From the perspective of Charles and Mary Beard in their *The Rise of American Civilization,* Anglo-Protestant southerners had disappeared from the nation sometime after 1830. This, too, was the view of the professors who were creating academic programs in American civilization in northeastern universities during the 1930s. Throughout that decade, northern academics could only imagine the Southern Agrarians as the most provincial of intellectuals. But, of course, all that changed when the aesthetic authority of the national landscape was destroyed and a national history was no longer a usable past. Participants in the aesthetic of a virtuous American civilization isolated from a corrupt European civilization were reluctant to convert to the aesthetic of an international marketplace. But the Southern Agrarians had no commitment to the aesthetic authority of an American civilization with its foundation in a national landscape. And they had an alternative international aesthetic authority to that of the marketplace. When Tate was asked in 1961 whether he still held the views he had expressed in *I'll Take My Stand* in 1930, he replied, "Yes, I do. That doesn't mean I think Southern Agrarianism will prevail. . . . I think that the point of view expressed in that symposium . . . represents the permanent values of Western society."

This was the message of hope that inspired the conversion of so many younger literary critics in the north to the New Criticism, whose leaders had been southerners. Capitalism destroyed national landscapes. But it had not and it could not defeat "the permanent values of Western Society," values that were not those of bourgeois nationalism.[5]

On the surface there seem to be significant parallels between the crisis of pastoralism expressed by Parrington, Matthiessen, and the symbol-myth school and the crisis of pastoralism expressed by the Southern Agrarians. But this is not the case. The virtuous agricultural world celebrated by the Southern Agrarians had, for them, a completely different relationship to space, time, and history from the agricultural world celebrated by Bancroft, Turner, the Beards, and northern literary critics such as Parrington and Matthiessen.

Warren and Tate had been part of a group, the Fugitives, who met regularly at Vanderbilt University in Nashville, Tennessee, during the 1920s. Many members of the group were students of John Crowe Ransom (1888–1974), who taught literature at Vanderbilt and was a major influence in the literary magazine, *The Fugitive.* Tate and Warren recognized their teacher as an inspiring poetic voice whose collected poems were published in *Poems about God* (1919), *Chills and Fever* (1924), *Grace after Meat* (1924), and *Two Gentlemen in Bonds* (1927). In their discussions of poetry, Donald Davidson, another member of the group, remembered that, for them, "a poem had to prove its strength. . . . In its cumulative effect this severe discipline made us self-conscious craftsmen, abhorring looseness of expression. . . . The poet, anxious to fortify his verses against criticism, strove to weed out anything 'loose'"[6]

The Fugitives emphasized discipline because they saw themselves as part of a heritage threatened by the fragmenting tendencies of capitalism. They believed they inherited a southern tradition that had the characteristics of the medieval world. This was a world of many local cultures. Members of these cultures found strength from being rooted in a particular place. Feeling the richness of the physical environment, its nuances and particularities, the Southern Agrarians also believed such people found strength in their sense of being links in a chain of generational continuity. One was united to one's ancestors and to one's descendants. Time, therefore, was experienced as generational. There was no sequence of past, present, and future. That was a modern notion that was false since it denied the fact of birth, death, and rebirth.

traditionals

So. Agrarian
view of
Modernity

In this traditional world people produced for use, not for the marketplace. Their economy, therefore, was in harmony with the generational rhythms of the land and of the family. Their religion also did not recognize modern time or the sequence of past, present, and future. Medieval religion emphasized that each moment is equally sacred. Sacred tradition was passed down through successive generations. The present was not more sacred than the past, and the future would not be more sacred than the present. But this harmonious world of tradition, in which members of the community experienced the organic relationship of their economic, social, and religious patterns, was not, for the Southern Agrarians, Eden. They were committed to the doctrine of original sin. All humans were fallen creatures, part angel and part devil. People in traditional societies recognized this tension and developed rituals of reconciliation. The organic unity they experienced was necessarily ironic because it constructed a balance of evil and good that could not be permanent.

The modern world, from the perspective of the Fugitives, was a romantic denial of the reality of traditional life. Modern people imagined that they could find an organic unity in the future in which harmony would be perfect and therefore permanent. Human beings were not evil; traditional societies were evil. The individual had the potential to be completely good. And so modern people constructed the romantic vision of history as progress from darkness to light. They tried to live within the illusion that they could escape from their embodiment of original sin. They expected to find a new Eden, but all they found was an earthly hell.

The contradiction of modern history, for the Southern Agrarians, was that the search for an organic unity that did not include evil led modern people into a society where they experienced greater and greater alienation. In starting an exodus to a promised land, they uprooted themselves from the particular places that had been their homes. They ceased to be in touch with the generational rhythms of the land. They also uprooted themselves from their social homes. It was only by imagining themselves free from the generational continuity of families that they could invent the discontinuity of past, present, and future. To be on the march toward utopia meant dependence on the capitalist marketplace. Without an economy rooted in a particular place, one had to participate in the marketplace. Working for money intensified alienation from a sacralized economy of production. Now modern people were alienated from place, family, and their own labor. In this profane environment, they were alienated from God.

In the mid-1920s, the Fugitives became aware that the business leaders of their region were committed to building a New South. Businessmen wanted to lead an exodus out of a backward past into a progressive future. They wanted the South to become part of the modern world. The Fugitives had discussed T. S. Eliot's poem "The Wasteland" when it appeared in 1922. They were in full agreement with him about the fragmentation and alienation of a transnational capitalist society. But they believed their region still embodied medieval characteristics: an appreciation for the generational qualities of nature and family.

To remind southerners (the Fugitives did not include African Americans as part of the southern people) that they had a history separate from capitalism, the Southern Agrarians began to write about the era of the Civil War. Tate, for instance, wrote biographies of "Stonewall" Jackson, Jefferson Davis, and Robert E. Lee. One of the most evil characteristics of modern society, for Tate and Warren, was its will to power. When one saw history as progress, one inevitably constructed a metaphor of the conquest of darkness by the forces of light. The Fugitives did not share the narrative that prevailed from Bancroft to the symbol-myth school in which the pastoral democracy of the United States of America-North in the 1830s was a gift from the national landscape—that it represented innocence and not power. Tate, in his novel *The Fathers* (1938), contrasts two men at the time of the Civil War. The southerner takes a humble stance toward his environment, which he sees as a complex web of particulars. His identity as a father is to be a link in the chain of generational continuity. The northerner sees a reconstructed South. Tate presents him as a man who could imagine social reality in terms of abstractions and generalizations, as a man who is willing to use military power to push people toward a world they could never reach because it denies the particularity of human existence. He is a father of a new world that denies generational continuity. He is the father of a world that is impossible for humans to inhabit.[7]

Warren repeats many of these themes in his novel *All the King's Men* (1946), written while he was at Minnesota. Here the man with the will to power is Willie Stark, a governor of Louisiana whom many readers identified with Huey Long, the charismatic governor and then senator

ATKM

from Louisiana who was assassinated in 1935. Stark believes that he can lead the people out of an old world of corruption into a new world of virtue. Stark represents a South dominated by the modern idea of progress. In the process of trying to reach the new world of abstractions, he neglects his relationships with his friends and loved ones. As a result he allows these relationships to wither, and he becomes responsible for the destruction of the lives of those friends and loved ones. He is killed by Adam Stanton, who can also imagine a perfect new world. When Willie Stark fails to be the Moses figure Adam expected him to be, Adam shoots him. Out of the wreckage, Jack Burden survives. Burden was a graduate student in history who could not complete his dissertation. He discovered the good man who was the subject of his research was also evil. Burden does not know at the beginning of the novel that all humans are a mixture of good and evil. For him if the world is not good it must be evil. And he refuses to act in an evil world. He will not complete his thesis. He will spend the rest of his life as an alienated observer.

But by the end of the novel he, like Melville's Ishmael, survives the death of most of his friends. He, like Ishmael and his shipmates on the *Pequod,* does not coldly observe the deaths of Willie Stark, Adam Stanton, and his biological father. He feels their deaths. And he knows that he, like them, is a mixture of good and evil. He embraces his two fathers, one legal and one biological. He had rejected them for their weaknesses. But at the end he celebrates generational continuity as he also embraces his mother, whom he had previously despised for her weakness. He sees himself as a link in a generational chain. He has rejected the way he had previously understood time as segmented into past, present, and future. He is able to celebrate life as generational continuity because he sees that there is a role to be played that is neither that of a Moses figure, nor that of a cynical observer. Willie Stark and Adam Stanton killed each other because they did not understand that the role of all humans should be to create a balance of good and evil. It is the responsibility of the individual to create unity out of complexity. One should acknowledge the particulars of the environment into which one is born and construct something beautiful out of them. One should acknowledge that this organic unity is necessarily complex, even contradictory, because it contains the flaw of original sin. Warren, as one of the fathers of the New Criticism, had made the Word of New Criticism flesh in the figure of his fictional son, Jack Burden. The New Critics wanted to find sons in their university classes who could learn from great literature what Jack Burden had learned in Warren's novel.[8]

For the Southern Agrarians, then, the idea of a national landscape filled with Adamic citizens was meaningless. From their perspective, the North of 1830 was part of the international pattern of industrial capitalism. And capitalists were ruthless invaders and conquerors. They had no respect for the integrity of local communities. All the world needed to be absorbed within their empire. They justified their wars of conquest as wars of liberation. They insisted they were freeing people from their bondage to an outmoded past. In 1861 Yankee capitalists and Yankee romantic utopians had joined to destroy what they saw as the darkness, the horror of a neo-medieval society in the South. Southerners had lost on the battlefield, but until the 1920s they had managed to preserve most of their traditional culture. Now the good southern sons who honored the sacred past because it should blend into present and future as a timeless unity were confronted by bad southern sons who wanted to replace the sacred past with a profane future. They wanted to replace unity with capitalist fragmentation.

Among many ironies, the publication of *I'll Take My Stand* in 1930 coincided with the onset of the Great Depression and the apparent collapse of international capitalism. These years between 1929 and 1935 were magical for bourgeois nationalists, all varieties of Marxists, and the many intellectuals who had constructed a synthesis of bourgeois nationalism and socialism. For this brief moment, opponents of international capitalism experienced political euphoria. It was a miracle that the all-powerful capitalism of the 1920s had died in 1929. The national democracy of 1830 would be embodied in the New Deal. An American civilization would preserve its autonomy from Europe. A socialist fraternal democracy would appear in the United States. And Southern Agrarians shared the euphoria of this fleeting moment. With the collapse of international capitalism, rooted local communities could be preserved. There would not be a New South. Since northern society had been an expression of the conquering spirit of international capitalism, northerners were now free to choose a different, more humble way of life. They could look to the South for a model of how to recreate vital areas of local life where it would again be possible to experience families and the land as sacred elements in the cycle of generational continuity, rather than as commodities in the marketplace. They could give up the religion of progress with its false promise of heaven on earth. They could accept the true religion, which embraced the fallen nature of man. They could develop rituals to reconcile the inevitable conflicts within each individual. Looking back to the medieval era as a usable past, many of these southern Protestants were troubled by the way the Reformation broke generational continuity. They were also troubled by the attempt of Protestants to predict the coming of the millennium and a heaven on Earth. Many of the Southern Agrarians expressed an intellectual appreciation of Anglo-Catholicism and Roman Catholicism as religions that sacralized generational continuity in an imperfect world. Allen Tate, however, was exceptional when he converted to Roman Catholicism in 1950.

But, even as the Southern Agrarians published another collection of essays, *Who Owns America?* (1935), which was a scathing attack on monopoly capitalism, they had come to believe that international capitalism had survived the Great Depression. There would be a New South. Into the foreseeable future the marketplace would fragment the lives of individuals as it alienated them from their labor, their families, and the places in which they were born.[9]

Faced with a future of capitalist domination, Matthiessen in 1940 had written *The American Renaissance.* The organic unity of truth, goodness, and beauty that was the national identity between 1830 and 1860 had been lost to a triumphant capitalism. The language of this perfect democracy, the language of the people, disappeared and was replaced by the language of the marketplace: individualism, competition, material success, the accumulation of commodities, new technologies leading to boundless futures. For Matthiessen, however, and his followers in the symbol-myth school, memory of that organic unity was kept alive by novelists such as Melville, who celebrated the good and beautiful of that lost Eden even as he accepted the reality of the fall into capitalism. This was a literature of complexity and irony that needed to be remembered if one was not going to be seduced into the language of capitalism, the fate suffered by most Americans after 1865.

Matthiessen associated his appreciation of that literature that combined complexity and irony with the writing of T. S. Eliot. But the Southern Agrarians did not read Eliot as their contemporary Matthiessen did. From the perspective of Tate and Warren, Matthiessen and the members of the symbol-myth school were romantics. They had forgotten that the nature of man was one of original sin. There was no fall from a recent

Eden. Melville, for them, was a great novelist who spoke the language neither of romantic nationalism, nor of capitalism. Melville knew that the individual was both good and evil. He developed a style that could deal with that complexity, a style that could hold these opposites together in a unity. He developed a style that expressed the irony of a reconciliation of conflicting opposites and weaknesses. Melville knew the reconciliation could not be permanent. Melville saw the possibility of a complex and difficult harmony in a world that would always be the same as it was at the moment of Adam's fall. The Southern Agrarians shared the view of T. S. Eliot that literary artists since the Renaissance and Reformation were divided between a romantic tradition and a metaphysical one and that Melville represented the transnational metaphysical tradition.

The romantics believed in the innate goodness of the individual. They wrote as an avant-garde whose publications would help liberate the innocent individual from corrupt society. But those in the metaphysical tradition believed in the innate sinfulness of the individual. They wrote warnings against the effort to escape the human condition. To imagine history as an exodus to a promised land meant a commitment to purges. It meant a will to power that would result in the slaughter of human beings, as in the case of Melville's Captain Ahab, of the Civil War, or of World War I. Now Hitler and Stalin were speaking the language of social purification as they promised to create perfect societies. But the metaphysical writers also demonstrated in their art that the inevitable presence of evil need not lead to a world without meaning. Opposites could be reconciled in society for a time as they were in a poem or novel that participated in the metaphysical tradition.

For centuries literary artists in the metaphysical tradition had been using the language of complexity and irony to confront the language of capitalism, with its false promises that if individuals would uproot themselves from a particular place and enter the boundless marketplace they would reach a better world filled with a cornucopia of commodities. Instead of complexity and irony they could enjoy simplicity and progress. For Tate, Warren, and other New Critics, this tradition did not find expression in national contexts. Their imagined reality was similar to that which Benedict Anderson believed was dominant before the creation of the modern nation. The imagined community of the modern nation found the sacred within national boundaries. That sacred was more powerful than the sacred of the universal religion of the medieval past. When the sacred of the modern nation became all powerful, it also denied the possibility of a variety of sacred localities within the nation's boundaries.

For the Southern Agrarians, however, the sacred was to be found simultaneously in the universal and the local, but not in the nation. Feeling in the 1920s that their local southern culture was sacred, they appreciated T. S. Eliot's affirmation that the sacred also was to be found in the universals of Catholicism. They disassociated literature from the erroneous belief of bourgeois nationalism that literature had meaning only as an expression of national culture. As the Southern Agrarians worked to develop a literary criticism that could explain the universal aspects of literature, they were in close contact with literary critics in England, such as I. A. Richards and William Simpson, who shared this viewpoint. These English New Critics also were rejecting the way in which the term "tradition" had been limited to a national context. Literary critics, they agreed, should not try to write about a national tradition in English literature or in American literature. When literary critics wrote about tradition, they should use the term to designate the universal tradition in literature that was critical of the antigenerational and utopian characteristics of the modern world.

The New Critics agreed, therefore, with Eliot's statement that "the historical sense compels a man to write not merely with his generation in his bones, but with a feeling that the whole of the literature of Europe . . . has a simultaneous existence and composes a simultaneous order. The historical sense is what makes a writer traditional." This was the basis for the New Critics' objection to the emphasis on biography in the historical method of the literary criticism of bourgeois nationalism. One of the things they had in mind when they used the term "romantic" in a derogatory way was the modern emphasis on the individuality of the artist. They rejected the Renaissance depiction of the artist as one who creates his own world. This artist was a Moses figure, an avant-garde leader, breaking generational continuity. This artist offered the abstractions of a utopia inhabited by autonomous individuals. Such an artist participated in the destruction of community.[10]

Against this figure of the artist as innovator, the New Critics argued that the artist who has a sense of tradition lets the tradition speak through him. The tradition existed before the artist was born and will exist after he dies. This is the meaning of Eliot's use of the term "simultaneous." An artist in 1550, 1650, 1750, 1850, or 1950 is working within the same tradition. An artist in 1750 is telling the same story as was told in 1550 or will be told in 1950. The New Literary Critic will focus on the particular work of literature as an expression of this antimodern tradition. The success or failure of the particular poem, play, or novel depends on how well it expresses this tradition, on how well it serves as a link in the generational activity that keeps the tradition alive from one generation to the next.

After 1935 Ransom, Tate, and Warren felt that they had lost their identity as Southern Agrarians. For them there no longer was a traditional South. With the victory of the disloyal southerners, who wanted a future of boundless capitalist expansion, there no longer was a southern culture because a culture was "the way of life of a particular people living together in one place." Writers, like themselves, could no longer be inspired by their vanished local culture to speak the truth about the fragmentation of modern society. And, for Tate, writers who lived in the capitalist wasteland "lacked a social basis of aesthetic independence." There is strong evidence, then, that when Tate, Warren, and their friend, Cleanth Brooks, went to the annual meeting of the Modern Language Association in 1936, they were considering the possibility that English departments might provide such "a social basis of aesthetic independence."[11]

The English department at Vanderbilt had, of course, been such an environment, but these southern literary critics no longer felt that there was a meaningful distinction between the North and the South. They could imagine taking positions in the English departments of northern universities. They could also imagine that the historical method of literary criticism had become so bankrupt that their new colleagues in these universities would quickly embrace the alternative theories they had developed within their peculiar region. They would persuade Yankee colleagues that the historical method of literary criticism did not offer an effective critique of capitalism. Tate contemptuously declared, "These attitudes of scholarship are the attitudes of the haute bourgeoisie that support it in the great universities; it is now commonplace to observe that the uncreative money culture of modern times tolerates the historical routine of the scholars. The routine is 'safe,' and it shares with the predatory social process at large a naturalistic basis."

Building on their paper given at the Modern Language Association meeting, "The Reading of Modern Poetry," Warren and Brooks published a book, *Understanding Poetry,* in 1938. Grant Webster, in his book *The Republic of Letters,* argues that the suddenness with which the New Criticism displaced the authority of the historical approach to literary analysis, making it within a decade the Old Criticism, can best be understood within the theoretical framework developed by Thomas Kuhn in his *The Structure of Scientific Revolutions* (1961). Kuhn's thesis was that historians of science should work from the assumption that there are two distinct periods in that history: revolutionary science and normal science. It was Kuhn's position that all science begins with a set of hypotheses about reality. Kuhn called these hypotheses paradigms. There was no science unless a community of scientists was prepared to work from a shared paradigm. They must be willing to use the paradigm to frame the questions they would try to answer in their research. There was no science unless the members of a community were willing to share the information gained from that research.[12]

According to Kuhn, as a community carried on this pattern of normal science, this pattern of puzzle solving within a shared pattern of hypotheses, anomalies were encountered that cast doubt on the explanatory power of the paradigm. The first reaction of a scientific community, for Kuhn, was to ignore this dissonance. If contradictions continued to be experienced, however, the community repressed that evidence. But as stress became more intense and the community lost coherence, members became willing to listen to other voices that presented other visions, hypotheses, about the nature of reality. Periodically in the history of science, a period of revolutionary science replaced a period of normal science. A new community committed to a new paradigm began to solve new problems. The period of revolutionary science was one when members of a community practicing a disintegrating pattern of normal science converted to the practice of another form of normal science. Reason and logic were defined by a particular paradigm. Within another paradigmatic community reason and logic would be defined differently. One could not use reason or logic to move from one community to another.

Using Kuhn's model, for Webster, can explain how a dramatic conversion of teachers of literature from the paradigm of historical analysis to the paradigm of New Criticism was possible between 1935 and 1945. One of the signs of a successful paradigmatic revolution, for Kuhn, was when a new community was able to establish a set of exemplars, such as textbooks. These could be used to initiate a new generation into its set of hypotheses. Textbooks gave a sense of authority, of inevitability, of naturalness, of normality to the revolution. When a scientific revolution was successful, it was presented as an established order. It became the only usable past. Webster sees Brooks and Warren's *Understanding Poetry* as such a crucial textbook, which began the shift of the New Criticism from a revolutionary challenge to the dominant paradigm of historical study to an established community whose paradigms defined what puzzles literary scholars would try to solve in their research.

Brooks and Warren presented the tradition of metaphysical poetry as providing the only adequate system of knowledge for humanity. For them, all other systems of knowledge were dangerously simplistic. Their fundamental paradigmatic assumption was that humans embodied both faith and reason, imagination and hard facts, soul and body, the universal and the particular, good and evil. Metaphysical poetry provided a language that embraced such dualisms. It took complexities and brought them into a unity filled with tension and irony. The metaphysical poem was a creative art form. It was not an art that falsely assumed it could represent reality. That assumption depended on the existence of a simplistic reality. But since reality was always complex, the artist had to be imaginative in constructing unity out of contradictions. Cleanth Brooks and another New Critic, W. K. Wimsatt, described the superiority of metaphysical poetry as a system of knowledge this way: "We can have our universals in the full conceptualized discourse of science and philosophy. We can have specific detail lavishly in the newspapers and in records of trials. . . . But it is only in metaphor, and hence it is par excellence in poetry, that we encounter the most radically and relevantly fused union of detail and the universal idea."[13]

Cleanth Brooks and Robert Penn Warren continued to make the New Criticism the established paradigm by publishing *Understanding Fiction* in 1943. Again they found an inferior fiction written by romantics that assumed the simplicity of reality. If there was complexity, the romantic author believed it was unnatural and would be left behind because progress toward unity was inevitable. If, however, the romantic author lost faith in progress, life became meaningless. Superior fiction was part of the antimodern metaphysical tradition that assumed the complexity of experience. It, therefore, provided the reader the knowledge necessary to live a productive life. One learned how to construct a

reject romantics

Mrs Dalloway

balance out of the opposites and contradictions that an individual now, as in the past and future, must inevitably encounter.[14]

The superiority of the language of complexity to the language of simplicity had been a central message of Warren's *All the King's Men.* Jack Burden had been initiated into the language of progress. He was taught to see the individual as innocent and society as corrupt. He was taught to believe that the old world of complexity would wither away and humans would achieve perfect harmony. When he was confronted by the fact that complexity was within the individual as a mixture of good and evil, he tried to escape participation in the contradictory world.

He then observed his friend Willie Stark speak the language of political progress. Acting within that language of simplicity, within the metaphor of old and new worlds, Stark caused great suffering and destroyed himself. For Warren, modern systems of knowledge, because they denied the complexity of existence, must inevitably create societies that were self-destructive. Adam Stanton, another of Jack's friends, spoke the language of science. As a system of knowledge, it also ignored the complexity of existence. It, too, did not give the individuals who worked within its boundaries enough knowledge to survive the complexities of the world.

If Jack Burden was Warren's fictional son, Warren was certainly John Crowe Ransom's intellectual son. Warren had learned from Ransom that "poetry, unlike science, does not seek purity and innocence. It does not seek refuge from society. Instead, it confronts the forms of social life and illustrates the limitations of social forms in a manner that calls for the construction of alternative ways of living. Most specifically, it recalls the richness and complexity of the world which is suppressed and forgotten by the scientific abstractions of the modern world." For the New Critics, then, the education of students into the language of the metaphysical tradition was literally a matter of spiritual life and death. Students needed to be persuaded that the dominant languages of the modern world would lead to destruction. Kuhn wrote of the way members of a paradigmatic community jealously guard its boundaries and insist that potential members accept the orthodoxy that is taught them. The New Critics saw this orthodoxy as more than an abstract language game. It was a redemptive orthodoxy. This is why Tate insisted that "[t]he study of literary texts could have little validity so long as reading was defined merely as a matter of the subjective response of individuals."

Or, as Brooks declared, "[T]he formalist critic assumes an ideal reader: that is, instead of focusing on the varying spectrum of possible readings, he attempts to find a central point of reference from which he can focus upon the structure of the poem or novel."[15]

When younger members of English departments converted to the New Criticism, they did so because it seemed to offer the only language that was a persuasive alternative to that of capitalism. The language of bourgeois nationalism, of art as the representation of national landscapes and national peoples, had become illegitimate. The language of Marxist aesthetics, of art as the representation of an international urban-industrial landscape and of an international working class, also had become illegitimate. In a world dominated by capitalism, it was reassuring to hear Cleanth Brooks assert that the "New Criticism separates literary criticism from the study of sources, social background, history of ideas, political and social effects." But literature segregated from the profane culture of capitalism was not a frail entity. "Literature," according to Tate, "is the complete knowledge of man's experience."[16]

And Tate and his fellow revolutionists assured their converts that one could embrace New Criticism without becoming a monarchist or a Catholic. One could be a vigorous critic of capitalism and a vigorous spokesman for the metaphysical literary tradition without talking about politics and religion. For Tate, "The specific task of the man of letters is to attend to the health of society not at large but through literature—that is, he must be constantly aware of the conditions of language in his age."[17]

The victory of the aesthetic of the boundless and materialist capitalist international marketplace over the aesthetic of the bounded and spiritual national landscape of bourgeois nationalism during the 1940s destroyed the cultural authority of the men from the Northeast and Midwest who, from the 1830s to the 1930s, believed that history as progress had culminated about 1830, when the national landscape had given birth to an American people. This people was imagined as an exclusive fraternity of Anglo-Protestants. Only Anglo-Protestant men had marched in the exodus from the profane traditions of a European Old World. The arts, the painting, the poetry, the novels, the histories of this sharply bounded "American" people would place only Anglo-Protestant men on the national landscape. These alone were the people with history—

the experience of time as progress from an Old to a New World, from a world of localism and internationalism to a world of nations.

With the Civil War, Anglo-Protestant men from the South were excluded from the national landscape and from the "American" people. Outside the narrative leading to the nation as the end of history, southern Anglo-Protestant men could be imagined as part of a local community or an international community. From the perspective of bourgeois nationalism, such communities lacked meaning since they needed to be superseded by a uniform and autonomous nation. It is an indication of the tremendous and sudden loss of the cultural authority of bourgeois nationalism in the United States that the Southern Agrarians could gain cultural authority by identifying their worldview with the local and the international.

It is an ironic truth, then, that the Southern Agrarians were the first group of the peoples without history in the United States who successfully challenged the aesthetic authority of the national canon. That canon expressed the narrative of a national literature prefigured by the Puritans, a national literature whose potential was fulfilled in the New England Renaissance. This is an ironic truth because the Southern Agrarians celebrated local and international texts written only by European and Euro-American men. The conflict in the English department at the University of Minnesota was between the symbol-myth group and the New Literary Critics. These exclusive white male groups had a common enemy in the white men of the marketplace. Neither could imagine that any other Americans—women, Native Americans, Mexican Americans, African Americans, Asian Americans—had agency in the 1950s or ever had exercised agency.

But when the aesthetic authority of bourgeois nationalism collapsed in the United States during World War II, the boundaries of the exclusive Anglo-Protestant democracy of the 1830s, that sacred time of national origins, also collapsed. As the boundaries disintegrated, it became possible for more groups than just the Southern Agrarians to claim that they had the right to define what American literature was in the past and is in the present. Now the symbol-myth scholars and the New Critics had another common enemy. All of the "minority" groups, representing a majority of the peoples living within the United States, saw the men of the symbol-myth school and the male New Critics as guardians of the

Key shift
The Moment
Watershed
Paradigm shift

boundaries of an exclusive and privileged white male academy and a
white male literary canon.

When the local and international began to achieve aesthetic author- KEY
ity during the 1940s and 1950s, the groups who had been denied a place
in the imagined center of the nation (because Anglo-Protestant males
defined them as peoples who were without history as progress) were
successful in defining both the symbol-myth school and the New Literary Critics as themselves particular groups. As the "minorities" were
victorious in breaking through the defensive walls of the ivory tower
and claiming their right to agency as literary critics, the invaders began to
smash the monumental convention with which the symbol-myth school
claimed to represent the universal national. And, as this academic mob
of "minorities" toppled the cultural monument of the universal national,
they also attacked the claim of the New Literary Critics to represent a
universal universal. Euro-American women pointed out that the universal universal represented only a particular gender of a particular class.
But dominant Anglo-Protestant men, in monopolizing the term *American* for themselves, had often justified their exclusion of the peoples of
color because those peoples had relationships to cultures outside the
national boundaries. There were African Americans, Mexican Americans,
Asian Americans who had such relationships. Even the Native Americans could be imagined as having links to indigenous peoples throughout the Americas. KEY

Now, as the New Literary Critics claimed that Americans (always implicitly or explicitly Anglo-Protestant) were Euro-Americans and participants in the universal universal of Western civilization, African American scholars could remind these white scholars that Western civilization
was a particular culture in a world with several civilizations. And that
reminder was strengthened by Asian American scholars, Mexican American scholars, and increasing numbers of immigrants from Central and
South America, who could also argue that Western civilization was itself
pluralistic. They could argue that given the dramatic cultural differences in Europe and the cultures of the Americas, there was not even a
Western universal universal. The New Literary Critics, therefore, had
won a victory over the national outlook of the symbol-myth school,
and they believed they had created an academic monastery that could
be kept pure from the barbaric darkness of capitalism. But their academic

refuge could not withstand the invasion of all those minorities who began to exercise their agency within the literary profession. These strangers studied and taught texts that had been repressed because they did not fit the aesthetic authority of the universal national or the universal universal. Literary criticism was moved into a world of cultural pluralism at both the national and international levels.

CHAPTER SIX

The Vanishing National Landscape: Painting, Architecture, Music, and Philosophy in the Early Twentieth Century

The New Literary Critics made literature into an abstract art when they no longer could see literature as an organic expression of a landscape that embodied the good, true, and beautiful. The promise of bourgeois nationalism that national landscapes could produce such an organic art was shattered in the 1940s. The Marxist promise that the urban-industrial landscape could produce an organic art also disintegrated in this revolutionary decade. Both bourgeois nationalists and Marxists believed that it was the responsibility of the arts to represent the reality of these landscapes and the reality of the democratic peoples who were the children of the landscape. But, for the New Literary Critics, the all-powerful landscape after World War II was that of international capitalism. This landscape was a wasteland of soulless materialism where there was no true, good, and beautiful. To escape this landscape of alienation and fragmentation, the individual had to turn to autonomous works of art that embodied within themselves that organic relationship of the true, good, and beautiful.

This literary philosophy of abstract art was similar to that expressed by many painters and critics of painting, by architects and critics of architecture, and by many musicians and critics of music in the 1940s. This expression marked a momentous paradigmatic conversion because the dominant criticism in these fields during the 1930s was that of bourgeois nationalism and Marxism. This conversion also characterized the field of philosophy, where the "realism" of bourgeois nationalism and

Marxism gave way to domination in the 1950s of a highly abstract mathematical approach to philosophy.

Most of the artists and critics who were turning to abstract art wanted to find an alternative to the ugly landscape of the marketplace. But the bourgeois elites who were leaders in the imaginative construction of the global marketplace believed that they could co-opt much of this art for their project. Unlike the art of bourgeois nationalism and Marxism, abstract art after World War II did not offer an alternative landscape as the foundation for anticapitalist politics. And the universalism of abstract art helped bourgeois elites undermine the sanctity of national boundaries. Its individualism also offered a critique of Marxist collectivism.

But the defensiveness of most abstract art after World War II, its reluctant acceptance of the triumph of capitalism, was in sharp contrast to the celebration of abstract art between the 1880s and World War I on both sides of the Atlantic. This was a celebration of an avant-garde that was overcoming bourgeois nationalism. The artistic avant-garde was breaking the boundaries that trapped so many individuals in a corrupt and dysfunctional society. Experimentations in art were leading an exodus to a promised land. Faith in progress was part of the first world of abstract art. This metanarrative of progress, however, was largely absent from the second world of abstract art. In that first world the landscape of the marketplace was entropic. In the second world the landscape of the marketplace was omnipotent.

Painting

Middle-class male painters in the United States during the nineteenth century participated in the bourgeois faith in the redemptive reality of the national landscape. They, like historians and novelists, had helped give this landscape a visible form. And, like bourgeois painters, historians, and novelists in other modern nations, they began to lose faith in the reality of their national landscape as they saw its plenitude become entropic when confronted by the incredible vitality of a transnational urban-industrial landscape. The crisis of space experienced, therefore, by the historian Frederick Jackson Turner and the author Mark Twain was the same crisis of space felt by their contemporary, the painter Winslow Homer.

At the beginning of the nineteenth century bourgeois painters in all the modern nations participated in the paradox of bourgeois nationalism by insisting on the uniqueness of each national landscape. Their paintings presented a majestic and benign nature free from rural poverty. This landscape, which had given birth to a national people with a homogeneous culture, was innocent of economic hierarchy and political power. In the case of Anglo-American painting, it minimized the presence of Native Americans who, if they were seen, were defined as a vanishing race. These paintings also excluded African Americans and Mexican Americans or placed them in a clearly subordinate position. And it was white men, not white women, who stood in these paintings, enchanted by the landscapes that were linked to the public world of the male citizen.[1]

In the generation before the Civil War, a Hudson River school of painters had evoked a national landscape that was boundless in its scope and also boundless in the energy and beauty it bestowed on its children, the citizens of the nation. Like their contemporaries, the historians George Bancroft and Francis Parkman, artists from the Northeast such as Asher B. Durand, Thomas Cole, and Frederic Church imagined they had the right and the responsibility to give the national landscape representation. Angela Miller has suggested that their paintings expressed a sense of "everywhere and nowhere." Given the multiplicity of local landscapes that existed within the political boundaries of the United States, paintings that claimed to represent a national landscape necessarily presented a universal national.[2]

But by the end of the nineteenth century, Anglo-American painters could no longer sustain the golden glow that had characterized the presentation of the national landscape before the Civil War. Winslow Homer, for example, painted an idyllic pond in the Adirondacks, expressing the peace and beauty of nature. Then he painted the same picture a second time. But now a hunter in a canoe was drowning a deer that had attempted to swim across the once peaceful pond. Increasingly the nature that Homer saw was similar to Mark Twain's vision in *Huckleberry Finn* of a Mississippi River that promised a refuge to Huck and Jim from the terrors of the timeful society on its banks. But the river did not provide permanent tranquillity. The brief moments of timeless harmony experienced by Huck and Jim were destroyed by continual episodes of death, violence, power, and corruption. The river pulled them steadily south, toward the heart of the darkness of slavery. This was the nature, the duplicitous national landscape that Homer evoked in his final series of paintings. Twain and Homer, as an older generation, shared the dismay of a younger generation of "naturalists," such as Stephen Crane, Frank Norris, and Theodore Dreiser, who became part of a "lost generation" in the 1890s. These writers were horrified to find ugliness not beauty, violence not peace, death not life in their national landscape.[3]

Charles Beard in the 1890s had been unwilling to dwell, like his elders Turner, Twain, or Homer, or like his contemporaries, the "naturalists," between two worlds, nostalgic for the beauty and goodness of a vanishing national landscape but appalled by the harsh truth of the incoming urban-industrial landscape. Instead Beard decided to find beauty and goodness in that new landscape. This decision was shared by a group of young painters who came to be called "The Eight." The leader, Robert Henri, had been inspired by Homer's contemporary, Thomas Eakins. Eakins had taught at the Pennsylvania Academy of Fine Arts until he was dismissed for using a nude male model in his classes. He had come to associate the artistic expression of the national landscape of the early nineteenth century with Europe. Identifying America with reality and the masculine, he defined pastoral painting as artificial and effeminate, the characteristics of the Old World of Europe. In his most famous landscape painting he had presented young men rowing on the Schuylkill River in Philadelphia. Here Eakins had not described the river as a false god that promised a supportive environment of strength and beauty. Unlike Twain and Homer, he simply presented the river as lifeless. Eakins's river did not betray his rowers because it offered them nothing but entropy. For Eakins, then, to paint the reality of the city was a way to achieve national independence from the lifeless world of the pastoral he now associated with Europe. He urged his students "to study their own country and to portray its life and types." They should not, he warned, "spend their time abroad obtaining a superficial view of the art of the old world."[4]

Robert Henri did study in Paris but returned a strident nationalist. In Philadelphia he was joined by William Glackens and John Sloan, who were illustrators for newspapers. Later Everett Shinn, interested in stage design, and George Luks, another newspaper illustrator, began to participate in discussions on how they could revolutionize and revitalize American painting.

After they moved to New York, they found that the National Academy of Fine Art would not show their paintings. They held their own showing, therefore, in 1908. The Eight—Henri, Glackens, Sloan, Shinn, Luks, Everett Lawson, Arthur Davies, and Maurice Prendergast—were concerned with presenting the many aspects of the new urban landscape. Like Beard they associated capitalism with an old world of chaos. In politics they blended their nationalism with both the republican traditions of productive small property and with socialism that would achieve rational productivity in large-scale industry. Robert Henri insisted, "I am not interested in art as art. I am interested in life." In this context Europe stood for the antidemocratic tradition of art for art's sake. America, in contrast, stood for art that expressed the democracy of the people, a democracy that was true, good, and beautiful. For Henri, then, a democratic art would "enter government and the whole material existence as the essential influence, and it alone will keep government straight, end war and strife, do away with material greed."[5]

The Eight gained the designation of the "Ash Can School" because their paintings presented the working-class people of the cities as filled with vitality. They used strong colors to suggest the beauty of working-class neighborhoods. They were constructing a national romance in which the urban landscape was not the antithesis of the pastoral landscape. Rather, it was revitalizing and therefore continuing the democracy that had emerged from that earlier national landscape.

The Eight believed that the representational techniques and spatial perspectives developed during the Renaissance were necessary to express the reality of the national landscape in its new urban form and for capturing the presence of the democratic people who were the nation's citizens. Seeing themselves as rebels against the artistic establishment, members of the Eight played a leadership role in bringing the painting of contemporary European artists to the United States for the notorious Armory Show in New York in 1913. In this circulation of ideas in the Atlantic world, the artistic experiments of expressionism, cubism, fauvism, and constructivism represented by men such as Picasso and Matisse were understood as iconoclastic. They were rebels who were overthrowing the world of aristocratic art. They were seen as potential allies of the American rebels in the struggle for a democratic future.

But at the Armory Show, the Eight were informed that they were conservatives. The future of painting, they were told, was with the nonrepresentational painters who were rejecting the vision of three-dimensional space constructed in the Renaissance. But, for the Eight, how could one defeat the foreign influence of capitalism unless one could remind Americans that a real national landscape existed and that it was the home of a democratic people? European abstract art, for the American new nationalists, gave support to the fragmentation caused by capitalism. Abstract art would confuse the people and lead them to believe that the chaos of capitalism could not be escaped. The new nationalists had been right when they advocated an American culture free from European influence. Ironically, then, the Eight had opened a Pandora's box by helping to bring the new European art to the United States. In later years they would lament that they "had unlocked the door to foreign art and thrown the key away. Our land of opportunity was thrown wide open to foreign art, unrestricted and triumphant; more than ever before, our great country had become a colony; more than ever before, we had become provincials."[6]

The Eight had been defined as out-of-date by a group of artists in New York that had formed around the photographer Alfred Stieglitz. For them the new urban landscape was more complex than the nineteenth-century agricultural landscape. This new reality, they argued, could only be expressed by the avant-garde techniques being developed in Europe. But Stieglitz, Marsden Hartley, Georgia O'Keeffe, and John Marin, as they embraced various abstract techniques, did not think of themselves as less committed to a national art than the Eight. They shared the optimism of the recently founded magazines—*The New Republic, The Seven Arts,* and *The Masses*—that an America built on an urban-industrial landscape would be independent of European culture and international capitalism. Herbert Croly, once editor of *The Architectural Record* and now an editor of *The New Republic,* declared that "what the United States needs is a nationalization of their intellectual life comparable to the nationalizing, now underway, of their industry and politics." Art, for him, "could convert the community into a well-informed whole." A young Walter Lippmann, joining *The New Republic,* agreed that "without a strong artistic tradition the politics of a nation sinks into a barren routine." James Oppenheim, an editor of *The Seven Arts,* added, "I believed that the lost soul among the nations, America, could be regenerated by art." Another member of *The Seven Arts* group, Paul Rosenfeld, stated that "[i]t is our faith that we are living in the first days of a renascent period, a time which means for America the coming of that national self-consciousness which is the beginning of all greatness."[7]

From the 1890s to the end of World War I, Charles Beard had not shared the belief of either the Henri group or the Stieglitz group that nationalism and the urban-industrial landscape were compatible. During those decades, for Beard, the choice was either the nationalism of the pastoral landscape or the internationalism of the urban-industrial landscape. But when he joined with Mary Beard to write *The Rise of American Civilization* in the 1920s, their narrative shared many aspects of the urban-industrial nationalism of these artists and intellectuals.

For some, like Randolph Bourne, World War I meant "one has a sense of having come to a sudden, short stop at the end of an intellectual era." There were painters, poets, novelists, and historians who became part of another "lost generation" in the 1920s. Their vision was of the permanent victory of corrupt and materialistic capitalism. The democratic nationalism of 1830 was gone, and the new democratic nationalism that had hoped to find vitality in the urban-industrial landscape had failed to restore the virtues of the republic. But, although much of the excitement and expectations of the years 1900–19 no longer characterized the 1920s, most painters of that decade did share the hope of the Beards that capitalism was external to national identity and ultimately would be defeated. They did not join Bourne in believing that they had become a lost generation. Not only did many hold fast to their vision of a new nationalism based on the new urban-industrial landscape, but others, who had been enchanted by the European scene before 1918, had, like Charles Beard, experienced a conversion from internationalism to nationalism.[8]

Indeed, the apparent victory of the Stieglitz group over the Eight by 1913, when it appeared that avant-garde abstract techniques rather than realism would become the dominant approach in celebrating the national landscape in the new century, began to be reversed in the 1920s. In this decade, the paintings of several members of the Stieglitz group—John Marin, Marsden Hartley, Georgia O'Keeffe, and Max Weber—became less abstract and more representational. More significant, however, was the emergence of a self-conscious group of artists who were committed to painting the "American Scene." Charles Sheeler and Charles DeMuth modified the techniques of cubism to paint such symbols of productivity as barns and factories. Their precisionist style emphasized a landscape constructed by the American people as a whole. It was not an art of heroic individuals. Edward Hopper was another artist who, on his return from study in Europe, felt compelled to paint the urban landscapes of the anonymous American people.[9]

Within this resurgence of a need to link art to a national landscape and its people, a particular group within the American Scene movement became known as the "Regionalists." Charles Burchfield, Thomas Hart Benton, John Stewart Curry, and Grant Wood were born in the Midwest. Before World War I, they all had been influenced by the variety of abstract techniques being developed in Europe and had experimented in those styles. After World War I, they felt that this experience was un-American and that they had been traitors to their national culture. Burchfield described his conversion out of cultural darkness into cultural light by pointing to this "early degeneracy in my art that I have never been able to explain." But, then, he continued, he realized that "I was forsaking my birthright" and "began to feel the great epic poetry of Midwest American life and my own life in connection with it." Burchfield, like Benton, then burned his early canvases done in what he had come to see as the decadent, alien, and undemocratic styles of Europe.[10]

The power of this surge of artistic isolationism in the 1920s can be seen at the Museum of Modern Art. It opened in New York in 1929 to demonstrate that painting in the twentieth century embodied forms of abstractionism that could speak to people in every nation. But the museum directors felt the need in 1930 to put on an exhibition of American folk art. Throughout the 1930s a continuous series of American folk art exhibitions was presented.

The Great Crash of 1929 became a miraculous moment for many painters, as it was for composers, novelists, literary critics, and historians. The most powerful narrative held by artists and other intellectuals in the 1920s was that the virtuous people, born of the national landscape by the 1830s, had become corrupted by an alien capitalist landscape after the Civil War. In this narrative the ethos of the nationalist landscape was one of honest production, while the capitalist landscape was characterized by dishonesty and exploitation. If one disassociated the industrial landscape from the capitalist landscape, as Charles Beard or socialists had done, then one could hope that the industrial landscape's ethos of honest productivity could subvert the capitalist landscape and restore vitality to the national landscape and its virtuous people. Now, suddenly and unexpectedly, the capitalist landscape had collapsed and the people were freed from their long period of imprisonment.

The ecstasy of the artists and intellectuals after 1929 came from their belief that they could now speak to and for the people. In this narrative it had been the artists and intellectuals who had kept alive the memory of those wonderful decades before the Civil War when the people and the artists and intellectuals had been able to express together the deep fraternity of the nation's citizens. Now this joyful period of democratic nationalism, lost in the Gilded Age, regained momentarily by Populists and Progressives, and lost again in the 1920s, was being restored. This was the narrative of the American Scene painters, but it was also the story told by many artists in New York City who identified themselves as socialists. William Gropper, Ben Shahn, and Jack Levine emphasized an American scene that was urban and virtuous.[11]

But Benton, Curry, and Wood, like the Beards, could not join a productive industrial landscape with an urban landscape. Like the Beards, they saw the popular culture of the city as that of the effeminate, irrational consumption characteristic of capitalism. When the Beards celebrated the triumph of a producer's economy in the 1930s, they repressed the problem of defining the new immigrants and their children, as well as African Americans, as part of the now liberated democratic people. The Beards in *The Rise of American Civilization* had denounced that popular culture in the Northern cities constructed at the end of the nineteenth century by Catholic and Jewish immigrants, as well as by African Americans. This, for them, was an un-American world of irrational leisure that contradicted the rational producer ethic of both the agricultural and industrial landscapes. Benton, Wood, and Curry shared this view of the city as the center of an unproductive, effeminate, and un-American culture. This would lead them to renounce their alliances in the 1930s with painters who were urban socialists.

Thomas Hart Benton, born in Missouri, entered into the world of American painting with this political memory: "I had been raised on the ideal that the big capitalist monopolies, centered in New York, were against the 'people's' interests." Returning from study in Paris, he became part of the community of artists in New York. There, immediately before World War I, he tried to communicate with the people of the city by joining John Weichsel's People's Art Guild. This group brought art to the settlement houses. But the Armory Show of 1913 caused Benton to rethink the question of what styles of art should be used to speak to and for the people. He rejected his education in France because "the new Parisian aesthetics" were "turning away from the living world of active men and women into an academic world of empty patterns." In contrast, he said, “We wanted an American art which was not empty, and we believed that only by turning the formative processes of art back to meaningful subject matter, in our cases specifically American subject matter, could we expect to get one.”[12]

Ironically Benton, now fearing urban culture, designed movie sets and painted backdrops between 1913 and 1918. The powerful use of stereotypes in movie narratives became a permanent element in his painting style. But he used the stereotypes of popular culture to reject urban popular culture. The panels of his mural, *The American Historical Epic,* done during the early 1920s, share many characteristics with the use of stereotypes by the Beards in *The Rise of American Civilization.* The Beards had used stereotypes of rugged pioneers in their prose poem about the settling of the trans-Appalachian West. Benton's mural also focused on the Anglo-American settlement of the national landscape. “I tried,” Benton wrote, “to show that the peoples' behavior, their action on the opening land, was the primary reality of American life.” Benton wanted to construct a public art “which reflected the American peoples' life and history in a way which the people could comprehend.”[13]

Benton then did a mural of ten panels for the New School of Social Research in New York. Scholars such as John Dewey and the Beards were active in starting this institution as a democratic alternative to what they saw as the elitism of the major universities. In these panels Benton celebrated the productivity of farmers and industrial workers. These men, as in the Beards' history, were represented as stylized heroes larger than life. But the panels representing activity in the city of New York evoked almost lifeless figures often engaged in mindless forms of popular entertainment.

In 1930 Benton called himself a socialist, but his acceptance of an industrial landscape did not imply Marxist internationalism. Rather, as with the Beards, a synthesis of the national and industrial landscape was used to celebrate American cultural exceptionalism. While younger people responded to the Great Depression by embracing a Marxist vision of a universal industrial landscape, Benton rejected his previous synthesis of progressivism and socialism. He told a meeting of the John Reed Club that there was no common humanity, but only a variety of national peoples. Again, like the Beards, he also became more self-conscious that the American people were Anglo-Americans like himself and his friends. Cutting his ties with a variety of New York socialist groups, whom he increasingly saw as representatives of alien populations, he returned to live in Missouri in 1935.

By the 1930s, then, Benton saw the Midwest, and the Midwest alone, as expressing the universal national. As an American scene painter, he was necessarily a regionalist painter because only the Midwest as a region contained the authentic American scene. Benton had done a huge mural to portray the history of the state of Indiana at the Chicago World's Fair in 1933. The fair was to represent a century of progress and Benton painted the progress of Indiana from a democratic society of agricultural producers to a democratic society of industrial producers. He repeated this theme in the mural he did for the Missouri state capitol in 1935 and 1936. Thus another Midwestern state provided the environment for the progress of a producer's democracy where, for Benton, "Capitalism is doomed."[14]

Benton was now the most famous artist in the United States, becoming the first to be featured on a cover of *Time* magazine for December 1934. When Henry Luce began *Life* magazine to add to his growing publishing empire, which included *Time* and *Fortune,* he asked Benton to go to Hollywood to capture the spirit of the film industry on canvas. Luce, however, refused to use Benton's paintings, which focused on Hollywood as a place of work and production, rather than as a place of play and entertainment.

But Benton, like so many of his generation, began to sense by 1937 that capitalism was not doomed. Suddenly he was thrust back into the world of Winslow Homer, Mark Twain, and Frederick Jackson Turner. The American landscape, agricultural and industrial, did not have the power to resist the chaos of capitalist self-interest and materialism. Once again the promise of the Virgin Land had not been fulfilled. Benton did four paintings between 1938 and 1945 that captured his dismay at a duplicitous national landscape. The first, *Persephone* (1938–39), found sexual lust to be a part of that landscape. He could no longer believe that the irrationality of sex was peripheral to American identity, isolated in the entertainment culture of cities.

If goodness and beauty were not part of the pastoral landscape, neither was truth. The promise of boundless vitality was also false. In *After Many Springs* (1940), Benton placed a skull and a revolver on a rural landscape. Violence and death, as in Homer's paintings or Twain's *Huckleberry Finn,* were signs that American nature was entropic. A future of perpetual winter, then, was the prophecy of *The Prodigal Son* (1943). Here an elderly man has returned to a farmstead from which all life—that of humans, animals, and plants—has vanished. In *Fantasy* (1945), Benton fled from this horrible desert into a completely abstract world of textures and colors.

When the national landscape in both its agricultural and industrial forms had vanished, Benton, of course, no longer could see an American people. In the foundational myth, the variation on bourgeois nationalism constructed by male Anglo-Protestants by the 1830s, the nation's people, its citizens, were born of the national landscape. When, for a Homer, Twain, or Turner, the national landscape died, so did the people as a homogeneous fraternity. Benton expressed his loss of this imagined community in these words: "My major painting themes, when I turned my attention to our native scene, were nearly always about the activities of people. Now, however, people began to be an accessory. Although I did not realize it at the time, I was thus myself moving away from Regionalism."[15]

A strident isolationist until Pearl Harbor, Benton responded to the attack by painting a series of eight pictures that characterized the Japanese and Germans as inhuman monsters. He hoped the government would use them to rally support for the war effort. But his offer was refused. The implication of these paintings was that the United States had plunged into a world that was totally hellish. The Roosevelt administration, of course, insisted that the revolutionary change from isolation to internationalism would lead to a better world. But Benton implied that the wider world was populated by monsters who would be demonic enemies until the end of time.

Jackson Pollack

It is no wonder, then, that Benton's favorite student, Jackson Pollock, would want to escape the world he inherited from his father figure. Born in Wyoming in 1912, Pollock came to study painting in New York with Benton and for several years became a member of his household. Pollock identified with the anticapitalist culture of both Benton's republicanism and the Marxism that was strong in the New York artistic community. He shared, therefore, the expectations that 1929 signaled the death of capitalism. He had been initiated into radicalism by his biological father, and his youthful criticism of the establishment earned him the name in high school of the "rotten rebel from Russia."[16]

But the young Pollock knew by 1937 that Benton's world, which had seemed so omnipotent in 1933, was disintegrating in the face of capitalist power. Remaining in New York, Pollock had a double experience of witnessing the death of a reality that had promised truth, goodness, and beauty. Unlike Benton, he had not turned his back on his Marxist contemporaries. They believed that the industrial landscape would call a democratic people, an international proletariat, into being. Then the ugliness, the mendacity, the selfishness of the capitalist marketplace would be defeated and left behind in the dustbin of history. But, by 1937, younger Marxists, whether Trotskyites or Stalinists, were losing hope that there was, or ever would be, a virtuous people who could resist the temptations of capitalism. Instead of a fraternity of producers, isolated consumers seemed to be the future.

Everything that Pollock had imagined was real—national landscape, industrial landscape, American people, international proletariat—now seemed ephemeral, merely a lovely dream. All he had left was himself. He now discovered that there was a considerable literature that focused on the individual rather than on society. Instead of emphasizing the conflict between positive and negative social groups, one should grapple with the conflict between the positive and negative aspects within each individual. And here, of course, was an environment where one could win. Here one could ignore the defeat of the people by capitalists; here one could ignore the displacement of national and industrial landscapes by the marketplace. Here one could still be a masculine hero. Most men did not have the strength to overcome their inner demons. But an exceptional few did.

As the United States entered World War II, Pollock, then, saw his painting entering into the realm of mythology. Such mythology, from his perspective, transcended national boundaries and was universal. He now argued that the representational painting invented during the Renaissance was time-bound. Painters in the representational tradition had tried to find meaning in particular landscapes and particular individuals. Only abstract painting could escape the boundaries of the particular; only expressive painting could capture the effort of the artist to construct order out of chaos.[17]

With the coming of World War II, art critics who, during the 1930s, had celebrated American scene painting converted to the international future proposed by the Roosevelt administration. They relegated the major regionalists—Benton, Wood, and Curry—to a discredited isolation. And the art critics pointed out that both the totalitarian German and Soviet governments demanded representational painting from their artists. Both governments associated abstract art with bourgeois decadence. Writing in 1946, Pollock stated his approval of this guilt by association. "There is an intelligent attack on Benton," he declared, "in this month's *Magazine of Art*—it's something I have felt for years." Internationalism, for Pollack in the 1940s, was the only legitimate position for an artist. "The idea of an isolated American painting, so popular in this country during the thirties, seems absurd to me. The basic problems of contemporary painting are independent of any one country."[18]

Ironically some of the influential art critics of the 1940s were former Marxists. They had surrendered their hope for the victory of the people as a proletariat over capitalism. But they continued to hate the consumer culture with which capitalism had seduced and corrupted the people. These critics saw in Pollock and other abstract expressionist painters an avant-garde that deliberately separated their art from popular culture and therefore from the corrupting influence of capitalism. This, of course, was very similar to the way the New Literary Critics wanted to disassociate literature from a capitalist-dominated popular culture. In the past, however, the theory of the avant-garde emphasized its redemptive role in leading the people out of bondage to a restrictive status quo. For Pollock, however, he and other abstract expressionist painters could not play such a liberating role. One could not imagine a better society; one could not imagine social progress.

But, for political and economic leaders in the United States, it was possible to imagine abstract expressionist painters as a positive avant-garde. Henry Luce had prophesied that World War II was ushering in "the American century." The United States, in his vision, was to be the leader of the world into an indefinite and unbounded future. This leadership, for Luce, was ushering in the triumph of the marketplace. A boundless space, the marketplace would liberate people everywhere from the boundaries—political, economic, social, and artistic—that had imprisoned them. By 1946 Luce was using his magazines, *Life* and *Time,* to identify Pollock as the leader of an artistic avant-garde that spoke the language of liberty.[19]

This image of Pollock ignored the major metaphors of his paintings—web, labyrinth, maze, vortex. It repressed his concern for the psychic darkness in which the individual was groping. It overlooked the way in which Pollock's outlook was similar to that of the directors and screenwriters of film noir in the 1940s. In these movies, the heroes found themselves trapped in a corrupt American society from which there was no escape. But, for Luce and other establishment image makers, New York was replacing Paris as the center of the art world because the abstract expressionists symbolized the boldness and energy of artistic pioneers who were smashing traditions. These artists gave hope to people throughout the world that they could share in the freedom and liberty these American artists symbolized. The role of the United States in the 1940s, like the role of the abstract expressionist painters, was to be an avant-garde leading people everywhere out of old worlds of tradition and restriction into a new world of endless liberty. Hating capitalism, Pollock and abstract expressionism were co-opted to provide legitimacy to the marketplace as the only meaningful space in which liberty was to be found.

But, of course, since the Renaissance, the marketplace had been seen as the antithesis of meaningful space. The marketplace was a space of constant flux. Individuals caught in that flux experienced nothing but alienation. It is significant that in his 1997 book, *After the End of Art*, Arthur Danto identifies the abstract expressionists as the last generation of artists who found meaning in art. They, and art critics such as Clement Greenberg, who celebrated them, could imagine that they represented a new and higher stage in the history of painting. Avant-gardes, made up of heroic male individuals, smashed the artificiality of existing conventions. They led, then, toward a realm beyond history. In the case of the abstract expressionists, the realm was the pure space of paint and canvas. They were modern artists who were still redeemer figures. But, for Danto, the next generation of artists identified with pop art could no longer make a distinction between art and convention. They could not imagine that artists could transcend the culture of the average person.[20]

It is Danto's belief that this current inability to imagine a redemptive role for the artist, a role for avant-gardes, suggests that we are experiencing a transition from that modern world born during the Renaissance, when the distinction between tradition and reality was imagined.

It is interesting to contrast Danto's book with another published in 1997, *Critical Condition: American Culture at the Crossroads* by Eleanor Heartney. Danto approaches the crisis of a progressive narrative from the perspective of patterns that have been dominant in the modern West since 1400. Heartney, however, discusses only a crisis in American painting. Danto does not believe that the modern narrative of a progressive succession of stages in painting can be restored. Heartney believes that a progressive narrative can be restored in American painting. She, then, is frustrated with art critics and painters who seem willing to accept that "art itself is being lost in an endless cycle of repetition and revival." She is angry that "art and its antithesis, Kitsch, which was once identified as the debased commercialization of high culture, have become one." She is dismayed then, that painters in the 1980s and 1990s feel they are artists when they explicitly imitate Pollock and other famous artists from the past. She is discouraged when painters say there is no national art, but only feminist, or African American, or Native American, or Chicano art. She thinks that it is scandalous that critics and painters see no alternative to the domination of the art world by the marketplace. But she cannot offer a space that is an alternative to that of the marketplace. She has no memory of a natural landscape, or an industrial landscape, or even the painter's autonomous space of canvas and paint. It is, then, a lament that can imagine no alternative to the space of the marketplace. And that, of course, is the cultural hegemony that the marketplace, that space defined as chaos as recently as the 1930s, has achieved since the 1940s.[21]

Heartney's lament was dismissed in 1998 by the economist Tyler Cowen in his book, *In Praise of Commercial Culture.* Cowen was confronting the fears of music and architectural critics as well as art critics. For Cowen the triumph of the marketplace over the ideological efforts to establish canonical hierarchies provided all artists with the liberty to be self-made and to have their art judged as the experience of each individual artist. Now art critics or politicians could no longer demand conformity to any particular style or school. In Cowen's utopian marketplace, there were no avant-gardes. Artists no longer had the responsibility to redeem the people. No artist tried to impose his or her style on other artists. One did not engage in hubris that one's personal style was responsible for the progress of civilization.[22]

But the rejection of the dangerous vision of artistic progress, for Cowen, did not lead to cultural chaos. Instead the marketplace provided a democratic environment in which artists enjoyed perfect liberty. Such liberty was the end of history because it denied the truth of all metanarratives. As the historian Richard Hofstadter had claimed in 1970, it was the attempt to impose grand ideological frameworks that had been the cause of major conflicts throughout human history. Cowen implicitly agreed with Hofstadter as he imagined a future without ideological conflict, a future of individual rather than cultural expression. At last the marketplace was making possible the triumph of state-of-nature anthropology. The problems, however, that Danto, Heartney, and Cowen saw in the world of painting were all defined by the paradigm that had been constructed in Renaissance Europe. This paradigm assumed a break between past, present, and future. Medieval culture, like all traditional cultures, was unusable because it was made up of artificial and ephemeral conventions. But heroic male individuals could lead people out of this timeful world into a timeless environment that expressed the laws of nature. And it was assumed that these heroic males only appeared among Europeans or among those on other continents who were of European descent.

There were debates in European countries and in the United States from the 1890s into the 1950s about whether art should represent national landscapes or should be "modern" nonrepresentational painting that expressed those universals that transcended national boundaries. But the dominant male art critics always assumed that the debate was between white men. They did not assume that paintings done by women could be part of that debate because women were biologically part of the dark premodern world. This was also true of Jews. In the United States, Native American, African American, and Mexican American artists also were seen as biologically incapable of meaningful activity in the modern world. This modern world born in the Renaissance was one where progress was achieved, and these artists represented peoples who were unprogressive by nature.

The major art critics who destroyed the aesthetic authority of the national landscape in the 1940s were male Jews—Harold Rosenberg, Clement Greenberg, and Barnett Newman. The revolution from isolation to internationalism liberated them from their identities as people who were permanently alien to the American national landscape. And they could now enthusiastically extol the virtues of the abstract expressionists as men who had transcended artificial national boundaries to achieve unity with timeless universals. Jonathan Freedman in *The Temple of Culture: Assimilation and Anti-Semitism in Literary Anglo-America* (2000) has pointed out that this first generation of male Jews who were allowed authority in the world of the arts and the academy proceeded to sustain the aesthetic authority that denied meaningful agency to women and to Native Americans, African Americans, and Mexican Americans. For these male Jews, now accepted as white men, as for male Anglo-Protestants, "others" were still "primitive" peoples incapable of making progress.[23]

Since the late nineteenth century, when some painters began to believe that representational painting did not express natural law but was, like the nation, an ephemeral convention, "modern" artists were attracted to the "primitive" art of Africans and Native Americans. Bill Anthes has described the complex and contradictory relationship of these twentieth-century painters to primitivism. They saw in the primitive an alternative to the artificial conventions of bourgeois nationalism. The primitive could express the universals of nature. But only European males or males of European descent could use the primitive to achieve harmony with the universal. Women, Asians, Africans, and Native Americans were natural primitives whose art was always limited by the boundaries of particulars. These natural primitives used their art to build ephemeral conventions. For example, white artists and art critics who were arguing the side of nonrepresentational art against representational painting were attracted to what they saw as the primitivism of the Harlem Renaissance in the 1920s. This primitivism could inspire white artists in their quest for the universal, but for them, black painters such as Aaron Douglas, Mailou Mailen Jones, Hal Woodruft, Malvin Gray Johns, and Jacob Lawrence could not contribute to the debate. Natural primitives, because of their race and gender, could not transcend cultural particulars to find the universal.[24]

This pattern also characterized the fascination with the primitive art of Native Americans on the part of the abstract expressionist painters of the 1940s and critics like Newman. These white men saw themselves as the avant-garde who would transcend timeful particulars to achieve harmony with the timeless universal. They believed they found inspiration in the primitive art of Indians. But they also believed that Native Americans were biologically incapable of leaving the past; they were inherently incapable of participating in a progressive future.

When this avant-garde failed to end history in the 1950s, their failure was linked by critics like Danto to a metaphor of entropy. For many postmodern theorists the vitality of all narratives was exhausted. Modern artists were no longer subjects capable of meaningful agency. But Hal Foster, in his book *The Return of the Real: The Avant-Garde at the End of the Century* (1996), has argued that "the death of the subject is now dead in its turn" because "the subject has returned—but in the guise of a politics of new, ignored, and different subjectivities." This is the vitality of all those peoples whose agency for centuries was repressed by the focus on a male Eurocentric avant-garde. Now, however, there is no longer an aesthetic authority either of a national landscape or a Eurocentric universal to deny meaning to the creativity of women or people of Asian, African, or Native American descent.[25]

Arif Dirlik in *The Postcolonial Aura* (1997) has pointed to the energy and self-confidence of many current groups who identify themselves with the local in contrast to the universal national or the universal universal. And this is certainly the case with Native American artists. Throughout the first half of the twentieth century, white women and men, especially at Santa Fe and Taos, had celebrated the primitive art of Native Americans. This was the tradition that the abstract expressionists and critics like Barnett Newman were participating in during the 1940s and 1950s. One respected the primitive, but understood that it had no role in the future except to inspire an avant-garde of white men. It was against this sometimes explicit but always implicit racism that painters such as George Morrison rebelled. Leaving his Ojibwa world in Minnesota for New York, he insisted that his paintings participated in modern abstraction. He denounced art critics who tried to find any aspect of his Indian background in his art. He, too, was an autonomous individual able to participate in the universal. But as it became clear that neither bourgeois nationalism nor Eurocentric civilization could sustain the aesthetic authority that defined American Indians as a vanishing race trapped in a primitive stage of evolution, some Native American artists felt that they could achieve dignity not by escaping their past, as Morrison had tried to do, but by embracing that past. Such a past would be alive and embodied in dynamic traditions that connected past, present, and future.[26]

Indian nations had been rooted in particular landscapes. With the death of the national landscape, one could reimagine the vitality of those local landscapes. Now native painters such as Fritz Scholder (b. 1937) and T. C. Cannon (b. 1946) insisted that they did not want their Indian identities to become invisible. They insisted that they did not want their art judged by white critics. They insisted that they wanted their use of Indian culture judged by Indian people. To be at home. Morrison, himself, decided to come home to Minnesota to die.

This celebration of a Native American heritage that differs so dramatically from that which developed in modern Europe has been recently expressed by the painter Rebecca Belmore, for whom the past, present, and future are one. "My heart," she declared, "is beating like a small drum, and I hope that you, mother earth can feel it. Someday I will speak to you in my language. I have watched my grandmother lie very close to you, my mother the same. I have watched my grandmother show respect for all that you have given her. Although I went away and left a certain closeness to you, I have gone in a kind of circle. I think I am coming back to understanding where I came from."[27]

Architecture

The Golden Day 1830–1860

When American studies scholars of the 1940s and 1950s incorporated Thomas Hart Benton and the composer Charles Ives into their elegies for the lost national landscape, they also incorporated the architects Louis Sullivan and Frank Lloyd Wright into their lament for the brief life and early death of a second American renaissance. In the 1940s, Lewis Mumford was one of the most influential cultural critics who discussed architecture. Mumford began to make his reputation in the 1920s with two books, *Sticks and Stones: A Study of American Architecture and Civilization* (1924) and *The Golden Day: A Study of American Literature and Culture* (1926). For Mumford, the period 1830–60 was the golden day. He used Mark Twain's term, "The Gilded Age," to describe the loss of the qualities of the American renaissance after the Civil War.[28]

For Mumford, the promise of the golden day was the development of arts that would express the uniqueness of the national landscape and the democratic people who were its children. In the 1920s Mumford was not writing an elegy for the golden day. He was certain that this declension after 1865 into a European world of undemocratic capitalism was temporary. He described the appearance of artists and intellectuals by 1900 in a variety of fields who rejected the abstract and rootless language of capitalism and were speaking the democratic language that had an organic relationship to the national landscape. In architecture, according to Mumford, the promise of an organic, national architecture had disappeared during the Gilded Age. Without a national language, Americans in the Gilded Age had experienced an architectural Babel. Americans were indiscriminate in their use of a variety of European architectural styles. But by 1900 at least two American architects had recaptured the vision of an organic, American architecture. Louis Sullivan and Frank Lloyd Wright were artists who could end the declension into the chaos of an international marketplace. They could provide redemptive leadership to restore the spiritual democracy of 1830.

Like his contemporary Charles Ives, Louis Sullivan shared the Renaissance tradition that defined the artist as a potential salvation figure. Like Ives, Sullivan's effort to be a national hero ended in tragedy. His second golden day would turn to darkness by 1920. Then, like Ives, his memory would enter into the academic's elegiac romance for the golden days of 1830, when there had been an American identity distinct from Europe.

Louis Sullivan was the son of an immigrant. Raised in the East, he, like George Bancroft and Frederick Jackson Turner, saw an authentic national landscape west of the Appalachian Mountains. He was aware of rapid urbanization in the Northeast and saw it as an alien threat to the national landscape. His hope, as an adult, was that American cities would emerge from the Midwestern national landscape that would be the American future as they overshadowed the un-American cities of the Northeast. Born in Boston in 1856, Sullivan spent his earliest years in Massachusetts on his grandfather's farm. In his autobiography, Sullivan wrote that as a young child he developed a great love of physical nature, and that his earliest memories were of an almost instinctive rejection of the message of the Catholic Church that man was a sinful and divided being, instead favoring the theological message, symbolized by the great trees on the farm, that there was a healthful and happy unity to all living things in the universe. Then he was taken back into Boston to be educated, and Sullivan described his trauma in these words:

> As one might move a flourishing plant from the open to a dark cellar... so the miasma of the big city poisoned a small boy.... Against the big city his heart swelled in impatient, impotent rebellion. Its many streets, its crooked streets, its filthy streets, lined with stupid houses, crowded

> together shoulder to shoulder like selfish hogs upon these trough-like lanes, irritated him, suffocated him; the crowds of people . . . hurrying here and there so aimlessly . . . confused and overwhelmed him, arousing nausea and dismay. . . . In the city all was contradiction, density, limitation, and a cruel concentration.[29]

He survived his adolescence in the city by dreaming of running away. "To run where? Anywhere to liberty and freedom!" And when opportunity came, he fled west to Chicago. As he crossed the Indiana prairie, as he felt the power and openness of the prairie, and the sky, and the great blue lake, he once more experienced the joy of communion with nature. Like Turner, Sullivan did not believe that the West had the power to keep America a nation of yeoman farmers. But the virgin land of the Midwest, Sullivan believed, did make possible the creation of American and not European cities, of garden cities and not the repetition of Old World cesspools like Boston, New York, and Philadelphia.

The key to this possibility was architecture. If cities were to be healthful and natural, the architecture of their buildings must be healthful and natural. For Sullivan, if the nation were to be saved, if it was to become healthful and natural, its salvation figure would be an architect. Shamelessly Sullivan offered himself to his country as its savior. "With me," he wrote, "architecture is not an art but a religion and that religion but part of democracy." He would reveal the fact that "American architecture is . . . ninety parts aberration, eight parts indifference, one part poverty and one part Little Lord Fauntleroy." He saw himself as an evangelist who would call the young architects away from this profane tradition to become, themselves, spokesmen for the sacred future. "Do you intend or do you not intend . . . to become architects in whose care an unfolding Democracy may entrust the interpretation of its material wants, its psychic aspirations?" He saw himself as a prophet and teacher who would reveal that the kingdom of God was within every man, because each man began life as an innocent child. To lose our corruption, we need only to become as little children again, as Emerson's generation had when they rejected their corrupt European fathers. "If the mind is left free to act with spontaneity, individuality of expression will come to you as the flower comes to the plant—for it is nature's law." Such innocence was universal to mankind, but Americans had a special opportunity to become as little children because, while the identity of Europe was cultural complexity, the identity of America was nature itself. America, Sullivan proclaimed, was "the garden of our world." Here "tradition is without shackles and the soul of man free to grow, to mature, to seek its own." This was "a new land, a Promised Land. Her destiny has decreed there shall be enacted the final part in the drama of man's emancipation—the redemption of his soul."[30]

All civilization, Sullivan wrote, could be characterized as feudal. "Glancing at our modern civilization," he continued, "we find on the surface crust essentially the same idea at work that has prevailed throughout the past." This was the dualism of the feudal idea, which "holds to the concept of good and evil" in contrast to the democratic idea, which is "single, integral. It holds to the good alone." Writing that "historic feudal thought . . . found its form in a series of civilizations resting upon a denial of man by the multitudes themselves," Sullivan explained man's tragic history as the failure of men to understand themselves as part of nature. Instead they had assumed the need to create an artificial environment by constructing an artful culture. They had imagined that they needed to replace childish simplicity by adult complexity. And so, cut off from the life-giving power of nature, they had lived lives of fear and inhibition.[31]

Now, however, the fruitful power of industrialism was reminding man of his organic unity with the fruitful power of nature. Sullivan wrote that when he was young and innocent, he had instinctively sensed the difference between the artificial and inhibited creativity that had constructed a city like Boston and the artless and fruitful creativity that was expressed in a great steel bridge, simple and honest in design. His childish response to the bridge was, "How great men must be, how wonderful, how powerful, that they could make such a bridge, and again he worshipped the worker."

If now Sullivan could teach Americans that all their buildings, like the bridge, should express the architectural principle that "form follows function," that every aspect of the community should express the simplicity and honesty of that rule that "form follows function," then he could lead them into that "garden of the heart wherein the simple, obvious truths, the truths that any child might consent to, are brought fresh to the faculties and are held to be good because they are true and real." He could restore "the child mind [which] can grasp an understanding of things and ideas supposed now in our pride of feudal thought to be beyond its reach."[32]

For Sullivan, industrialism was best able to restore man to his child-like understanding of his instinctive harmony with nature in the Midwest where, unlike the corrupt and complex East Coast, the factory and the virgin land came together in a direct face-to-face partnership, a marriage of productive partners. This was why Chicago, unlike Boston or New York, was a city of joy. In the old cities, men huddled together, inhibited by fear because they were separated from nature. Their buildings were fortresses or prisons. But in Chicago men had rediscovered that as natural men, they, like nature, were producers. Like the trees, they could plant themselves in the ground and reach toward the sky. This, Sullivan insisted, was why "the architects of Chicago welcomed the steel frame and did something with it." This was why "the architects of the East were appalled by it and could make no contribution to it." This was why the skyscraper was born in Chicago. It was the architecture of joy.[33]

Skyscraper part of Garden city

Sullivan designed high buildings made possible by the use of the steel framework, and he covered them with elaborate decorations of carved leaves. For Sullivan there was no contradiction between his emphasis on simplicity and honesty in architecture based on his rule that "form follows function" and this complex decoration. He hoped Chicago and ultimately all cities would be "garden cities," organic outgrowths, like trees, from the earth itself. In his mind his decoration was artless, not artful. It was not the decoration of civilization imposed by the human imagination. It was natural decoration implicit in the organic unity of the building and its natural environment.

Sullivan could escape Jefferson's fear that all cities must be sores on the body politic not only because he distinguished between artificial cities and artless garden cities, but also because he accepted the political philosophy of Rousseau. For Sullivan, the Founding Fathers, including Jefferson, had feared the conflict between majority and minority interests, between the group and the individual. But Sullivan, like so many of his contemporaries, affirmed the position of Rousseau that in a perfect society there would be a "general will" in which organic consensus among all individuals would be expressed. Sullivan, too, was trying to shift his generation away from a vision of the state of nature as the home of atomistic individuals toward a vision of the state of nature filled with men committed to the social good. Sullivan saw his organic architecture as one aspect of a larger recovery of the true meaning of the state of nature. This revolution, for him, was most fully embodied in the new science of sociology, which he describes as "the art, the science of gregarious men. . . . This is the unity, science, poem, and drama of Sociology, the precursor of Democracy."[34]

In 1890 Sullivan saw the force of industrialism and sociology leading to the destruction of feudal civilization. He was certain that in 1893 at the Columbian Exposition at Chicago, the new architecture would begin the final education and liberation of the American people. It would illustrate the organic functionalism of productive physical nature and human nature. Here, at Chicago, there would be "a superb revelation of America's potency—an oration, a portrayal to arouse that which was hidden, to call forth into the light." The new, organic democratic architecture would demonstrate how there could be created "out of the cruel feudal chaos of cross purposes, a civilization, in equilibrium, for free men conscious of their power."[35]

But in Chicago there was an architect, Daniel Burnham, who, Sullivan wrote, "was obsessed by the feudal idea of power." And Sullivan believed that Burnham conspired to have the architecture of the exposition dominated by architects from the East Coast. For Sullivan, progress from complexity to simplicity was natural, but change from simplicity to complexity, the coming of decadence, must be the result of deliberate, unnatural conspiracy. Sullivan, unlike Frederick Jackson Turner in 1893, had seen Chicago as the beginning of a new frontier of hope. But the years between 1893 and 1917 were ones of disillusionment for Sullivan. He had prophesied the truth of organic architecture, American architecture, but he witnessed the continued dominance of what he believed was feudal, European architecture. He had prophesied a new reformation and renaissance for America, but, instead, he saw the corruption of the Midwest, the national landscape, by an Eastern conspiracy. Personally his importance as an architect declined. Clients stopped coming. He was ignored. He grew old alone, alienated, and impoverished. Like Charles Ives, he had tilted at the windmills of European hierarchy and capitalist materialism, and he, like Ives, had been defeated. The people refused to listen to the democratic language of his architecture. He could only lament, "Thus architecture died in the land of the free and the home of the brave."[36]

Like Sullivan, Frank Lloyd Wright was one of the heroes for whom the symbol-myth school wrote elegies. Like Sullivan, Wright imagined himself as an artistic hero whose architecture would rescue the American people from their un-American existence. Like Sullivan, Wright found the authentic America in the generation before the Civil War. Like Sullivan, Wright wrote an autobiography in which he celebrated his heroic persona and lamented that the people had not yet embraced him as a redeemer figure. There is no surprise in the fact that Wright, like Sullivan, described himself as a child of the national landscape. The landscape gave them the strength and inspiration they did not find in their biological fathers.

Wright was born in 1867 on his grandfather's farm near Spring Green, Wisconsin. But Wright's father kidnapped his son from the landscape that was true, beautiful, and good, the real America of the yeoman farmer. Wright's father took his wife and his son eastward across the Appalachians to dwell in the culture of a Massachusetts made decadent by its association with Europe, rather than in the America of the Midwest. His biological father was a Baptist minister whose sermons spoke of the beauty and goodness found in heaven. But Wright had seen the true heaven in the landscape of his grandfather's farm. Each summer Wright escaped the weakness of his biological father to regain strength from the rural countryside of Spring Green. Seeing strength in her son and weakness in her husband, Wright's mother had the courage to overcome propriety and get a divorce. Living in Madison, Wisconsin, Wright, after graduation from high school, enrolled at the University of Wisconsin. According to his autobiography, he then disappointed his mother by leaving the University of Wisconsin because it did not have the resources to encourage his genius. He went to Chicago.[37]

Here, according to his story, it was inevitable that he would go to work for Louis Sullivan. He shared with Sullivan the metaphor of two architectural worlds. The Old World had architects who imitated European styles. The New World would have architects whose buildings would express the characteristics of the American people. Sullivan had said that "the American architect must himself become indigenous . . . he must absorb into his heart and brain his own country and his own people." Wright believed that he was destined to be that architect. In 1901 Wright gave a lecture at Hull House, "The Active Craft of the Machine." Like the historian Charles Beard and like his fellow Chicagoans economist Thorstein Veblen and philosopher John Dewey, Wright argued that the machine was compatible with the democracy that grew out of the pastoral landscape. His vision was of an industrial landscape wedded to the national landscape. Beard, Veblen, and Dewey all saw the self-interest and materialism of capitalism as the antithesis of the producer ethic embodied in both the national and industrial landscapes. Wright agreed with them that while capitalism had captured the industrial landscape at the beginning of the nineteenth century, the productive nature of industrialism was too strong to remain trapped within the exploitative nature of capitalism. Wright believed that he as an artist could help liberate industrialism from the greed of capitalism. "My God is machinery," he declared. "The Art of the future will be the expression of the individual artist through the thousand powers of the machine, the machine doing all the things that the individual cannot do, and the creative artist is the man that controls all this and understands it." By separating the machine from the greed of businessmen, the architect could provide the city with "soul."[38]

Wright left Sullivan's firm and became famous by designing houses for businessmen in the Chicago suburb of Oak Park. Implicit in Wright's move was his inability to imagine how he could control the chaos that was Chicago. He had seen the nuclear family as the essential social unit on the pastoral national landscapes. If he, at the moment, could not fuse the pastoral and urban landscape, he could, however, fuse the pastoral and suburban landscapes. Here in Oak Park were Americans, not the immigrants from Europe who filled Chicago and most other major cities in the United States. The citizens of Oak Park, for Wright, were good people, "most of whom had taken asylum there to bring up their children in comparative peace, safe from the poisons of the great city." He hoped to liberate these "good people" from undemocratic European influences by offering them an alternative to the hierarchical Victorian house whose several floors and many private rooms frustrated the functioning of the democratic American family. His Prairie Style linked a one-story house to the landscape and the openness and flow of the interior encouraged the integration of the family.[39]

But Wright in 1935 looked back in his autobiography to his private success and his public failure. He had attracted the attention of architects in Europe, and he had become wealthy from the many houses he designed for businessmen. But he could not imagine redeeming the chaos of inner Chicago. He was, he remembered, "up against a dead wall. I could see no way out." With his utopian hopes for the city at an impasse, he

his affair

also experienced an impasse with his utopian expectations for the nuclear family. This family needed to be based on affection. And he had fallen out of love with his wife, the mother of his six children. He had fallen in love with a married woman. Suddenly he saw his neighbors as prisoners of conventions, of a rigid set of laws, of a greater concern for property than for love. Trapped in an enclosure of artificial European culture, he and Mrs. Cheyney engaged in the irony of fleeing to Europe to be free. When they returned in 1911, Wright went to his grandfather's farm. "I turned to the hill in the valley as my grandfather before me had turned to America—as a hope and a heaven." Here, at Taliesin, he would combine an architectural studio, a home, and a farm that would provide food, water, and power. But when Mrs. Cheyney was killed in a fire at Taliesin in 1916, Wright fled to Japan. He had been invited to design the Imperial Hotel in Tokyo. He remained in Japan for six years. As it had for Sullivan, the period of World War I seemed to mark the end of Wright's redemptive dreams. But, like his contemporary, Charles Beard, he was able to restore some of his hope. This was remarkable because, in the 1920s, he received almost none of the attention and admiration that he had experienced between 1900 and 1908.[40]

Taliesin

Friends rescued Taliesin from bankruptcy, and he survived another scandal. He had married again in 1923, but he soon began to live with another woman. His wife charged him with criminal adultery and violation of the Mann Act. But the charges were dropped when his wife granted him a divorce, and he remarried in 1928. He then began to write the autobiography published in 1935 and to draw up the plans for Broadacre City.

The Great Crash of 1929 revitalized Wright's hopes that capitalism would disappear and Americans could live in a world of private property dedicated to production and not profits. Somehow a miracle would occur and the European cities in the United States, such as Boston, New York, and Chicago, would vanish. Broadacre City would fulfill Jefferson's dream of a nation of small farmers. And it was twentieth-century technology that would make this possible. Every American family would own a farm, but family members could use the automobile to do work also in factories and offices. But there would be small-scale factories and offices scattered throughout the countryside. There would be no need for the concentration of humanity in the central city—that horror of "Tier upon tier, the soulless shelf, the interminable empty crevice

his vision

along the winding ways of the winding, unhealthy canyon. The heartless grip of selfish, grasping universal structure. Box on box beside boxes. Black shadows below with artificial lights burning all day long in little caverns and squared cells. Prison cubicles." But automobiles, electricity, machines would dissolve all such monstrous cities and everyone would live in a decentralized environment where the national landscape gave birth to a democratic society of nuclear families who shared abundance. There would be no significant gap between the rich and the poor. In 1935 Wright envisioned that perfect bourgeois society of classless, middle-class people free from the greed of international capitalism. Broadacre City was an environment in which every house had an organic relationship to the land. Houses "should grow as the trees around the man himself grow." The American citizen would "make his house a harmonious whole."[41]

But then, as for Charles Beard, Wright saw the possibility of another world war. Wars, Wright lamented, demand centralization. He, like Beard, believed that it was the continuing influence of England in the United States that was the major threat to pull us into a European war. Again, for him, it was the people of the East Coast who most wanted war because they had never become independent of European culture. It is "that eastern part of us that is already an out-and-out pseudofascist Europe reflecting the great disappearing British Empire." The East, he continued, "was never really agrarian." In desperation he advocated splitting the country into three parts—the Northeast, the South, and a combined Midwest and West. The capital for this real America would be "placed mid-way on the rolling prairies of the Mid-West beside the Father of the Waters—our Mississippi—there where the amplitude, rectitude, and impartiality that might characterize the greater part of our nation, could, unburdened by congenital prejudice or the equivocal influence of foreign power, be free to initiate and grow the ways and means to live a good life as the independent democracy this country was designed to be."[42]

But the war came and so did more and more centralization. Wright, like the much younger Jackson Pollock, now believed that there was no hope that the creative artist could redeem the people. "A nation industrialized beyond proper balance with its own agronomy is a menace to its own peace and the peace of the world," he lamented. "The artificiality of our mechanized society," he said, "is helplessly drifting toward a bureaucracy so top-heavy that the bureaucracy of Soviet Russia will seem honest and innocent by comparison." In the 1930s, Wright, like Charles Beard and Thomas Hart Benton, could imagine a national romance in which an urban-industrial America was an organic outgrowth of agrarian America. But now he saw two Americas, the real America—the democratic, decentralized America of the pastoral national landscape that had died during World War II—and the new urban-industrial America—centralized and undemocratic, which controlled the future. With the death of the national landscape, his belief in a virtuous American people, children of the landscape, also died. His book of 1949, *Genius and the Mobocracy,* overtly spoke of the tragedy of Louis Sullivan. The people had not appreciated his genius. But this book spoke covertly of Wright's belief that the people had not appreciated his genius. The tradition of the avant-garde artist had been that of the genius who was able to lead the people to a better world. But there could be no avant-garde if the people could not be led. The people were a permanently corrupted mob. The artist had hoped that there was a corrupt elite whom the artist, with the help of the people, could defeat. But now Wright saw the genius, whether a Sullivan or a Wright, alienated from both the corrupt elite and the corrupt people. All the genius could do was remember the America when the organic was more powerful than the artificial. "So this new democratic architecture we call organic and is original," Wright lamented, "may again be swamped by the same heedless mobocracy or more likely by official statism (the two gangsterisms do work together) and our hope of organic culture will be left to die with principle in this Western Wasteland."[43]

Although Wright found that he had personal fame during the final years of his life, he could not avoid the pain that the architects who became dominant during the 1940s celebrated the central city. He must have felt the terrible irony that these architects were born in Europe and that under their leadership American urban architecture came to be defined as the "International Style."

The political and economic leaders of the revolution that took the United States from the isolation demanded by bourgeois nationalism into the sacredness of the international marketplace embraced the revolutionary architecture self-consciously created by European architects as a response to the horror of World War I. These architects saw their art providing an international alternative to the destructive forces of nationalism and capitalism that they believed had caused the bloodbath of 1914–18. Once more, then, political and economic leaders in the United States co-opted the work of artists who were anticapitalist to promote the United States as the cultural center of international capitalism.

Going into the 1920s, many architects in the Scandinavian countries, as well as in Holland, France, Italy, Austria, and Germany, envisioned themselves as an avant-garde who could help redeem Europe from its suicidal culture. They embraced the vision of Karl Marx that the industrial revolution offered the possibility of a productive and rational international community in place of the unproductive and irrational world of bourgeois nationalism and capitalism. Architecture, therefore, should bring the honesty of the factory, a design for rational productivity, into the design of office buildings and apartment houses. Unlike Sullivan and Wright, these European architects did not imagine a synthesis of national landscapes with urban-industrial landscapes. Increasingly during the 1920s and 1930s, these architects associated national landscapes with the development of fascist politics.

And, indeed, the political victory of fascism in Germany and Austria in the 1930s drove many of these architects into exile in the United States. Hitler demanded an architecture that grew out of the German soil. Early in the 1930s, before Hitler, the American architects Russell Hitchcock and Philip Johnson had gone to Germany and had come home committed to the school of "international architecture" that they found there. This alternative architectural position to the national organicism of Frank Lloyd Wright had been taken up in the 1930s by a number of American corporate leaders. It fitted their vision of a marketplace freed from national boundaries. The European exiles, especially those from the German Bauhaus School, such as Walter Gropius, immediately, therefore, found academic positions in major universities in the United States and commissions from its major corporations. The symbolism of their square, glass corporate office buildings was that their buildings, like mathematics and physics, represented universal, not particular, principles. These were buildings free from the local and particular; they represented a universal universal, rather than a universal national.

The artistic avant-gardes of bourgeois nationalism and international Marxism promised that they could lead the people out of the chaos of international capitalism into a harmonious world where truth, goodness, and beauty would be unified. Now, however, the hopes of the Bauhaus

School, like the hopes of the abstract expressionists, that the purity of their art would overcome the chaotic eclecticism of the popular arts, were dissolved in the endless circulation of styles in the marketplace. As postwar architects quickly abandoned the austerity of the international architecture imagined in 1920, one could apply to architecture all of the laments of Eleanor Heartney's *Critical Condition: American Culture at the Crossroads.* Architects felt free to use ornamentations borrowed from any number of earlier architectural styles. Or one could apply the celebration of Tyler Cowen's *In Praise of Commercial Culture.* One could celebrate the vitality and freedom of expression of "postmodern" architecture, where architects no longer believed they had a responsibility to use their art to redeem humanity. At least Frank Lloyd Wright's sense that he had lost control of the flow of history would be shared by his hated enemy from Europe, Walter Gropius, who once had thought that the United States could be the promised land for an architecture that symbolized rational productivity.[44]

Music

Like Charles Beard, a group of New England men who were to play an important role in defining what was and was not American music were born in the 1870s. Like Beard, then, they came of age in the 1890s, and they, too, saw their nation in crisis. Arthur Farwell, Edward Burlingame Hill, Daniel Gregory Mason, John Alden Carpenter, David Stanley Smith, and Charles Ives were members of the first generation of college students for whom music was part of the liberal arts curriculum. Studying music in schools such as Harvard and Yale, they were reminded that no American had produced a symphony comparable to those composed by Europeans. They were taught that the greatest of Europeans were Bach, Beethoven, and Brahms. They were aware that the elite audiences for symphonic music, which were developing in the major cities, listened to European music usually conducted by Europeans.[45]

This dependence on European music and musicians was, for these young Americans, evidence of the crisis of the 1890s. They shared with Turner, Beard, and Parrington the narrative that an independent national culture had been achieved by the 1830s. Born from the national landscape, there was a virtuous and democratic American people. Like their contemporaries, the historians, they defined the essence of the people as spiritual. The nation had a religious identity. Like the painters, they shared, therefore, the historians' story of the corruption of the people after the Civil War and the hope that the people could be redeemed. Redemption meant a rejection of the materialism of the marketplace and a return to the spirituality of the national landscape.

But they did differ from the positions held by Turner and Beard in the 1890s. They ignored the commitment of the historians to the universal laws of evolution. For Turner, those laws meant the death of the national landscape and the democratic people who were its children. Beard, in the 1890s, refused to accept Turner's pessimism. Turner had linked capitalism to evolution, but Beard saw evolution pushing past the stage of capitalism to culminate in a worldwide industrial democracy. For these New England men, who by the 1920s would head the music departments at Harvard, Yale, Princeton, and Columbia and also would be important composers or influential music critics, redemption of the people could be achieved if a musical avant-garde taught the people that they were speaking the false language of materialism and revealed to them the true language of spiritual nationalism—the language the people spoke before the Civil War. To accomplish this, an American symphony equal to those of Beethoven and Brahms needed to be written. And this symphony needed to break down the class division between the elite concertgoers and the ordinary individual who listened only to popular music.[46]

elements of pop culture

As much as Thomas Jefferson, these New England men hated cities as environments alien to the national landscape. When they were born in the 1870s, Boston, New York, and Philadelphia were exploding in size as immigrants from southern and eastern Europe, Catholics and Jews, flooded into them. As part of the crisis in the 1890s, these alien cities with their foreign populations threatened to blur the memory of the pastoral landscape whose inspiration was necessary for national redemption. For the New England men in the 1890s, as for Charles and Mary Beard and Thomas Benton in the 1930s, the popular culture of the cities was corrupting. This was true not only of the urban entertainments created by Catholics and Jews, but also of the ragtime, blues, and jazz brought into northern cities by African Americans migrating out of the rural South. Sometimes implicitly, sometimes explicitly, the New England men defined the people of 1830 as male Anglo-Protestant citizens. By the 1920s the Beards were writing about the insidious alliance between capitalist materialism and urban popular culture. But this was a central truth for the New England musical establishment from the 1890s to the 1930s.

The ideal bourgeois citizen, for them, was a man who controlled his emotions and was thus guided by his rationality. Such rationality, however, was not an alternative to spirituality. The spirituality of the religion of the nation was, like rationality, an expression of a man's best qualities. Natural spirituality, like rationality, was opposed to the irrational, the emotional. It was opposed to a life of bodily appetites. The New England group was obsessed, therefore, with the need to be an ideal bourgeois citizen. That citizen was a potential warrior because the nation needed to be defended by a citizen army. But since the time of Emerson, male artists in America knew that the men of the marketplace defined themselves as warriors and male artists as effeminate. Artists were men who dwelled in the irrational, the emotional, bodily world of women. They were not part of the male world of production; they were part of the female world of consumption. They were not rational; they had slid down into the world of fantasy.

This was the complex and frightening cultural burden that Charles Ives carried with him as he set out to compose the great American symphony. If he were successful, America would be musically independent of Europe. If he were successful, Americans would become a classless society in which the language of a symphony brought elite and ordinary listeners together. If he were successful, he would remind his listeners that the only music that had sprung from the national landscape of 1830 was the folk music of Anglo-Protestants. If he were successful, he would demonstrate that the male Anglo-Protestant artist could play a more heroic role than a businessman could. Who could be more of a manly success than the artist who redeemed the nation? This was a role that no businessman could play. Businessmen would be followers of this patriotic musical genius as he led them out of the fragmentation of capitalist self-interest into the unified community of national interest. Such a composer would be the most powerful symbol of a productive America.[47]

His contemporaries, Hill, Mason, and Smith, became major figures in the music departments of Ivy League universities. But Ives could not imagine how he or anyone could play a heroic and redemptive role from within the academy. Businessmen were right that academic men were effeminate. Like women, they were committed to tradition and convention. Like women, they spent their time talking rather than producing. To support himself and his wife, Ives went into the insurance business in New York City. Coming from a family in Connecticut that was not wealthy, Ives knew he was a self-made man. He was a success. He became wealthy enough to buy an estate in Connecticut and commute to his work in the city. He hated the noise, the dirt, the crowds of the city. Every evening and every weekend he could escape this chaotic landscape, which was ugly, corrupt, and false, to return to the rural landscape of Connecticut, which was beautiful, good, and true, because it represented the essence of American national identity.

This was the landscape he wanted to represent in the music he would compose. But Ives's New England generation was also part of a transnational generation of bourgeois artists who were participating in a crisis of representation. Everywhere in the Atlantic world, painters could no longer find inspiration in the national landscape or in the ideal bourgeois citizen. Like the painters, composers now felt trapped within a pattern of sterile conventions. Many, such as an Arnold Schoenberg in Europe or a Charles Ives in the United States, rejected in 1900 what had seemed in 1850 to be the natural and eternal laws of tonality and rhythm. Ives, like Schoenberg, would experiment with atonality and polyrhythms. But Ives was not seen, as Schoenberg was, as an iconoclast because Schoenberg's music was known and discussed by his contemporaries. Ives's music, however, did not become public knowledge until it was played after World War II.

In 1900 the best-known American composer was Edward MacDowell. Trained in Europe from the age of fifteen until he was twenty-seven, MacDowell returned to the United States in 1888 to write romantic music in the German tradition that he admired so greatly. For the music critics of his day, his compositions were so sophisticated and skillful that he was accepted immediately as the first American to compose at an equal level of technique with Europeans. Aaron Copland remembered that "[i]t was the music of MacDowell that we knew best."[48]

There is a dramatic parallel between MacDowell's mastery of musical technique learned in Europe and that of his contemporaries in painting. And there is a dramatic parallel between the use of that technique in MacDowell's music, as in the popular paintings of the 1890s, to provide stability for a genteel middle-class establishment. As the artists painted "pretty" pictures in their portraits and landscapes, so MacDowell composed "pretty" musical pieces. And as the artists tended to draw ever smaller and more artificial landscapes, so MacDowell's music tended to find inspiration in a fantasy world that had no relation to the economic and political conflicts that were so savagely dividing America in the 1890s. This escapism was expressed in the very titles of his major compositions:

Op.17. *Two Fantastic Pieces, for Piano* (1884)

1. Legend
2. Witches' Dance

Op.19. *Forest Idylls, for Piano* (1884)

1. Forest Stillness
2. Play of the Nymphs
3. Revery
4. Dance of the Dryad

For Ives, MacDowell's second suite for orchestra, the *Indian Suite* of 1897, came no closer to reality, nor did his "New England Idylls" of 1902. His songs of 1900, "To a Wild Rose," "From Uncle Remus," "Of Br'er Rabbit," "From a German Forest," all expressed what Ives would call a "dainty" gentility.[49]

While Ives was exposed to this kind of music at Yale, he already had been trained by his father, the town bandmaster in Danbury, Connecticut. This training had prepared Ives to challenge the academic music establishment by teaching him to consider the possibility of polytonality, polyrhythms, and atonality. George Ives, his father, was a most unusual musical innovator who taught his children to listen to several keys, and to listen to two bands as they approached each other playing different tunes. From his father, Charles Ives also learned to consider much of the academic music too "sweet," too "easy," too "sissified," too "feminine."

hmm

At Yale, however, under the direction of academic musicians, Ives composed songs similar to those of MacDowell; they accepted German dominance with titles like "Feldeinsamkeit" and "Ich Grolle Nicht," and they accepted genteel sentimentality with words that read:

O'er the mountains toward the west
As the children go to rest,
Faintly comes a sound,
A song of nature hovers round,
'Tis the beauty of the night;
Sleep thee well till morning light.

or

Marie, I see thee forest one
As in a garden fair, a garden fair
Before thee flowers and blossoms play
Tossed by soft evening air,
The Pilgrim passing on his ways
Bows low before thy shrine;
Thou art, my child, like one sweet prayer,
So good, so fair, so pure, almost divine.

Ives remembered that in his childhood he had a spiritual experience that revealed to him the unity of the universe. In the 1890s at Yale he was taught that this unity was expressed best in nineteenth-century patterns of rhythm and tonality, in genteel poetry, and not through the band music, the circus tunes, and the evangelical hymns of the common people of his childhood.[50]

Then, around 1900, he experienced another spiritual crisis. He now saw the genteel tradition as European not American, aristocratic not democratic, feminine and not masculine. Now doubting dominant forms, he could fall back on his father's teachings and expand them to cover every aspect of American life. All present cultural forms should be rejected in the name of experimentation. He would write symphonic music that could speak to and for democratic Americans. Unity with God must be experienced through a new democratic folk music that was free from the artificial restraints of aristocratic music. This music could help men everywhere to transcend the imperfect status quo to achieve unity with God.

His successful career in insurance would allow him to compose freely without the need to please current musical critics and the audiences who wanted to listen to nineteenth-century music. Ives defined his music as an expression of theology and politics. His unfinished *Universe Symphony* was to include these three movements:

1. Formation of the countries and the mountains.
2. Evolution in nature and humanity.
3. The rise of all to the spiritual.[51]

For Ives, then, the first decades of the twentieth century marked the end of a corrupt, materialistic, and undemocratic America and the restoration of the spiritual democracy for which Thoreau and Emerson had been spokesmen. He was certain of the transition when he wrote

> The Hog-Mind and its handmaidens in disorder . . . cowardice and suspicion; all a part of the minority (the non-people) . . . will give way more and more to the great primal truths, that there is more good than evil; that good is on the side of the majority (the people), that he has made men greater than man, that he has made the universal mind and the over-soul greater and a part of the individual mind and soul, that he has made the Divine a part of all.[52]

Ives had turned back to Emerson to find the philosophical justification for transcendence of the establishment. It is ironic that he agreed with Emerson that the greatest prophet of transcendence yet to appear was Beethoven. For Ives, there is an "oracle" at the beginning of the Fifth Symphony. He wrote that in those

> four notes lies one of Beethoven's greatest messages. We would . . . strive to bring it toward the spiritual message of Emerson's revelations . . . the soul of humanity knocking at the door of divine mysteries, radiant in the faith that it will be opened—and the human become divine.[53]

Ives, then, would embody the philosophy of Beethoven and Emerson. His music, he declared, needed to be composed "fervently, transcendentally, inevitably, furiously," and then it would have "sincerity, strength, nobility, and will be American."[54]

For Ives, Americans, the people, were closer to God than people anywhere else in the world. But this was only because Americans were freer of corrupting institutions and traditions. Americans, then, had the responsibility of helping the rest of the world to escape their burden of historical corruption. And Ives had the greatest responsibility of any American because it was through music alone that men could be unified in a natural and not an artificial community. Spoken and written languages were themselves historical institutions and traditions and served to divide men. But music, Ives declared, "is beyond any analogy to word language and . . . the time is coming . . . when it will develop possibilities inconceivable now, a language so transcendent, that its heights and depths will be common to all mankind."[55]

Furiously Ives composed in isolation from a corrupt world in order to save that world. He refused to listen to other music so that he would be free to find the key to that sacred music that would lift mankind into a heaven on earth. As he experimented with the expression of Anglo-American folk music, especially hymns, in patterns of polytonality, atonality, and polyrhythm, trying to find the formless music that would unite all humanity, he became more and more frustrated with traditional instruments and traditional musicians. "The Instrument," he cried out, "There is the perennial difficulty. There is music's limitations. Is it the composer's fault that man has only ten fingers?" And his impatience exploded against the men who must perform his compositions. "I began to feel that if I wanted to write music that was worthwhile (that is, to me), I must keep away from musicians."[56]

Writing music with simultaneous rhythms, concurrent melodies, complex patterns of syncopation that orchestras rejected as unplayable, Ives continued to compose at a furious rate because the world he needed to save was so corrupt, because the people he needed to save were so crushed by suffering. In 1912, he used words by Matthew Arnold for a song expressing this view:

> Crowded on the pavement, close to Belgrave Square
> A tramp I saw, ill, moody, tongue-tied
> A babe was in her arms, and at her side
> A girl; their clothes were rags, their feet were bare.
> Some laboring men whose work lay somewhere there,
> Passed opposite; she touched her girl, who hied
> Across and begged, and came back satisfied.
> The rich she had let pass with frozen stare,
> Thought I: "Above her state this spirit towers;
> She will not ask of aliens, but of friend,
> Of sharers in a common human fate.
> She turns from the cold succor, which attends
> The unknown little from the unknowing great,
> And points to a better Time than ours."[57]

Like so many of his contemporary artists and intellectuals, Ives began to see the millennium rising out of the darkness around 1914. He sensed a spiritual awakening among the people. He saw the rejection of the gospel of self-interest in favor of the new social gospel of community salvation and brotherly love. In 1914, then, he composed his most triumphant song, "General William Booth Enters into Heaven." Against the complacent sterility of the aristocracy, he contrasted this leader of the common man who, preaching a gospel of love for the people, had transcended churchly institutions and churchly dogma. Booth was a leader who transcended conformity to respectable norms that ignored the needs of the people. This was the fruitful leader who was bringing his motley, ragtag democratic army "washed in the blood of the lamb," into a New World. For Ives in 1914

> The Masses are yearning, are yearning, are yearning
> Whence comes the hope of the world;
> The Masses are dreaming, dreaming,
> The Masses are dreaming,
> When comes the vision of God!
> God's in His Heaven,
> All will be well with the world.[58]

These lines from his song, "Majority," express his faith that a constitutional amendment giving the people the right to vote on all important decisions, to participate directly as a general will, would allow them to vote themselves into a heaven on earth.

Then the war came. For Ives, as for a number of his contemporaries, it destroyed his millennial expectations. The materialism and selfishness of the marketplace was going to continue. The national landscape did not have the power to call the people out of the false language of self-interest and back to the true language of democracy and national interest. It was useless for Ives to try to create a musical language to help redeem the people. "My things," he was to write, "were done mostly in the twenty years between 1896 and 1916. In 1917, the war came on and I did practically nothing in music. I did not seem to feel like it." He did compose another song, however, using the words of Lord Byron; it was an elegy for the national landscape. This was "A Farewell to Land," in which the voice and the piano were to start at the top of the voice's range and descend steadily to the lower limits of the voice:

> Adieu, Adieu! My native shore
> Fades o'er the waters blue;
> The night winds sigh, the breakers roar
> And shrieks the wild sea-mew,
> You sun that sets upon the sea,
> We follow in his flight;
> Farewell while to him and thee,
> My native land, good night.[59]

After 1945 the symbol-myth school helped bring Ives's music out of total obscurity. Ives's music, ironically, would be kept alive within the walls of the academy. The men of the symbol-myth school did not expect Ives's music to speak to a people permanently trapped in capitalist culture. But they could enrich their elegy for the national landscape by incorporating that of Ives. They could remember that once the national landscape had produced heroes. It was only a hero who developed a vision of his redemptive role. It was only the defeat of such a gigantic figure that was worthy of being called a tragedy. The elegy written by the symbol-myth scholars would sustain the memory of these heroes and their tragedies. Ives would be part of that pantheon that included the American Scene painters and the architects Louis Sullivan and Frank Lloyd Wright.

almost Greek Tragedy

Going into the 1920s, then, Ives had abandoned his hope of writing symphonic music that would speak to and for the people. The other men from New England who were Ives's contemporaries also found it increasingly difficult to sustain their hope that an American symphonic music would appear and redeem the people by returning them to the national spirituality of Emerson and Thoreau. Instead, the danger of urban popular music, which they had perceived in the 1890s, had become much more powerful in the 1920s. Jazz had become popular among large numbers of the younger Anglo-Protestant generation. Jazz, for the members of the academic musical establishment, such as Daniel Gregory Mason, expressed the sensual culture of Negroes. It was the antithesis of the spiritual American culture created by Anglo-Protestants. It was a contradiction to the values of the responsible bourgeois citizen. For Mason, the urban landscape was not only characterized by the un-American sexuality of Negro music, but jazz also expressed the fragmentation of life within the urban landscape. Living within the unity of the pastoral, national landscape, citizens achieved an organic wholeness. They were a people—a deep fraternity. But, for Mason, the urban landscape depended for existence on the machine. The urban landscape expressed a mechanical, not an organic, foundation. Jazz also gave voice to the ugliness and corruption of an environment dominated by the machine. Jazz was dangerous because it was both sensual and mechanical.[60]

pop music

Even more dangerous than the Negro, however, was the Jew. In the founding myths of bourgeois nationalisms, which insisted that a national people had emerged from a national landscape, Jews were permanent aliens, un-English, un-French, un-German, un-American. Emphasizing the distinction between private property made virtuous by the discipline of the national interest on each citizen and private property made corrupt by the self-interest of capitalists for whom the international marketplace was more important than the national landscape, bourgeois nationalists defined the Jew as the prototype of the capitalist. Alienated from the spirituality of the people, the Jew was always a materialist. Alienated from the national interest, the Jew was always committed to self-interest. Jews were the entrepreneurs who were spreading jazz to young Anglo-Protestants. They encouraged these unsuspecting youths to speak the un-American language of sensuality and materialism. As the critic Gilbert Seldes wrote, "Can the Negro and the Jew stand in the relation of a folk to a nation? And if not, can the music they create be the national music?" And Mason lamented that "[o]ur whole contemporary aesthetic attitude toward instrumental music, especially in New York, is dominated by Jewish tastes and standards, with their Oriental extravagance, their sensuous brilliancy and intellectual facility and superficiality, their general tendency to exaggeration and disproportion."[61]

But the New Englanders who dominated academic and critical discussions had not been able to create the redemptive music they wanted. Now in the 1920s they were challenged by a generation of young composers born around 1900. Many came from the urban wasteland so despised by the musical establishment. And some were Jews. These younger men imagined themselves as an avant-garde. They, however, would escape the tired conventions of the New Englanders born in the 1870s. They, too, would, for the first time, compose American music that was the equal of, if not the superior to, European music. The New Englanders born in the 1870s were horrified in the 1920s when music critics in England, Germany, and France suggested that jazz represented the future of American music. For the Europeans, jazz represented the vitality of a young nation, and they hoped it might revitalize their old nations. In France a group of composers—Airíe, Honegger, Tailleferre, Durey, Poulenc, and Milhaud—were given the name "the Six" in part because of their interest in using jazz in their compositions. The New Englanders had looked to Germany for models; the generation of 1900 went, instead, to Paris, where they were encouraged to imagine a synthesis of symphonic music and jazz.

Most of these younger Americans studied in Paris with Nadia Boulanger. She rejected the extremism of Schoenberg but wanted her students to revitalize symphonic music by experimenting creatively with traditional patterns. One of her American students was Aaron Copland.

He was born in 1900 in Brooklyn of parents who were Jewish immigrants from Russia. Copland and George Gershwin, another Jewish composer from New York, became, in the 1920s, the two most important American synthesizers of jazz and classical music. Gershwin, unlike Copland, did not seek formal musical training. Indeed, Boulanger thought his genius was so great that she hoped he would not inhibit it by listening to teachers.[62]

Copland returned to the United States strongly committed to a metaphor of two worlds, European and American. He appreciated the modern music to which he had been exposed in Paris. He saw himself as a participant in this musical modernism. But he believed that modern music needed to be rooted in particular national cultures. French composers had vitality because they were sustained by a vital national culture. "The relation of French music to the life around me," he wrote, "became increasingly manifest. Gradually, the idea that my personal expression in music ought somehow to be related to my own back-home environment took hold of me. The conviction grew inside me that the two things that seemed always to have been separate in America—music and the life about me—must be made to touch. This desire to make the music I wanted to write come out of the life I had lived in America became a preoccupation of mine in the twenties."[63]

Like Charles Ives a generation earlier, Copland imagined that his compositions would combine experiments in tonality and rhythm with American folk music. But for him, as for George Gershwin, this folk music was jazz. "I want frankly," Copland declared, "to adapt the jazz idiom and see what I could do with it in a symphonic way." Unlike Ives, Copland had his first major work, *Symphony for Organ and Orchestra* (1924), performed immediately. In Paris, Nadia Boulanger had praised Copland to Serge Koussevitsky, who then came to the United States to become the director of the Boston Symphony. He used his influence to have Copland's works performed. Most critics found his compositions from the 1920s to be too experimental and too difficult. Audiences agreed with the critics. Copland's effort to develop a symphonic language that would speak for and to the American people seemed to have failed almost as completely as Ives's effort.[64]

Toward the end of his long life, Copland looked back on his career and saw a seamless flow. He acknowledged that there were stylistic changes, but he saw them as minor variations. Like Charles and Mary

Beard, he was a historian against history. Like America, he had an essential identity that survived superficial change.

But Copland in the 1930s did develop a symphonic style that many believed spoke for and to the American people. He achieved popularity when he discarded jazz as the folk music he would use to create an authentically American music. Instead he turned to the Anglo-American folk music on which Ives had based his symphonies. Unlike Ives, however, Copland also abandoned the atonal and polytonal experiments of modern music. Copland, however, did not make these dramatic changes to achieve personal popularity. Instead, he changed because he had become a participant in that narrative that saw an egalitarian democracy in 1830. This fraternity of equal citizens disciplined by their commitment to the national interest was temporarily lost after the Civil War. The capitalist marketplace corrupted the language of fraternity and persuaded the people to speak the language of self-interest. Now, however, capitalism had collapsed. The language of self-interest was no longer persuasive. Once again artists of all kinds could return to the world of Emerson. They could help the people regain their true language, that of a fraternal democracy. They would see and feel that this language was the gift of the national landscape. They would understand the difference between the fragmentation of the marketplace and the organic unity of nature's nation.

First, however, Copland would have to move with his leftist friends from their belief in the early 1930s that revolutionists inspired by Marx needed to use a new music to liberate Americans from the capitalist language of self-interest. Revolutionary music would teach the people that they were part of an international proletariat and that the language of this proletariat was one of equality and fraternity. An important New York community of Jewish intellectuals and artists in 1930 imagined that an international industrial landscape was succeeding the capitalist marketplace. The industrial landscape was characterized by rationality and productivity in contrast to the irrationality and consumerism of the marketplace.[65]

Associated with this group was the Anglo-American Charles Seeger. He helped found the New York Composers Collective. Seeger had been asked by Thomas Hart Benton to participate in the dedication of Benton's murals at the New School for Social Research. Benton had

Anglo-American folk music played for the occasion. Seeger's familiarity with Anglo-American folk music was deepened when in 1932 he edited John and Alan Lomax's *American Ballads and Folk Songs.* But until 1935, Seeger and most of his friends in the Composers Collective assumed that the rural past was irrelevant to the industrial future. Unlike Charles and Mary Beard and Benton, they did not have a narrative in which the democratic rural world of the nineteenth century was a usable past for the democratic industrial world that was being born in the twentieth century. Members of the Collective even rejected the powerful heritage of revolutionary songs used by the International Workers of the World (the Wobblies) before World War I. Most members of the Collective believed that a New World needed a new musical style. The Collective published a *Worker's Song Book* in 1933 that contained a song by Copland, "Into the Streets May First." "To write a fine mass song," according to Copland, "is a challenge to every composer. It gives him a first-line position on the cultural front, for in the mass song he possesses a more effectual weapon than any in the hands of the novelist or even the playwright."[66]

After 1935 the leaders of the Communist Party committed themselves to a popular front, an alliance with all groups who were struggling to replace corporate capitalism. Earl Browder, the head of the party, now declared that "communism is twentieth-century Americanism." Before this shift in strategy, leftist writers such as Michael Gold, who saw a usable past in Jefferson and Lincoln and Whitman, were on the periphery. Now Gold, who wanted arts rooted in the American vernacular, became mainstream. Leftists could now share with the Beards and Benton the belief that the pastoral national landscape was the foundation of the urban-industrial landscape and that capitalism had always been alien to the essential American identity.[67]

This vision of gaining strength from a rural and democratic past to overcome the economic crisis of the 1930s was also used by the image makers in the Roosevelt administration. They worked at presenting Roosevelt as the reincarnation of Lincoln. An Anglo-American composer, Virgil Thomson, a member of the generation of 1900, had written a symphony on a *Hymn Tune* in 1928. Here, in contrast to Ives, he had used traditional tonality. In 1936 and 1937, he wrote scores for the government-funded films, *The Plow That Broke the Plains* and *The River.* His music was a nostalgic use of Anglo-American folk songs. Thomson believed that his music helped Aaron Copland to use Anglo-American folk songs in his successful ballet of 1938, *Billy the Kid*.[68]

Until the mid-1930s, Copland had seen two Americas, his urban world of a musical avant-garde, his Jewish community, and jazz versus a rural world of an irrelevant musical heritage and Anglo-American nostalgia. Now he could believe that this other America was part of his heritage. Copland solidified his reputation as a composer who could reach a mass audience with another ballet, *Rodeo,* in 1942. Again his use of folk songs was presented in traditional tonality. His fullest ability to identify with the Anglo-American rural past came in 1944 with the performance of his ballet *Appalachian Spring,* for which he won a Pulitzer Prize in 1945. From 1944 to the present, he has been identified as the most important American composer. Copland's deep commitment to the pastoral national landscape gave him something like immortality because, by the late 1930s, he had stopped identifying capitalism as alien to that landscape. Thomas Hart Benton and Charles and Mary Beard had their reputations destroyed in the 1940s because they never stopped identifying capitalism as the enemy of a native democracy. But Copland's pastoral compositions in *Billy the Kid, Rodeo,* and *Appalachian Spring* had no political message other than that the United States had a rich and beautiful heritage of Anglo-American music; this music had become the heritage of everyone, including New York Jews. This vision of national consensus, a national romance, was expressed by the New York composers Rodgers and Hammerstein in their extremely popular musical of 1943, *Oklahoma.*

The image makers of the wartime Roosevelt administration wanted to obscure the revolutionary discontinuity that replaced the sacredness of the national landscape with the sacredness of the international marketplace. Copland's popular ballet music gave support to the image that American history had always been and always would be a seamless flow. It is poetic, then, that Copland's last major effort to sustain his national romance was a failure. He wrote the music for an opera, *The Tender Land,* performed in 1954. Neither the audience nor the critics liked it. In contrast to the atmosphere of happiness and fulfillment evoked in the wedding on which *Appalachian Spring* focused, this opera found tragedy in the pastoral environment. The heroine loses her love and then abandons her family. Here there is dissonance and discontinuity, rather than harmony and continuity. Dissonance and discontinuity were major characteristics of the music composed by a younger generation starting in the 1940s. Copland's response was dismay that these young men had abandoned his concern in the 1930s and 1940s with reaching a mass audience.

But if younger composers in the 1940s felt at some level that their environment was the chaos of the marketplace, then chaos would be central to their music. All of this, for Copland, was a mistake. "With reckless disregard for what players like to play, and for practicalities of the instruments," he wrote with regret, "composers have been providing music that is, at times, playable by only a handful of specialists in contemporary music." He was unaware that these composers could not imagine a people to communicate with, since the idea of a homogeneous people was a construct of bourgeois nationalism and Marxism. He lamented that younger composers were able to do without audiences because they were supported by academic salaries. In a world of fragmentation and alienation, "the worst feature of the composer's life is the fact that he does not feel himself part of the musical community."[69] Ironically, however, Copeland's last composition returned to the polytonality of the music he wrote in the 1920s.

Charles and Mary Beard are the last great American historians; Aaron Copland is the last great American composer; Jackson Pollock is the last great American painter. At least a half century separates us from such figures. In our world of marketplace flux, we do not seem to expect that figures will appear who can provide a coherent narrative. Speaking of painting, Arthur Danto saw the abstract expressionists as the last artists who believed they were an avant-garde who were leading their art to a higher stage. Critics like Clement Greenberg had made the distinction between those artists who were part of history because they were making progress and those who were outside of progressive history, those relegated to the dustbin of history, those who were without history. But, for Danto, subsequent painters were unwilling or unable to discriminate, to say this is really art but that art does not fit the criteria; that this art is relevant and that irrelevant.

This denial of progress and boundaries also took place among composers in the 1940s and 1950s. This was the situation Copland lamented when he saw no community, no shared language among the younger musicians. How shocked he must have been when, in the 1940s, John Cage became the most discussed composer.

Cage was born in 1912, and, as a young man, unlike Copland, he chose Schoenberg as his hero and studied with him. By the late 1930s, Cage had worked out his understanding of the world. It was chaos. As a composer he could not create order. His music would not contain the chaos, but express it. He was conscious that his position opposed the entire tradition of music from the Renaissance to the present. For him, we needed to "give up illusions of order, expressions of sentiment, and all the rest of our inherited aesthetic claptrap." He began to present a series of "imaginary landscapes." In one of them, twelve portable radios were played on stage. All were on simultaneously. Each was "played" by two performers, one who constantly changed the volume and tone, the other who constantly changed stations.

Cage explained these imaginary landscapes when he wrote, "I believe that the use of noise to make music will continue and increase until we reach a music produced through the aid of electrical instruments which will make available for musical purposes all the sounds that can be heard." And so he concluded, "I have nothing to say and I am saying it and that is poetry." He saw himself, therefore, as an American innocent who rejected European experience. "I want to be as though newborn," he declared, "knowing nothing about Europe, almost in an original state."[70]

Cage saw his revolutionary position as that of a participant in an avant-garde. Like the New Literary Critics, the logical positivists, the International School of Architecture, and the abstract expressionist painters, he saw himself saving the world from the artificial patterns of nationalism. Composers who were modern nationalists had not liberated the individual from the restrictive patterns of human conventions. They had merely replaced premodern traditions with modern traditions.

Cage, therefore, linked himself with those European composers who, likewise, were trying to liberate musicians from convention. The autonomous individual was, for Cage, the ideal of Western Civilization, not the ideal of a nation that emphasized its boundaries. More quickly, however, than his revolutionary colleagues in painting, architecture, and philosophy, Cage realized that the rejection of the aesthetic authority of Anglo-Protestant bourgeois nationalism was opening a Pandora's box of new aesthetic authorities.

From the 1890s to the 1940s, Yankee musical critics had denied that the African American music that had become the dominant popular music during this half century was legitimate music. But in the 1940s, when the aesthetic authority of Anglo-Protestant bourgeois nationalism was being rejected as an expression of an isolationist culture that needed to be replaced by a new culture of internationalism, many establishment musical critics found it necessary to accept the legitimacy of African American music.

But Cage, as a self-defined leader of an avant-garde, continued to make a distinction between the people with history and those without history. He now described the advocates of spontaneity in music in Europe and America as people with history. They were making progress from an Old World of convention to a New World of musical liberty. One of the things he was aware of in the new set of musical expectations in the 1940s was that some African American musicians were developing a self-conscious theory of musical improvisation.

Charlie "Bird" Parker, Dizzy Gillespie, Thelonious Monk, Bud Powell, and Kenny "Klook" Clarke were creating a pattern of improvisation in jazz that they called "bebop." Cage quickly and vehemently denied that there was any similarity between the spontaneous music of Europe and America and the improvisation of jazz. "Improvisation," Cage insisted, "is generally playing what you know" and it "doesn't lead you into a new experience." He added, "The form of jazz suggests too frequently that people are talking—that is, in succession—like in a panel discussion."[71]

Using an aesthetic of impersonal art similar to that of the New Literary Critics, the logical positivists, the abstract expressionist painters, and the International School of Architecture, Cage denounced the African American composers like Parker and Gillespie for their primitive commitment to tradition and personality. He knew that they were explicitly proud of making variations on African American tradition; that they were proud that they expressed their personal identities in their music; that their music was an expression of the political struggle of black Americans to find justice in a nation that had oppressed them.

All of these affirmations of the personal, social, and political meaning of improvisation proved for Cage that African American composers were not part of his exodus from a lower stage of music to a higher stage where music would be segregated from everything personal, social, and political, and where it would be appreciated only for its intrinsic qualities. It followed, for Cage, that "[m]y notion of how to proceed in a society to bring change is not to attack the thing that is evil, but rather to let it die its own death." To the end of his life, Cage was loyal to the idea of negative revolution first imagined by the bourgeoisie in the Reformation and the Renaissance.[72]

Philosophy

When Richard Hofstadter wrote *Social Darwinism in American Thought, 1860–1915* in the early 1940s, John Dewey was one of its heroes. For Hofstadter, Dewey was one of the major figures among the reform Darwinists who was attacking and defeating the conservative Darwinists during the period from the 1890s to World War I. The crucial issues in this ideological war, as Hofstadter had interpreted them, were between the democratic fraternity that characterized the United States in the generation before the Civil War and the capitalistic environment imported from England after the Civil War. This destructive environment had replaced public interest with self-interest; it had replaced unity with fragmentation; it had replaced the spirituality of the nation with the materialism of the marketplace. But Hofstadter reported in 1944 that Dewey's generation of reform Darwinists had restored the organic unity of the nation and defeated the effort to replace the democracy born of the national landscape with an alien identity. Dewey promised, however, that the revitalized democracy of 1900 represented the dynamic force of an evolutionary nature. The democracy of 1900 would be better than the democracy of 1830, but it would express the organic growth of that original democracy. The American nation would always grow in time, but it would not die in time because it was in harmony with the progressive patterns of evolution. American democracy was the gift of nature; it did not represent cultural conventions that were born in time and died in time. Dewey was committed to the national romance.

But Hofstadter in 1944 shared the view expressed by Charles and Mary Beard in *The Rise of American Civilization* that the participation of the United States in World War I had temporarily stopped the victorious march of democracy. During the war, capitalism had once more gained control of the nation and imposed its fragmentation and materialism on the people. Nevertheless, Hofstadter hoped that the collapse of capitalism in 1929 and the commitment to democracy by Roosevelt's New Deal would once more restore the narrative of history as democratic progress. John Dewey was born in 1859 and was a major public intellectual in the 1930s and 1940s. During those decades he produced a constant stream of essays as well as publishing a book every other year.

I have suggested that Hofstadter's *Social Darwinism* was an extended footnote to the Beards' *The Rise*. But it also was an extended footnote to the narrative that Dewey, a friend of the Beards, had constructed from the 1890s to the 1930s.[73]

When Hofstadter began his implicit rejection of Charles Beard in *The American Political Tradition* of 1948, he also was rejecting Dewey because Dewey, like Beard, had believed that there was a distinction between virtuous private property that worked in the national interest and corrupt private property that worked only for self-interest. After Dewey's death in 1952, Hofstadter in his subsequent writings would explicitly present Dewey as part of a provincial and unusable past. And, indeed, Dewey, like Beard, would be symbolically slain by the generation of which Hofstadter and I were members. The gigantic figure in American philosophy from 1900 into the 1940s, Dewey's writings vanished from academic departments of philosophy in the 1950s. He joined the other victims of my patricidal generation—Charles Beard, F. O. Matthiessen, Thomas Hart Benton, Frank Lloyd Wright. We killed them because all shared the crime of seeing capitalism as the enemy of the American democratic nation. All shared the crime of declaring capitalism a threat to the organic arts that grew out of the national landscape.

During the revolutionary shift of the national foreign policy from isolation to internationalism in the 1940s, one saw an abrupt deemphasis on courses in philosophy departments that traced a line of development from the colonial New England of Jonathan Edwards, to the New England renaissance of Ralph Waldo Emerson, to the New England academic philosophers, Charles Sanders Peirce, William James, and John Dewey. Within philosophy departments, graduate students were now required to focus on analytic philosophy that segregated philosophy from the moral and political concerns that had always been Dewey's central concern. Now in the 1950s the philosophers to be emulated were logical positivists from Europe—Englishmen, Germans, or the members of the Vienna Circle. Rejecting Dewey's belief that there was an organic relation of the true, good, and beautiful, they wanted to save the truth of science from corruption by the emotional and ephemeral values of the good and beautiful. Their analytic philosophy, like physics, would be universal and, therefore, transnational. As in the case of architecture, several of the leaders of American philosophy departments in the 1950s were men who had fled Nazism in the 1930s because they rejected its commitment to an organic national philosophy and, like the Bauhaus architects, wanted their subject matter to speak a universal and rational language.[74]

Ironically Dewey as an undergraduate and graduate student in the 1880s had looked to Germany and Hegel and to England and the neo-Hegelian, T. H. Green, to give him hope that the terrible fragmentation and alienation he believed characterized America after the Civil War could be overcome.

"There is a greater richness and greater variety of insight in Hegel," Dewey declared, "than in any other single systematic philosopher." Hegel promised Dewey that the fragmentation he was experiencing was a temporary phenomenon. A divine spirit was leading humanity toward the organic unity when the true, the good, and the beautiful would be one. Hegel verified for Dewey the vision of bourgeois nationalism that there could be a classless fraternity of citizens who were the children of the national landscape. Embracing this civil religion, Dewey now saw his Protestant heritage as an alien and unwanted presence that made it difficult for citizens to participate in the organic harmony of a national democracy. In a democracy, he wrote, "the distinction between the spiritual and the secular has ceased, and the divine and the human organization are one." With the help of Hegel and Green, Dewey could see the whole in spite of the "sense of divisions and separations that were... borne in upon me as a consequence of a heritage of New England culture, divisions by way of isolation of self from the world, of soul from body, of nature from God." It will be in democracy, Dewey declared, as an organic community, "that the incarnation of God in man... becomes a living, present thing, having its ordinary and natural sense."[75]

As Dewey went into the 1890s he had faith that history was a progressive movement in which the passage of time was redemptive. He was certain that progress was leading toward a democratic community characterized by harmony and prosperity. In this decade, however, he shifted the agency behind progress from God to nature. He became a reform Darwinist. Nature did not, as the Enlightenment had theorized, embody a set of timeless and universal laws. Nature was a living, growing body. Like Frederick Jackson Turner and Charles Beard in the 1890s, Dewey had developed a vision of progressive history as an expression of an evolutionary physical nature. And, like them, he saw human beings suffering from cultural lag because they did not understand that their natural environment was always in motion. Having constructed cultures at one point in the evolutionary process, they tried to preserve them in the face of a new natural environment. Leaving the University of Chicago for Columbia University in 1905, Dewey became the colleague of Beard and James Harvey Robinson and enthusiastically embraced their "New History." Like them, he believed that the major obstacle to progress was ignorance of the dynamism of nature. "One of the main difficulties in understanding the present and apprehending its human possibilities is the persistence of stereotypes of spiritual life which were formed in old and alien cultures." With an "intelligent understanding of past history," he insisted, we have "a lever for moving the present into a certain kind of future." And, he continued, "The study of History can reveal the main instruments in the discoveries, inventions, new modes of life, etc., which have initiated the great epochs of social advance." History can also set before the student "what have been the chief difficulties and obstructions in the way of progress."[76]

Until his generation, Dewey saw those men who had been labeled "philosophers" as major figures in defending outmoded cultures. "It became the work of philosophy," he lamented, "to justify on rational grounds, the spirit, though not the form, of accepted beliefs and traditional customs." But thousands of years of philosophical error were about to end when Dewey's generation embraced the truth that nature was dynamic and no longer attempted to defend an irrelevant past. This conversion would mean the end of wars because, Dewey said, "all that institutions have ever succeeded in doing by their resistance to change has been to dam up social forces until they finally and inevitably manifested themselves in eruptions of great, and usually violent and catastrophic change."[77]

Modernity

In his history of progress Dewey especially celebrated the movement from the medieval to the modern world. Because Dewey by 1900 had put aside the divine within physical nature, he was delighted by modern secularism, which "tended to wean men from preoccupation with the metaphysical and theological" and encouraged them to "turn their minds with newly awakened interest to the joys of nature and this life." Central to this trend toward modern secularism, for Dewey, was the scientific revolution. "Given the free individual, who feels called upon to create a new heaven and a new earth, and who feels himself gifted to perform this task to which he is called," Dewey declared, "the demand for science, for a method of discovery and verifying truth, becomes imperious."[78]

But Dewey felt the need to call for a second scientific revolution because the first had mistakenly defined nature as a fixed set of timeless principles. The first scientific revolution was also in error because it saw discovery as an individual rather than a community experience. Dewey was certain that human nature was inherently social. Throughout history humans had joined together in the creation and re-creation of their communities. Individualism, therefore, was an example of false consciousness. Unfortunately, he declared, people "ascribe all the material benefits of our present civilization to their individualism—as if machines were made by the desire for money profits, not by impersonal science." In the current second scientific revolution, then, scientists would recognize that nature was constantly in evolutionary change. They would recognize that values entered into their decisions about what aspects of nature to study. They would recognize that in participating in this dynamic process, they were creating meaning. They were not passively finding truth, but they were constructing a truth that was also good and beautiful. It was a truth that caused society to move toward a better, more harmonious future. This was the time, Dewey insisted, for a philosophy "which shall be empirically idealistic, proclaiming the essential connection of intelligence with the unachieved future—with possibilities involving a transformation."[79]

By 1900 Dewey was focusing on education as the environment in which it would be possible for children to escape the false consciousness that had been imposed on them by their society. They needed to escape a whole set of dualisms—mind versus body, spirit versus matter, subject versus object, society versus nature, individual versus society. If children were freed from these false traditions, they would discover their biological identities in which all the false dichotomies were resolved into organic unity. They would learn that nature had given them intelligence so they could engage in an experimental relationship with the dynamic processes of nature. Using experimental intelligence, they could learn how best to cooperate with and participate in the processes of evolution. Teachers, therefore, should not impose fixed patterns of knowledge on children. All such patterns always became irrelevant to the future. Instead, creative children needed to be encouraged to work in groups with the experimental method. They needed to learn that education is an active process in which they, working together with their natural environment, create meaning.

It is no wonder, then, that Dewey saw teachers as priests of the civil religion that he believed was replacing all the traditional religions in the world, including all the Protestant denominations in America. "I believe," Dewey declared, "that the teacher is engaged, not simply in the training of individuals, but in the formation of the proper social life. I believe that every teacher should realize the dignity of his calling; that he is a social servant set apart for the maintenance of proper social order and the securing of the right social growth. I believe that in this way the teacher always is the prophet of the true God and the usherer in of the true kingdom of God."[80]

From the 1890s to World War I, Dewey shared the optimism of Charles Beard. He, too, believed that the industrial revolution was an expression of an evolutionary nature. Industrialism shared the plenitude of nature; like nature, it encouraged cooperation among humans; like nature, it taught humans to be forward looking, to be prepared to surrender current social patterns and to participate in the creation of new patterns. Like Charles Beard and Karl Marx, Dewey saw the industrial revolution as an expression of a universal nature. He expected that a universal democracy was emerging. Like Beard and unlike Marx, he expected that the transition from a hierarchical past to a democratic future would be peaceful. He agreed with Beard that there was virtuous private property that worked in the national interest and that the owners of such property would form a democratic revolution and do away with the self-interest of capitalism.

Until 1919, Dewey preached, therefore, the need for a policy of internationalism. "Facts have changed," he declared. "In actuality we are part of the same world as that in which Europe exists and into which America is coming. Industry and commerce have interwoven our destinies. To maintain our older state of mind is to cultivate a dangerous illusion." Like Beard, Dewey expected an end to the long history of human conflict. He expected the end of class hierarchy and self-interest. Self-interested elites had been in control of nations and taken their countries into competition with other countries. This competition had escalated into wars.[81]

This was the imaginative context with which Dewey interpreted the explosion of World War I in Europe in 1914. This catastrophe was, for

WWI

him, the last gasp of the old order. He had expressed his millennial expectations when he wrote, "A tremendous movement is impending when the intelligent forces that have been gathering since the Renaissance and Reformation shall demand free movement, and, by getting their physical leverage in the telegraph and printing press, shall, through free inquiry in a centralized way, demand the authority of all other so-called authorities." Now Dewey saw the possibility that the war would speed the replacement of all the undemocratic authorities that had caused it. His contemporary, the economist Thorstein Veblen, wrote *Imperial Germany and the Industrial Revolution.* For Veblen, as for Beard and Dewey, the industrial revolution was creating a society of democratic producers. In Germany, the most industrial of European nations, the ordinary people had become such democratic producers. But for Veblen, they were ruled by an undemocratic feudal aristocracy. And Veblen hoped the war would sweep away this war-loving elite and liberate the German people, who would instantly become a peaceful fraternity.[82]

In 1915 Dewey published *German Philosophy and Politics.* He agreed with Veblen as he explained how the commitment of German philosophy to unchanging absolutes was expressed in the inflexible hierarchy of German politics. This pattern of German politics inevitably led to war because German leaders believed they were absolutely right and their enemies were absolutely wrong. They could not imagine that the good might be created out of compromise and cooperation. Dewey, like Veblen, hoped that the United States would enter the war and help liberate the German people from the destructive culture lag defended by their leaders.[83]

Dewey had begun to expand his audience beyond the academic world and had commenced writing for the *New Republic* magazine. Here Dewey explained the difference between a just and an unjust war. An unjust war was a defense of the status quo. It tried, as in the case of the German aristocracy, to block the inevitable course of evolution. This antiprogressive war, Dewey declared, was characterized by meaningless violence. But a war fought to facilitate evolutionary progress was just. Progressive war makers engaged in meaningful force, not meaningless violence, as they defeated reactionary enemies. Dewey was so sure of the need for the United States to use progressive force against the reactionary violence of the German aristocracy that he had Randolph Bourne fired from the *New Republic.* Bourne, a young admirer of Dewey's views on education and democracy, did not agree with Dewey that war and democracy were compatible.

As in the case of Beard and Veblen, Dewey was certain that American participation in the war was bringing about the final transition in the United States from partial to full democracy. This would be an easy and peaceful transition because the essential America was democratic and was challenged only by a small capitalist hierarchy. The competition between capitalist self-interest and democratic national interest was ending because "the war, by throwing into relief the public aspect of every social enterprise, has discovered the amount of sabotage which habitually goes on in manipulating property rights to take a private profit out of social needs." But while this peaceful revolution of 1917 was placed in the United States, Dewey celebrated the use of progressive military force in the Russian Revolution. "The rule of the workmen and the soldiers," he declared, "will not be confined to Russia; it will spread through Europe, and this means that the domination of all upper classes . . . is at an end."[84]

When the war ended in 1918, however, Dewey participated in the disillusionment expressed by so many of his academic generation. Sixty years old in 1919, he was a prophet whose prophecies, like those of Beard and Veblen, had failed. World War I had not brought the democratic millennium. Dewey again shared the discovery of so many of his contemporaries that the war had not been fought to further democracy, but to make capitalism more powerful. Like Beard, he now dramatically rejected the vision of an industrial revolution that was an expression of the universal laws of evolutionary nature. He shared Beard's rejection of internationalism. He, too, retreated from a commitment to a redemptive international landscape to a redemptive national landscape. Like Charles and Mary Beard in the 1920s, Dewey no longer saw world history as progressive. He was on the defensive. He now asserted that only by coming to the United States had Europeans been able to escape their undemocratic conventions and achieve the childlike innocence that enabled them to experience nature directly. "The American environment," he was happy to say, "with its constant beginning over again and its comparative lack of traditional background of law and social institutions demands a philosophy of experience." Dewey declared, therefore, that the United States should not join the League of Nations. Americans, he asserted, would be contaminated by associating with nations whose politics were "still conducted upon a basis that was instituted before democracy was heard of." Because Dewey now saw no evolutionary power that could move people from an old to a new world, he rejected any future use of war by the United States. In an unprogressive world all war was violence. There was no distinction between violence and force when one could not facilitate progress from an old to a new world. For the rest of his life, Dewey, like the Beards, was an opponent of internationalism. Like them he hated the possibility that the United States might enter the war that began in Europe in 1939.[85]

Between 1919 and 1939, between the ages of sixty and eighty, Dewey published an amazing number of major books: *Reconstruction in Philosophy* (1920), *Human Nature and Conduct* (1922), *Experience and Nature* (1925), *The Public and Its Problems* (1927), *The Quest for Certainty* (1929), *Individualism: Old and New* (1930), *Philosophy and Civilization* (1931), *Art and Experience* (1934), *A Common Faith* (1935), *Liberalism and Social Action* (1935), *Experience and Education* (1938), and *Logic: The Theory of Inquiry* (1938). I suggest that Dewey's incredible outburst of artistic creativity expressed his terrible fear that his beloved American democracy was being defeated by capitalism. No longer able to believe that industrialism was a symbol of the immediate presence among humans of the productive and cooperative force of evolutionary nature that inevitably must push capitalism into the dustbin of history, Dewey's flow of books seemed to be his attempt to substitute his personal energy for that of industrialism. He would provide the energy that would show Americans how they could escape from the artificial and undemocratic culture of capitalism. He would be the Moses figure leading his American people out of their enslavement by capitalism. He needed to destroy the cultural hegemony of capitalism. He needed to demonstrate how unnatural, undemocratic, and ugly it was. He needed to construct a powerful, persuasive vision of how beautiful an American promised land of evolutionary nature was. He would paint word pictures of how in this promised land the individual would no longer experience fragmentation and alienation. Here the individual would experience the wholeness of a fraternity where every citizen would know and feel the good, the true, and the beautiful.[86]

For Dewey, then, the nation needed "a more manly and more responsible faith in progress than that which we have indulged in the past." His call in *Reconstruction in Philosophy* was for philosophy to become "an instrument for the conscious and deliberate improvement of men's everyday lives." This philosophy would carry over into any inquiry into human and moral subjects the kind of method (the method of observation, theory as hypothesis, and experimental test) by which the understanding of physical nature has been brought to its present point.[87]

When he called for such an activist philosophy to further the course of history as progress, however, Dewey was on the defensive. Another young colleague from the *New Republic,* Walter Lippman, had joined Dewey in calling for the redemptive use of military force in World War I. But when the war failed to make not only the world but even America safe for democracy, Lippman, unlike Dewey and Beard, gave up on American democracy as well as world democracy. The people, for Lippman, as for a growing number of academic political scientists, had proved to be too irrational, too emotional, to make constructive choices. Participation in politics by the masses needed to be discouraged. Informed and rational elites needed to be allowed to make decisions for their nations.

Dewey answered this upsurge of antidemocratic theory in his book of 1922, *Human Nature and Conduct.* Human beings, he insisted, are not by nature irrational. Human nature expresses itself within the patterns of the culture in which individuals find themselves. The pattern of cultural habits in which most individuals found themselves in the 1920s was irrational and self-destructive. There were two kinds of habits, Dewey declared, "routine unintelligent habit and intelligent habit, or art." Art was becoming a more and more important topic for Dewey because he no longer had his pre-1917 belief that the schools were working with the evolutionary forces of industrial democracy. He no longer believed that the habits of our capitalist society were so ephemeral that the school could "see to it that each individual gets an opportunity to escape from the limitations of the social group in which he was born, and to come into living contact with a broader environment." This was why he felt the need to reassert what he had been arguing since 1900 that evolutionary nature was the environment in which individuals could become a democratic fraternity expressing the good, true, and beautiful. This was the message of his 1925 book, *Experience and Nature.* Clearly, for him, the experience of most of his fellow citizens was impoverished by their habits, which were shaped by capitalist domination. But he wanted to remind them that their experience was not authentic. They were not experiencing the reality of nature, an experience that could take them out of their spiritual wasteland and make them whole.[88]

His frustration that the people were not able to escape from the fragmentation of capitalist culture led him back to a critique of that culture in *The Public and Its Problems* (1927). Again he called on his readers not to give up hope that capitalism could be defeated. Once more he evoked a vision of a promised land. "The Great Society was marked by extensive webs of interdependence," he proclaimed. "The Great Community would be marked by a shared understanding of the consequences of this interdependence." Dewey, however, was dismayed that academic philosophers had not left the Ivory Tower to help in the reconstruction of philosophy. Dewey expressed his frustration and anger with his university colleagues in *The Quest for Certainty* (1929). He was aware that a number of English analytical philosophers were becoming influential in American philosophy departments. These foreigners, for Dewey, had given up on the unity of the good, true, and beautiful; they were injecting "an irrelevant philosophy into interpretation of the conclusions of science that the latter thought to eliminate qualities and values of nature."[89]

But capitalism was failing in the Great Crash of 1929, and Dewey regained hope that he could persuade Americans to escape the bad habits of their current society. In *Individualism: Old and New* (1930), he again talked about the old individualism as an example of culture lag. He repeated what he had been writing since the 1890s, that the old individualism had been functional in destroying medieval society, but it had become dysfunctional in an urban-industrial environment where a new individualism, which saw the individual as a cooperative member of the community, was necessary. And in *Philosophy and Civilization* (1931) he again appealed to philosophers to participate in the redemption of their American civilization. Like Charles and Mary Beard, he defined the United States as a civilization separate from and superior to European civilization. When he wrote about the democratic potential of this civilization, he, like the Beards, ignored all other American nations. His exclusion of the Catholic nations of the New World, with their large populations of indigenous and African American peoples, was also an exclusion, as in the case of the Beards, of Native Americans, African Americans, Mexican Americans, and Asian Americans within the United States. When Dewey contrasted American innocence with European power, he, like the Beards, ignored the Euro-American conquest of the Native Americans and Mexican Americans; he ignored the Euro-American enslavement of African Americans. The men who began American civilization programs in Ivy League universities in the 1930s could be inspired by Dewey as well as the Beards.[90]

In 1934 and 1935 Dewey published *Art and Experience* and *A Common Faith.* In *A Common Faith,* which asserted that a civil religion was the necessary basis of American civilization, he wrote about the need to translate a search for spiritual life and the need to have a sense of one's soul into secular terms. All activity, he reminded his readers, is practical. Our need for a spiritual life, therefore, is practical. We instinctively understand the need to escape a sense of fragmentation. Since we live in a fragmented society, we need to have faith that an organic society is possible. "The whole self," he declared, "is an ideal, an imaginative projection." Our definition of soul is the vision of achieving unity out of chaos. But how could he free Americans from the "unreligious attitude" that attributes human achievement to "man in isolation from the world of physical nature and his fellows"?[91]

Dewey, after his loss of faith that industrialism as an expression of evolution would teach men to replace the self-interest of capitalism with the common interest of democracy, turned more and more to art as a transcendent experience. It was only through art that the people could find unity in a national civil religion. This was the message of *Art as Experience.* Since the Renaissance, artists had seen beyond the falsity and corruption of the cultural patterns in which they found themselves. They had seen that if they could achieve a direct experience with nature they could share in nature's organic unity. Their soul would feel the good, the true, the beautiful. But in a capitalist society, works of art were bought by the rich and put in museums. There, as commodities, they could not inspire the viewer to follow the artist into the redemptive heart of nature. And, indeed, artists trapped in the current materialistic society did not appreciate that they could be Moses figures and lead the people out of their bondage. They hoped only to save themselves. Trapped within the capitalist emphasis on self-interest, "Artists find it incumbent," he lamented, "to betake themselves to their work as an isolated means of 'self-expression.' In order not to cater to the trend of economic forces, they often feel obliged to exaggerate their separateness to the point of eccentricity."[92]

Because the average worker worked with machines, he had no sense of himself as an artist. He did not know or appreciate the products that flowed out of the assembly line. Cut off even from the best works of artists that were hidden in museums as trophies of the rich, workers lived in a "cheap and vulgar" environment, characterized by "the movie, jazzed music, the comic strip." They lived with the "experience of an almost incredible paucity, all on the surface."[93]

Dewey's only hope for escape from capitalism, therefore, was through an art that was the antithesis of the popular arts. Only such art that rejected popular culture could imagine "experience in its integrity." Art, Dewey continued, was "experience freed from the forces that impede and confine its development as experience." Since it is so difficult for us to transcend our corrupt and ugly society and see the goodness, truth, and beauty of nature, Dewey now insisted that it was to pure art that "the philosopher must go to understand what experience is."[94]

Dewey, however, like Charles Beard, hoped that the apparent collapse of capitalism after 1929 would recreate the wartime conditions of 1917 and 1918, when they had expected that the needs of wartime planning would force people out of the habits of self-interest and into the habits of national interest. Dewey's other book of 1935, *Liberalism and Social Action,* was an expression of that hope. Dewey had personally responded to the failure of his wartime expectations by engaging in public activities that might stem the reactionary tide of capitalism. He had helped create the New School for Social Research in response to the refusal of most university faculties to participate in public affairs. He was a leader of the American Association of University Professors in defending academic freedom. He was a leader in establishing a League of Industrial Democracy, a League for Independent Political Action, a Farmer-Labor Political Federation, and an American Commonwealth Political Federation. Now in *Liberalism and Social Action,* he spelled out what needed to be done to end the catastrophes of the Great Depression.[95]

After supporting the third-party movement of Robert LaFollette in 1924 and the candidacy of Al Smith in 1928, Dewey had declared himself a socialist in 1932. He called for the socialization of "the forces of production." He wanted the nationalization of banking, public utilities, transportation, communications, and natural resources. He demanded high taxes on the rich in order to redistribute the wealth in the country. He wanted to purge this "idle, luxurious, predatory group." He was horrified by Roosevelt's sweeping victory in 1936 because he believed the Democrats were as much a tool of big business as were the Republicans.

But he wanted no part of the Popular Front because of the influence of the Communist Party. After he had rejected his commitment to internationalism in 1919, he could no longer accept the internationalism of the Russian Revolution. The Communist Party, for him, was a threat to the integrity of the American nation. It did "not speak the American idiom or think in terms relevant to the American situation." Communists claimed that they had a scientific understanding of the forces of evolution and they could predict an inevitable revolutionary defeat of capitalism. Such prophecies, Dewey now declared, were evidence that communism was a false religion committed to "a fanatical and doctrinaire inflexibility." Dewey was so angry at the Communists that, in his late seventies, he agreed to chair, in 1937, the Commission of Inquiry into the charges made against Leon Trotsky in the Moscow Trials.

For Dewey, Roosevelt's reelection in 1936 was evidence that the people had not abandoned capitalism and embraced a democratic socialism. It also appeared to him that an alien communism was the strongest opponent of capitalism within the United States. Defeated as a public intellectual, Dewey felt the need to publish *Logic: The Theory of Inquiry* in 1938. It, too, was an expression of his defensiveness. American academic philosophers were not listening to his arguments that they should abandon talking to themselves and become, like Dewey, public philosophers. They were seduced by foreigners like the Englishman A. J. Ayer and his 1936 book *Language, Truth and Logic.* Ayer warned philosophers to stay away from statements about the good and the beautiful and to focus on truth statements that could be verified. These logical positivists from England, Germany, and Austria, Dewey lamented as late as 1946, had made "the practical neglect of modern philosophers of political and moral subjects into a systematic theoretical denial of the possibility of intelligent concern with them."[96]

When Dewey died in 1952, nothing about the America he had seen in 1900 had changed. Capitalism was still dominant. It still forced most Americans into self-destructive habits so that they did not even imagine a democratic community where they could experience organic unity. Distracted by a set of false popular arts, Americans did not see that in true art "one confronted experience as a complex yet unified whole steeped in values." Perhaps philosophers in the United States were choosing to make logical positivism the dominant academic philosophy in the 1940s because, like Dewey, they saw a capitalist culture in which the good and the beautiful were replaced by the evil and the ugly. Perhaps if they could not save the good and the beautiful from the corruption of capitalism, they could at least segregate the true from the chaos of the marketplace. The New Literary Critics had hoped to create an academic monastery that would protect a saving remnant from the new dark ages. Perhaps this was the goal of the logical positivists after men like Dewey had tried and failed for a half century to lead the people out of their bondage to capitalist culture.[97]

The architects who were exiles from Europe hoped that in the United States they could establish an architecture based on the universal laws of science, an architecture that would transcend the constant flux of ephemeral styles. But this public world of architecture, like the public worlds of painting and composing, could not defend the boundaries of a pure and timeless art from the flux of popular culture. But philosophers who had fled from the demands of fascism for a philosophy that was an organic expression of a national people were able to shape philosophy departments in the United States into monasteries where philosophy as an expression of the universal and timeless truths of science could be protected from the surrounding flux. The price for philosophy departments, however, was their increasing isolation from the major debates in the larger culture. For most academic philosophers, the debates about the identity and role of nations in the international marketplace were irrelevant, as were the debates about the identities of the variety of cultures within each nation. They also have ignored the issues of the relationship of the international marketplace constructed by capitalists to issues of social justice and to the health of the environment. As Dewey feared, academic philosophy has been very successful in being academic.

CHAPTER SEVEN

The Disintegration of National Boundaries: Literary Criticism in the Late Twentieth Century

Having joined the history department at Minnesota in 1952, I was fortunate to have the opportunity to participate in the American Studies Program. I believe this participation was crucial to the development of my focus on the role of a concept of space for the dominant culture. In contact with colleagues and graduate students who were interested in painting, architecture, music, and philosophy, I was able to theorize how the parallel crises in these separate academic disciplines were interrelated with the crisis of the national landscape in the 1940s and 1950s. I was also fortunate to be in such close contact with the men who taught American literature.

As I pointed out in chapter 3, teachers of American history who had been initiated into the paradigm of the national landscape in the 1930s had this aesthetic authority shattered in the 1940s and 1950s. But the response of my colleagues in American history to the death of the national landscape differed from that of my colleagues in American literature. Survey courses on the history of the United States did implicitly make American exceptionalism into a sacred, whose boundaries should be guarded. But the debates among historians about American exceptionalism did not, in my experience, achieve either the focus or the intensity of the debates among literary critics. I did not feel the same level of distress about the loss of the national landscape among my colleagues in history that I felt among my colleagues in American literature.

I believe that Bill Readings, in *The University in Ruins* (1996), is able to explain why the death of the national landscape had a more dramatic impact in American literature than in American history, as well as in American art, architecture, and philosophy. Readings has argued that the purpose of higher education during the period of bourgeois nationalism was to create refined citizens. They were to be initiated into the civil religion of the nation. Because this was essentially a spiritual education, it became the responsibility of literature, more than any other discipline, to replace theology at the center of higher education and reveal the beauty, goodness, and truth of the nation—to present its organic wholeness. Using materials drawn primarily from the experience of German nationalism, Readings proposed that this central role of literature and thus the deep significance of a literary canon were to be found in all modern nations. The dominant metaphor of these new national canons was purity. The purity of a nation's literature was to be defended against the influence of other national literatures. Since the nation was masculine, its body politic consisting of a fraternity of citizens, literature written by women needed to be excluded. The purity of the national canon also needed to be protected from literatures that expressed local cultures within the nation's political boundaries. Although modern nations were imagined as having a uniform national culture, there were anomalies of particular local cultures or enclaves of resident aliens. The internal boundaries of the authentic nation needed to be zealously guarded against contamination by these others, these people who existed outside the uniform and sacred national culture.[1]

Readings has proposed that the larger responsibility of modern universities to educate citizens and the particular role of literature to accomplish this task began to end with World War II. The civil religion of the nation was being replaced by the higher sacred of the international marketplace. Proponents of the culture of international capitalism wanted to do away with patterns of isolation based on visions of national purity. And they could tolerate a variety of local cultures throughout the world as long as they were not enemies of capitalism. Teaching impersonal standards of excellence, objectivity and cost-effectiveness, universities were now preparing students to transcend the national homeland and be capable of successful circulation in the world marketplace.

One can observe this change by comparing the positions of Parrington and Matthiessen with those of the symbol-myth school and the New Literary Critics. Parrington and Matthiessen had believed that only literature could redeem the nation's soul. They did not see an active threat to

role of lit

This is the answer.

Old threat

the purity of the canon from the local cultures, which contradicted the ideal of a uniform national culture. The major enemy, for them, was international capitalism, which threatened to replace the spirituality of the nation with materialism and the uniformity of national culture with social fragmentation. For the symbol-myth school and the New Literary Critics, those fears had been fulfilled. The only hope for the symbol-myth group was to segregate the sacred texts of the national canon within the university since the civil religion of a uniform national culture had been destroyed by capitalist barbarians. For the New Literary Critics the university also would be the monastic refuge for a trans-Atlantic body of sacred texts. In the pure environment of the Ivory Tower, a saving remnant of faithful professors hoped to convert enough undergraduates so that they, too, would want to become members of the academic cult who found their meaning in life by celebrating that body of sacred texts that expressed the organic unity of the good, true, and beautiful that once characterized nations before their defeat by international capitalism. Literature could not redeem citizens who had become capitalists.

But as graduate students in the 1950s and 1960s began to achieve academic power in the 1970s and 1980s, they questioned the relevance of a canon that no longer had the authority to represent a nation's people. Living in the culture of the international marketplace, they did not see a homogeneous American (or English, or French, or German) people. They did not see a national landscape that had given birth to the nation's people. What they saw was a canon whose texts had been enshrined in Matthiessen's *American Renaissance* and that was being defended by the established professors in English departments as a means for their personal secular salvation.

One of these younger scholars was Russell Reising, whose book, *The Unusable Past: Theory and the Study of American Literature*, was published in 1986. When he looked at America, Reising did not see the country imagined by bourgeois nationalists. He did not see a uniform culture whose boundaries coincided with the political boundaries of the nation. He did not see the people as the fraternity of Anglo-Protestant citizens of the pre–Civil War era. When he looked at the American past, he saw writers who were women and he saw writers who were African Americans. He saw particulars, rather than a universal national. The aesthetic authority that he was using to decide what writing produced within the United States ought to be taught in courses in American literature was dramatically different from that used by Matthiessen to validate certain canonical works. Matthiessen had seen the literature written by anyone other than male Anglo-Protestants in the Northeast as ephemeral particulars that were outside the meaning found in the universal national. But for Reising, the concept "universal national" held no meaning. He, therefore, found no good reason to exclude books written by Anglo-Protestant women and by African Americans from courses on American literature. He did not believe that he had a responsibility to guard the purity of Matthiessen's canon.[2]

When Reising analyzed the writings of eleven men who, for him, were the most influential literary critics from the 1940s to the 1970s, he found their critical theories unusable because they did not deal with the particulars of American literary expression. F. O. Matthiessen, Charles Feidelson Jr., Richard Poirier, Perry Miller, Yvor Winters, Richard Chase, Leslie Fiedler, Sacvan Bercovitch, Lionel Trilling, R. W. B. Lewis, and Leo Marx were irrelevant to future literary critics because "these theorists project[ed] a vision of American literature as an isolated body of texts, estranged from, or only vaguely related to American social or material reality." They accomplish this isolation, according to Reising, when they "devalue, often suppress, writers and varieties of writing that do reflect interest in a historically determined social milieu" and "they either deemphasize what social references exist in the writers and works they study, or they turn them into non- or even anti-referential elements."[3]

Reising was aware that Gene Wise, in his book, *American Historical Explanations* (1973), had used Thomas Kuhn's model of paradigm revolution in *The Structure of Scientific Revolutions* to clarify the rejection of Charles Beard and Vernon Louis Parrington in the 1940s by a group of scholars whom Wise called "counter-Progressives." He also was aware that Grant Webster had borrowed Kuhn's model for his book, *The Republic of Letters: A History of Postwar American Literary Opinion* (1979), to discuss the sudden triumph of the New Literary Critics. But Reising felt uncomfortable placing his analysis within such a formal structure. Perhaps this was because he chose not to discuss in detail how his group of literary critics differed from the dominant paradigm of the 1930s.

But all the elements of Kuhn's model are present in Reising's analysis. He saw his group rejecting the social realism of Parrington. He did not ask, however, what specific historical realities were important to Parrington. He saw Lionel Trilling as leading the attack on Parrington, but he did not ask what Trilling had defined as reality in the 1930s. Trilling's conversion from social realism, therefore, is not important to Reising. Instead he starts with the Trilling who was attacking Parrington. In his collection of essays written in the 1940s and published in 1950 in book form as *The Liberal Imagination,* Trilling, according to Reising, "inverts the nationalist scheme of values, in each case turning literary and critical attention away from public, social issues, toward private issues of individual consciousness." Reising quoted Trilling's distinction between American novels and European novels: "American fiction," Trilling wrote, "has nothing to show like the huge, swarming, substantial population of the European novel, the substantiality of which is precisely the product of class existence."[4]

But Trilling does fit Kuhn's model precisely because he, like so many of the men discussed by Reising, had had a conversion experience. In 1939 Trilling had written, "There is a superb thickness about the feel of American life." It has been my argument that the conversions taking place in the 1940s were related to the symbolic defeat of both bourgeois nationalism and Marxism by the new culture of international capitalism. If one accepted Trilling's argument that there are no classes in the United States, one could avoid reporting that a capitalist class had triumphed during World War II. And Trilling was part of a group in the 1930s, now identified as the New York Intellectuals, who had been strongly influenced by Marxism. Reising, then, was not interested in explaining what he recognized as an intense, perhaps desperate, desire on the part of the group he was studying to separate the literature of bourgeois nationalism, the canon of Matthiessen's *American Renaissance,* from the dominant social reality of capitalism. He pointed to Richard Poirier's *A World Elsewhere: The Place of Style in American Literature* (1966) as the most eloquent expression of the desire. He quoted Poirier as saying that "style is always bound to struggle against immitigable pressures of place, time, and nature and against literary form as a product of these." When he appealed to Emerson's transcendentalism as a model for escaping the complexities of everyday life, Poirier, however, did not have, at that time, the memory of Emerson's national landscape, which provided Henry Nash Smith, R. W. B. Lewis, and Leo Marx with a spiritual alternative to the power and ugliness of capitalism. Each author, for Poirier, had to create his own personal refuge; each had to weave a beautiful cocoon of style in which to find shelter from social reality.[5]

Like the New Critics and the symbol-myth school, Reising's authors were trying to salvage liberty from the disappearing hope for a national democracy of equality and fraternity. Like the liberty proclaimed by the capitalists they hated, it was ironically only for a privileged few.

Reising, in contrast, was like Parrington and Matthiessen, who wanted literature to represent society, but Reising wanted a more inclusive society. He noticed, then, that all the major postwar literary critics were white males and that they excluded the novels of white women and African Americans from the canon. But Reising was not self-conscious in 1986 that the aesthetic authority for defining the American people as male, white Anglo-Protestants from the Northeast had been shattered in the 1940s. He was not explicit that this changing style of defining who the people were had been the inspiration for his book. Perhaps he was not persuaded of Kuhn's model of paradigmatic revolution because he accepted the argument of the group of theorists he was studying that the shift of literary authority in the 1940s from social realism to the interior structure of the novel was one merely of literary style. Reising, like Lionel Trilling, would not associate a dramatic shift in literary authority with a dramatic shift in politics.

Reising, then, in the 1980s, like Lionel Trilling in the 1940s, did not call attention to the fact that in the 1930s the dominant group of male Anglo-Protestants defined Jews as outside the fraternity of the nation's citizens. Ivy League universities in the 1930s had public quotas on the number of Jews who would be admitted as freshmen. And Jews were discouraged from teaching American literature and American history, those sacred expressions of the nation's civil religion. It did not seem significant to Reising, therefore, that the white males of the literary canon in the 1950s—Emerson, Thoreau, Melville, Hawthorne, Whitman, Twain, Henry James, and Faulkner—were all Protestants but that many of the major white male literary critics of the 1950s, starting with Trilling, were Jews.[6]

The Nazi commitment to purge Jews as aliens who corrupted the German body politic brought an end by 1945 to the legitimacy and respectability of anti-Semitism in England, France, and the United States, as well as many other Western democracies where Jews had been considered outside the fraternity of the people. The sudden willingness of Ivy League universities at the end of World War II to recruit Jews to teach American history and literature was a dramatic sign that the aesthetic boundaries of the bourgeois nation as a homogeneous people with a uniform culture could no longer be legitimately defended. The revolutionary shift of aesthetic authority from the sacred space of the bourgeois nation to the sacred space of the international marketplace is most powerfully expressed in the immigration policy of the United States. Since the 1790s Congress had legislated that only white people could be naturalized as citizens. In 1882 Congress legislated that Chinese could no longer enter the country as resident aliens. When the failed internationalism of World War I was followed by a resurgence of nationalism, Congress in the 1920s ended almost all immigration from southern and eastern Europe, which meant the immigrations of Catholics and Jews. It also ended the immigration of Japanese resident aliens. Congressional policy coming into the 1940s was intended to protect the purity, the racial integrity of Anglo-Protestants, the authentic American people. But the new aesthetic authority of international capitalism defined space as a marketplace in which all the cultures of the world could (must) participate. Beginning in the 1950s, Congress began to lift restrictions on Chinese immigration. The Immigration Act of 1964 made it possible for people of color to become citizens, and the country began to experience large-scale immigration from Asia and Latin America.

It is understandable, although ironic, that many male Jews, the first group of unclean outsiders (after the southern male Anglo-Protestant New Critics) to become part of the academic establishment, chose to obscure the dramatic shift from the extreme racial definition of the American people as Anglo-Protestants in the 1920s and 1930s to the new pluralistic definition of Americans that began during World War II. A number of these male Jews became the leaders of the consensus school of historical interpretation that was challenging the conflict school of the 1930s. These men included Lionel Trilling and his *The Liberal Imagination* (1950), Daniel Boorstin and his *The Genius of American Politics* (1953), Richard Hofstadter and his *The Age of Reform* (1955), Louis Hartz and his *The Liberal Tradition in America* (1955), Leslie Fiedler and his *An End to Innocence* (1955), and Daniel Bell and his *The End of Ideology: On the Exhaustion of Political Ideas in the Fifties* (1961). These men wanted to believe that the tradition of nationalism in the United States did not share a commitment to racial exclusiveness with Nazi Germany. Another possible reason that these men chose to argue that American history was marked by consensus and continuity rather than conflict and change was a desire to minimize the significance of Marxism in the 1930s, a Marxism that many of them had found persuasive during that decade. It was clear by 1948 that consensus, the enforced dominant cultural paradigm of cold war America, defined Marxists and possible Marxist sympathizers as the most dangerous others, the most dangerous un-Americans within the nation's boundaries. Escaping from their definition as racial aliens by bourgeois nationalism in the 1930s, these men, as new insiders, did not want to be pushed outside of the circle of national respectability because of their Marxist pasts. Stressing the constant of consensus, they obscured both the magnitude of the conflict between American bourgeois nationalism and international capitalism and the intensity of the conflict between a variety of American Marxisms and international capitalism.[7]

When male Jews suddenly became leading interpreters of American literature, they, therefore, had two important reasons to preserve the canonical writers enshrined in Matthiessen's *American Renaissance.* Keeping the canon intact would mask the revolutionary changes in national identity taking place in the 1940s. Keeping the canon intact would also preserve the sacred texts that Matthiessen had seen as a refuge from capitalism. Losing the Marxist hope for a society of wholeness in which the good, true, and beautiful could be one in contrast to the fragmentation, ugliness, and exploitation of capitalism, men like Lionel Trilling could share the hope of the New Literary Critics and the symbol-myth school that those canonical works would be a world elsewhere, where one escaped corrupt society. And, as in the case of these other critics, the canon expressed their commitment to fraternity. This defense of the canon by the male Jews also fits the argument of Jonathan Freedman in *The Temple of Culture: Assimilation and Anti-Semitism in Literary Anglo-America* (2000) that many Jewish intellectuals throughout the first decades of the twentieth century had venerated a high culture dramatically segregated from popular culture.[8]

But, of course, as Reising's book indicated, one could not sustain a national canon on the basis of personal preference. These literary critics were not able to argue that the canon represented a homogeneous and exclusive national culture. They would not argue that it expressed the conflict between national democracy and international capitalism. Their only aesthetic authority was an appeal to a long but now rootless tradition, one without social context and social meaning. It was this fragile,

Challenge

even ephemeral, tradition that European American women and male and female African American literary critics began to attack by the 1970s. These two formerly excluded groups were the first to begin the decon-struction of the canon that represented only white, Protestant males.

The new and official pluralism that was a central part of the shift from isolation and bourgeois nationalism to internationalism and the culture of international capitalism meant that the exclusive democracy of the 1830s was no longer legitimate. All of the groups excluded in Matthiessen's vision of American democracy—American Indians, African Americans, Mexican Americans, Anglo-Protestant women—needed to be seen now as citizens who were symbolically equal to male Anglo-Protestants. As the men who controlled English departments in the 1930s could no longer keep white southern men and then male Jews from teaching American literature, they also could not justify the continued exclusion of European American women and African Americans. This was com-parable to the way in which President Truman ordered the desegrega-tion of the armed services in 1947 and the way that the owners of major league baseball teams felt, at the same time, the need to desegregate the national game. Academic gatekeepers felt compelled to desegregate their disciplines. In challenging the authority of the canon keepers of the 1970s, Reising had drawn on the increasingly important criticism being written by European American women who now were teaching American literature at major universities. They, unlike the southern crit-ics and the male Jews, had no compelling reason to see the literary canon as a body of sacred texts. They had many good reasons to find the male Anglo-Protestant canon oppressive.

Women

In her essay "Women, Literature, and National Brotherhood" (1991), ✷ Mary Louise Pratt discussed how the development of modern bour-geois nations threatened the feminism that existed in Europe and the European colonies at the end of the eighteenth century. Building on Anderson's *Imagined Communities,* Pratt emphasized how modern na-tions were officially constructed in masculine terms, as their peoples were imagined to be deep fraternities of male citizens. Within the mod-ern nation, then, only citizens were imagined as having agency. Women, who were outside the public realm of citizenship, could not be imagined by dominant males as being agents within the nation's history. They could not be imagined as participating in the nation's public life. The only place for bourgeois women was the home. In this private sphere

only citizens been seen as agents

their function was to be republican mothers who would produce future generations of citizens. Feminists in the Atlantic world resisted their segregation from the public sphere; they were not successful. But some bourgeois women did manage to retain their participation in the print culture that had been expanding rapidly at the end of the eighteenth century.[9]

This meant, for Pratt, that, although bourgeois women lacked

> political rights, they remained able to assert themselves legitimately in national print networks, engage with national forms of self-understanding, maintain their own political and discursive agenda, and express demands on the system that denied them full status as citizens. To a great extent, this entitlement was achieved in class privilege, which the women of letters shared with their male counterparts. One might suggest four elements, then, that in part came to define the conflicted space of women's writing and women's citizenship: access to print culture (class privilege); denial of access to public power (gender oppression); access to domesticity (gender privilege); and confinement to domesticity (gender oppression).

In the United States it was middle-class, Anglo-Protestant women who experienced this conflicted situation in the nineteenth century. Their novels were published and outsold those of the nineteenth-century men who were enshrined in the canon defended by Reising's group of literary critics in the 1970s. Pratt's hypothesis about this double experience of bourgeois women in the nineteenth century helps explain why some of the leaders of the generation of women who became major literary critics in the 1970s, such as Nina Baym and Jane Tompkins, focused on the restrictions placed on nineteenth-century women novelists, but ignored their important privileges.[10]

In 1981 Nina Baym published an essay, "Melodramas of Beset Manhood: How Theories of American Fiction Exclude Women Authors." She had recently written a study of nineteenth-century women authors, *Women's Fiction: A Guide to Novels by and about Women, 1820–1870* (1979). Now her explicit purpose was to analyze the value judgments used by male literary critics to exclude women novelists from the canon. She wanted her readers to see that current male critics were working with a set of arbitrary and often contradictory conventions. Implicitly she was desacralizing the canon she had been taught to revere as a graduate student. Writing before the publication of Benedict Anderson's *Imagined*

Communities, Baym was trying to understand why women had been excluded from the canon. Unlike Pratt, she did not have the language of public and private spheres and the way bourgeois nationalism limited citizenship to men. She began by pointing out that during the 1970s, her first decade of college teaching, no women novelists were included in the canon. She then proposed that the major reason for this exclusion was nationalism. Male literary critics, she continued, insisted that the American novel be totally independent from the English novel. In her own graduate education she had been confronted with books by male literary critics that assumed this autonomy—*American Renaissance, The Romance in America, Form and Fable in American Fiction, The American Adam, The American Novel and Its Tradition.* Male literary critics, she argued, made this distinction by insisting that English novels dealt with society while American novels (always written by men) dealt with a male individual who stood outside of society. She believed that the following quotation from Joel Porte symbolized this position: "Students of American literature," Porte wrote, "have provided a solid theoretical basis for establishing that the rise and growth of fiction in this country is dominated by our authors' conscious adherence to a tradition of nonrealistic romances sharply at variance with the broadly novelistic mainstream of English writing."[11]

This argument, she pointed out, meant that most novelists writing in the United States since 1789 were defined as un-American. Any American novelist writing about transnational universals or internal particulars was not writing an American novel. Identifying Lionel Trilling as the most important spokesman for American literary exceptionalism, she asked what gave Trilling the authority to define Theodore Dreiser as an un-American novelist or Vernon Louis Parrington as an un-American literary critic. Trilling's position, she decided, had authority "because it represented a long-standing tradition among male literary critics to find canonical writers" who were members of "the dominant middle-class white Anglo-Saxon group" and who experienced a "modest alienation" from their group. "I will," she wrote, "call the literature they produced, which Trilling assesses so highly, a consensus criticism of the consensus."[12]

When Bill Readings discussed in *The University in Ruins* how bourgeois nationalists privileged the novel as the most important art form in the education of the ideal citizen, he argued that young men studying their nation's canonical literature would be taught to see the gap between the ideal and immediate reality. All bourgeois literary criticism, for him, assumed a tension between the ideal and the practice of citizenship. Pratt, in her essay, pointed out that the ideal citizen was sovereign and fraternal and that women threatened both male sovereignty and citizenship. They threatened the practice of citizenship. These characteristics were an implicit part of Baym's explanation for the tradition of misogyny that she found among male literary critics. These men, for her, were working with a "myth" that "[n]arrates a confrontation of the American individual, the pure American self divorced from specific social circumstances, with the promise offered by the ideal of America." This ideal was symbolized by a feminine national landscape that promised to be a passive environment in which a man "will be able to achieve complete self-definition." At this point Baym was explicitly borrowing from Annette Kolodny's book, *The Lay of the Land* (1975), which desacralized the myths that Henry Nash Smith, R. W. B. Lewis, and Leo Marx had found to be the essence of American national identity. They, of course, had not been self-conscious that these were myths that gave men absolute power over the feminine. But Kolodny had analyzed their vision of a virgin land as a male fantasy.[13]

For Baym, however, as for Kolodny, men in their everyday lives experienced women as mothers, sisters, wives, and daughters. These women, unlike those in the male fantasies, had agency that frustrated the male desire for omnipotence. From the perspective of the male canonical novelists, then, these women were "entrappers and domesticators." In this narrow, exclusive tradition of a solitary male seeking perfection, which white male literary critics in the 1970s were insisting was the only valid American literary tradition, "there is no place for the woman author," Baym declared. "Her roles in the drama of creation are those allotted to her in a male melodrama: either she is to be silent, like nature; or she is the creator of conventional works, the spokesperson of society."[14]

Baym believed this tradition of American literary exceptionalism was bankrupt because she perceived that the boundaries that were supposed to separate the American nation from her mother country, England, were weakening. Male literary critics stressed that the English novel dealt with society and did not celebrate the sovereign male individual. If middle-class, white, Anglo-Saxon women in the nineteenth century wrote social novels celebrating the family and not the sovereign male individual, their novels were European and not American. According to American male literary critics, Englishmen were the sons of their mothers, while American men were self-made. They were free from both mothers and fathers. They were American Adams. But if we assume that in all bourgeois families sons are to become independent of both mothers and fathers, that to be bourgeois is to be self-made, it is not surprising that Baym found two recent books about English novels, Harold Bloom's *Anxiety of Influence* and Edward Said's *Beginnings,* that implicitly denied the male tradition of American literary exceptionalism. Both Bloom and Said, she reported, found the major tradition among male English novelists to be the effort of a young man to become self-made. Focusing on this English national tradition, Bloom and Said did not find it worthwhile to analyze novels written by English women. Baym had achieved the ironic authority of being able to say that American canonical texts were linked to the mother country, even as male critics had found the novels of American women to be part of a trans-Atlantic community. The implicit logic of her argument was that these men share a transnational bourgeois culture.[15]

deconstruct

When Jane Tompkins published *Sensational Designs: The Cultural Work of American Fiction* in 1985, she joined Annette Kolodny and Nina Baym as part of the first generation of European American women literary critics who were successfully challenging the male canon that they, as graduate students, had been asked to accept. Not aware of the growing scholarship on nationalism, Tompkins, like Baym, was engaging in an implicit rather than an explicit deconstruction of the link between the canon and nationalism. At the same time Anderson was arguing that modern nations had been constructed by men of a particular class at particular times, Tompkins was arguing that the American canon had been constructed by men of a particular class at a particular time. As Anderson was stripping the nation of its illusion of immortality, Tompkins, like Kolodny and Baym, was stripping the canon of its claim to be eternal. They disrobed the male canonical figures to disclose these figures' mortality.[16]

Nina Baym had been hesitant in her essay to use the term "universal national," which Anderson's analysis was to make part of standard vocabulary about modern nationalism. Tompkins also did not explicitly use the term, but her attempt to deconstruct the existing canon depended on her implicit rejection of the canon as representative of a universal national. Like Baym, Tompkins found that a universal national that did not include women was a contradiction of terms. "I am," she declared, "a woman in a field dominated by male scholars" and therefore "I have been particularly sensitive to the absence of women's writing from the standard American literature curriculum." Her historical strategy was to persuade her readers that novels "should be studied not because they manage to escape the limitations of their particular time and place, but because they offer powerful examples of the way a culture thinks about itself, articulating and proposing solutions for the problems that shape a particular historical moment." Implicitly, like Baym, she was rejecting state-of-nature anthropology and was using cultural anthropology.[17]

In her first chapter she examined the construction of Nathaniel Hawthorne's position as one of the major canonical writers. "The reputation of a classic author arises," she insisted, "not from the 'intrinsic merit' of his or her work, but rather from the complex of circumstances that make texts visible initially and then maintain them in their preeminent position." Hawthorne was given his reputation, according to Tompkins, by "the circle of well-educated, well-connected men and women" who controlled New England's cultural life at mid-century. This elite wanted to honor a novelist who was "spiritually and culturally suited to raise the level of popular taste and to civilize and refine the impulses of the multitude." Benedict Anderson's argument in *Imagined Communities* would be in agreement with Tompkins that it was elites, not the masses, who were constructing the modern nation. But Tompkins, unlike Baym and Anderson, did not see how novelists, like Hawthorne, were chosen by elites to represent a universal national that deliberately excluded the majority of the people dwelling in the United States and that this was the pattern of exclusion in other modern nations.[18]

After analyzing in depth the novels of Charles Brockden Brown, James Fenimore Cooper, Harriet Beecher Stowe, and Susan Warner—writers who were excluded from the canon in the 1970s—Tompkins declared that she believed these writers were more important for understanding American culture than the canonical writers were. "It is the notion of literary texts as doing work, expressing and shaping the social context that produced them," she insisted, "that I wish to substitute finally for the critical perspective that sees them as attempts to achieve a timeless, universal ideal of truth and formal coherence."[19]

Perhaps it was because Tompkins was not in awe of the vision of the modern nation as characterized by a homogeneous culture theoretically shared by all the citizens—a universal national—that she could not imagine that the cultural work of canonical texts was to create the illusion of a uniform fraternity that transcended the particulars of region, class, race, ethnicity, and gender—a uniform fraternity that, like the nation, was timeless. Unlike Kolodny and Baym, who believed that canonical novels shared a common mythology and a common Adamic persona, Tompkins saw the noncanonical novels she was celebrating as valuable because they, unlike those of the canon, dealt with stereotypes. "A novel's impact on the culture at large depends not on its escape from the formulaic and derivative," she declared, "but on its tapping into a storehouse of commonly held assumptions, reproducing what is already there in a typical and familiar form."[20]

Nina Baym, in her essays and books, joined Tompkins in arguing that the best-selling novels written by women during the nineteenth century deserved serious scholarly analysis. Both, however, seemed to ignore Pratt's theoretical position that nineteenth-century women writers were both oppressed and privileged. In the 1980s neither Tompkins nor Baym stressed that the middle-class, Anglo-Protestant women novelists accepted their world as hegemonic, as natural and inevitable, as the norm from which all other Americans of different classes, ethnicity, and race were to be judged and found wanting. But literary critics who were African American women did point out this implicit hierarchy. And soon lesbian literary critics would point out that Tompkins and Baym also accepted the inevitability, the naturalness of the bourgeois heterosexual family. It is not surprising, then, that in an essay in 1998, "Manifest Domesticity," Amy Kaplan focused attention on how Anglo-American women writers in the nineteenth century worked to sustain Anglo-American cultural hegemony at home and abroad.[21]

It is important, then, to notice that one of the first major African American literary critics, Houston A. Baker Jr., celebrated the particular nature of African American literature as Tompkins was celebrating the particular nature of literature written by Anglo-American women in the nineteenth century. In his book of 1984, *Blues, Ideology, and Afro-American Literature: A Vernacular Theory,* Baker explicitly rejected the demand of Matthiessen and the generation of male literary critics in the 1950s and 1960s for a literature that represented a universal national.[22]

Because the collapse of the aesthetic authority of national landscapes was a transnational experience in the 1940s, a group of French intellectuals immediately after World War II saw a relationship between the national landscape as an expression of timeless natural law and the faith of the Enlightenment in the existence of universal natural law. They then discovered that the German philosopher Friedrich Nietzsche had challenged the authority of the Enlightenment in the late nineteenth century. Now, in the 1980s, as many American literary critics came to doubt the existence of timeless universals, they discovered the writing of these French theorists.

Tompkins, therefore, was aware that her scholarship was built on the assumptions that a number of social realities exist and that there were no extrahuman, no natural, no rational standards that could be used to justify the argument that some social realities were natural and rational and some were unnatural and irrational. To justify her scholarly attention to noncanonical texts she appealed, then, to the authority of the French intellectuals and some of their American disciples. "The critical perspective that has brought into focus the issues outlined here," she wrote, "stems from the theoretical writings of structuralist and poststructuralist thinkers: Lévi-Strauss, Derrida, and Foucault; Stanley Fish, Edward Said, and Barbara Herrnstein Smith." In particular she thanked Stanley Fish, who had become, perhaps, the most influential American literary critic as he argued that we use language to create our concepts of reality, knowledge, and truth. For Fish, we always live within the contingency of language. He called this verbally constructed world "rhetorical." He insisted that literary critics must always call this rhetorical reality into question, but their criticism must not be "performed in the service of something beyond rhetoric. Derridean deconstruction does not uncover the operations of rhetoric in order to reach the truth; rather it continually uncovers the truth of rhetorical operations, the truth that all operations, including the operations of deconstruction itself, are rhetorical." Breaking the boundaries of the canon celebrated by Matthiessen, these women scholars continued, however, to be constrained by disciplinary boundaries. They were not aware that their criticisms of a canon defined exclusively by males were interrelated with a transatlantic crisis of bourgeois nationalism. They did not see how their debates about theory were interrelated with the decreasing persuasiveness of state-of-nature anthropology and the increasing persuasiveness of cultural anthropology. They did not see how powerfully the traditional distinction between art and politics was undermined by cultural anthropology.[23]

The 1980s, then, were the decade when the ramifications of the collapse of the bourgeois nation as a timeless reality that had replaced the timeful traditions of prenational cultures led in the United States as in other bourgeois nations to a self-conscious and widespread crisis about how we can know what is true. Paul Jay in his book, *Contingency Blues* (1997), wanted to refute the argument of literary critics such as Giles Gunn in *The Culture of Criticism and The Criticism of Culture* (1987) and *Thinking across the American Grain: Ideology, Intellect, and the New Pragmatism* (1992) and Richard Poirier in *The Renewal of Literature* (1987) and *Poetry and Pragmatism* (1992) that this "legitimation crisis" was caused by the recent and unfortunate influence of foreign, especially French, philosophers. But, as with Baym and Tompkins, the scholarly resources Jay drew upon for his argument were largely those from within the discipline of literary criticism. In developing his arguments, he, therefore, did not draw upon Benedict Anderson's *Imagined Communities* or the more recent *Rescuing History from the Nation* by Prasinjit Duara. But he did recognize what they, especially Duara, make clear—that people in modern nations are torn apart by their commitment to their nations as timeless space and their commitment to endless progress.[24]

Jay began his book with an analysis of Emerson, who saw a contingent world where current patterns must and should be replaced by better patterns. This was Emerson the pragmatist, who believed in the inevitability of progress. But, for Emerson, the American nation as a new creation that had replaced the Old World of Europe must never be replaced by another new order. This, for Jay, was Emerson the transcendentalist. America was a sacred space; its civil religion must be an eternal orthodoxy. Jay, then, traced this contradictory pattern down through John Dewey. He argued that Dewey also was both a pragmatist who believed in ceaseless progress and a transcendentalist who wanted the United States to be an eternal entity. Jay, however, did not take into account that Dewey and his transcendental nationalism were symbolically destroyed in the 1940s. This had left only the pragmatic world of constant change, a world of endless contingency. But until the 1980s, the survival of Matthiessen's transcendental canon in literary criticism obscured the revolution of the 1940s, and it was a revolution that Jay did not stress in 1997.

But Jay did believe that the contradiction between timeless truth and constant supercession was a characteristic of what he called "modernity" and that the current crisis of legitimation caused by a self-consciousness about contingency was the intellectual heritage of Emerson's modern America, a crisis shared with, but not imported from, modern France. He was critical, therefore, of the proposal of Gunn and Poirier that Americans return to Emerson to escape their current crisis. Gunn and Poirier seemed to be making an implicit effort to revive the narrative of the national romance as they argued that the flow of experience celebrated by Emerson was different from the meaningless flux of experience in Europe. America, the New World, was free from the artificial conventions of the Old World. These traditions and conventions could be deconstructed. But change in America always kept contact with the American world as it had begun with Emerson's generation. In celebrating Emerson's world as mutable and yet eternal, Poirier and Gunn were implicitly excluding Anglo-Protestant women from that America, as well as American Indians, African Americans, Mexican Americans, and Catholic and Jewish immigrants. It seems as if they hoped to bring the memories of the symbol-myth school back to life.

Jay called Gunn and Poirier "redemptive" critics who hoped Emerson could inspire American men to escape the current atmosphere of indecision, ambiguity, and uncertainty. Inspired by Emerson, American men once again would have the will to act and restore order out of chaos. Jay also analyzed the writings of the philosopher, Richard Rorty. For Jay, Rorty's self-image was that of a superior man with a culturally redemptive role to play. Rorty had rejected the Enlightenment project of using reason to discover truth. He believed that truth is constructed by particular linguistic communities. Claiming John Dewey as his inspiration, he announced that philosophers were now irrelevant. It was poets who best understood the contingent character of all statements about reality. Poets understood that scientists, like philosophers or literary critics, were always artists. But only poets were aware of the irony that their creations were contingent and survived only for a moment. As I interpret Jay's analysis, Rorty seems to be a belated adherent of the New Literary Criticism. According to Jay, Rorty saw this appreciation of irony as "open only to a class of male Brahmins sufficiently removed from ordinary life to be able to focus their attention on the complex of epistemological contingencies underlying it." Rorty seems to share the belief of the New Literary Critics that one could learn this heroic viewpoint from a group of trans-Atlantic giants, "Blake, Arnold, Nietzsche, Mill,

Marx, Baudelaire, Trotsky, Eliot, Nabokov, and Orwell." And like the New Literary Critics, Rorty was prepared to defend the sacred boundaries of his exceptional community.[25]

For Jay, however, this crisis of legitimation was irrelevant to the future of literary criticism in the United States. He believed that critics like Fish and Rorty were caught in a situation where they kept repeating the same questions about how we know what we know. He believed that they were trapped in a contradiction when they insisted that they knew what we cannot know. And Jay refused to accept the attempt of Gunn, Poirier, and Rorty to return to the contradiction of Emerson's commitment to a timeless America that experienced endless development. Implicitly Jay rejected their attempt to revitalize the national romance. Implicitly, then, Jay was choosing change as discontinuity, rather than as organic development. Implicitly, then, he was refusing the attempt of Gunn, Poirier, and Rorty to restore the belief in the modern nation as the end of history. Their perception of a crisis of legitimation depended on a belief that the nation was the source of truth as well as the source of the good and beautiful. Implicitly Jay was questioning the modern dualism that found meaning in the modern nation as an embodiment of natural law and found nothing but chaos in the traditions of cultures outside the nation's boundaries.

Jay, therefore, was accepting the reality of the cultural patterns of all the peoples whom modern nationalists had defined as being without history. Jay's proposal for a constructive future for literary criticism did not assume a meaningful history that was a progressive purge of meaningless history. He was imagining a world in which a variety of cultures were always engaged in complex patterns of interrelationships. Reality was embodied in these dialogues. In this world there were no absolute boundaries that protected a pure and timeless entity. Jay, unlike modern nationalists, did not imagine the inevitable patterns of cultural border crossings both within the nation and between nations as symbols of contamination. Hybridity, not purity, was, for Jay, the reality of human experience. And hybridity did not mean chaos as the adherents of the national romance insisted.

It was implicit in Jay's position that modern nationalists had written their histories as rituals of purification. They had created literary canons that supposedly represented the purity of that national identity. They had been able to impose this pattern of imagined purity because they had greater military power than did the peoples, the others, whom they dominated. But this power had not been able to stop a cultural dialogue between the conquerors and the conquered. To establish this position Jay appealed to Mary Louise Pratt's book *Imperial Eyes: Travel Writing and Transculturalism* (1992). Here she had written about a "contact zone," which refers "to the space of colonial encounters, the space in which peoples geographically and historically separated come into contact with each other and establish ongoing relations, usually involving conditions of coercion, racial inequality, and intractable conflict. . . . By using the term 'contact,' I aim to foreground the interactive, improvisational dimensions of colonial encounters [which] . . . emphasizes how subjects are constituted in and by their relations to each other."[26]

This theme that the boundaries established by the dominant culture are places of cultural dialogue rather than impervious walls was central to Carolyn Porter's long essay "What We Know That We Don't Know: Remapping American Literary Studies" (1996). She argued that her colleagues had begun to doubt the usefulness of a focus on a national literature and were searching for alternative paradigms. The term "American," she insisted, had become problematic. In the essay she discussed many recent texts by literary critics but focused on four books. The first was *The American Ideal: Literary History as a Worldly Activity* (1991) by Peter Carafiol. He saw a dominant literary tradition stretching from Emerson to Matthiessen that asserted that the essence of the American nation was a unity of the good, true, and beautiful. It was the purpose of literature to help readers find this ideal amidst the many contradictions they experienced.[27]

Carafiol was critical of his older colleague, Sacvan Bercovitch, who had been arguing since the 1970s that there was a national culture dominated by what Bercovitch defined as *The American Jeremiad.* For Bercovitch, Americans in the late twentieth century continued to define experience within the jeremiad used by seventeenth-century Puritans. This jeremiad, according to Bercovitch, announced the achievement of an ideal society. The passage of time caused a declension from the ideal as sons of the Founding Fathers chose to create new and inferior patterns rather than preserving the original, sacred patterns. But some loyal sons rejected the declension caused by the disloyal sons and prophesied that the perfect time of origins would be restored. I interpret this jeremiad as a form of the national romance.[28]

For Bercovitch this jeremiad of the Puritans had been appropriated by the Founding Fathers and used by every subsequent generation of Americans to sustain the belief that no matter how much they experienced change, they remained within the national home created by the Founding Fathers. To a large extent Carafiol had borrowed from Bercovitch for his concept of "The American Ideal" and the way literary men from Emerson to Matthiessen had been obsessed by that ideal. Bercovitch, as Carafiol understood him, had separated himself from Matthiessen because Bercovitch, unlike Matthiessen, did not see the ideal nation as a historical reality, but rather as an ideological construct. But for Carafiol, Bercovitch was, nevertheless, sustaining the American Ideal by arguing that this ideology, this imaginative construction, remained so powerful that it did not seem possible to establish alternative worldviews within the United States. Carafiol argued, however, that the writings of men like Emerson and Thoreau could and should be read in ways that were an alternative to Bercovitch's forcing them within the pattern of the American jeremiad.

In her discussion of Carafiol, however, Porter found it ironic that while his book was a manifesto to free literary criticism from a tradition that focused on national identity, he went back to canonical male Anglo-Protestants, Emerson and Thoreau. He remained within the framework that Reising had called an unusable past—the framework that ignored the writing of all those Americans who were not male Anglo-Protestants from the Northeast. The national romance seemed to provide the structure for Carafiol's narrative.

In discussing the American Jeremiad and the American Ideal, neither Bercovitch nor Carafiol, therefore, saw World War II as a dramatic moment in which the bourgeois elites of the Atlantic nations rejected those essential elements of bourgeois nationalism—the national landscape and its children, the nation's people. They did not see the development by these elites of a culture of international capitalism. They did not see that in the new culture there would be no role for national canons in the construction of national citizens. They did not see the erosion of modern universities as centers of national culture that Bill Readings discussed in *The University in Ruins.*

But this revolutionary shift in aesthetic authority from the national landscape to the international marketplace was the implicit theme in *The New American Studies* (1991), edited by Philip Fisher, the next book analyzed by Porter. It is indicative of how successful the symbol-myth school, the New Literary Critics, and the male Jews were in insulating the canon from capitalism that Fisher, writing in 1990, could bring arguments into the debates among literary critics that Hofstadter had developed in the 1950s. When Hofstadter converted from his belief that there had been a conflict between an American national democracy and international capitalism, his new consensus position was that capitalism was the necessary foundation for democracy. This democratic capitalism, the real America, was characterized by liberty. The unreal America imagined by Hofstadter's teachers was supposed to be one of equality and fraternity as well as liberty. But Hofstadter had come to believe that equality and fraternity were threats to liberty. They represented Old World ideologies.[29]

This vision, that the authentic America was the embodiment of democratic capitalism with its gift of liberty, was Fisher's contribution to the conversation among literary critics in the 1990s. Hofstadter had argued that the capitalist marketplace, when it was first developed in Europe, had been frustrated there by the many powerful cultural boundaries of that continent. These encircled the individual and kept him from enjoying the freedom of the marketplace. This now, thirty years later, was Fisher's position. Hofstadter had argued that when the marketplace was brought to the New World it escaped those rigid borders and the individual was now free to create himself. Fisher repeated this thesis. America, he said, was a democratic space because it had no culture, only an economy. Ours, Fisher declared, is "a national life that is economic rather than religious or, in the anthropological sense, cultural." For Fisher, then, what I have called the culture of bourgeois nationalism never characterized the United States. It had, for him, characterized Germany. In contrast to this Old World country, America was "without a Volk, without a single environment or climate, without a culture, and without the deep romantic sense of a language." And, he continued, "even to the present there is no poetry, music, or philosophy that plays a significant part in what we think of as American identity."[30]

But this democratic social space, for Fisher, repeating the consensus historians of the 1950s, had, in contrast to German organic unity, a remarkable uniformity. Free individuals, moving through space, tended to build similar houses, to construct similar plans for towns and cities, to wear similar clothes. This standardization facilitated the logic of the marketplace, which was that of constant expansion. This boundless space, then, in which these uniform individuals moved, was so transparent that it was easily understood by the individual. In this democratic social space, therefore, the individual created no traditions, no myths, no ideologies that might inhibit the growth of the marketplace. In this constant experience of liberty and expansion, individuals were always participants and never observers. Within the marketplace, "there are no outsiders, no intellectuals, no critics, no utopian imaginations."[31]

There is for Fisher, however, constant conflict between individuals within the marketplace. It is this competition that drives the expansion of the economy. In 1944, Hofstadter, in *Social Darwinism in American Thought,* had argued that the celebration of the marketplace was an ideology imported from England after the Civil War. It marked the declension from the pre–Civil War democracy of equality, fraternity, and liberty. But in 1948 Hofstadter, in *The American Political Tradition,* argued that the Civil War marked no such declension because Americans had always been capitalists rather than democrats. At that moment he was horrified to discover this "democracy of cupidity." By 1970, however, he was celebrating the necessity of capitalism for a democracy characterized by liberty, rather than an oppressive equality and fraternity. In the 1950s, then, Hofstadter, like Schlesinger, had rejected the idea that the 1930s were a decade that promised to restore the democracy of the 1830s by defeating the capitalism imported from Europe in the 1870s.

Consensus School

Fisher's presentation of the history of American literary criticism focused on these three moments—the pre–Civil War renaissance, Civil War capitalism, and the renaissance of the 1930s. Because, for him, capitalism had been the reality of America since the first English settlements, the two renaissances were figments of an academic imagination. This, of course, was what Hofstadter had claimed in 1948 as he rejected what he then saw as the fictional history written by the Beards and by his dissertation director, Merle Curti. As a literary critic, Fisher focused on the academic imaginations of F. O. Matthiessen and Perry Miller, who, as the major figures in the 1930s, had created the illusion of a renaissance in the 1830s—one they hoped would be repeated in their time.

Fisher now had to qualify his assertion that there was no ideology in America. Within the authentic America of the marketplace there was no ideology. But literary critics had constructed an adversarial culture within the walls of the academy. Their ideological critique of capitalism was, from Fisher's perspective, impotent. And Fisher wanted to rescue his fellow literary critics from the fantasyland of the Ivory Tower so they could place the teaching of literature within the capitalist reality of American experience. This also meant that he had to qualify his affirmation of history as the inevitable progress of capitalism.

If the Civil War, rather than two false renaissances, was the reality of American history, as Fisher claimed, then there was conflict within that history. In a sense he reversed the cycles of Turner, the Beards, and the Schlesingers. They had seen the public interest of democracy periodically challenged by the self-interest of capitalism. But always, for them, democracy emerged victorious and stronger from the confrontation. Fisher's variation on this history of cycles, which was a progressive upward cycle, was to argue that the national uniformity of the capitalism of individual competition was periodically challenged by the formation of groups that wanted to draw boundaries around themselves. This was the case with the Civil War, where capitalist uniformity had been challenged by southern slaveholders. But capitalist uniformity had emerged from this conflict stronger than ever.

For Fisher, American studies scholars of the 1930s had imagined a national unity, an organic body, rather than the uniformity of independent individuals. They wanted to isolate the country within national boundaries. It was ironic, for Fisher, that this vision echoed German nationalism, rather than American nationalism. And there was poetic irony, for him, that this alien ideology was both challenged and reinforced by the identity politics of minority groups. As minorities entered English departments, they added to the distortions of American literature. The uniformity of capitalist experience was now obscured by the unrealistic cultural pluralism insisted upon by "departments of black or Afro-American studies, Jewish studies, women's studies, Native American studies, Chicano and Asian-American studies, and in some cases, gay studies." But since the boundaries of group identity are contradictory to the individualism of the marketplace, it was inevitable that these temporary fabrications would be reabsorbed into the essential uniformity of the marketplace.[32]

The vision of capitalism as the engine of a progressive history of liberty that Fisher shares with Hofstadter is the position that William Appleman Williams had tried to destroy. Where Williams saw capitalists using power to destroy the boundaries of local cultures to force their peoples to produce for the marketplace, Fisher saw capitalism liberating individuals from the cultural prisons of those local cultures. Capitalists, for Fisher, only used power defensively to preserve the uniformity of the marketplace, where every individual had a chance to become self-made. Fisher, therefore, could not imagine economic, political, and cultural power used by Anglo-Protestant men to impose the stigma of inferiority on Anglo-Protestant women, Native Americans, African Americans, Mexican Americans, Catholics, Jews, Asian Americans, homosexuals, and lesbians. He could not imagine that members of these groups felt a sense of otherness imposed on them. If they did, according to Fisher, it had been imposed on them by academics who had themselves chosen their identities as outsiders, as nonparticipants in the normal society in which the vast majority of Americans participated.

From my perspective, Carolyn Porter, along with Carafiol and Fisher, had not placed their debates about the current crisis among literary critics within the developing scholarship on bourgeois nationalism. They had no theoretical explanation for the importance of the inward-looking nationalism of American studies in the 1930s. They had no explanation for why only male, Anglo-Protestant literary figures from the Northeast had been chosen to represent the American people. They had no explanation for the development of cultural pluralism as a challenge to the male, Anglo-Protestant canon. But they all agreed with Reising that this tradition was an unusable past. Porter expressed her fear that given the political hegemony of capitalism in the 1990s, Fisher's demand that literary critics interpret American writers as participants in the marketplace would be all too persuasive. She, however, would devote most of her long essay to literary critics who were concerned with replacing the canon embodied in Matthiessen's *American Renaissance* with a canon or canons that expressed the voices of all those writers excluded by the sexism and racism of the democracy of Jackson and Emerson, Roosevelt and Matthiessen.

It was with relief, then, that Porter turned away from Fisher to the 1991 essay by Gregory Jay, "The End of American Literature: Toward a Multicultural Practice." Jay has said that he took the title of his essay from my *The End of American History*. And certainly he shared my belief that the concept of a national people with a uniform culture—a universal national—no longer had aesthetic authority. Jay declared that "it is time to stop teaching American literature and replace it with 'Writing in the United States.'" This would allow literary critics to study "the acts of writing committed within and during the colonization, establishment, and ongoing production of the U.S. as a physical, sociopolitical, and multicultural event, including those writings that resist and critique its identification with nationalism." These writings would not necessarily be poems or novels, and they would not necessarily be writings in English. Teachers would present "hybrid forms and texts that come from African-, Hispanic-, Jewish-, Native-, and Asian-Americans. These would remind students that the U.S. has always been a multicultural society." Porter necessarily had to choose a limited number of texts to discuss in her essay. But, as she was writing in the mid-1990s, other literary critics had become self-conscious of how the disintegration of bourgeois nationalism was forcing literary critics to choose new paradigms that would give focus to their particular research problems. Donald Pease, for example, had edited a collection of essays, *National Identities and Post-Americanist Narratives,* that was published in 1994; Priscilla Wald, in her *Constituting Americans: Cultural Anxiety and Narrative Form* (1995), had focused on the instability of nationalism; and John Carlos Rowe, in his *At Emerson's Tomb: The Politics of Classic American Literature* (1997), had taken that literature out of the realm of a timeless universal national and placed it within the context of the debates in which the major authors were involved.[33]

Although Porter applauded Jay's concern that literary scholars show "how various cultural groups and their forms have interacted during the nation's ongoing construction," she criticized his willingness to continue to use national boundaries to define "Writing in the United States." If, for her, those political boundaries were constructed by what Jay designated as a "white patriarchy," then the cultural hegemony of the privileged men remained even if one studied the writings of those who were not members of that white patriarchy. If one acted as if the United States was an essential national entity, one's belief that the boundaries had become problematic were irrelevant. It was not enough, for Porter, to break down the internal national boundaries established by dominant male Anglo-Protestants to segregate their pure public world from the impurities of the majority of peoples who lived within the political boundaries of the United States.[34]

Implicitly, then, Porter was calling into question the connection between the ways that male Anglo-Protestants justified their monopoly of the term "American" both within the United States and within the Western Hemisphere. All the peoples in those other so-called "American" nations shared the impurities of the segregated groups within the nation. The dominant Anglo-Protestant culture, therefore, segregated their America from these other nations. And like those segregated within the United States, these American people beyond the boundaries of the United States were not really American. But, of course, if one could not sustain the aesthetic authority of Anglo-Protestant purity within the United States, if the formerly internally segregated groups now claimed the term "American," why should not the externally segregated groups also claim the term "American" for themselves? Why was Mexico or Cuba or Brazil not an American nation? If this was true, what did the term "American literature" mean?

Porter now turned, therefore, to a book by José David Saldívar, *The Dialectics of Our America: Genealogy, Cultural Critique, and Literary History* (1991). Saldívar agreed with Fisher that capitalism was central to the history of the United States. But where Fisher shared the later Hofstadter's benign view of capitalism as the source of liberty, Saldívar's view was similar to that of William Appleman Williams. For Saldívar, capitalism meant power, inequality, and exploitation. Saldívar did agree with Fisher, however, that capitalism was a transnational phenomenon and that literature should be analyzed within that framework.[35]

One major consequence of such a perspective, for Saldívar, would be to focus on Chicano literature as a variety of Latin American literature, rather than as the writing of a minority within the United States. The dominant Anglo-Protestant culture had expressed its sense of racial superiority to the cultures of Native Americans, African Americans, and Mexican Americans within the boundaries of the nation. And Anglo-Protestants had seen all Latin American cultures as necessarily inferior because their populations were largely mestizo, mixtures of Indians, Africans, and Europeans. But male Anglo-Protestants, who were a minority within the United States, were an even greater minority within the world of all North, Central, and South American nations. Now, in the 1990s, Anglo-Protestants no longer had the aesthetic authority of bourgeois nationalism, which defined some nations as superior and necessary agents of the progress of civilization.

As long ago as the 1890s, when Frederick Jackson Turner had expressed his fears that the unique history of the United States as an Anglo-Protestant nation was ending, the Cuban writer José Martí agreed with this conclusion. Demanding the end of Spanish rule in Cuba, Martí had spent many years in exile in the United States. In 1891 he published *Nuestra América.* Here he confessed that once he had identified "Our America" as including all the nations of the Americas. These New World countries were, for him, in conflict with the oppression of the Old World countries of Europe. But, he said, he had been wrong. The greatest threat to the nations of the Americas came from the imperialism of the United States. This, for him, was a cultural as well as a political and economic threat because Anglo-Americans had nothing but contempt for the peoples of Latin America. "The scorn of our formidable neighbor who does not know us," Martí wrote, "is Our America's greatest danger."[36]

Now, for Saldívar, a group of Latin American writers, including Chicanos in the United States, were reviving Martí's critique. Some of them identified themselves as a School of Caliban. There was deliberate irony in their use of the term. They wanted to dramatize the barbaric use of oppressive power by the dominant culture of the United States with its self-image as the most civilized people in the world. For Saldívar, if Martí's Havana were imagined as the center of the Americas rather than Washington, scholarly perspective on the boundaries of American literature would change dramatically.

Saldívar's arguments are evidence of the extent to which the aesthetic authority of bourgeois nationalism had weakened by the 1990s. For Saldívar, the denial by bourgeois nationalists that their nations were committed to a boundless marketplace made no sense. He did not accept the narrative of bourgeois histories that defined capitalists as resident aliens within the nation. In contrast to bourgeois citizens, capitalists supposedly were soulless materialists who lusted after power. And, like José Martí a hundred years earlier, Saldívar saw the ideal of the bourgeois citizen as a way for the dominant bourgeois culture in the United States to deny its use of colonial power, both internally and externally.

Like Martí, Saldívar saw the commitment of Anglo-Protestant literary critics to the protection of the spiritual purity of the national literary canon from the corrupting and fragmenting influence of capitalism as part of that larger pattern of cultural hypocrisy. Such literary critics sustained the belief that there was an essential nation eternally committed to liberty. They reinforced the convention, therefore, that any exercise of national external power by the nation was an anomaly.

In rejecting this bourgeois aesthetic authority, Martí and Saldívar were implicitly rejecting that vision that linked the history of bourgeois nations to the history of cultural progress. Only by isolating the nation from international patterns, only by segregating the nation's homogeneous people from those groups within the nation's political boundaries who were not part of the universal nation, could bourgeois nations further the advance of civilization. Linking himself to the School of Caliban, Saldívar, however, saw no evidence that pure bourgeois nations had ever existed. The entire set of bourgeois dichotomies was false. There were no pure nations; there were no pure peoples.

In terms of literature, this meant that the particular dichotomy of independence and dependence was not valid. Bourgeois nationalist literary critics had insisted that only males of the dominant culture were capable of significant agency. But, for Saldívar, Martí had exercised significant agency. Dominated peoples did not fit that ideal of perfect passivity that Nina Baym had rejected in 1980. The external and internal boundaries of nations were always, as Mary Louise Pratt argued, areas of interchange. Influence did not flow only from the dominant to the dominated.

These arguments symbolized a massive crisis for the way bourgeois nationalists had defined space. Linear progress was, for them, possible only within the space of the bourgeois nation. Only citizens of the nations participated in meaningful history as progress. Only such citizens were capable of meaningful agency. But when one did not find such a spatial vision believable, the flow of human energy was no longer seen as linear. Now one could imagine flows of energy from many centers, flows that intermingled and ultimately redefined the existing centers. This was why critics like Saldívar could dismiss claims of historians from Bancroft to Hofstadter that only the United States was America, a new world whose space encouraged linear progress. This was why leading scholars in the discipline of American studies were demanding in the 1990s that American studies, which had developed out of the American civilization programs of the 1930s, now must break out of the national boundaries of the United States. For current American studies scholars, such as Annette Kolodny and Janice Radway, the term "American" needed to include all the nations of the Western Hemisphere. Saldívar published *Border Matters: Remapping American Cultural Studies* in 1997. He was able to link the breakdown of the sacred boundaries created by Anglo-Protestants within the United States so they could monopolize the identity "American" for themselves to the breakdown of the external boundaries they had created so they could claim to be the only Americans in the Western Hemisphere. This dialogue between internal and external boundaries also was central to Mary Helen Washington's presidential address to the American Studies Association in 1998, "Disturbing the Peace: What Happens to American Studies If You Put African-American Studies at the Center?"[37]

With the breakdown of the aesthetic authority of bourgeois nationalism and its corollary state-of-nature anthropology, literary scholars were, therefore, now imagining culture as a time-space continuum that as timeful process inevitably changed, whether it was rooted in a particular place or transplanted to another place. They were rejecting the concept that, in order to be authentic, a culture must be timeless. These were the assumptions on which the African Englishman, Paul Gilroy, had built his narrative in *The Black Atlantic* (1993). He saw bourgeois elites from Europe creating an international marketplace that moved millions of people out of Africa to provide slave labor on plantations established by Europeans throughout the Americas. These human beings from a variety of African cultures survived being scattered throughout the Western Hemisphere, according to Gilroy, by putting together pieces from their various African cultures and by creating new cultural patterns that were both local and international.[38]

Because Gilroy saw culture as itself a timeful space, he believed culture was a process, necessarily changing from generation to generation. From this position he criticized those Africans and African Americans who, for him, were using a paradigm of timeless space comparable to that expressed by bourgeois nationalists. He rejected the claim of those he called "Afrocentrists" that it was possible for peoples who had been forced into a diaspora from the African continent to retain an essential identity rooted in a timeless African space. For Gilroy the current descendents of the African diaspora had shared memories of this social catastrophe. The memory of this pain had inspired, in Gilroy's analysis, rich musical and literary expressions on both sides of the Atlantic. But these expressions, for him, did not have a metaphysical relationship to a lost African space. They grew out of the timeful experience of the diaspora. Now these memories were interacting with the current experiences of the peoples of African descent on both sides of the Atlantic.

For Gilroy the traditions of the diaspora were carrying these peoples into a future that they would help construct; these living traditions were not carrying them back to an unchanging Africa.

Gilroy had urged scholars to consider linking their definition of the origins of the modern world to the origins of the trans-Atlantic slave trade. And a Brazilian scholar, Stelamaris Coser, in her book *Bridging the Americas: The Literature of Paula Marshall, Toni Morrison, and Gayle Jones* (1995), argued that the writings of these novelists incorporated a memory of the slavery, colonialism, and racism that had been imposed on the people who became black Americans in North and South America. These novelists, for Coser, were engaged in creating a countermemory and a counterhistory that denied the official history of the modern world written by Europeans and European Americans. They were denying the position of spokesmen for the dominant white culture that the coming of the modern world had ushered in a history of liberty. They pointed out that modern white people had created the new political category of citizenship, which promised equal rights for every citizen, but then created social and economic hierarchies.[39]

The Asian American scholar, Lisa Lowe, in her book *Immigrant Acts: On Asian American Cultural Politics* (1996), also challenged the superficiality of this vision of citizenship. She shared the position of Gilroy and Coser that literature should be placed within a context of economic power. When readers approach literature written by Asian Americans, these readers should remember that corporations controlled by Anglo-Protestants had brought Chinese men in the mid-nineteenth century to the United States to build the transcontinental railroads. These workers, of course, could not become citizens, as no immigrants from Asia could until after World War II. For Lowe, the uprooting of Asian populations to provide cheap labor in the United States continues down to the present. She sees women from a variety of Asian countries working in sweatshops on both sides of the Pacific to produce clothing they cannot afford to buy.[40]

The race and gender of exploited Asian American workers, she argues, helps obscure the major pattern of class exploitation. Here she finds that novels written by Chinese Americans, Japanese Americans, Korean Americans, Filipino Americans, and Americans from India illuminate how the ideal of an equality of homogeneous citizens is contradicted by powerful class, racial, ethnic, and gender divisions. She hopes that as these novels from different Asian American communities illuminate patterns of racial and gender discrimination, they will also teach their readers how each group, in its own way, experiences economic exploitation. She hopes that a recognition of complexity and hybridity in each community will make it possible to imagine coalitions between the various groups. The emergence of Asian American literatures since World War II adds, then, more voices to those from the African American and Hispanic American communities that are providing countermemories that contradict those of the dominant culture. These countermemories contradict the claim that the United States has been a classless democracy whose citizens enjoy equality.

The Anglo-Protestants who defined themselves as a democracy with a homogeneous culture that had emerged out of the national landscape during the nineteenth century imagined that African Americans, Asian Americans, even Mexican Americans were permanent outsiders. These aliens could not become part of the people. But Native Americans posed a special problem. They had been part of what Anglo-Protestants called the national landscape for thousands of years. This meant, for the Anglo-Protestants, that American Indians had to be removed from that landscape. This could be done by physical genocide or by cultural genocide. By the 1880s, many Anglo-Protestants believed that if Indian cultures were purged from the landscape, the surviving people could be integrated into Anglo-Protestant culture. What was essential, however, was that the memories of separate Indian cultures, once deeply embedded in the landscape, vanish. Going into the twentieth century, the Anglo-Protestant vision of the vanishing Indian meant the death of Indian cultures and their burial in unmarked graves.

But then Anglo-Protestant political and economic elites decided in the 1940s to destroy their commitment to a sacred national landscape and to replace it with a sacred international marketplace. Following F. O. Matthiessen's suicide, his celebration in *American Renaissance* of the writings by Anglo-Protestant men as art that had grown organically out of the national landscape was replaced by elegies for that art written by his students, Henry Nash Smith, R. W. B. Lewis, and Leo Marx. For them this literature was no longer a living presence because the national landscape from which it had emerged had been killed by international capitalism and replaced by the international marketplace. All literary critics could do now was to preserve the memory of the pure and spiritual democracy found in the writings of Emerson, Thoreau, and Whitman.

As these cloistered academics established academic rituals for mourning this dead past, a powerful irony began to emerge. Native Americans could reclaim the national landscape for themselves. The landscape they reclaimed, of course, did not have the characteristics of the universal national. Indians, who had not lost their tribal cultures, saw many particular landscapes in which their many particular cultures had been rooted for thousands of years. This was the reality of localism, which bourgeois nationalists had hoped to eradicate. As the roots of Anglo-American culture withered in the now lifeless soil of the national landscape, it was clear that Native American roots continued to live and grow.

This was the momentous context for the publication of Kenneth Lincoln's book, *Native American Renaissance* (1983). Nine novels written by Native Americans were published between the 1850s and the 1960s. From the 1960s to the present, however, many novels by American Indians have appeared in print. One of the first expressions of this renaissance, N. Scott Momaday's *House Made of Dawn* (1968) was awarded the Pulitzer Prize.[41]

When Anglo-American literary critics lost their authority to guard the boundaries of the canon, when they could not longer identify it with Anglo-American myths of origin, they, of course, also lost their authority to guard the boundaries of English departments. American Indian literary critics were able to enter the academy and speak with authority. Louis Owens, one of the first nationally recognized American Indian literary critics, pointed out in his *Other Destinies: Understanding the American Indian Novel* (1992) that the two major novels written by Indians in the 1930s—John Joseph Matthews's *Sundown* (1934) and D'Arcy McNichols's *The Surrounded* (1930)—presented protagonists who were lost between their tribal cultures and the dominant culture, and they could not escape their alienation. It was important for Owens, therefore, that a generation later, in Momaday's *House Made of Dawn,* the protagonist escapes his alienation and returns to his tribal culture. It also was important to Owens that when Bill Ashcroft, Gareth Griffiths, and Helen Tiffin published *The Empire Writes Back: Theory and Practice in Post-Colonial Literature* (1989) they did not include writings by Native Americans. For Owens and other American Indian literary critics, this omission was amusing because they, of course, saw American Indians as one of the first colonized peoples. And certainly critics like Owens and novelists like Momaday saw themselves as writing back. They wanted white people to know that they were not passive objects, artifacts of a vanished past. They wanted white people to know that they had the agency to create their own future.[42]

The current collapse of the aesthetic authority of bourgeois nationalism from the peak of its persuasive power in the nineteenth century is dramatized by comparing Cheryl Walker's *Indian Nation: Native-American Literature and Nineteenth-Century Nationalism* (1997) with Craig S. Womack's *Red on Red: Native American Literary Separatism* (1999). In contrast to the struggles of Native Americans with a vital Anglo-American nationalism a century and a half ago, Womack felt free to construct a new vision of literary criticism. Bourgeois nationalists in 1830 saw literature as helping to create the political identity of modern nations when literature was accepted as a universal national. Now Womack saw literature helping to create local political identities for the various Indian nations. He quotes a Métis scholar, Howard Adams, from Canada: "We must have Aboriginal nationalism, an understanding of the state's capitalist ideology and its oppression, and, ultimately a counter-consciousness." For Womack, then, "We are not victims but active agents in history, innovators of new ways, of Indian ways, of thinking and being and speaking and authoring in the world created by colonial contact."[43]

Womack is angry at postmodern theorists who argue that all positions are contained within language and cannot possibly represent a reality outside of that language. He proposes that postmodernism represents a loss of certainty by the dominant culture of Europe and America. But Womack is certain that "there is the legal reality of tribal sovereignty, recognized by the U.S. Constitution and defined over the last 160 years by the Supreme Court, that affects the everyday lives of individuals and tribal nations and, therefore, has something to do with tribal literature." And, he continues, "I will seek a literary criticism that emphasizes Native resistance movements against colonialism, confronts races, discusses sovereignty and native nationalism, seeks connections between literature and liberation struggles, and, finally, roots literature in land and culture."[44]

The death of that national landscape in which the Anglo-Protestants of Emerson's generation hoped to root their "American" literature indeed has provided the possibility of a rebirth, a renaissance, for Native American cultures. But current American Indian literary figures, unlike Emerson's generation, are aware of how capitalism was always a central part of bourgeois nationalism. They are aware that the individualism of bourgeois artists reinforced the individualism of bourgeois businessmen. This was a philosophy that separated the individual from the land because it did not teach the individual to give up his autonomy to become an interdependent participant in the rhythms of nature. This is why the Indian public intellectuals who have emerged since the 1960s, such as Vine Deloria Jr., as well as literary critics such as Louis Owens, believe that Native Americans have much to teach the dominant culture about ecological issues, about how to live in harmony with the landscape rather than to mine and discard it. At the turn of the twenty-first century, they are certain that American Indian cultures are intellectually and morally superior to the modern cultures of bourgeois nationalism and international capitalism.[45]

CHAPTER EIGHT

The End of American History

My generation of historians, who came of age in the 1940s and 1950s, responded to the crisis of bourgeois nationalism in the United States in a dramatically different way than did our contemporaries who taught American literature—the symbol-myth school and the New Literary critics. Both of those groups continued to hope that the purity of literary texts written by male Anglo-Protestants could be segregated from the corruption and fragmentation of capitalism. But Richard Hofstadter, who had defended the purity of the imagined spiritual fraternity of the democracy of 1830 against the materialism of international capitalism in his first book, *Social Darwinism in American Thought* (1944), had insisted that capitalism was always an essential part of the American nation in his second book, *The American Political Tradition* (1948). In contrast to the celebration of the mythic world of 1830 by his contemporaries—Henry Nash Smith, R. W. B. Lewis, and Leo Marx—Hofstadter, in the *American Political Tradition,* had directly attacked the myth that there was a pure, spiritual nation locked in conflict with capitalism.

In explicitly defending a national literary canon against the chaotic and corrupting internationalism of capitalism, the symbol-myth critics also were implicitly defending this canon against the literatures written by the peoples living within the United States who, for them, were without history. Implicitly Marx, Smith, and Lewis were working with the explicit distinction made by Bancroft, Prescott, Motley, and Parkman, which found the agency of people who were not ideal citizens, who were not part of a homogeneous national fraternity, to be meaningless.

For these Anglo-Protestant historians, Jews and Catholics were members of traditions that preceded the modern nation. They could not contribute, therefore, to history as progress. Now Hofstadter, in rejecting the foundational myths of Anglo-American bourgeois nationalism, could no longer imagine Jews and Catholics as permanent aliens who were incapable of constructive agency.

Hofstadter represented many of us who were becoming aware that the culture of isolation expressed by Charles and Mary Beard in *The Rise of American Civilization* defined Catholics and Jews as permanent aliens who needed to be kept outside the cultural boundaries of the nation. And we were rejecting the cultural authority of this segregation. Many of us, therefore, were enthusiastic about Hofstadter's third book, *The Age of Reform* (1955), where he explicitly identified and rejected a myth of national purity created by Anglo-Protestants. He described the children of the New Immigrants—Catholics and Jews concentrated in the cities of the Northeast and Midwest—as creators of a pluralistic national identity in the 1930s. This inclusive America, for him, was replacing the exclusive America of Anglo-Protestants, who were becoming a provincial culture surviving primarily in rural, small-town environments of the South and West. Hofstadter had turned the Beards' *The Rise of American Civilization* upside down. The aesthetic authority to define the boundaries of the nation had passed, for Hofstadter, from Anglo-Protestants to some of those who previously had been outside the homogeneous people imagined by bourgeois nationalism.

This new aesthetic authority celebrated that urban-industrial frontier that Turner had seen coming from England to New England in the 1830s. This was that terrible alien energy that Turner had feared would change the national landscape from an environment of spiritual plenitude to one of spiritual entropy. And, indeed, Hofstadter in 1950 saw a South and West populated largely by Anglo-Protestants as an area of cultural entropy.

When I started graduate studies at the University of Wisconsin in February 1948, older graduate students told me that the most impressive members of their cohort were William Appleman Williams and John Higham. Higham's dissertation was published as *Strangers in the Land: Patterns of American Nativism, 1860–1925* (1955). It, too, turned *The Rise of American Civilization* upside down. The Beards had celebrated the legislation of the 1920s that severely restricted the immigration of Catholics and Jews from southern and eastern Europe. Higham shared the revolutionary shift in aesthetic authority with Hofstadter. For the Beards, Anglo-Protestants were the center of the nation, and Catholics and Jews were on the periphery. But Higham wrote as if Anglo-Protestant nativism was an irrational tradition that was on the periphery of the nation, which now had a pluralist center in the Northeast. Nativism, for Higham, represented culture lag. He endowed pluralism with cultural hegemony when he related it to an inevitable historical progression.[1]

But those of us who participated in the Hofstadter-Higham rejection of the exclusion of Catholics and Jews from the body of the American people did not declare that we were engaged in a paradigm revolution in which we were trying to replace an exclusive with an inclusive democracy. The theoretical boundaries of the history profession insisted that in order to be objective, scientific historians, we needed to segregate our rationality from our values. We could say that we were rejecting our professional elders because we discovered that they were not writing objective history. They had shaped their narratives with a set of values, rather than from an examination of the facts. We could not say that we had replaced those values with different values. We could not say that we were shaping our narratives with our own values. When Kenneth Stampp published *The Peculiar Institution: Slavery in the Antebellum South* in 1956, reviewers did not emphasize how this book expressed a revolution in values. Since the creation of the American Historical Association in the 1880s, Anglo-Protestant historians from the South had written most studies of slavery. They had painted a picture of a benign institution. Now Stampp wanted to call attention to much harsher realities. He, unlike Turner and Beard, could not imagine African Americans as people outside of national history.[2]

Reviewers of Stampp's book emphasized the movement of scholarship from the southern periphery to the northern center, from a provincial past to a sophisticated present. A developing civil rights movement in the South strengthened this new critique of slavery. White northerners were finally becoming critical that most African Americans in the South of the 1950s were not allowed to vote and that Jim Crow segregation in public places was based on an intense and extensive caste system. But this rejection of racist values by my generation was also leading some historians to a belief that racism was part of Anglo-Protestant culture in the North. As the civil rights movement led by southern African

Americans gained increasing support from white northerners, Congress in 1965 passed civil rights legislation that outlawed the methods used in the southern states to keep African Americans from voting. Paralleling this dramatic decade of racial conflict was the appearance of a cluster of books in which historians explored the history of white racism as a national, rather than a southern phenomenon. *Race, The History of an Idea in America* by Thomas A. Gossett appeared in 1963; *North of Slavery: The Negro in the Free States* by Leon Litwack came out in 1965; Eugene Berwanger's *The Frontier against Slavery: Western Anti–Negro Prejudice and the Slavery Extension Controversy* was published in 1967; *White over Black: American Attitudes toward the Negro, 1550–1812* by Winthrop Jordan followed in 1968; *The Black Image in the White Mind* (1971) by George Fredrickson took up Jordan's story and applied it to the nineteenth century. There was little focus, however, on how this new self-consciousness about a national tradition of white racism could be used to analyze such major northern historians as Frederick Jackson Turner and Charles Beard. The question of why northern historians had ignored slavery and permitted southern historians to monopolize the writing of an apologetic narrative about their peculiar institution was not asked.[3]

For Turner and Beard, the major drama in American history was a conflict between the democratic people who were the children of the national landscape and the undemocratic capitalists who were the children of the international marketplace. This was a conflict carried on by adult white males. Implicit in the writing of Turner and Beard was the explicit attitude of the Founding Fathers toward Native Americans and African Americans. For Washington and Jefferson, these groups were perpetual children. Women, for the founders, were also barred from the public sphere in which adult males exercised their civic responsibility because females were perpetual children. Only adult white males, therefore, achieved rationality and could exercise agency in protecting the nation's boundaries from external and internal corruption.

For Charles and Mary Beard in *The Rise of Civilization,* the Civil War was a conflict between undemocratic capitalists in the North and undemocratic planters in the South. Northern capitalists were able, for the Beards, to co-opt the support of democratic agrarians from the Midwest in their effort to impose capitalist patterns on southern society. Reconstruction, for them, was the effort of those victorious northern capitalists to force their economic interests on white southerners. This economic penetration of the unwilling body of the white South was a symbolic rape that might plant alien cultural seeds in that region. The Beards, however, were more concerned that capitalism would create a new international and undemocratic society in the North. Their disciple, Hofstadter, in his *Social Darwinism in American Thought,* had reaffirmed the Beards' message in *The Rise of American Civilization* that Populism and Progressivism had successfully aborted this possibility. Because the aesthetic authority of the bourgeois nationalism that informed the Beards' narrative, like that of Turner, placed African Americans outside the nation's history, they were not concerned about the African American experience in slavery. Nor were they interested in any roles African Americans played in Reconstruction.

I was aware as I started graduate school that W. E. B. DuBois, an African American sociologist, novelist, poet, dramatist, essayist, and historian, had published *Black Reconstruction* in 1935. When I asked one of my professors at Wisconsin about DuBois's thesis that African Americans had exercised crucial and constructive agency in the southern states during Reconstruction, he replied that DuBois could not be an objective historian because he was a Negro and a communist. Implicit in his answer was that rationality was to be found within the public sphere of the nation and that DuBois was doubly outside that sphere because of his race and his radicalism. But as my generation applauded the constructive agency of southern African Americans in the civil rights movement, which would soon be called the Second Reconstruction, historians began to rewrite the First Reconstruction. Starting with *After Slavery: The Negro in South Carolina during Reconstruction, 1861–1877* (1965) by Joel Williamson, historians began to provide footnotes to DuBois's *Black Reconstruction.* In 1988, when Eric Foner, one of the leading historians of Reconstruction, published his *Reconstruction: America's Unfinished Revolution, 1863–1877,* he shared DuBois's sense of tragedy that a creative attempt at biracial democracy had been destroyed by a politics of white racism. It was Foner's hope that the Second Reconstruction that began after World War II could complete the revolution of the 1870s and end a national tradition of white supremacy.[4]

When Hofstadter had shared the aesthetic authority of the Beards' *The Rise of American Civilization,* one could read his narrative in *Social Darwinism in American Thought* as a drama in which English capitalism and its American followers had tried to penetrate the body of the democratic people so that the seeds of an alien culture could be implanted within the political boundaries of the nation. The historians who awarded Hofstadter's book a prize were heartened by his reassurance that Populists and Progressives had engaged in a prophylactic politics that kept the alien culture from growing and restored the purity of the pre–Civil War American democratic body. But Hofstadter had insisted in his second book, *The American Political Tradition,* that the presidential heroes of the Beards—Jefferson, Jackson, Lincoln, Theodore Roosevelt, Wilson, and Franklin Roosevelt—could not protect democracy from capitalism because they were capitalists. Capitalism did not represent a foreign invasion. Our national leaders fathered it.

As many of us participated in the symbolic revolution that made democracy dependent on capitalism, the tradition of bourgeois nationalism that defined the nation as a defender of liberty against external power now became problematic. If the presidents from Jefferson to Franklin Roosevelt were not defending the liberty of the democratic nation from the power of international capitalism, what were they doing? Hofstadter's first answer was that they were the agents of capitalist power. But Hofstadter quickly moved away from his criticism of capitalism as a system of both national and international power to argue in his later books that capitalism coming from Europe was the source of liberty. When he made this shift he also ceased his analysis and critique of the power used by a dominant Anglo-American culture to enforce the subordination of other groups of Americans.

I believe, however, that while many of us shared Hofstadter's rejection of the metaphor of an American cultural virginity that had to be defended against seeds of change brought from Europe, we also had become aware of the power used by a dominant male Anglo-Protestant culture to protect its cultural virginity against the agency of all the groups in the United States who were imagined as outside the fraternity of citizens in the 1830s. From the perspective of our new aesthetic authority, we saw an inclusive democracy as the essential national identity that needed to now be achieved. We would celebrate, therefore, the agency of those who were previously seen as un-American. Many of us would use this perspective to criticize Hofstadter's revitalization of American history as the history of liberty. The historiography of Reconstruction provides major evidence for this important shift in perception and values. We had been taught in the 1930s and 1940s by liberal northern professors that the white South had successfully resisted radical Reconstruction. In our academic culture, which defined capitalism as an expression of the alien power of Europe, this successful defense was to be celebrated and we understood that these alien economic rapists had encouraged African American men to be rapists and impregnate white women. Their children would be alien monsters.

But when our values changed and we analyzed the caste system that was created by Anglo-Protestants in the English colonies, we saw a pattern in which white men monopolized violence in their relationship to blacks. White men could use violence against black men, but black men, defined as perpetual boys and dependent children, could never use violence against white men on pain of death. White men could engage in the rape of black women at will and deny black men the right to protect their mothers, wives, and daughters. White men could deny their children born of these unions because the children were eternal aliens. The post-1945 generation of historians of Reconstruction, as they rejected the authority of the caste system, found that blacks in the 1870s had engaged in very little violence but that white men had used extensive violence against African Americans to drive them from politics as they continued to rape African American women.

Looking at the Beards' presidential heroes, whom Hofstadter had wanted to desacralize in 1948, and asking what their relationship was to the caste system dramatically destabilized, then, the dominant metaphor that American history was the history of liberty, in contrast to European history as the history of power. The culture of Washington and Jefferson was one in which they saw themselves as defenders of liberty while they exercised tyranny over their slaves, including their children born of slave mothers. Committed under the caste system to preserving the purity of the Anglo-Saxon American people against the infiltration of unclean peoples, their culture declared that children of mixed ancestry were more dangerous than those whose parents were either African or Anglo-American. The children of white fathers might pass as white and plant the seeds of their hidden black blood within pure white bodies. Hofstadter in 1948 had seen Jefferson and subsequent presidents disguising their hard, aggressive capitalist side behind a soft persona that celebrated spirituality over materialism and public interest over self-interest. Now those of us who were members of Hofstadter's generation but who were committing ourselves to the Second Reconstruction were discovering another hard side to our presidents, one that they had learned from their colonial ancestors as they exploited male and female slaves.

One of the leading colonial historians of my generation, Edmund Morgan, had initially, in his writings, celebrated the pragmatism, the absence of ideology among colonial Anglo-Protestants throughout the seventeenth century. But he dramatically ended his participation in the consensus school when he published *American Slavery, American Freedom: The Ordeal of Colonial Virginia* (1975). Earlier, when Morgan had rejoiced that colonial Anglo-Americans (he called them "Americans") experienced a minimum of conflict among themselves, he did not include African Americans and Native Americans within the people he saw on the landscape. They were people without history. But by 1975 he no longer could dismiss African Americans as irrelevant actors in American history. Now he emphasized in *American Slavery, American Freedom* the terrible irony that colonial Anglo-Americans were working with a racial metaphor of two worlds. They defined their world of liberty by contrasting it to the world of their slaves. They were free because they had slaves.[5]

When William Appleman Williams came, like Hofstadter, to believe that capitalism was brought across the Atlantic by the first English colonists, he, unlike Hofstadter, denied that it was a system of liberty. Like the Beards and Turner before him, Williams saw capitalism as a system of power. But since he saw capitalism as an essential element of the dominant Euro-American culture from its beginning, he did not believe that capitalism coming from Europe could engage in the cultural rape of a liberty-loving, white democracy as Turner and the Beards had believed and as F. O. Matthiessen, Henry Nash Smith, and Leo Marx also had believed.

For Williams, the first English colonists were participants in a capitalist culture that taught them that as they had left their homes in England, so they also needed to leave their new homes along the Atlantic coast. Their lives would have no meaning unless they engaged in constant economic expansion. Williams believed that this commitment had driven Euro-Americans westward to the Pacific. But he was primarily interested in how this commitment began to drive them overseas after the 1890s. He wanted to focus on the attempt of the dominant culture to gain control of an international marketplace. He believed that in this environment one could no longer defend the innocence of the sacred men of the national landscape.

Williams and others of his generation, therefore, were implicitly destroying the aesthetic authority of the national landscape, that sacred space that Anglo-Protestants had imagined was their home. Bourgeois elites in European countries had invented sacred national landscapes to destroy the rootedness of aristocracies and peasants in sacred local landscapes. Such peoples would not have a home in the national landscape that belonged to the bourgeoisie. In the United States the Anglo-Protestant middle class had removed the Native Americans from their rootedness in local landscapes. The Indians vanished as a sacred national landscape displaced their profane local landscapes. But as the aesthetic authority of the national landscape began vanishing in the 1940s, the Anglo-Protestant bourgeoisie no longer had a home to defend against alien invaders. They had become defenders of an international marketplace in which any concept of home must be temporary.

Anglo-Protestant historians who used narratives comparable to those of Turner, Parrington, and the Beards suddenly had difficulty, therefore, in sustaining the story of English settlers becoming liberty-loving Americans when they lost their adult identities as Europeans and became the American children of the national landscape. Such a narrative had to culminate in an American Revolution that completed the separation of nature's nation from the conventions and traditions of Europe, the final separation of sons from fathers. But if one did not see the promised land of the national landscape and its homogeneous people as the culmination of this exodus out of Egyptian bondage, what would colonial historians see? Increasingly they saw a variety of local landscapes inhabited by Indians. They saw Europeans invading these homelands, using their superior military power to drive the native peoples from their homes. Responding to the collapse of the aesthetic authority of the national landscape, Francis Jennings published *The Invasion of America* in 1975. When the bourgeois nation no longer had the aesthetic authority that persuaded historians that it was the end of history, the people defined outside of the history of the bourgeois nation suddenly achieved dignity in the eyes of historians. If Jennings no longer believed that a bourgeois national landscape was destined by the course of history as progress to replace local landscapes, he also could not see bourgeois

Europeans discovering a virgin land, a New World, destined to become their national landscape. They were not actors within the inevitable course of history as progress. They, like the Native Americans, were participants in particular cultures that did not represent universal and timeless laws.[6]

Vanishing Indians, therefore, were no longer an abstract aspect of the inevitable course of progressive history. It was European invaders and their Euro-American descendants who were willing to use guns and swords to create a New World, a virgin land. Already in 1973 Richard Slotkin had published *Regeneration through Violence: The Mythology of the American Frontier*, which was followed by Richard Drinnon's *Facing West: The Metaphysics of Indian Hating and Empire Building* (1980). The benign memories of a colonial past where the only meaningful conflict was between the European past and the American future, between European fathers and American sons of liberty, were being replaced by countermemories of a dark and bloody ground. For Slotkin, Drinnon, and many of their contemporaries, the image of terrible power rather than delightful liberty characterized the European conquest of the continent. Colonial historians became curious, therefore, about how the Indians vanished and how many of them had been purged. Suddenly scholars saw a significant population of Indians. The Atlantic coast had had many Indian towns. Steadily guesses about Indian population increased. Estimates about the length of time Indians had been living in the Americas also increased. The largest number proposed as living within what are now the political boundaries of the contiguous United States is about ten million. The American Indian scholar, Russell Thornton, in his *American Indian Holocaust and Survival: A Population History since 1492* (1987), discusses this scholarship. The complex relationships between the European populations with North and South American environments is discussed by Alfred W. Crosby Jr. in *The Columbian Exchange: Biological and Cultural Consequences of 1492* (1972). Included in his story is the metaphor of the penetration of germs brought by Europeans into the bodies of Indians. It is guessed that European diseases played a major role in decimating native populations and creating what one historian has called "The Widowed Land." By the 1990s the rejection of the innocence implicit in the concept of the discovery of a New World seemed almost commonplace in books like David Stannard's *American Holocaust* (1991) and Ian Steele's *Warpaths: Invasions of North*

America (1994). It was possible for a younger scholar, Kerwin Lee Klein, to explore this dramatic change in historical interpretation in his *Frontiers of Historical Imagination: Narrating the European Conquest of North America, 1890–1990* (1997).[7]

By the 1970s, then, Anglo-Protestants had lost their claim to represent the universal national and to monopolize agency within the history of the English colonies and the United States. As the new historians of Reconstruction wanted to focus on the agency of African Americans, colonial historians became interested in the agency of the Native Americans, as well as the large colonial African American population. Gary Nash's *Red, White, and Black: The Peoples of Early America* (1974) was an early discussion of the dialogue among these groups. This was followed by James Axtell's *The Invasion Within: The Contest of Cultures in North America* (1985). More detailed discussions of Indian agency were written, for example, James H. Merrill's *The Indians' New World: Catawbas and Their Neighbors from European Contact through the Era of Removal* (1989) and Matthew Dennis's *Cultivating a Landscape of Peace: Iroquois-European Encounters in Seventeenth-Century America* (1993). This trend to see the Indians as having a meaningful history, in contrast to their dismissal by Bancroft, Turner, and the Beards as peoples without history, was expressed by William Cronon in his *Changes in the Land: Indians, Colonists, and the Ecology of New England* (1983). Here he analyzed in depth the farming and hunting practices of the Indians and contrasted them with what he saw as the essentially capitalist economy of the colonists. The new paradigm—that Indians were peoples with agency—had been dramatized as early as 1969 by Anthony F. C. Wallace in his *The Death and Rebirth of the Seneca,* an explicit refutation of the myth of the vanishing Indian.[8]

Bancroft, Turner, and the Beards had celebrated the movement across the Appalachians as the moment when the nation, reaching the virgin land of the Mississippi Valley, had escaped the complex presence of European culture in the colonial period. Part of the complexity that these historians were, themselves, escaping in their narratives was the multiple relationships of the French, English, Spanish, and colonial governments with the Indian communities. Until the Revolution, the Indians had such military and economic power that European and Euro-American governments were forced into extensive diplomatic, economic, and cultural relations with the native peoples. The aesthetic authority of bourgeois nationalism had defined a world of absolutes. Either the nation was dependent or independent. Either the people were pure or impure. But Richard White could use an aesthetic authority that defined a landscape where interdependence existed, where hybridity rather than autonomous racial units was the pattern. This was his argument in *The Middle Ground: Indians, Empires, and Republics in the Great Lakes Region, 1650–1815* (1991).[9]

When Bancroft, Turner, and the Beards had celebrated the exodus after 1789 into the virgin land of the Mississippi Valley, when they saw a national landscape free at last from all vestiges of European culture, they were also imaginatively escaping White's middle ground, where Indians as well as Europeans had agency on the landscape of North America. West of the Appalachians, Americans (Anglo-Americans) would no longer have to negotiate with Indian nations. There no longer would be dialogue and hybridity. It is poetically right, then, that Jefferson and Jackson, heroes for Bancroft, Turner, and the Beards because they credited them with achieving the imagined foundations of bourgeois nationalism, an autonomous national landscape and a homogeneous people, should, according to current scholarship, have indeed prophesied that the middle ground would not characterize the history of the United States west of the Appalachians.

Reversing the pattern of the nineteenth-century anthropologists who, as agents of Anglo-American imperialism, had studied the myths of "savage" peoples, contemporary historians are studying the mythic worlds of Jefferson and Jackson to understand their compulsion to use violence to sweep Indians out of the path of the nation's Manifest Destiny. Jefferson did imagine a national landscape extending to the Pacific, and he did imagine the cultural and racial homogeneity of the Anglo-American people on this continental expanse. *The White Man's Indian: Images of the American Indian from Columbus to the Present* (1979) by Robert F. Berkhofer Jr. was the first major overview of this intellectual imperialism. But colonial historians had begun to make specific case studies of this imperialism before Berkhofer's book appeared. They shared William Appleman Williams's belief that the conquest of the Indians was a central part of the diplomatic history of the United States. Reginald Horsman had published *Expansion and American Indian Policy, 1783–1812* in 1967. *Seeds of Extinction: Jeffersonian Philanthropy and the American Indian* by Bernard Sheehan followed in 1973. When *Jeffersonian*

Legacies, edited by Peter S. Onuf, appeared in 1993, it was clear that the group of historians gathered at a conference to discuss Jefferson saw him more as a figure who exercised power than as an apostle of liberty. If one asked what Jefferson's relationships to African Americans, Native Americans, and Anglo-American women were—those major groups excluded from the fraternity of citizens in Jefferson's new nation—one saw his belief that he had the right to exercise power over these inferior human beings, that because they were irrational he did not need to listen to them. He could exploit the labor of his male slaves and invade the bodies of his female slaves. He could father children who, for him, belonged to their mother, but not to him.[10]

By 1990, then, it seemed natural for scholars who specialized in diplomatic history to focus on the relationships that the national government developed with the Indian nations during the age of Jefferson. A group of these books are Robert Tucker and David C. Hendrickson, *Empire of Liberty: The Statecraft of Thomas Jefferson* (1990); Bradford Perkins, *The Creation of a Republican Empire, 1776–1865* (1993); William E. Weeks, *Building the Continental Empire: American Expansion from the Revolution to the Civil War* (1996); Frank L. Owsley Jr. and Gene A. Smith, *Filibusters and Expansionists: Jeffersonian Manifest Destiny, 1800–1821* (1997); Lawrence S. Kaplan, *Thomas Jefferson: Westward the Course of Empire* (1999); and Anthony F. C. Wallace, *Jefferson and the Indians: The Tragic Fate of the First Americans* (1999).[11]

When Arthur Schlesinger Jr. published *The Age of Jackson* in 1945, he saw Jackson as Bancroft, Turner, and the Beards had seen him. Jackson symbolized the continued effort of Americans to dissociate themselves from the oppressive hierarchy of Europe. They needed that liberty to enjoy the equality and fraternity of their democracy. When Schlesinger's elders awarded his book a prize, they continued to share the aesthetic authority of the bourgeois nationalism created by the Anglo-Protestants of both Jackson's and Bancroft's generation. This aesthetic authority defined a national landscape that was the home only of Anglo-Protestants. This authority created boundaries around this home, where the members of the national family enjoyed equality and fraternity. Within this family of equal citizens, no one had more power than anyone else.

Schlesinger's Jackson, like Beard's Jefferson, therefore, could not be an imperialist when he drove the "civilized" Indian nations in the south-eastern states of Georgia, Alabama, Mississippi, Florida, and Louisiana from their homes and forced them into a wilderness beyond the Mississippi. Schlesinger did not talk about Jackson as an Indian fighter before he became president because Schlesinger assumed it was the destiny of Indians to vanish from the national landscape, the home of a white American people. Like the Beards and Turner, Schlesinger also did not focus on Jackson as a slaveholder. In the aesthetic authority of Anglo-Protestant bourgeois nationalism, the issues of liberty, equality, and fraternity were found only within the history of a racially uniform American people, and African Americans were outside the boundaries of that people.

Hofstadter, between 1944 and 1948, had reversed his views about Jackson. Influenced by the Beards, he had seen a Jacksonian democracy where virtuous private property sustained equality and fraternity among the people. In 1944 he had seen international capitalism coming from England with a doctrine of self-interest that threatened the equality and fraternity of the national family. But in 1948, when he published *The American Political Tradition,* he argued that Jackson was a capitalist committed to self-interest, not national interest. Hofstadter explicitly had rejected that aspect of the aesthetic authority of bourgeois nationalism that described the nation as a home rather than a marketplace. But he implicitly continued to use that aspect of bourgeois aesthetic authority that defined Native Americans, African Americans, and white women as being outside the public sphere. In that sphere only white men had agency.

But for the generation of scholars who succeeded Hofstadter it was impossible to sustain the racism and sexism of bourgeois nationalism once the marketplace became a more sacred space than the national landscape. Historians did not associate cultural homogeneity with the marketplace. Historical writing about the age of Jackson, therefore, now followed two major trends. One emphasized that the importance of free-market capitalism expanded dramatically between the presidencies of Jefferson and Jackson. In contrast to Bancroft, Turner, and the Beards, whose narrative was that the exodus across the Appalachians had left the vestiges of European class hierarchy behind on the East Coast, scholars such as Edward Pessen, in his *Riches, Class, and Power before the Civil War* (1973), now argued that class divisions among whites intensified during the age of Jackson. This rewriting of the Jacksonian period as the age of capitalism was consolidated in *The Market Revolution: Jacksonian America, 1815–1846* (1991) by Charles Sellers.[12]

The other approach to this period expressed the self-consciousness of how racially exclusive Jacksonian democracy was. Reginald Horsman, in his *Race and Manifest Destiny: The Origins of American Racial Anglo-Saxonism* (1981), had indicated that the racism of the dominant culture in the United States was as intense and widespread as that of any European nation. It was a racism that employed elaborate philosophical and scientific arguments. Ronald Takaki had already argued the centrality of racism in the world of Jefferson and Jackson in his *Iron Cages: Race and Culture in Nineteenth-Century America* (1979). When the symbol-myth school had celebrated the age of Jackson and Emerson, they had connected the writings of Emerson and Whitman to the folktales of the common people. These scholars did not write about the popular culture of African Americans, nor did they write about the popular culture in the cities dominated by the New Immigrants and their children. But, a later generation of scholars who rejected the racism implicit in the symbol-myth school also rejected the explicit racism of the Anglo-American popular culture of the democracy of the 1830s. Alexander Saxton, in *The Rise and Fall of the White Republic: Class, Politics, and Mass Culture in Nineteenth-Century America* (1990), and Eric Lott, in *Love and Theft: Blackface Minstrelsy and the American Working Class* (1993), both explored the cultural hybridity between Anglo-American and African American popular culture. Both, however, found that whites could use African American popular culture for their own enjoyment and, at the same time, use it to define their superiority, their humanity in contrast to the inferiority, the subhuman nature of blacks. Reversing Arthur Schlesinger's celebration of the creative role of labor in constructing Jacksonian democracy, David R. Roediger, in *The Wages of Whiteness: Race and the Making of the American Working Class* (1991), wrote about a tragedy that has continued to divide the labor movement down to the present. Laborers, for Roediger, had created a collective identity for themselves by distinguishing themselves from African Americans. They were not becoming powerless in factories owned by capitalists because their whiteness set them apart from black slaves. With Jefferson and Jackson they identified whiteness with liberty.[13]

When many historians implicitly or explicitly renounced the racism that was central to the profession into the 1940s, they began a process of replacing the metaphor that had identified liberty with national history with a metaphor that identified the dominant culture with power. This deconstruction of one set of metaphors and the construction of another symbolized that many historians of my generation and the next generation were implicitly replacing state-of-nature anthropology with cultural anthropology. Bourgeois nationalists assumed that citizens had achieved independence and autonomy. They were individuals who were free to use their reason to find the truth, unencumbered by artificial traditions and conventions. After bourgeois nationalists created national history as an art form to help construct their nations, they created anthropology in the nineteenth century to give them authority over the traditional peoples they were colonizing. Anthropologists used their imagined gaze as independent, rational individuals to define the inferiority of traditional peoples trapped within their irrational conventions and superstitions. All of these anthropologists were, of course, white. Only white men on both sides of the Atlantic had achieved individual autonomy and rationality.

For nineteenth-century anthropologists, white men, as autonomous individuals capable of rational agency, were citizens of nations whose people were capable of rational agency. Both the white citizen and his nation were segregated from inferior people by the distinction between rationality and irrationality. The white, bourgeois citizen had achieved autonomy and rationality by stepping out of irrational traditions. He had fulfilled his essential individuality by coming into organic harmony with the laws of nature that were embodied in his national landscape. But by the beginning of the twentieth century, anthropologists found it more and more difficult to see themselves and their modern societies as standing apart from traditions and conventions that had been created in time and would change in time. They were losing the ability of bourgeois nationalists to make a distinction between space and time. Applying the perspectives of cultural anthropology to modern nations, one could argue that they were expressions of traditions and conventions created in time, and they would change in time. The agency of bourgeois citizens, therefore, was not different from the agency of members of traditional cultures. Both used their imaginations to create institutions and traditions that, in the language of bourgeois nationalism, were not progressive. If there was no dichotomy between individual and society or between society and nature, individuals could not step outside of culture and engage in an epic quest for the timeless ground of natural law. Individuals could participate in changing their cultures, but they could not leave them to discover a state of nature. Nineteenth-century anthropologists and historians, from this perspective, were creating traditions that whiteness could be identified with rationality, and they were helping to create an institutional hierarchy in which whites exercised power over people of color.

Working implicitly from the position of late twentieth-century cultural anthropology, most historians, however, no longer accepted this definition of African Americans, Native Americans, white women, and all other minority groups as incapable of constructive agency because they were by nature irrational. Scholars, like Saxton and Roediger, who no longer could see whiteness as a natural category, had begun to study the history of whiteness as a convention created in time and that would change in time. Whiteness, for them, first had been imagined and then given expression in a complex pattern of conventions and institutions.

By the 1990s, some historians in the United States were beginning to identify the paradigmatic revolution in which they were participating with the term "postcolonialism." Some were becoming aware that when the aesthetic authority of bourgeois nationalism began to be replaced with the aesthetic authority of the international marketplace during the 1940s, this shift had freed indigenous scholars throughout the British and French empires from the cultural hegemony of the concept of progressive history achieved only by modern nations. If one identifies Anglo-Protestants as the most important colonizers in the United States and also identifies as colonized those peoples who were imaginatively excluded from the homogeneous body of the nation's citizens, one can see the parallels with the situation in the British and French empires. All the peoples in those colonies were imaginatively excluded from the body of English and French citizens. Since, according to bourgeois nationalism, progress could be made only by national citizens, who alone were capable of rationality, the peoples in the British and French empires, because they were not rational, could not exercise constructive agency. And just as in the United States, where Mexican American, African American, and Native American intellectuals could teach in major universities by the 1970s because these institutions were no longer centers committed to the creation of uniform national citizens, so also the voices of intellectuals and artists from the former colonies in Asia and Africa were now given respect, having achieved authority in universities throughout Europe and the United States.

One of those scholars who has had a major impact in the United States is Edward Said. His book *Orientalism* (1978) played a major role in persuading American academics to consider the relationship of the United States to postcolonialism. Said analyzed the ways in which Western Europeans had imposed stereotypes on the peoples they colonized, stereotypes that defined them as peoples without history. The shift from a national to an international perspective can be seen by comparing Stanley Elkins's *Slavery: A Problem in American Institutional and Intellectual Life* (1959) and George Fredrickson's *White Supremacy: A Comparative Study in American and South African History* (1981). When Elkins, like others of my generation, lost the aesthetic authority of bourgeois nationalism, he could no longer see the history of his nation as that of unconditional liberty. Suddenly rejecting the racism of our elders in the historical profession, we now saw, as Kenneth Stampp had, the brutal power of slavery. But Elkins, like many of us in the 1950s, was also rooted in a tradition of national isolation. He was not able, then, to see slavery in the United States as part of the larger pattern of colonialism that had spread out of early modern Europe. To express his anger at the way the horrors of slavery had been suppressed by the historical profession of the 1930s, he asked his readers to compare it to the outrages imposed by Nazis on Jews in the concentration camps of World War II.[14]

Since the citizens of the United States had been asked to see World War II as a defense of liberty against totalitarianism, Elkins's metaphorical linking of American history to Nazi history was shocking. But as the aesthetic authority of bourgeois nationalism continued to weaken, it became possible for some of us in Elkins's generation to imagine that slavery and racism could be placed in other comparative frameworks. When the aesthetic authority of bourgeois nationalism began to break in the 1940s, bourgeois elites in Western Europe, Canada, and the United States renounced their anti-Semitism and racism. Within the United States, however, this was not true in the southern states. It also was not true of the bourgeois elites who controlled South Africa. It seemed plausible, then, for George Fredericksen to expand his earlier study of racism in the United States into a comparative study with South Africa. His book, *White Supremacy: A Comparative Study in American and South African History* was published in 1981. As the new aesthetic authority of the international marketplace increasingly shaped the questions historians asked, questions about race were placed in the larger context of the colonial expansion of modern Europe. Here the ideology of race was linked to the economic, political, and cultural power that Europeans exercised over the peoples they had conquered in Asia, Africa, Australia, New Zealand, and North and South America. A recent synthesis of this scholarly argument is *Race: The History of an Idea in the West* (1995) by Ivan Hannaford.[15]

The metaphors of postcolonialism have achieved their greatest aesthetic authority from the 1970s to the present in the areas of what has been called colonial American history. Postcolonialism symbolized the rejection of the tradition that only modern nations have cultures with historical agency and that cultures that do not participate in the space of the modern nation are without meaning. From the perspective of bourgeois nationalism, the long history of the English colonies from the early seventeenth century to the American Revolution was meaningless. Bancroft, Turner, and the Beards had given negative meaning to the colonial period by arguing that what was important was the way that colonists escaped English traditions and conventions. What was important was the growing power of the natural landscape, which became the national landscape after 1789. From the 1890s to the 1940s there had been a few historians, such as Herbert Osgood and Charles McLean Andrews, who argued the vitality of an English presence down to the Revolution, but they failed to attract a paradigmatic community. This also was true of Herbert Bolton, who insisted that the history of the United States could be understood only in comparison to other American nations.

The Beards' *The Rise of American Civilization* represented, then, the dominance of a culture of isolation between 1919 and 1941 within the historical profession. For the men who formed American civilization programs in the 1930s, state-of-nature anthropology provided the paradigm to argue the isolation of the United States from the unnatural cultures of Europe and the Americas, which was, for them, achieved about

1830. It also justified ignoring the colonial past, when European culture had been in competition with the natural landscape. The culture of isolation was so strong going into the 1940s that many major universities—Johns Hopkins, Princeton, Pennsylvania, Chicago, and California-Berkeley—did not offer graduate training in colonial history.

But when the new culture of internationalism began to be constructed during World War II, a number of younger historians joined Hofstadter in denouncing the Beards' vision of a fundamental conflict between national democracy and international capitalism. It became important for these consensus historians to prove that there was no conflict between a democracy born of the natural landscape and capitalism brought from Europe. In the 1950s, then, many articles and books appeared arguing for the absence of conflict in the English colonies. These studies, however, like those of the Beards, continued to ignore Native Americans and African Americans. They focused largely on the governmental and economic activities of white men.

Implicitly, however, the consensus historians had accepted the new reality that the modern nation was not the end of history and that the international marketplace would, in the future, be a more important space. The readers of the Beards' *The Rise of American Civilization* would have understood that one did not put colonial history in an international context because one should focus on the patterns leading to the appearance of the absolutely independent and autonomous nation with its homogeneous fraternity of citizens. To imagine in the 1940s, then, that the international economy was more important than a bounded national economy meant renouncing this interpretation of the colonial experience as prefiguring the emergence of an isolated nation. Such current major colonial historians as Gordon Wood and Joyce Appleby, therefore, use the imagery of a new colonial history that has achieved independence from national history. One of the leading consensus historians of the 1950s, Louis Hartz, participated in this shift when he published *The Founding of New Societies: Studies in the History of the United States, Latin America, South Africa, Canada, and Australia* in 1964. As the belief in the national landscape as a sacred space began to collapse in the 1940s and the metaphor of two worlds was rejected, it became impossible, therefore, to imagine that the influence of English culture was becoming entropic throughout the colonial period. This new perspective denied the logic of the American civilization programs in the

1930s, which argued that the plenitude of an American natural landscape had destroyed all ancient and decrepit English traditions and institutions.[16]

Bernard Bailyn, for example, had implicitly rejected the metaphor of an entropic old England in *The Ideological Origins of the American Revolution* (1967), in which he argued that the Founding Fathers had justified the Revolution in terms of republican theory developed in England in the seventeenth and eighteenth centuries. Then J. G. A. Pocock, in *The Machiavellian Moment: Florentine Political Thought and the Atlantic Republican Tradition* (1975), insisted that the Anglo-American distinction between profane time and sacred space should be traced back to the Renaissance. Pocock saw the irony that the scholarly exponents of an isolated American civilization in the 1930s were using concepts of space and time that had been an important European tradition for five hundred years. Subsequent scholars have analyzed the intimate relationship between English politics, economics, and society and the English peoples in the North American colonies. This scholarship assumes that these traditions and institutions were developed in time and were changed in time. It assumes the creativity and dynamism of cultures in England and the participation of the English colonists in that creativity. This is the perspective presented by Ian Steele in *The English Atlantic* (1986) and by Daniel W. Howe in *American History in an Atlantic Context* (1993).[17]

One of the major themes in these histories is the development of bourgeois culture on both sides of the Atlantic. This is the subject of Carole Shammas's *The Pre-Industrial Consumer in England and America* (1990), Richard L. Bushman's *The Refinement of America* (1992), and *Consumption and the World of Goods* (1993), edited by John Brewer and Roy Porter. Implicitly these historians were building their narratives on the foundation of cultural anthropology, rather than state-of-nature anthropology. They assumed that the actors in their stories were creators of cultural patterns, rather than avant-gardes leading an exodus from timeful culture to timeless space. They assumed change rather than progress. They were fulfilling, therefore, the fears of historians who were or are bourgeois nationalists that history that does not focus on the independence of particular nations is not a history of progress.[18]

This was certainly true of histories such as *Albion's Seed: Four British Folkways in America* (1989) by David Hackett Fisher and *Adapting to a*

New World: English Society in the Seventeenth-Century Chesapeake (1994) by James Horn. Both said that individuals cannot leave society because their identities are created by the cultures into which they are born. In direct contrast to Bancroft, Turner, and Beard, Fisher wrote as if it was natural for English colonists to bring their cultures with them in order to give meaning to their lives. In *Imagined Communities,* Benedict Anderson had related how historians who were bourgeois nationalists found no meaning in the international and local, both of which contradicted their vision of an autonomous and homogeneous nation. Fisher was challenging this aesthetic authority on both the international and local levels. He did not send English settlers across the Atlantic; rather his migrants came from four local cultures that existed within the political boundaries of England. It was these local cultures that continued to be recreated in the colonies. And, Fisher insisted, these living cultures did not die when the United States replaced the colonies. He reminded his fellow historians that there was no homogeneous national culture between 1789 and 1861; otherwise, how could they explain the explosion of the Civil War in 1861? Indeed it was Fisher's hypothesis that the continuing differences between the four local English cultures that crossed the Atlantic help explain that national catastrophe.[19]

interesting

Nineteenth-century anthropologists had seen all the peoples of the world as participants in cultures that they had created, with the great exception of the citizens of bourgeois nations. They saw cultures of traditional peoples as weak and ephemeral because they were products of human imagination. Born in time, they would die in time. These anthropologists were so committed to the progressive separation of rational nations from the irrational peoples without history that they could not imagine that traditional cultures were constantly reconstructed and revitalized. These anthropologists, like the historians who were their contemporaries, went into the 1940s, then, assuming not only that Native American cultures were dying, but also that African American cultures were vanishing. Indeed, it was difficult for them to imagine that Africans, brought as slaves, had the capacity to create new cultures that made use of the African heritage, but also incorporated aspects of Anglo-American culture.

proof that challenged the paradigm

But, of course, all this changed when anthropologists and historians began to believe that modern nations were creations of human imagination and that they, too, were always in the process of recreation and revitalization. Since this artful activity took place within the dimension of time, it could not claim to be leading toward a timeless space. It became possible for historians, then, to imagine that African American culture was dynamic and meaningful. They also were willing to study African American culture because they no longer shared the view of their professional elders that everything associated with blacks was dirty and worthless. After World War II, therefore, colonial historians began to imagine that African peoples as well as English peoples had crossed the Atlantic as participants in cultures. They could imagine that in North America these cultures, as in Europe and Africa, were in a constant process of recreation and revitalization.

Colonial historians, as we have seen, were able by the 1970s to see Native Americans on the landscape. Colonial historians also achieved the ability during this decade to see African Americans. Gerald W. Mullin's *Flight and Rebellion: Slave Resistance in Eighteenth-Century Virginia* appeared in 1972, followed by Peter H. Wood's *Black Majority: Negroes in Colonial South Carolina from 1670 through the Stono Rebellion* (1974). Sidney Mintz and Richard Price published *The Birth of African-American Culture: An Anthropological Perspective* in 1976. Because historians now imagined a variety of cultures rather than the homogeneous cultures seen by bourgeois nationalists, they became interested in the variety of African American cultures that developed in the colonial period. Daniel Littlefield's *Rice and Slaves: Ethnicity and the Slave Trade in Colonial South Carolina* was published in 1981 and was followed by Allan Kulikoff's *Tobacco and Slaves: The Development of Southern Cultures in the Chesapeake, 1680–1800* (1986). This trend has continued with books such as *Slavery in North Carolina* (1995) by Michael Kay and Lorin Lee Cary. Bourgeois nationalists had feared that the local and international would corrupt the purity of national homogeneity. From the perspective of bourgeois aesthetic authority, only the modern national culture had firm boundaries. This was the frightening aspect of the international and local: they represented flows of energy that did not respect boundaries. They ignored the distinction between the legitimate and illegitimate, between purity and impurity.[20]

Working implicitly with the logic of postcolonialism, which denied the sanctity of the boundaries of the bourgeois nation, Mechel Sobel could imagine *The World They Made Together: Black and White Values in Eighteenth-Century Virginia* (1987) and Michael Mullin could imagine *Africa in America: Slave Acculturation and Resistance in the American South and the British Caribbean* (1992). Mullin broke the boundaries of Anglo-American bourgeois nationalism by placing a dynamic African American culture in dialogue with Anglo-American culture in the colonies that would become the United States and by claiming that one could understand that culture more fully by comparing it with British colonies in the Caribbean. This powerful rejection of the claim made by the aesthetic authority of bourgeois nationalism that there were people without history can be dramatically seen in John Thornton's *Africa and Africans in the Making of the Atlantic World* (1992). Slavery, Thornton argued, was an important part of several African cultures. European nations, according to him, did not have the military power, until the latter nineteenth century, to dominate African societies. Through the colonial period, Europeans who wanted slaves for plantations in the Americas had to trade, therefore, with African political leaders on terms of equality. This was a middle ground comparable to that which Richard White had seen in North America.[21]

Within this Atlantic world, which included Western Europe, Western Africa, and North and South America, it no longer made sense to many colonial historians to segregate English and Anglo-American history from the histories of the other major European imperial powers—France, Spain, and Portugal. In these comparative histories, the authors focused especially on the imaginative worlds of the colonists. This was particularly true of *Ceremonies of Possession in Europe's Conquest of the New World* (1995) by Patricia Seed and *Lords of All the World: Ideologies of Empire in Spain, Britain, and France* (1995) by Anthony Pagden. But as the vision of nations as the only containers of historical meaning disintegrated, other historians wanted to go beyond comparison of cultures within the geographic space of the Atlantic. The aesthetic authority of bourgeois nationalism had restricted progressive history to the nations of Western Europe or the United States. It was these nations that were the driving force for the advance of Western civilization. It followed, then, that, if the bourgeoisie in each modern nation could no longer claim to monopolize historical agency, then one could no longer claim that historical agency was limited to the Atlantic world. If there were no peoples without history, historians needed to be willing to make comparisons throughout the entire globe. This was the argument of historians such as William H. McNeill in his *Polyethnicity and National Unity in World History* (1986) and *The Global Condition: Conquerors, Catastrophes, and Community* (1993). Other important discussions are Marshall G. S. Hodgson, *Rethinking World History* (1993); Paul Costello, *World Historians and Their Goals* (1993); and Bruce Mazlish and Ralph Buultjens, editors, *Conceptualizing Global History* (1993).[22]

These historians of empires and the historians of global patterns did not expect, in contrast to historians who were bourgeois nationalists, to find uniformity. Indeed bourgeois historians had always feared the world outside their nations' boundaries because they saw it as chaotic. Only within the nation could one hope to overcome the chaos of local and international cultures and see a progressive history leading to unity and uniformity. But the emphasis on the international and local that has characterized the study of the colonial era by historians in the United States since the 1970s continued to fulfill the fears of historians who were bourgeois nationalists that there were no permanent patterns when one experienced either the international or the local. An example of this fluidity is the way that colonial historians expected the boundaries between Native American cultures and African American cultures to be porous because these cultures were always in the process of recreation. An overview of this experience is *Black Africans and Native Americans: Color, Race, and Caste in the Evolution of Red-Black Peoples* (1988) by Jack D. Forbes. More particular studies are *Indians, Settlers, and Slaves in a Frontier Exchange Economy: The Lower Mississippi Valley before 1783* (1992) by Daniel H. Usner Jr. and *Lumbee Indian Histories: Race, Ethnicity, and Indian Identity in the Southern United States* (1993) by Gerald M. Sider. Naomi Zack has edited a collection of essays, *American Mixed Race: The Culture of Microdiversity* (1995).[23]

The aesthetic authority of postcolonialism that found significance in the agency of all groups gave new meaning to the American Revolution as the concluding moment for the colonial history of the United States. Equating political power with the power of traditions to entrap the individual within the boundaries of culture, Bancroft, Turner, Parrington, and the Beards had wanted the Revolution to symbolize the escape of European settlers from European culture and power to find liberty as free individuals in the environment of the natural landscape. But as historians began to see a powerful Anglo-American culture in the process of recreating itself between 1776 and 1789, they also saw it in conflict with the cultures of African Americans and Native Americans. Historians in the 1990s could empathize with the way in which most African Americans and Native Americans understood the Revolution. They saw it as tightening the bonds of slavery or of accelerating the white invasion of Indian lands. Many blacks and Indians, therefore, saw more hope for dignity within the British empire than in an independent United States. This irony is expressed in books such as Gary Nash's *Race and Revolution* (1990), Sylvia R. Frey's *Water from the Rock: Black Resistance in a Revolutionary Age* (1991), Tom Hatley's *Dividing Paths: Cherokees and South Carolinians through the Era of Revolution* (1993), and Colin G. Calloway's *The American Revolution in Indian Country: Crisis and Diversity in Native American Communities* (1995).[24]

This ironic perspective on the bourgeois nationalist definition of the Revolution as the beginning of a national history of liberty has another more powerful dimension when one looks at the history of women. When the bourgeois nation was imagined as a fraternity of equal citizens sharing a homogeneous culture, bourgeois men could not imagine that bourgeois women had any meaningful agency. As noncitizens, they were people without history. When the historians of my generation (almost all were males, as were our teachers) began to imagine a more inclusive democracy, we thought about Jewish and Catholic males becoming authentic citizens. And we then began to consider that the segregation of male Native Americans, African Americans, and Mexican Americans from the public sphere should cease and that they should be included in the national story. My generation of male historians was much more reluctant, however, to begin to write about the history of women. But we could not continue to justify the exclusion of women from the history profession once the exclusiveness of a male Anglo-Protestant fraternity of citizens had lost its aesthetic authority.

It was the significant number of women who entered the history profession by the 1970s, then, who began to write the history of women in the colonial and national periods. Seeing themselves as having historical agency, they brought women from the past out of the category of people without history. But as many of the first generation of women literary critics, such as Nina Baym and Jane Tompkins, focused on the writings of Anglo-Protestant women from New England, so did many of the first generation of women historians. They, too, came out of that tradition, described by Mary Louise Pratt as one of both oppression and privilege. Women historians who wrote about women before World

War II, such as Mary Beard, participated in the mythology of Anglo-American nationalism and were committed to state-of-nature anthropology. They had argued that American women (meaning middle-class Anglo-American women) during the colonial period had escaped from many of the restrictive conventions still experienced by English women (meaning middle class). The first generation of women historians who followed Beard's cohort continued to identify American national identity with the Northeast in general and New England in particular. It was possible for the women historians of the 1960s and 1970s, therefore, to talk about American women in the colonial period, when they really meant only middle-class, Anglo-American women primarily from New England.

But the women historians of the 1960s and 1970s had been able to enter the profession because the aesthetic authority of Anglo-American bourgeois nationalism was collapsing. These postwar women historians did not accept it as natural and inevitable that women would provide leadership only for other women. They would teach men through their research and writing and in their classrooms. In contrast to the vision held by Mary Beard's generation that there was increasing liberty for middle-class women in the colonial period, they focused instead on the paradox that the formation of the republic incorporated an explicit political ideology that identified citizenship with males. Women historians of the 1960s and 1970s analyzed and criticized the pattern of bourgeois nationalism that segregated the public sphere of men from the private sphere of women. They focused on the irony that the creation of the nation meant the creation of conventions that restricted middle-class women within the home.

This first generation of post–World War II women historians celebrated the Anglo-American middle-class women from the Northeast who in the 1830s and 1840s began the movement to win the vote for women. These historians identified their own agency as new participants in the public sphere of higher education with the desire of the pioneers of the suffrage movement to participate in the public sphere. What these post-1950 historians did not recognize, however, was that the Anglo-American women reformers of the nineteenth century had wanted to bring the virtues of the middle-class home dominated by women into the public sphere. They had wanted to reform the political world of men without losing the unique identity of the middle-class

Centrality of home

home. In contrast to the postwar women historians, the suffrage leaders before the Civil War, like the men of George Bancroft's generation, saw the modern nation as the climax of an inevitable historical process. And they also saw the bourgeois nuclear family standing at the end of history. The middle-class Anglo-American women of the Northeast during the American renaissance, therefore, did not want to escape the bourgeois family; they only wanted to bring its virtues into the public sphere.

but some of this was a good idea

But the second generation of post–World War II women historians did not see the issue of women's liberation as one of redefining and revitalizing an eternally bounded nation. Instead, as they lost their loyalty to bourgeois nationalism, they began to imagine that there were bourgeois patterns of culture that had circulated on both sides of the Atlantic. Now one could argue that the nuclear family was a major element in the bourgeois nationalism that claimed cultural hegemony over aristocrats and peasants in Europe and indigenous peoples in the Americas. Replacing the local landscapes of peasants, aristocrats, and Indians with a national landscape, the middle classes also wanted to replace the extended families of those groups with the nuclear family. Modern nations were pure and virtuous compared to the peoples without history, and the nuclear family was pure and virtuous compared to the sexual laxness of the families of less civilized peoples.

a 2nd wave

In imagining history as progress from savagery through barbarism to civilization, the bourgeoisie saw the nuclear family as an essential progressive institution. To the extent that backward races could be civilized, their conversion to the purity of the nuclear family was necessary. From the 1830s to the 1940s, therefore, Anglo-American middle-class women reformers, including the leaders of the suffrage movement, felt the responsibility to teach Native American, African American, and Mexican American women the virtues of the bourgeois patriarchal family. It also was the mission of middle-class women to use the spiritual power of their homes to contain the materialism that threatened the spirituality of the public sphere. Men, unable to sustain the civil religion of the nation by themselves, needed the help of their mothers, wives, sisters, and daughters. And since civilization depended on the nuclear family, middle-class women were more effective than men were as missionaries who could lift the women of backward cultures, cultures without history, out of their antiprogressive extended families. Becoming progressive, these women could then lead their sons into civilization.[25]

Central concern over African Am. family is not nuclear; no fathers; many fathers. But maybe the problem is the econ. culture which does not support alternate family structures.

But as women historians of the 1960s and 1970s, who were white and middle-class, experienced the collapsing aesthetic authority of bourgeois nationalism in the United States, they also experienced the collapsing aesthetic authority of Western civilization. The transnational bourgeoisie had insisted that specific bourgeois nations were necessary engines to push and pull humanity out of the darkness of the evolutionary stages of savagery and barbarism into the light of civilization. Now if one did not hold the modern nation as sacred, one also could not hold modern civilization as sacred. And, of course, one could not continue to hold the nuclear family as sacred.

This commitment to the nuclear family as the culmination of history as progress was also based on a commitment to state-of-nature anthropology. It was the nuclear family that made it possible for the individual to escape the artificial and corrupting patterns of all those cultures that had stood between the essential individual and the artless rationality of Western civilization. But now these women historians were losing the aesthetic authority that had kept them from seeing themselves as participants in a culture that itself was in the process of historical change. They were no longer able to define themselves as observers who, from their privileged position in the timeless space of Western civilization, could objectively study the inferior people who lived in the flux of time. Women historians were part of a particular culture, and their agency was not superior to that of the women who lived in other particular cultures. These women historians were no longer writing the history of liberty for Anglo-Protestant women. They were no longer ignoring the power that middle-class Anglo-Protestant women had exercised over lower-income white women as well as Native American, African American, Mexican American, and Asian American women.

Younger women historians in the 1990s, therefore, such as Kathleen M. Brown in her essay, "Beyond the Great Debates: Gender and Race in Early America" (1998), spoke about their increasing interest in anthropology. It is my argument that these historians implicitly replaced the aesthetic authority of state-of-nature anthropology with the aesthetic authority of cultural anthropology. This means that they see the "subjectivity" of individual women as a process. A woman's identity comes from her interaction with the values, traditions, and institutions of her community. Identity is a timeful creation and it changes through time as community values, traditions, and institutions are reconstructed. In contrast to imagining a golden age for women (Anglo-Protestant middle class) in the colonial era when they escaped the English past, Brown sees her generation expecting the flow of culture from England to New England. They see the institution of the family brought from England as powerfully patriarchal. And the values and traditions of this patriarchal family continued to be recreated and revitalized throughout the seventeenth and eighteenth centuries. The patriarchy of the early nineteenth century, therefore, was a variation of English families.[26]

If one broke out of the aesthetic authority of Anglo-Protestant exceptionalism, one could become interested in the role of Native American and African American women and how the traditions of their families differed from those of the English colonists. The publication of Mary Beth Norton's *Founding Mothers and Fathers: Gendered Power and the Forming of American Society* in 1996 symbolized the authority of an alternative narrative to that of the history of liberty. It suggested the context in which books such as *Negotiators of Change: Historical Perspectives on Native American Women* (1995), edited by Nancy Shoemaker, and *More Than Chattel: Black Women and Slavery in the Americas* (1996), edited by David Barry Gaspar and Darlene Clark Hine, would appear.[27]

It was this ability to see the identity of individuals as the product of the dialogues in which they were engaged that had changed women's studies into gender studies. Women were in constant conversation with men. And if the identities of women were expressions of those conversations, so were the identities of men. The literary critic Nina Baym, in her "Melodramas of Beset Manhood," had pointed to the refusal of male literary critics to acknowledge that male authors and their male protagonists experienced an environment of dialogue. Instead, they insisted on the authenticity of the author's monologue and the purity of their protagonists' autonomy. A decade later, the historian Kenneth A. Lockridge published *On the Sources of Patriarchal Rage: The Commonplace Books of William Byrd and Thomas Jefferson and the Gendering of Power in the Eighteenth Century* (1992). If men, for Lockridge, lived in families but insisted on their autonomy, this quest for perfect liberty must have resulted in great frustration.[28]

The concept that individual identity was the creation of the dialogue a person experienced with other individuals within a context of traditions and institutions brought about a reunion of social and political history. It is conventional wisdom among historians that during the

Shift in historical interest

does DN agree or disagree w/ S. Berkovitch

1960s political history was replaced by social history as the area that most interested historians. In the argument that I have developed, this change symbolizes the dwindling aesthetic authority of bourgeois nationalism. For Turner, the Beards, and the two Schlesingers, political history was where the drama of the cycles of national history was played out. They worked within what Sacvan Bercovitch defined as the American Jeremiad, the sense of a timeless promise, a declension into timeful chaos and a prophecy that this chaos would be transcended and the original promise restored. As the historical profession developed after the 1880s, the study of American history began to be divided up into this sequence of generations. One specialized in the American Revolution, or Jacksonian Democracy, or the Civil War and Reconstruction, or the Gilded Age and Progressivism, or the 1920s and the New Deal. By limiting their research to autonomous generations, historians could avoid the terrible possibility that the history of the United States was one of change in time and that the nation was not the end of history.

all had agency

 The growing interest in social history symbolized, therefore, the implicit definition of history as the environment in which the actions of the people without history were as important as those of the people with history because these avant-gardes could no longer guarantee that history was progressive. Many of the social historians of the 1960s and 1970s turned their backs on what they now called the history of elites. They wanted to study lower-income people as well as those excluded from the national story because of racial, ethnic, or gender considerations. But as women historians moved toward a redefinition of their field as that of gender studies, they could no longer ignore the world of elite politics. If the identities of women and men were social constructions, an important element in those constructions came from the legal and political institutions existing at any given time. If social history in the 1960s and 1970s was an implicit attempt to ignore the existence of power, gender studies insisted that power was always present. Recent books, such as *Women before the Bar: Gender, Law, and Society in Connecticut: 1639–1789* (1995) by Cornelia Hughes Dayton and *Courts and Commerce: Gender, Law, and the Market Economy in Colonial New York* (1997) by Deborah A. Rosen, reminded their readers that there was no autonomous sphere for women.[29]

will to power

 The perception of the role of law in defining gender roles became especially important in the developing scholarship on gays and lesbians.

George Mosse had argued in *Nationalism and Sexuality* (1985) that when the middle classes had the power to create bourgeois nationalism they rejected as unclean and abnormal the sexual practices of peasants and aristocrats in Europe and in traditional cultures throughout the world. The state-of-nature anthropology of the bourgeoisie insisted that the essential individual was heterosexual and destined to participate in the nuclear family. Gays and lesbians, therefore, were deviant within the culture of bourgeois nationalism. They were people without history and found no representation in the history of the American people or in the histories of other bourgeois nations. Laws in all bourgeois nations defined homosexuals as outlaws.[30]

When bourgeois nationalism began to come apart in the United States during the 1940s, one of the responses of the dominant culture was to try to keep homosexuals from becoming one of the groups who were escaping from the category of people without history. The government ordered the outing of homosexuals in the military and their discharge. The Eisenhower administration demanded an oath from government employees that they were not homosexuals. *Homosexuality in Cold War America* (1997) by Robert J. Corber presents much of this story. The crucial importance of law is the theme of *Making History: The Struggle for Gay and Lesbian Equal Rights, 1945–1990* (1992) by Eric Marcus; *Sex Wars: Sexual Dissent and Political Culture* (1995) by Lisa Duggan and Nan Hunter; *A Nation by Rights: National Culture, Sexual Identity Politics, and the Discourse of Rights* (1998) by Carl Stychin; and *Freedom to Differ: The Shaping of the Gay and Lesbian Struggle for Civil Rights* (1998) by Diane Helene Miller.[31]

Those who were rejecting the political synthesis believed that, looked at from the perspective of privileged middle-class, Anglo-Protestant men, all other peoples were victims of their power. Focusing only on the social history of these formally excluded peoples, one could celebrate their agency, their liberty. But gender studies emphasized a both/and logic in contrast to the either/or logic of the social historians of the 1960s. Excluded groups were victims, and they had agency. One could only understand their agency if one saw how it worked with and against those who had power over them. This was the perspective of books such as *Ar'n't I a Woman: Female Slaves in the Plantation South* (1985) by Deborah Gray White; *Labor of Love, Labor of Sorrow: Black Women, Work, and the Family from Slavery to the Present* (1986) by Jacqueline Jones;

Gendered Strife and Confusion: The Political Culture of Reconstruction (1997) by Laura F. Edwards; *To 'Joy My Freedom: Southern Black Women's Lives and Labors after the Civil War* (1997) by Tera Hunter; and *Living In, Living Out: African American Domestics in Washington, D.C.* (1994) by Elizabeth Clark-Lewis.[32]

The aesthetic authority that gave dignity to the histories of the peoples whom bourgeois nationalists had defined as without history assumed that it was natural for individuals to be participants in communities. This aesthetic authority, rejecting the state-of-nature anthropology of bourgeois nationalism, found that individuals gained strength from their relationships to other individuals. This was the message of this group of books about black women. But the persuasive power of this alternative aesthetic authority built on the naturalness of cultural anthropology found its most dramatic expression, perhaps, in the field of immigration history. Turner, like the Beards, had feared the "new" immigrants from southern and eastern Europe because they were bringing antiprogressive Jewish and Catholic traditions with them. These Anglo-Protestant historians believed that only Protestants from northern Europe could fulfill their potential to become autonomous individuals. When this "new" immigration was ended by the congressional legislation of the 1920s that the Beards celebrated in their *Rise of American Civilization,* historians who participated in the culture of isolation in the 1930s could write as if the "new" immigrants, like African Americans or Mexican Americans or Asian Americans, had never entered the virgin land that was the national landscape.

The writing of immigration history in the 1930s, therefore, was done by historians such as George Stephenson, Theodore Blegen, Carl Wittke, and Marcus Lee Hanson. These Scandinavian and German American historians wrote that their ancestors had easily been assimilated into the national melting pot. But their ability to repress the existence of the "new" immigrants ended dramatically in the 1940s, when it was the policy of the Roosevelt administration to recognize male Catholics and Jews as equal citizens with Protestants. Oscar Handlin, the first Jew to achieve tenure at Harvard as a Professor of American History, had published *The Uprooted: The Epic Story of the Great Migrations That Made the American People* in 1951. The narrative of this prize-winning book, like those on immigration written by Protestant historians of the 1930s, expressed the authority of state-of-nature anthropology. But its reassuring message was that all immigrants from Europe—Catholics and Jews as well as Protestants—could step out of their culture. Again, he assumed, like his predecessors, that the avant-garde was made up of males.[33]

But, of course, the same new culture of internationalism that was being constructed in the 1940s, which had made popular Handlin's inclusion of Catholics and Jews from Europe as first-class citizens, also was destroying the aesthetic authority of the national landscape and the homogeneous culture it supposedly had produced. As the vision of a national landscape and a national people became less persuasive, so did the state-of-nature anthropology they embodied. In 1964 Rudolph Vecoli explicitly attacked Handlin's thesis that European immigrants had become separated from their Old World cultures when they came to the United States. Implicitly using the outlook of cultural anthropology, Vecoli saw the survival of traditions and institutions in a community of Italian immigrants in Chicago. The revolution of aesthetic authority among historians of immigration was so rapid that by 1985 John Bodnar published *The Transplanted,* a synthesis of the scholarship that implicitly used cultural anthropology. The Vecoli-Bodnar generation was self-consciously influenced by the writings of European historians such as Frank Thistlewaite and Dirk Hoerder, who had argued against the metaphor of two worlds that had informed both the isolationist historians of the 1930s and Oscar Handlin. Walter Nugent used the insights of Thistlewaite and Hoerder in his *Crossings: The Great Transatlantic Migrations, 1870–1914* (1992). Here he compared migrations to Canada and Argentina with that to the United States. In 1993 Mark Wyman published *Round Trip to America: The Immigrants' Return to Europe, 1890–1930,* which presented a stark contradiction to Handlin's metaphor of the uprooted.[34]

As usual, attention to the role of women lagged, coming in studies of European emigration only recently, as in *From the Other Side: Women, Gender, and Immigrant Life in the United States, 1820–1990* (1994) by Donna Gabaccia. Because most immigrants since the legislation of 1965 have come from Asia and Latin America, historians representing these groups have been shifting the focus of immigration history away from Europe. Some books representing this trend are *Occupied America: A History of Chicanos* (1988) by Rodolfo Acuña; *Strangers from a Different Shore: A History of Asian-Americans* (1989) by Ronald Takaki; and *Margins and*

Mainstreams: Asians in American History and Culture (1994) by Gary Okihiro. Accompanying this aesthetic affirmation of the reality of the local, in contrast to the universal national envisioned by bourgeois nationalists, was the affirmation of the international in contrast to the bounded nation. The emphasis in colonial history on the crucial importance of transatlantic markets in moving millions of people across the Atlantic was becoming the most powerful interpretive model for migrations in the nineteenth and twentieth centuries. Expressions of this hypothesis are found in such studies as *Labor Migration in the Atlantic Economies: The European and North American Working Classes During the Period of Industrialization* (1983), edited by Dirk Hoerder; *Migration, Migration History: Old Paradigms and New Perspectives* (1997), edited by Jan Lucassen and Leo Lucassen; and *Global History and Migrations* (1997), edited by Wang Gungwu.[35]

problem w/ "implicit"

In discussing the challenge to the aesthetic authority of bourgeois nationalism in the writing of history since the 1940s, I have frequently used the word "implicit." I have pointed to many historians who implicitly reject the bourgeois nation as the end of history. They have implicitly rejected the aesthetic authority of a national landscape and its children, a homogeneous people. They have implicitly rejected state-of-nature anthropology. They have implicitly found the local and the international to be more significant spaces to study than the modern nation. Because much of the debate among historians who defend bourgeois nationalism as the focus of historical research and historians who want to focus on the local and/or international rests on implicit rather than explicit hypotheses, historians tend to talk past each other. It is difficult for them to explicitly identify how their paradigms differ from each other's.

latest historians

It is not surprising that I find that the postnationalist historians have achieved greater clarity, however, than the nationalist historians. No longer persuaded by the aesthetic authority of bourgeois nationalism, postnationalist historians are deconstructing its assumptions. They see evidence that contradicts the hypothesis that there is a bounded nation and a homogeneous people. They present evidence that the local and international are spaces in which the actions of individuals have great meaning. At the moment this position has been expressed most fully in a number of articles, rather than books. Some of these are "The Autonomy of American History Reconsidered" (1979) by Laurence Veysey;

"American Exceptionalism in an Age of International History" (1991) by Ian Tyrrell; "Of Audiences, Borderlands, and Comparisons: Toward the Internationalization of American History" (1992) by David Thelen; "Recovering America's Historic Diversity: Beyond Exceptionalism" (1992) by Joyce Appleby; "Neither Exceptional Nor Peculiar: Towards the Comparative Study of Labor in Advanced Society" (1993) by James E. Cronin; "From Exceptionalism to Variability: Recent Developments in Cross-National Comparative History" (1995) by George M. Fredrickson; and "Exceptionalism" (1998) by Daniel T. Rogers. Rogers was in the position to summarize twenty years of scholarship on the local and international, which he found strongest in the colonial period. But he pointed to important scholarship that placed nineteenth-century religious, gender, labor, immigration, and political cultural patterns in an international context. Rogers had just published *Atlantic Crossings: Social Politics in a Progressive Age* (1998).[36]

I find that the younger defenders of bourgeois national history share many of the contradictions that I found in the writings of Arthur Schlesinger. In 1986, Thomas Bender, in his essay "Wholes and Parts: The Need for Synthesis in American History," lamented that there had been no successful synthesis since the Beards' *The Rise of American Civilization.* But he did not ask why the Beards' synthesis was not relevant to historians in the 1980s. And he did not suggest how a focus on a bounded nation and a homogeneous national culture could be achieved in the face of all the local cultures and the international patterns being written about by his contemporaries. In "The Price of the New Transnational History" (1991) Michael McGerr warned that historians who eroded national boundaries would lose readers from the general public who were committed to the vision of a bounded nation. Michael Kammen, like Bender a leader of the generation immediately behind mine, warned in his "The Problem of American Exceptionalism" (1993) of the dangers of incoherence that faced those who rejected a national narrative. And John Higham from my generation echoed this warning in his "The Future of American History" (1994). Given my point of view, it is not surprising that I am struck by the pragmatic tone of this defense of national history. The defenders don't express a sense that their theories, hypotheses, and paradigms are intellectually superior or that they explain more of the data. They seem to me to be defending a tradition because without it there is no meaning. But this has always been the position of bourgeois nationalists. History has no meaning if it is about people who have no history, people who are not part of the universal nation. But, of course, bourgeois nationalists claimed that their position was the antithesis of tradition. Tradition was fluid but not progressive. Bourgeois nationalists claimed they were superior to peoples who lived within tradition because bourgeois nationalists had the method to discover timeless truths. Defending tradition, bourgeois nationalists, therefore, inadvertently place themselves within the dimension of time as unpredictable change, the world they feared and hoped to escape from. They can defend an inherited tradition, but then they cannot prophesy that their national story will be one of progress from the irrational to the rational. Losing the metaphor of two worlds, they must link national exceptionalism to a vision born in time. Without the high ground of objectivity, the timeless space of nature's nation, they must explain why it is not probable that their tradition will change in time. They must also explain why it is not possible that their tradition born in time will also die in time.[37]

Epilogue

The story I have told about the triumph of cultural anthropology in the writing of literary criticism and history since the 1960s is filled with irony. In contrast to these academic cultures, the dominant political culture in the United States from the 1940s to the present has been characterized by a revitalization of state-of-nature anthropology. Bourgeois nationalism had qualified the imagined autonomy of the essential and natural individual who supposedly existed before the artful construction of society. Bourgeois nationalists insisted that this individual place national interest above self-interest. Building on this premise, these nationalists were able to link the liberty of citizens with an ideal of fraternity and equality. Bourgeois nationalists believed that the nation was as natural as the individual. They believed that the nation's society had grown organically out of the national landscape. Such a society, in contrast to all other societies, could not oppress the individual because it, too, emerged out of the state of nature.

This was why bourgeois nationalists feared the self-interest of the capitalism that, in the name of the boundless international marketplace, denied the bounded sanctity of the national landscape. But bourgeois nationalists, of course, were covert believers in the boundless marketplace, and it has been my argument that bourgeois elites in many parts of the world had begun, by the 1940s, to renounce the vision of bounded and sacred peoples who were the children of bounded and sacred national landscapes.

It was this desacralization of the paradigm of national peoples who had sprung from national landscapes that made it possible for historians and literary critics to interpret bourgeois nationalism as a cultural construction. They could now appreciate the dignity of all the other cultures whose existence had been repressed either by the aesthetic authority of bourgeois nationalism or by the aesthetic authority of Western civilization. The assumed superiority of Western civilization to all other cultures was dependent on the aesthetic authority of bourgeois nationalism because modern Europeans and European settlers throughout the world believed that Western civilization was the sum of the autonomous cultures of modern nations. Western civilization could not advance, according to this view, unless it was propelled forward by particular nations. It followed, then, that when the aesthetic authority of bourgeois nationalism disintegrated during the 1940s, so did the aesthetic authority of Western civilization. The postcolonial era emerged when bourgeois elites could no longer claim a natural cultural superiority over the unnatural cultures of colonized peoples within the nation's boundaries or the colonized peoples within an external empire.[1]

But the dismissal of the vision of a sacred people also meant that bourgeois elites were no longer committed to linking liberty with equality and fraternity. In the realm of the new sacred international marketplace, there was only liberty. Self-interest was no longer disciplined by national interest. The new dominant political culture of the 1950s no longer found it legitimate for the national government to engage in economic planning. In the 1960s, the sociologist Robert Bellah feeling the disintegration of bourgeois nationalism, began to argue for the existence of a national civil religion. For him, civil religion signified the existence of a community of shared national values. Implicitly he described these values as liberty, equality, and fraternity. But in his book of the 1970s, *The Broken Covenant,* Bellah lamented that many people were forgetting the need for a vision of equality and fraternity. Focusing only on liberty, they were allowing the social cohesion of national interest, the civil religion of community, to dissolve. Bellah was engaged in a jeremiad as he tried to recall his fellow Americans to their national church.[2]

His jeremiad culminated in a book, *Habits of the Heart: Individualism and Commitment in American Life* (1985), that he coauthored.[3] Here Bellah and his colleagues lamented that most Americans were so blinded by a false individualism that they did not understand how their lives were not only enriched by their participation in community, but actually depended on the existence of community. Bellah was only one of many contemporary academics who lamented the declension of the United States from what they saw as the powerful public philosophy of the 1930s to the current situation, in which both the Republican and Democratic parties reject the heritage of Franklin Roosevelt's New Deal.[4] For example, Michael J. Sandel, a professor of political science at Harvard, published *Democracy's Discontent: America in Search of a Public Philosophy* in 1996. It, too, is an elegy for the nineteenth-century tradition of republican virtue. As one reviewer wrote, "American history is, in Mr. Sandel's telling, a story of the tragic loss of civic republicanism." Michael Schudson, however, in his *The Good Citizen: A History of American Civic Life* (1998), rejects the pessimism of scholars like Bellah and Sandel. His rhetorical strategy is to place them in a framework of cultural lag. The nation, for him, is a living entity, and, with World War II, it entered a new stage of political identity. Sounding like the apologists for art as a marketplace commodity, Schudson is enthusiastic that citizens have become liberated from the constraints of political parties. To an extent they are even free from the constraints of governmental institutions. Joining with small groups of like-minded citizens, they can use the initiative to pass legislation. They can thus avoid executives, legislatures, and judiciaries as they pursue their self-interest in a political marketplace of autonomous individuals. Schudson, rejecting the outmoded values of equality and fraternity, is celebrating liberty as the necessary logic of the marketplace. The tradition of bourgeois nationalism that Schudson was renouncing had feared capitalism because it threatened the sacred boundaries of the nation. Capitalism was also feared because it was believed that its doctrine of self-interest would endanger the equality and fraternity of the people; capitalism would introduce class hierarchy and power. From Bancroft in the 1830s to the Beards in the 1930s, Anglo-Protestant historians had presented a mythic vision of a classless middle-class society in conflict with an alien capitalism. In this way Anglo-Americans were always victims of power. It has only been since the 1950s that historians, breaking free from the aesthetic authority of bourgeois nationalism, have been able to confront the power that Anglo-Americans used to segregate the other Americans from their monopoly of the national identity.[5]

But since Anglo-American bourgeois nationalists also were the anonymous twins of the capitalists whose power they supposedly feared, the power they exercised over other Americans was always economic as well as cultural. Indeed it was their focus on the defense of the boundaries of a homogeneous Anglo-American people that rendered largely invisible the way in which cultural segregation was always linked to economic exploitation. In this way the existence of class hierarchies from 1789 to the present was repressed both by scholars and politicians.

This disassociation of race, ethnicity, and gender from class has continued to shape the outlook of the historians who have celebrated, since the 1950s, the destruction of the imagined boundaries of the exclusive male, Anglo-Protestant citizenship established in the 1830s. They have not focused on the economic benefits that Anglo-American men have gained and continue to gain from the complex pattern of economic exploitation of those who were not considered part of the people. Because the people were defined as a classless middle class, the exploitation of white male workers was also repressed in the histories from Bancroft to the Beards. Now, as members of the dominant political culture join academics in celebrating the liberation of individuals from the restraints of racial, ethnic, and gender prejudices, these political spokesmen find it easy to define democracy much as Schudson does. They, too, see a land of liberty where every individual is free. Like Schudson, most American voters, therefore, do not see the flow of institutional patterns of economic exploitation and power from before the 1930s to the present. They are able to revitalize the Beards' commitment to the real America as a classless middle-class society.

As George Lipsitz argues, however, in *The Possessive Investment in Whiteness: How White People Profit from Identity Politics* (1998), participants in the dominant political culture, emphasizing the autonomy of individuals, have no notion of how government policies—national, state, and local, as well as policies of private banks—have put restrictions on the freedom of Americans who are not white to choose places to live. Zoning laws and the lending policies of banks have forced many of these Americans into ghettos in the central cities. This is also true of government-funded public housing. Meanwhile, government loans for new homes and the building of highways made it possible for whites to move out of the inner cities to the suburbs. It is difficult for minorities to find decent jobs in their ghettos, and they don't have the public transportation to follow the jobs created in the suburbs. The de facto segregation of the public schools guarantees fewer resources for the children of the ghetto. And cultural critics who celebrate a postmodern situation in which all master narratives have been broken down and one is free to choose one's own narrative are also complicit, therefore, in repressing the continuity of institutional power out of this past, into the present, and on into the future.[6]

Working from the perspective of Lipsitz, one might suggest that bourgeois nationalism was an episode in the history of capitalism. The European empires that began the conquest of the world during the Renaissance and Reformation were informed by the new bourgeois faith in the endless growth of the marketplace. And this faith assumed that surpluses, not scarcity, were the law of nature. In this respect the collapse of bourgeois nationalism since the 1940s has not undermined the master narrative of the bourgeoisie. The faith in the boundless marketplace and inevitable surpluses that characterizes dominant political cultures in most of the world today was there in the late eighteenth century, when bourgeois nations were first constructed.

It is the marketplace and its surpluses that are the ground for the bourgeois ideology of liberty. But the existence of the faith in the boundless marketplace and the surpluses that it demands has always depended on the use of military and political power to bring surpluses into the marketplace. Surpluses are not the innocent gift of nature; they come from the artful construction and use of political and military institutions. A term for the use of these institutions to conscript surpluses for the marketplace is "imperialism." European imperialists organized the slave trade to force people to produce for the marketplace. European settlers in North and South America, South Africa, Australia, and New Zealand destroyed the subsistence economies of the indigenous peoples to force them to produce for the marketplace. Peasant cultures were destroyed in Europe itself to force people to produce for the marketplace.

During the period of bourgeois nationalism the reality of the continued uprooting of populations by capitalist imperialism and their forced migrations was obscured by the vision that bourgeois nations were establishing boundaries and their populations were becoming rooted. It was obscured by the ability of bourgeois nationalists to persuade themselves that imperialism was an expression only of the international capitalism that existed outside of national boundaries. In this way bourgeois nationalists could link mass migrations from and within Europe to developing patterns of citizenship, rather than to the social dislocations caused by developments in the structure of capitalism. It has been the

[margin notes: Globalization / not new / now seen]

breakdown of the aesthetic authority of bourgeois nationalism, therefore, that makes it possible for us to imagine the existence of a new era of globalization. Because all bourgeois nations insisted on their isolation, their sacred autonomy, World War II was a revolution that suddenly made the international marketplace more sacred than national landscapes.

This means that as some scholars since the 1940s continue to believe the real America is a classless middle-class society, other scholars continue to believe that the era of bourgeois nationalism, 1790–1940s, was not one of a global economy. We continue to be influenced, then, by the way in which bourgeois nationalists saw themselves withdrawing from eighteenth-century internationalism. But each bourgeois nation, believing that the progress of Western civilization depended on the initiative of particular modern nations, was committed to spreading its unique form of civilization to the world.

This civilizing mission was, of course, interrelated with the belief of bourgeois elites that the prosperity of their nations depended on foreign markets and foreign raw materials. But because of the aesthetic authority of bourgeois nationalism, bourgeois elites did not see themselves participating in a common pattern of cultural and economic expansion. France alone would spread its unique culture to its colonies and seek new markets in those colonies. This would also be the pattern for England or Germany or the United States.

[margin note: "New" is really a return to 18c.]

What is new about the so-called postmodern era, then, is that bourgeois elites, rejecting their artistic heritages that supposedly grew organically out of their national landscapes, have no arts to offer the non-Western world. With the breakdown of the social discipline of bourgeois nationalism, these elites also can no longer offer the nuclear heterosexual family to "backward" peoples. Since the 1940s, then, Western elites can only offer their "superior" science and technology to the "underdeveloped" world. This, too, is a symbolic return to the universalism envisioned by bourgeois elites in the eighteenth century, before they created their modern nations supposedly rooted in particular states of nature. The promise of Western civilization now, freed from the boundaries of bourgeois nationalism, is that Western science and technology can create the economic miracle in which every individual in the world can become a middle-class consumer.

Because economic imperialism during the era of bourgeois nationalism was so powerfully connected to cultural imperialism both within and outside any particular nation, it has been difficult for postmodern theorists to see the continued flow of economic imperialism after World War II. Operating now through multinational corporations, this imperialism demands, however, as it did in 1500, the mobilization of populations to produce for the marketplace. And this imperialism assumes, as it did in 1500, that people must migrate to meet marketplace imperatives.[7]

There is an apparent novelty, however, in this pattern of postmodern migration. During the period of bourgeois nationalism, immigrants, responding to the demand of the marketplace, expected to become citizens of the nations to which they were drawn. Now, however, because of the way in which bourgeois nationalism has lost its aesthetic authority, it is possible for immigrants in any large city in the world to imagine that they will continue to construct and reconstruct the cultures they brought with them. Or they can imagine blending their cultures with those of other immigrant groups. Given the current disarray of bourgeois national cultures, it has become more difficult to imagine giving up one's culture to participate in what once had been a powerful symbol system. But this condition of cultural pluralism again is not completely novel in the sense that it existed before bourgeois nationalism was constructed. In the European empires from 1500 to 1800, it was not expected that the peoples uprooted by imperialism would become part of a homogeneous national culture. And, of course, during the period of bourgeois nationalism, many immigrants, as in the case of those from Asia coming to the United States, were barred from citizenship and had no choice but to construct alternative cultures within the nation. Beyond that, many immigrants whose whiteness made them eligible for citizenship chose not to accept Anglo-Protestant culture as a sacred center toward which they were making a pilgrimage.

An irony of our current situation, therefore, is that the explicit and implicit boundaries on citizenship began to be deconstructed in the 1940s when bourgeois elites, choosing to make the international marketplace more sacred than the national landscape, redefined citizenship as something pragmatic and secular, rather than sacred. It then became possible to challenge the implicit or explicit gender, ethnic, and racial barriers to citizenship because the aesthetic authority of a sacred homogeneous people no longer existed.[8]

The presidents of the United States during the period of bourgeois nationalism saw their political authority linked to economic growth. So have the presidents during the period of international capitalism. But the presidents of the current era, which began in the 1940s, are explicitly committed to the international marketplace as the source of national prosperity. They, therefore, no longer present themselves as leaders who will engage in national planning to sustain the health of the nation. They no longer use the rhetoric of equality and fraternity, as Franklin D. Roosevelt had once done in the presidential campaign of 1936. Since Roosevelt shifted his focus from domestic reform to internationalism in 1940, presidents have argued that government economic regulations hinder the efficient working of the marketplace. Into the 1970s these presidents, however, supported government regulation to overcome the political and social barriers that restricted the liberty of women and racial minorities.

But the new political culture of the marketplace had become so persuasive by the 1980s that there was a backlash against affirmative action legislation. If the marketplace was a state of nature where each individual should have the liberty to develop his/her essential identity, then affirmative action legislation, as much as government regulation of the economy, was a violation of the laws of the marketplace. The national and international marketplaces, however, were dominated by corporations and not individuals. Corporate leaders moved factory jobs out of the United States to countries where labor was cheaper. Union membership declined with the loss of what had been unionized workplaces. And, in the climate that demanded autonomy for the individual, unions were defined as part of the archaic restrictions of the 1930s.

Corporations, however, were largely immune from this kind of analysis. In the dominant political culture of the 1930s, corporations were defined as threats to the liberty, equality, and fraternity of the people. The national government was the spokesman and defender of the people against the hierarchical privilege of corporate capitalism. By 1980, however, Ronald Reagan, in his successful presidential campaign, helped reverse this perception as he identified government, not corporations, as the major threat to the liberty of the people. Another irony, therefore, was that the dominant role of corporations in the economy was obscured by this focus on the way that government was defined as the major threat to the liberty of the individual. Now dominating a nonunionized workforce and free of the concern of government regulation, corporate leaders had kept the buying power of the average American from increasing during the 1970s through the 1990s. Meantime, the salaries of corporate leaders skyrocketed. During these twenty years the richest 1 percent of Americans were able to increase their share of the national wealth from 20 percent to 40 percent.[9]

Presidents and corporate leaders christened these decades as ones of unprecedented prosperity. But, if you were an average white man during these years, you wondered why you were not sharing in the booming economy. One could not blame the corporations because somehow they were part of a marketplace of free individuals. The national government, however, was outside the now sacred international marketplace. One could be persuaded that it was profane government affirmative action that gave unfair advantage to women and to ethnic and racial minorities. It was the government that was keeping most white men from sharing in the economic miracle brought by an unfettered market. At its most extreme, this anger at the national government for devouring its own people, meaning white men, could lead to events such as the bombing of the Alfred G. Murrah Federal Building in Oklahoma City.

But for those of us who do not share the belief in a sacred marketplace, even the economic power of multinational corporations was not sufficient to artfully construct an international marketplace. From the beginning of the European empires in the Renaissance, military and political power was used to force resources into the marketplace. The political leaders of the United States had used military force to begin to construct the international marketplace in World War II. The presidents continued to use force to protect the marketplace from what they perceived as the threat of communism. With the end of the cold war, the presidents have used military force against "rogue" states that are seen as threats to world stability.

It is interesting, then, to analyze how Presidents Reagan, Bush, and Clinton worked to deconstruct the concept of a homogeneous people who should share economic equality, while they constructed the alternative concept of a people who must stand as a unified whole against "rogue" states. Because the international marketplace is not a state of nature that was discovered, it is an art form that needs constant reconstruction and revitalization. National armies continue to be necessary for that process of reconstruction. Scholars have been impressed by the way presidents have used television and the movies to manufacture the image of a unified people, symbolized by military regiments, who stand together against an artfully crafted and demonized enemy. A homogeneous people can participate in a particular kind of equality and fraternity while defending liberty because all individuals can participate vicariously in the organic unity of the military.

The promise of the international marketplace is a regime of perpetual peace. A continuing irony, however, is that one must be prepared for perpetual war to achieve the goal of peace. The culture of international capitalism seems, therefore, to be deeply divided. Within this culture one is asked to accept the rational working of the natural laws of the marketplace, but one is also encouraged to develop a personality that is stronger and more aggressive than that of the leaders of the "rogue" states. One must always be ready to make the sacrifices demanded by war. The repressed identity of violence as a characteristic of the international marketplace is also present within the nation. In the 1890s John Dewey had feared the doctrines of Herbert Spencer, which, for Dewey, meant the constant war of everyone against everyone. In 1944 Richard Hofstadter, in his *Social Darwinism in American Thought,* had celebrated the victory of reform Darwinists, like Dewey, over the Darwinists who believed that evolution meant a world of perpetual and unlimited competition. Hofstadter in 1944 thought that doctrine of the survival of the fittest and its implicit racism was only an irrelevant moment in the national past.

If, however, the dominant political culture in the United States at the end of the twentieth century and the beginning of the twenty-first century is one that sees us living in a marketplace that allows the individual to express her or his essential identity, then difference can only be explained by heredity. Our current dominant political culture, which shares many ideological aspects of the nineteenth century, vehemently rejects, as did the scientific racists of 1850, cultural anthropology. It, therefore, has encouraged a revitalization of white racism. Many marginalized white men have turned to right-wing groups that preach white supremacy. But a number of intellectuals also have been attracted to a racism that offers a simple, noninstitutional explanation of why, on average, racial minorities experience more poverty than do white Americans. It had become legitimate by 1994 for Charles Murray and Richard Herrnstein to argue in *The Bell Curve* that it was because African Americans were inherently less intelligent than whites that they had lower incomes.[10]

war & peace.

political culture

this feels more like the last gasp.

If women, ethnic, racial, and gay/lesbian minorities were once kept outside of the sacred circle of "the people" defined by bourgeois nationalists, they now seem to be in the process of being defined outside the current dominant political culture. According to this culture, the new world of international capitalism has given every individual the opportunity to make something of oneself. When a hierarchy emerges out of this competition, the unsuccessful individual can only blame him or herself. And if this survival of the fittest is true within the United States, it is also true among the world's nations. If the peoples of Africa or South America cannot lift themselves up to the economic level of the United States and Western Europe, it is their fault; they are inherently weak people who do not have the ability to climb the marketplace ladder.

[margin note: denial of institutional discrimination]

Much of academic culture at the beginning of the twenty-first century, therefore, is separated from the dominant political and economic culture. Academics who are committed to cultural anthropology find it difficult to communicate with a public committed to state-of-nature anthropology, and many lament that they cannot, therefore, become public intellectuals. I believe it is of crucial importance, then, for those of us in higher education to become self-conscious that we are part of a bourgeois heresy that began to be created in the late nineteenth century—that we are part of a heretical paradigm that includes more than the social sciences and humanities.[11]

[margin note: academics]

[margin note: David's call]

It was in the 1880s and 1890s that the cultures of bourgeois nationalism experienced a crisis when national landscapes were challenged by an urban-industrial landscape that seemed to promise an international future. Bourgeois music, painting, and architecture responded to the dissonance of these competing spaces. So did bourgeois novels, poetry, and drama. So also did bourgeois psychology and philosophy. It was during this crisis that some heretical anthropologists began to challenge state-of-nature anthropology. They began to argue that as language-speaking animals, humans are always members of a community. To be human is to participate in the shared and collectively constructed art form that is language. Because language is created by the community, it is always in the process of recreation. When one says that language is living, one has defined a community as having both the characteristics of space and time. The space of a language community has boundaries, but those boundaries change through time.

[margin note: heresy starting 1880's]

[margin note: cultural anthropology centrality of language communities]

[margin note bottom: → a beautiful definition]

The space-time relativism of the cultural anthropologists was a challenge to the bourgeois nationalists' faith in their nations as timeless spaces. It was because bourgeois nations were states of nature that they were seen as homes for the essential individuals who existed in the original state of nature. These individuals were themselves spaces without time. Cultural anthropology, therefore, challenged such individual identity and insisted that the boundaries of individuals also changed through time. But since World War II the new culture of the international marketplace has revitalized state-of-nature anthropology by arguing that the marketplace transcends the boundaries of a particular culture. Unlike the bourgeois nation as a bounded space, however, the international marketplace is a constantly expanding space. But, like the space of the bourgeois nation, it is supposedly timeless because it claims to be eternal. The international marketplace, like the bourgeois nation before it, insists that it is not limited by death. The boundless marketplace symbolizes perpetual youth.[12]

Many of us who are in the humanities and social sciences are not aware that the paradigm of the international marketplace, unlike the paradigm of bourgeois nationalism, cannot claim that it represents the authority of Newtonian physics. As we have participated in the deconstruction of bourgeois nationalism, we have argued the interrelationship of state-of-nature anthropology and state-of-nature physics. We have argued that both are untrue. But to a large extent we ironically now share with the spokesmen of bourgeois internationalism a commitment to an anthropology that is segregated from the natural sciences. The state-of-nature anthropology of bourgeois internationalism does not argue that it represents the laws of nature. But the bourgeois heresy of cultural anthropology also does not argue that it shares the logic of a heretical physics that was constructed simultaneously with it at the end of the nineteenth century. But some physicists, confronted in the 1890s with the vision of the two spaces, national and international, pastoral and urban-industrial, began to imagine that space and time were a continuum. Physical spaces, like language communities, changed their shapes through time. The observations of a physicist were not timeless because the physical world observed was a process. When observed at a later time, it would be a different environment. In Newton's timeless space, the forms of nature were not living or dying. In the alternative physics that became associated with the name of Albert Einstein,

there is birth and death. It is this dramatic paradigm revolution that
makes it possible to talk about our solar system as having been born
and eventually dying. It is this paradigm that led Kuhn to imagine that
scientific communities are born, have a life cycle, and die. The physics
that Thomas Kuhn had learned and that implicitly informed his *The
Structure of Scientific Revolutions* theorized that one always observes
from within a physical environment. Kuhn was not self-conscious that
when he argued that scientists always observe from within a social environment, he also was using the theory of cultural anthropology. But
both twentieth-century physics and anthropology share the metaphor
that we are always within a circle.

we are always within the Circle

 I believe, then, that the bourgeois heresy of cultural anthropology is
part of a larger pattern of cultural heresy that also includes twentieth-
century physics. Imagining this larger pattern, one can consider the
parallels between the space-time continuum proposed by cultural anthropology and by Einsteinian physics. It has been difficult for academic humanists and social scientists to think of themselves as sharing
a common culture with natural scientists. Such a culture, however, presents an alternative paradigm to bourgeois internationalism. And academic humanists and social scientists will find that they can communicate with a larger public if they can show how they are interrelated with
a more comprehensive critique of international capitalism shared by
many parts of the academic community, including the sciences.

a shared theoretical point of view

 It is this definition of the Earth as a living body that has made possible the current ecological movement. The belief of this movement that
the Earth, as a living body, has limits is, of course, absolutely incompatible with the belief in the boundless expansion of the marketplace. For
ecologists, this doctrine of necessary and inevitable expansion will disrupt the current rhythms of the Earth and cause severe disruptions. For
example, the rapid development of global warming, ecologists warn,
can have catastrophic consequences.[13]

ecology

 When the claims of bourgeois nationalists and Marxists that their
positions represented natural law were discredited during the 1940s, this
seemed to leave the culture of international capitalism free from scientific criticism. But the alternative vision of natural law held by ecologists has gained a voice in popular culture. Throughout the United States
and in many other countries, local governments demand environmental
impact studies before new buildings or new dams may be constructed.

It is now accepted in the United States that the use of fertilizers as well as pesticides can have a destructive impact on the quality of the air, land, and water. At the local level, it has become common sense that there are limits on our use of air, land, and water. These actions, however, are widely understood as minor compromises with the normal world of constant and inevitable economic growth. For many, they are not seen as expressions of a worldview that denies the legitimacy of the commitment of international corporations to perpetual growth.

But there are people everywhere in the world who do see the logic of the Earth as a living body as a direct confrontation with the logic of the international marketplace. People from Europe, Asia, Africa, and South America with an ecological commitment to the necessary limits to growth joined in 1999 with ecological activists in the United States to protest the globalization controlled by international corporations. They saw the World Trade Organization meeting in Seattle in fall 1999 as a voice of those corporations. There they were joined by trade unionists who also were ready to protest the policies made by men who had little concern for what happened to workers in local communities. Other protesters were people who did not want their local communities in Asia, Africa, or South America forced into producing for the international marketplace. They feared the disruption of complex social systems that gave their members a sense of meaningful community. This outlook was similar to that of ecologists who feared the disruption of complex natural systems that provided meaningful communities for plants, animals, and humans. Here was an example of how the principles of cultural anthropology and the principles of twentieth-century physics formed a holistic way of interpreting the social and physical environment. Here was a conversation between bourgeois heretics and indigenous peoples made possible because there were similarities between the anthropology and science held by both groups.[14]

It is the hope of many critics of the international marketplace that the Seattle coalition, which was present in spring 2000 at protests against a meeting of the International Monetary Fund (IMF) and the World Bank in Washington D.C., can expand to include more and more groups who have been excluded from the limited prosperity of the global economy. It is a coalition that believes in an international alliance whose groups want to preserve local cultural diversity even as local diversity in nature must also be preserved. It is a coalition that, if it grows in strength, will force the exponents of the boundless international marketplace to make their implicit commitment to state-of-nature anthropology explicit. It will reveal that bourgeois internationalists have no scientific authority for their faith in perpetual growth. Perhaps, then, people can be persuaded that the international marketplace is not a new world to be discovered but, like the New World of 1492, is an artful construction. Perhaps, then, more people will be persuaded that the most important tools used in the creation of the new worlds of 1492 and World War II were political and military. Perhaps, then, we can finally free ourselves from those metaphors that encourage us to flee the timeful complexity of a locality to find liberty in the timeless abstractions of the marketplace. Perhaps, then, we will be able to construct metaphors that will allow us to live at home within the circle of the Earth.

Notes

Foreword

1. Joyce V. Millen, Alexander Irwin, and Jim Yong Kim, "Introduction: What Is Growing? Who Is Dying?" in *Dying for Growth: Global Inequality and the Health of the Poor,* ed. Jim Yong Kim, Joyce V. Millen, Alexander Irwin, and John Hershman (Monroe, Maine: Common Courage Press, 2000), 5. Jean-Bertrand Aristide, *Eyes of the Heart: Seeking a Path for the Poor in the Age of Globalization* (Monroe, Maine: Common Courage Press, 2000), 5. Philip Martin and Jonas Widgren, "International Migration: A Global Challenge," *Population Bulletin* 51, no. 1 (1996): 2. Sidney E. Plotkin and William E. Scheuerman, *Private Interest, Public Spending: Balanced-Budget Conservatism and the Fiscal Crisis* (Boston: South End, 1994), 29.

2. William K. Tabb, *The Amoral Elephant: Globalization and the Struggle for Justice in the Twenty-first Century* (New York: Monthly Review Press, 2001), 21.

Introduction

1. John Carlos Rowe, ed., *Post-Nationalist American Studies* (Berkeley and Los Angeles: University of California Press, 2000), 5.

2. Ibid., 3.

3. Carole Pateman, in *The Sexual Contract* (Stanford: Stanford University Press, 1988), and Charles W. Mills, in *The Racial Contract* (Ithaca: Cornell University Press, 1997), place the sexism and racism of the Founding Fathers in the context of transnational bourgeois culture.

4. See my discussion of issues of gender, race, and class in American studies scholarship from the 1930s to the 1960s in chapters 4, 5, and 6 of this book.

5. See my discussion of the way historians shifted from the metaphor of the discovery of America to the invasion of America in chapter 8 of this book.

6. Thomas S. Kuhn, *The Structure of Scientific Revolutions* (Chicago: Chicago University Press, 1962).

7. Benedict Anderson, *Imagined Communities: Reflections on the Origins and Spread of Nationalism* (London: Verso, 1983).

8. Carl L. Becker, *The Heavenly City of the Eighteenth-Century Philosophers* (New Haven: Yale University Press, 1932).

9. David W. Noble, "The New Republic and the Idea of Progress," *The Mississippi Valley Historical Review* 38, no. 3 (December 1951): 387–402, and *The Paradox of Progressive Thought* (Minneapolis: University of Minnesota Press, 1958).

10. David W. Noble, *Historians against History: The Frontier Thesis and the National Covenant in American Historical Writing Since 1830* (Minneapolis: University of Minnesota Press, 1965), and *The Eternal Adam and the New World Garden: The Central Myth in the American Novel Since 1830* (New York: Braziller, 1968).

11. David W. Noble, *The Progressive Mind, 1890–1917* (Chicago: Rand McNally, 1970).

12. Peter N. Carroll and David W. Noble, *The Restless Centuries: A History of the American People* (Minneapolis: Burgess Publishing Co., 1973), and *The Free and the Unfree: A New History of the United States* (New York: Penguin Books, 1977).

13. J. G. A. Pocock, *The Machiavellian Moment: Florentine Political Thought and the Atlantic Republican Tradition* (Princeton: Princeton University Press, 1975).

14. Gene Wise, *American Historical Explanations: A Strategy for Grounded Inquiry* (Homewood, Ill.: Dorsey Press, 1973).

15. David W. Noble, *The End of American History: Democracy, Capitalism, and the Metaphor of Two Worlds in Anglo-American Historical Writing, 1880–1980* (Minneapolis: University of Minnesota Press, 1985).

16. For the economic worldview brought to North America by the English middle class, see Karl Polanyi, *The Great Transformation* (New York, Toronto: Farrar & Rinehart, Inc., 1944); Alan MacFarlane, *The Origins of English Individualism* (Oxford: Basil Blackwell, 1978); and C. B. MacPherson, *The Political Theory of Possessive Individualism: Hobbes to Locke* (Oxford: Oxford University Press, 1962). William Cronon discusses the conflict between the English middle-class view of private property and the Native American view of communal property in seventeenth-century New England in his *Changes in the Land: Indians, Colonists, and the Ecology of New England* (New York: Hill and Wang, 1983). The hostility of the English colonists toward the communal property system of Native Americans is directly linked to the hostility of the English middle class toward the subsistence economy of English peasants. See, for example, Michael Perelman, *The Invention of Capitalism: Classical Political Economy and the Secret History of Primitive Accumulation* (Durham: Duke University Press, 2000). An overview of the shift from the medieval to the modern worldview is provided by Daniel Philpott in his *Revolutions in Sovereignty: How Ideas Shaped Modern International Relations* (Princeton: Princeton University Press, 2001). He also discusses the erosion of Western political imperialism that occurred with World War II.

17. A useful overview of the way modern Europeans were separating a rational nature from an irrational society is Thomas DaCosta Kaufmann, *The Mastery of Nature: Aspects of Art, Science, and Humanism in the Renaissance* (Princeton: Princeton University, 1993). My views on the development of the modern middle-class perspective on space have been influenced by the cultural geographer Yi-Fu Tuan, especially his books *Topophilia: A Study of Environmental Perception, Attitudes, and Values* (Englewood Cliffs: Prentice Hall, 1974) and *Space and Place: The Perspective*

of Experience (Minneapolis: University of Minnesota Press, 1977). Denise Albanese, *New Science, New World* (Durham: Duke University Press, 1996) is a recent study of the ways in which early modern Europeans were defining medieval culture and all traditional cultures throughout the world as populated by irrational and dangerous Others. She calls attention to the importance of Michel de Certeau's argument in *The Writing of History,* trans. Tom Conley (New York: Columbia University Press, 1988), where he describes the ways that writers of modern history depend upon the creation of Others to sustain their thesis of modern exceptionalism.

18. When the metaphor of two worlds, an American New World separated from a European Old World, began to fall apart in the 1940s, scholars became aware of the way in which the European middle classes had imposed their vision of a limitless future on the American continents. Durand Echeverria, *Mirage in the West: A History of the French Image of American Society to 1815* (Princeton: Princeton University Press, 1957) and Charles Sanford, *The Quest for Paradise: Europe and the American Moral Imagination* (Urbana: University of Illinois Press, 1961) are two early studies. Edmundo O'Gorman, in *The Invention of America* (Bloomington: Indiana University Press, 1961), describes the transfer of the medieval view of Europe as the center of the world to the Renaissance view that the Americas would be the center. Developing this theme is an essay by Mircea Eliade, "Mythical Geography and Eschatology," in *Utopias and Utopian Thought,* ed. Frank E. Manuel (Boston: Houghton Mifflin, 1966). More recently, scholars, influenced by an ecological point of view that unites space and time, began to analyze the assumption that the European middle class imposed on the nature that they hoped would provide limitless bounty. Carolyn Merchant, in *The Death of Nature: Women, Ecology, and the Scientific Revolution* (San Francisco: Harper & Row, 1980), focused on the early modern denial that nature was characterized by cycles. She followed the transfer of this viewpoint across the Atlantic in her *Ecological Revolutions: Nature, Gender, and Science in New England* (Chapel Hill: University of North Carolina Press, 1989). Another overview is Donald Worster, *The Wealth of Nature: Environmental History and the Ecological Imagination* (New York: Oxford University Press, 1993). Annette Kolodny, in *The Lay of the Land: Metaphor as Experience and History in American Life and Letters* (Chapel Hill: The University of North Carolina Press, 1975), had argued that the men of the symbol-myth school had imposed a male fantasy on a landscape that had no independence. Frieda Knobloch, in *The Culture of Wilderness: Agriculture as Colonization in the American West* (Chapel Hill: The University of North Carolina Press, 1996), has taken Kolodny's metaphor and applied it to the development of the pattern of agriculture in early modern Europe that was focused on the market, rather than subsistence. She argues that this pattern, brought to the English colonies, assumed the possibility of limitless growth in production. She sees the issue of power in this agricultural paradigm. As humans were coerced into producing for the marketplace, so was nature coerced. But as recent scholars have come to argue that dominant groups were incapable of removing all agency from those people whom they dominated, Knobloch argues that the middle class has not been able to remove all agency from nature.

19. As recent scholars have lost their ability to accept the aesthetic authority of a negative revolution, many have come to accept the aesthetic authority of positive revolution. This is why Thomas Kuhn's *The Structure of Scientific Revolutions* had such a major impact in many academic disciplines. Kuhn dismissed what he saw as

the dominant tradition in the writing of the history of science. This tradition argued that beginning in the Renaissance, individuals escaped their cultural traditions and superstitions and were able to use their reason to directly see a piece of nature. This history of science saw a pattern of progress as more and more pieces of nature were observed. But it was Kuhn's position that scientists are always members of communities who study nature through a set of hypotheses that they share. Imagination is the source of these hypotheses, and what we know as reason is defined by the hypotheses. Participating in the same cultural revolution as did Kuhn, art historians began to argue that Renaissance artists had not found a way to see nature directly. They were attacking the dominant paradigm represented in the books of E. H. Gombrich, *The Story of Art* (New York: Phaidon Publishers, 1950) and *Art and Illusion: A Study in the Psychology of Pictorial Representation* (London: Phaidon Press, 1959). Gombrich had used the phrase "the conquest of nature" to describe Renaissance painting. Landscape, for the new alternative paradigm in art history, was something imagined and constructed by a particular group of painters at a particular time. Landscape was not a timeless space. Finding or discovering a landscape implied an innocent role for the painter. Creating a landscape implied that the painter was exercising power. One of the most powerful analyses of the use of landscape painting by the middle class to remove peasants and aristocrats from a landscape in Europe monopolized by the middle class and to remove indigenous peoples from landscapes in America, Africa, or Australia so they could be monopolized by European settlers is W. J. T. Mitchell's *Landscape and Power* (Chicago: University of Chicago Press, 1994). Another important study is John Barrell, *The Dark Side of the Landscape: The Rural Poor in English Painting, 1730–1840* (Cambridge: Cambridge University Press, 1980).

20. The European bourgeoisie had constructed an aesthetic authority in anthropology, painting, and science that gave them the sense of cultural superiority to members of medieval cultures and members of the indigenous cultures on other continents that modern Europeans were conquering. The bourgeoisie assumed they had learned that all traditional peoples were trapped within the unreality of culture. But the bourgeoisie were free from the limits of those cultures and were now able to see nature in all its limitless plenitude. Why, then, were these modern people of Western Europe able to escape these unusable pasts? It must be that they could achieve harmony with nature because their biological inheritance was stronger than, more in harmony with, the plenitude of nature. As the children of nature, they were racially superior to the peoples of traditional societies. Ivan Hannaford, in *Race: The History of an Idea in the West* (Baltimore: The Johns Hopkins University Press, 1996), demonstrates how racism—like state-of-nature anthropology, the physics of Galileo and Newton, and landscape painting—was a major element in the construction of a modern European worldview.

21. See, for example, William G. McLaughlin, *Revivals, Awakenings, and Reform: An Essay on Religion and Social Change in America, 1607–1977* (Chicago: University of Chicago Press, 1978).

22. The Anglo-Protestant vision of Jews as materialistic aliens is explored in Bryan Cheyette, ed., *Between "Race" and Culture: Representations of "the Jew" in English and American Literature* (Stanford: Stanford University Press, 1996); Jonathan and Daniel Boyarin, eds., *Jews and Other Differences: The New Jewish Cultural Studies*

(Minneapolis: University of Minnesota Press, 1995); and David Gerber, ed., *Anti-Semitism in American History* (Urbana: University of Illinois Press, 1986).

23. See, for example, Robert Berkhofer, *Beyond the Great Story: History as Text and Discourse* (Cambridge: Harvard University Press), 1995.

1. The Birth and Death of American History

1. David W. Noble, *Historians against History: The Frontier Thesis and the National Covenant in American Historical Writing Since 1830* (Minneapolis: University of Minnesota Press, 1965), and *The End of American History: Democracy, Capitalism, and the Metaphor of Two Worlds in Anglo-American Historical Writing, 1880–1980* (Minneapolis: University of Minnesota Press, 1985).

2. See Shlomo Avineri, *Hegel's Theory of the Modern State* (Cambridge: Cambridge University Press, 1972); Raymond Plant, *Hegel: An Introduction* (Oxford: Basil Blackwell, 1983); Robert Wuthnow, *Communities of Discourse: Ideology and Social Structure in the Reformation, the Enlightenment, and European Socialism* (Cambridge: Harvard University Press, 1989); and Jonathan Boyarin, ed., *Remapping Memory: The Politics of TimeSpace* (Minneapolis: University of Minnesota Press, 1994). Because most scholars no longer take nationalism for granted as a natural given, there has been an explosion of scholarship on the subject. This desacralization project is expressed by Emily S. Apter in her book *Continental Drift: From National Characters to Virtual Subjects* (Chicago: University of Chicago Press, 1999), where she looks at the ways the collapse of bourgeois nationalism in France has caused French scholars to reexamine issues of class, race, ethnicity, and gender within France and the former French empire. She links these new perspectives on nationalism to scholarship in England, Germany, and the United States, as well as to the writing of scholars from former European colonies. Prasenjit Duara, in his book *Rescuing History from the Nation: Questioning Narratives of Modern China* (Chicago: University of Chicago Press, 1995), discusses the ways the model of bourgeois nationalism has informed the writing of historians in India and China. Some other recent books are Ernest Gellner, *Nations and Nationalism* (Ithaca: Cornell University Press, 1983); E. J. Hobsbawm, *Nations and Nationalism Since 1780: Programme, Myth, Reality* (Cambridge and New York: Cambridge University Press, 1990); Étienne Balibar and Immanuel Wallerstein, eds., *Race, Nation, Class: Ambiguous Identities*, trans. Chris Turner (London: Verso, 1991); Homi K. Bhabha, ed., *Nation and Narration* (London: Routledge, 1990); Paul Gilroy, *"There Ain't No Black in the Union Jack": The Cultural Politics of Race and Nation* (Chicago: University of Chicago Press, 1991); Anne McClintock, Aamir Mufti, Ella Shohat, eds., *Dangerous Liaisons: Gender, Nations, and Postcolonial Perspectives* (Minneapolis: University of Minnesota Press, 1997); Arjun Appadurai, *Modernity at Large: Cultural Dimensions of Globalization* (Minneapolis: University of Minnesota Press, 1996); Partha Chatterjee, *The Nation and Its Fragments: Colonial and Postcolonial Histories* (Princeton: Princeton University Press, 1993); Andrew Parker et. al., eds., *Nationalisms and Sexualities* (New York: Routledge, 1992); Geoff Eley and Ronald Grigor Suny, eds., *Becoming National: A Reader* (Oxford, New York: Oxford University Press, 1996); Anthony W. Marx, *Making Race and Nation: A Comparison of South Africa, the United States, and Brazil*

(New York: Cambridge University Press, 1998); Jinqi Ling, *Narrating Nationalism: Ideology and Form in Asian American Literature* (New York: Oxford University Press, 1998); Maghan Keita, *Race and the Writing of History: Riddling the Sphinx* (New York: Oxford University Press, 2000); and Anthony Smith, *National Identity* (London: Penguin, 1991). In 1995 Jean-Marié Guéhenno published *The End of the Nation-State* (Minneapolis: University of Minnesota Press, 1995). That same year Kenichi Ohmae published *The End of the Nation-State: The Rise of Regional Economies* (London: Free Press, 1995).

3. Motley, Prescott, Parkman, and Bancroft are discussed in David Levin, *History as Romantic Art* (Stanford: Stanford University Press, 1959), and Philip Wayne Powell, *Tree of Hate: Propaganda and Prejudices Affecting United States Relations with the Hispanic World* (New York: Basic Books, 1971). Robert Young, in *White Mythologies: Writing History and the West* (London, New York: Routledge, 1990), relates the beginning of postcolonial cultural analyses in the United States to the publication of Edward W. Said's *Orientalism* (New York: Pantheon Books, 1978). Said implicated the work of European scholars in creating a representation of Asia and Africa that justified European imperialism as a necessary paternalistic role. Clearly the same argument can be applied to representations of "Latin" America by Anglo-Protestant scholars in the United States. See, for example, William Prescott, *History of the Conquest of Mexico* (Philadelphia: J. B. Lippincott, 1864), 85–86, and *History of the Conquest of Peru* (Philadelphia: J. B. Lippincott, 1874).

4. John L. Motley, *The Rise of the Dutch Republic: A History* (New York: Harper & Brothers, 1859).

5. Francis Parkman, *The Jesuits in North America in the Seventeenth Century* (Boston: Little, Brown, and Company, 1867), 135.

6. George Bancroft, *History of the United States: From the Discovery of the Continent [1789]*, vol. 3 (Boston: C. C. Little and J. Brown, 1846), 478. See the discussion of Bancroft in Noble, *Historians against History.*

7. George Bancroft, *Literary and Historical Miscellanies* (New York: Harper, 1855), 449. I have been influenced by Bruce Greenfield's discussion of aesthetic authority in "The Problems of the Discoverer's Authority in Lewis and Clark's History," in *Macropolitics of Nineteenth-Century Literature: Nationalism, Exoticism, Imperialism*, ed. Jonathan Arac and Harriet Ritvo (Philadelphia: University of Pennsylvania Press, 1991). See also Myra Jehlen, *American Incarnation: The Individual, the Nation, and the Continent* (Cambridge: Harvard University Press, 1986).

8. See my discussions of Turner in Noble, *Historians against History* and *The End of American History.* See also Jack D. Forbes, *Frontiers in American History and the Role of the Frontier Historians* (Reno: Desert Research Institute, University of Nevada, 1966); John T. Juricek, "American Usage of the Word 'Frontier' from Colonial Times to Frederick Jackson Turner," *Proceedings of the American Philosophical Society* 110 (1966): 10–34. Lee Clark Mitchell, *Witnesses to a Vanishing America: The Nineteenth-Century Response* (Princeton: Princeton University Press, 1981), is an overview of public attitudes toward the frontier.

9. Frederick Jackson Turner, *The Frontier in American History* (New York: H. Holt, 1920), 229.

10. Frederick Jackson Turner, *The Rise of the New West, 1819–1829* (New York and London: Harper & Brothers, 1906), 331–32.

11. Frederick Jackson Turner, *The United States, 1830–1850: The Nation and Its Sections* (New York: Holt, 1935).

12. David Brion Davis, *Slavery and Human Progress* (New York: Oxford University Press, 1984).

13. George Bancroft, *Memorial Address on the Life and Character of Abraham Lincoln* (Washington, D.C.: Government Printing Office, 1866), 16–17, 34–35.

14. Marlon Ross, "Romancing the Nation-State: The Poetics of Romantic Nationalism," in *Macropolitics of Nineteenth-Century Literature*, ed. Arac and Ritvo, 56–85.

15. Turner, *The Frontier in American History*, 18; *The United States, 1830–1850*, 30; *The Frontier in American History*, 261.

16. Turner, *The United States, 1830–1850*, 86, 89.

17. Turner, *The Frontier in American History*, 11. Lee Benson, *Turner and Beard: American Historical Writing Reconsidered* (Glencoe, Ill.: Free Press, 1960, discusses the influence of Loria on Turner.

18. Gene Wise, in *American Historical Explanation: Strategy for Grounded Inquiry* (Homewood, Ill.: Dorsey Press, 1973), provides an excellent analysis of Turner's inability to embrace fully the urban-industrial future.

19. For Twain's pessimism, see Roger B. Salomon, *Twain and the Image of History* (New Haven: Yale University Press, 1961), and Harold P. Simonson, *The Closed Frontier: Studies in American Literary Tragedy* (New York: Holt, Rinehart, and Winston, 1970). Books that interpret Beard as part of a generation that was looking to England and Germany for ways of understanding and controlling the new urban-industrial world are Ernst A. Breisach, *American Progressive History: An Experiment in Modernization* (Chicago: University of Chicago Press, 1993); James T. Kloppenberg, *Uncertain Victory: Social Democracy and Progressivism in European and American Thought, 1870–1920* (New York: Oxford University Press, 1986); and Daniel T. Rodgers, *Atlantic Crossings: Social Politics in a Progressive Age* (Cambridge: Harvard University Press, 1998).

20. See William F. Fine, *Progressive Evolutionism and American Sociology, 1890–1920* (Ann Arbor: University of Michigan Research Press, 1979).

21. James Harvey Robinson and Charles A. Beard, *The Development of Modern Europe*, 2 vols. (Boston, New York: Ginn and Company, 1907).

22. Charles A. Beard, *American Government and Politics* (New York: The MacMillan Company, 1910); *The Supreme Court and the Constitution* (New York: The MacMillan Company, 1912); *An Economic Interpretation of the Constitution* (New York: The MacMillan Company, 1913); *The Economic Origins of Jeffersonian Democracy* (New York: MacMillan Co., 1915).

23. Charles A. Beard, "Jefferson and the New Freedom," *New Republic* 1 (November 14, 1914): 19.

24. Charles A. Beard, *American City Government: A Survey of Newer Tendencies* (New York: The Century Co., 1912), and Charles A. Beard and Mary R. Beard, *American Citizenship* (New York: MacMillan, 1914), 6.

25. See my discussion of Beard, Dewey, and Veblen in Noble, *The Progressive Mind*.

26. The enthusiasm of most historians for World War I is discussed in George T. Blakey, *Historians on the Homefront: American Propagandists for the Great War* (Lexington: University Press of Kentucky, 1970), and in Carol S. Gruber, *Mars and*

Minerva: World War I and the Uses of Higher Learning in America (Baton Rouge: Louisiana University Press, 1975).

27. Charles A. Beard and Mary R. Beard, *The Rise of American Civilization,* 2 vols. (New York: MacMillan, 1927) and *America in Midpassage* (New York: The MacMillan Company, 1939); Charles A. Beard, *The American Spirit: A Study of the Idea of Civilization in the United States* (New York: The Macmillan Company, 1942).

28. See Warren I. Cohen, *The American Revisionists: The Lessons of Intervention in World War I* (Chicago: University of Chicago Press, 1967); and Thomas C. Kennedy, *Charles A. Beard and American Foreign Policy* (Gainesville: University Presses of Florida Press, 1975).

29. Charles A. and Mary R. Beard, *The Rise of American Civilization,* vol. 1, 328.

30. Charles A. and Mary R. Beard, *The Rise of American Civilization,* vol. 2, 514, 516–17, 534–35.

31. Charles A. and Mary R. Beard, *The Rise of American Civilization,* vol. 1, 53, 105.

32. Ibid., 198.

33. Charles A. Beard with George H. E. Smith, *The Idea of National Interest: An Analytical Study in American Foreign Policy* (New York: The Macmillan Company, 1934), 85.

34. Charles A. and Mary R. Beard, *The Rise of American Civilization,* vol. 1, 247, 397

35. Ibid., 399.

36. Charles A. and Mary R. Beard, *The Rise of American Civilization* vol. 2, 568–69.

37. Ibid., 568–69.

38. Charles A. Beard with George H. E. Smith, *The Future Comes: A Study of the New Deal* (New York: The Macmillan Company, 1933), 161–64.

39. Charles A. Beard, "Rushlights in Darkness," *Scribner's* 90 (December 1931): 578; Charles A. Beard, "Written History as an Act of Faith," *American Historical Review* 39 (January 1934), 225.

40. See my discussion in Noble, *The End of American History.*

41. Charles A. Beard with Smith, *The Idea of National Interest,* and Charles A. Beard, *The Open Door at Home: A Trial Philosophy of National Interest* (New York: Macmillan, 1934).

42. Charles A. and Mary Beard, *America in Midpassage.*

43. Charles A. Beard, *Giddy Minds and Foreign Quarrels: An Estimate of American Foreign Policy* (New York: MacMillan, 1939); Charles A. Beard, *A Foreign Policy for America* (New York: Knopf, 1940); Charles A. and Mary R. Beard, *The American Spirit.*

44. Charles A. and Mary R. Beard, *The American Spirit,* 164.

45. Ibid., 538.

46. Ibid., 594. Major studies of Beard include Howard K. Beale, ed., *Charles A. Beard: An Appraisal* (Lexington: University of Kentucky Press, 1954); Bernard C. Borning, *The Political and Social Thought of Charles A. Beard* (Seattle: University of Washington Press, 1962); Richard Hofstadter, *The Progressive Historians* (New York: Knopf, 1968); David W. Marcell, *Progress and Pragmatism: James, Dewey, Beard, and the American Idea of Progress* (Westport, Conn., and London: Greenwood Press, 1974); Robert Allen Skotheim, *American Intellectual Histories and Historians* (Princeton: Princeton University Press, 1966); Cushing Strout, *The Pragmatic Revolt in American History: Carl Becker and Charles Beard* (Ithaca: Cornell University Press,

1958); and Ellen Nore, *Charles A. Beard: An Intellectual Biography* (Carbondale: Southern Illinois University Press, 1983).

2. Historians Leaving Home, Killing Fathers

1. Richard Hofstadter, *The Progressive Historians: Turner, Beard, Parrington* (New York: Alfred A. Knopf and Random House, 1968); Charles A. and Mary R. Beard, *The Rise of American Civilization*, 2 vols. (New York: Macmillan, 1942); David W. Noble, *Historians against History: The Frontier Thesis and the National Covenant in American Historical Writing Since 1830* (Minneapolis: University of Minnesota Press, 1965). In this chapter I will refer to *The Rise of American Civilization* as *The Rise.*

2. Hofstadter, *The Progressive Historians,* xiv; Arthur M. Schlesinger Jr., *The Age of Jackson* (Boston: Little Brown & Company, 1945); Richard Hofstadter, *Social Darwinism in American Thought, 1860–1915* (Philadelphia: University of Pennsylvania Press, 1945). The crisis of Hofstadter's generation is discussed in Edward A. Purcell Jr., *The Crisis of Democratic Theory: Scientific Naturalism and the Problem of Value* (Lexington: University Press of Kentucky, 1973); Robert Booth Fowler, *Believing Skeptics: American Political Intellectuals, 1945–1965* (Westport, Conn.: Greenwood Press, 1978); John W. Coffey, *Political Realism in American Thought* (Lewisburg, Penn.: Bucknell University Press, 1977); and Marion J. Morton, *The Terrors of Ideological Politics: Liberal Histories in a Conservative Mood* (Cleveland: Press of Case Western Reserve University, 1972). Dana D. Nelson, in *National Manhood: Capitalist Citizenship and the Imagined Fraternity of White Men* (Durham: Duke University Press, 1998), clarifies the conflict between the bourgeois nationalist commitment to fraternity and its commitment to competition and hierarchy. Hofstadter and many of his generation tried to escape this conflict by rejecting the association of democracy with fraternity and, instead, insisting that the essence of democracy was liberty. See also Susan Stout Baker, *Radical Beginnings: Richard Hofstadter and the 1930s* (Westport, Conn. and London: Greenwood Press, 1985).

3. Richard Hofstadter, *Social Darwinism,* 50, 30,

4. Ibid., 144.

5. Ibid., 101, 145, 175.

6. Richard Hofstadter, *The American Political Tradition* (New York: Alfred A. Knopf and Random House, 1948). Daniel Joseph Singal provides a useful intellectual biography of Hofstadter in his article, "Beyond Consensus: Richard Hofstadter and American Historiography," *American Historical Review* 89 (October 1984): 976–1004. The most powerful study of the impact of World War II is Peter Novick, *That Noble Dream: The "Objectivity Question" and the American Historical Profession* (Cambridge and New York: Cambridge University Press, 1988).

7. Hofstadter, *The Progressive Historians,* 452 n. 9.

8. Hofstadter, *The Age of Reform* (New York: Alfred A. Knopf and Random House, 1955).

9. See my discussion in David W. Noble, *The End of American History: Democracy, Capitalism, and the Metaphor of Two Worlds in Anglo-American Historical Writing, 1880–1980* (Minneapolis: University of Minnesota Press, 1985).

10. Hofstadter, *The Age of Reform,* 203.

11. Ibid., 326.

12. Richard Hofstadter, *Anti-Intellectualism in American Life* (New York: Alfred A. Knopf and Random House, 1962), 154–55.

13. Hofstadter, *The Progressive Historians*, 444.

14. Richard Hofstadter, *The Idea of a Party System in America: The Rise of Legitimate Opposition in the United States: 1780–1840* (Berkeley and Los Angeles: University of California Press, 1970), xii. Bernard Bailyn, *The Ideological Origins of the American Revolution* (Cambridge: Belnap Press of Harvard University Press, 1967).

15. Richard Hofstadter, *America at 1750: A Social Portrait* (New York: Alfred A. Knopf and Random House, 1971), xvi.

16. Paul M. Buhle and Edward Rice-Maximin, *William Appleman Williams: The Tragedy of Empire* (New York: Routledge, 1995).

17. William Appleman Williams, *American-Russian Relations: 1781–1947* (New York: Rinehart, 1952), 106. For the powerful influence that Williams exercised for his generation, see Robert W. Tucker, *The Radical Left and American Foreign Policy* (Baltimore: The Johns Hopkins University Press, 1971), and Joseph M. Siracusa, *New Left Diplomatic Histories and Historians: The American Revisionists* (Port Washington, N.Y.: Kennikat Press, 1973). Bradford Perkins's informative essay, "The Tragedy of American Diplomacy: Twenty Five Years Later," *Reviews in American History* 12 (March 1984): 1–8, provides an overview of Williams's influence—through his writings, students, and supporters—on the historiography of American diplomacy and a bibliography of writings about this Williams school.

18. Williams, *American-Russian Relations*, 157, 192.

19. William Appleman Williams, "The Frontier Thesis and American Foreign Policy," *Pacific Historical Review* 24 (November 1955): 379, 380, 383.

20. Ibid., 390, 395.

21. William Appleman Williams, *The Tragedy of American Diplomacy* (Cleveland: World Publishing Company, 1959).

22. Ibid., 49.

23. Ibid., 83.

24. Ibid., 158–59, 185.

25. Ibid., 205–6.

26. William Appleman Williams, *The Contours of American History* (Cleveland: World Publishing Company, 1961).

27. William Appleman Williams, *The Great Evasion: An Essay on the Contemporary Relevance of Karl Marx and on the Wisdom of Admitting the Heretic into the Dialogue about America's Future* (Chicago: Quadrangle Books, 1964), 19–20.

28. Ibid., 114, 164.

29. William Appleman Williams, *Some Presidents: Wilson to Nixon* (New York: New York Review of Books, 1972) and *America Confronts a Revolutionary World, 1776–1976* (New York: Morrow, 1976).

30. William Appleman Williams, *Americans in a Changing World: A History of the United States in the Twentieth Century* (New York: Harper and Row, 1978) and *Empire as a Way of Life: An Essay on the Causes and Character of America's Present Predicament Along with a Few Thoughts about an Alternative* (New York: Oxford University Press, 1980), 58, 213.

31. The best analysis of Schlesinger's writings is Stephen P. Defoe, *Arthur M. Schlesinger, Jr., and the Ideological History of American Liberalism* (Tuscaloosa and

London: University of Alabama Press, 1994). Arthur M. Schlesinger Jr., *The Age of Jackson* (Boston: Little, Brown and Company, 1945).

32. Ibid., 32.
33. Ibid., 43.
34. Ibid., 312.
35. Ibid., 367.
36. Ibid., 23.
37. Ibid., 510.
38. Arthur M. Schlesinger Jr., *The Vital Center: The Politics of Freedom* (Boston: Houghton Mifflin, 1949).
39. Ibid., 39.
40. Ibid., xxiv.
41. Ibid., 29.
42. Ibid., 245.
43. Ibid., 255.
44. Arthur M. Schlesinger Jr., *The Crisis of the Old Order: 1919–1933* (Boston: Houghton Mifflin, 1957); *The Coming of the New Deal* (Boston: Houghton Mifflin, 1958); and *The Politics of Upheaval* (Boston: Houghton Mifflin, 1960). See the discussion of the theory of cycles expressed by Arthur M. Schlesinger Sr. in Arthur M. Schlesinger Jr., *The Cycles of American History* (Boston: Houghton Mifflin, 1986), 24–25.
45. Arthur M. Schlesinger Jr., *A Thousand Days: John F. Kennedy in the White House* (Boston: Houghton Mifflin, 1965).
46. Arthur M. Schlesinger Jr., *The Crisis of Confidence: Ideas, Power, and Violence in America* (Boston: Houghton Mifflin, 1969), xi, 81.
47. Ibid., 239.
48. Arthur M. Schlesinger, *Robert F. Kennedy and His Times* (Boston: Houghton Mifflin, 1978) and *The Imperial Presidency* (Boston: Houghton Mifflin, 1973).
49. Arthur M. Schlesinger Jr., *The Disuniting of America* (New York: W. W. Norton, 1991).
50. Allan Bloom, *The Closing of the American Mind: How Higher Education Has Failed Democracy and Impoverished the Souls of Today's Students* (New York: Simon and Schuster, 1987); Roger Kimball, *Tenured Radicals: How Politics Has Corrupted Our Higher Education* (New York: Harper & Row, 1990); and Dinesh D'Souza, *Illiberal Education: The Politics of Race and Sex on Campus* (New York: The Free Press, 1991). See also Jeffrey Williams, ed., *PC Wars: Politics and Theory in the Academy* (New York: Routledge, 1995). Schlesinger, *The Disuniting of America.*
51. Schlesinger, *The Disuniting of America,* 53, 72.
52. Ibid., 43.
53. Ibid., 103.
54. Ibid., 122.
55. Ibid., 137.

3. The Crisis of American Literary Criticism from World War I to World War II

1. Vernon Louis Parrington, *Main Currents in American Thought,* vol. 1, *The Colonial Mind, 1620–1800,* vol. 2, *The Romantic Revolution in America, 1800–1860*

(New York: Harcourt, Brace, 1927), and vol. 3, *The Beginnings of Critical Realism in America, 1860–1920* (New York: Harcourt, Brace, 1930). F. O. Matthiessen, *American Renaissance: Art and Expression in the Age of Emerson and Whitman* (New York: Oxford University Press, 1941). Discussions of Parrington are to be found in Gene Wise, *American Historical Explanations: A Strategy for Grounded Inquiry* (Homewood, Ill.: Dorsey Press, 1973); Richard Hofstadter, *The Progressive Historians: Turner, Beard, Parrington* (New York: Alfred A. Knopf and Random House, 1968); and David W. Noble, *Historians against History: The Frontier Thesis and the National Covenant in American Historical Writing Since 1830* (Minneapolis: University of Minnesota Press, 1965). The most recent study of Parrington is H. Lark Hall, *V. L. Parrington: Through the Avenue of Art* (Kent, Ohio: Kent State University Press, 1994). Discussions of the academic context in which Parrington developed his ideas are Marcus Klein, *Foreigners: The Making of American Literature, 1900–1940* (Chicago: University of Chicago Press, 1981); Richard Ruland, *The Rediscovery of American Literature: Premises of Critical Taste, 1900–1940* (Cambridge: Harvard University Press, 1967); Kermit Vanderbilt, *American Literature and the Academy: The Roots, Growth, and Maturity of a Profession* (Philadelphia: University of Pennsylvania Press, 1986); and David R. Shumway, *Creating American Civilization: A Genealogy of American Literature as an Academic Discipline* (Minneapolis: University of Minnesota Press, 1994). Walter Benn Michaels, *Our America: Nativism, Modernism, and Pluralism* (Durham, N.C.: Duke University Press, 1995) discusses the aesthetic authority that kept Parrington and Matthiessen from seeing any American literature that was not male and Anglo-Protestant.

2. Howard Mumford Jones, *The Theory of American Literature* (Ithaca: Cornell University Press, 1948).

3. Books that discuss the political imagination of artists and intellectuals in the 1930s are Warren Susman, *Culture as History: The Transformation of American Society in the Twentieth Century* (New York: Pantheon, 1984); Richard H. Pells, *Radical Visions and American Dreams: Culture and Social Thought in the Depression Years* (New York: Harper and Row, 1973); Michael Denning, *The Cultural Front: The Laboring of American Culture in the Twentieth Century* (New York: Verso, 1997); Lary May, *The Big Tomorrow: Hollywood and the Politics of the American Way* (Chicago: University of Chicago Press, 2000); Alan M. Wald, *The New York Intellectuals: The Rise and Decline of the Anti-Stalinist Left from the 1930s to the 1950s* (Chapel Hill: University of North Carolina Press, 1987); and Alexander Bloom, *Prodigal Sons: The New York Intellectuals and Their World* (New York: Oxford University Press, 1986).

4. Parrington, *Main Currents in American Thought,* vol. 1, 120.

5. Ibid., 184.

6. Ibid., 401.

7. Parrington, *Main Currents in American Thought,* vol. 2, 389.

8. Parrington, *Main Currents in American Thought,* vol. 3, 17.

9. Ibid., 81–82.

10. Ibid., 86.

11. Ibid., 401.

12. Ibid., 403.

13. Books about Matthiessen are Frederick C. Stern, *F. O. Matthiessen: Christian Socialist as Critic* (Chapel Hill: University of North Carolina Press, 1981); Paul M. Sweezy and Leo Huberman, eds., *F. O. Matthiessen (1902–1950): A Collective Portrait*

(New York: Henry Schuman, 1950); Giles B. Gunn, F. O. *Matthiessen: The Critical Achievement* (Seattle: University of Washington Press, 1975); and William E. Cain, F. O. *Matthiessen: The Politics of Criticism* (Madison: University of Wisconsin Press, 1988). ✗

14. See, for example, Thomas Hill Schaub, *American Fiction in the Cold War* (Madison: University of Wisconsin Press, 1991).

15. Parrington, *Main Currents in American Thought*, vol. 3, 100.

16. See, for example, Ruland, *The Rediscovery of American Literature;* Vanderbilt, *American Literature and the Academy;* and Shumway, *Creating American Civilization.*

17. F. O. Matthiessen, *Translation: An Elizabethan Art* (Cambridge: Harvard University Press, 1931).

18. F. O. Matthiessen, *Sarah Orne Jewett* (Boston: Houghton Mifflin, 1929), 20.

19. Matthiessen, *American Renaissance*, 434.

20. John Rackliffe, ed., *The Responsibilities of the Critic: Essays and Reviews by F. O. Matthiessen* (New York: Oxford University Press, 1952), 210–11.

21. Granville Hicks, *The Great Tradition: An Interpretation of American Literature Since the Civil War* (New York: Macmillan, 1933). Rackliffe, ed., *The Responsibilities of the Critic*, 189.

22. F. O. Matthiessen, *The Achievement of T. S. Eliot: An Essay on the Nature of Poetry* (Boston and New York: Houghton Mifflin Company, 1935), 20–21.

23. David Simpson, *The Politics of American English, 1776–1850* (New York: Oxford University Press, 1986).

24. Matthiessen, *American Renaissance*, ix

25. Ibid., 626.

26. Ibid., 625.

27. Ibid., 514.

28. Ibid., ix, x.

29. F. O. Matthiessen, *From the Heart of Europe* (New York: Oxford University Press, 1948).

30. F. O. Matthiessen, *Henry James: The Major Phase* (London and New York: Oxford University Press, 1944).

31. Sweezy and Huberman, eds., *F. O. Matthiessen*, 91–92.

32. F. O. Matthiessen, *Theodore Dreiser* (New York: Sloane, 1951). See the discussion of Matthiessen's involvement in the Wallace campaign in Cain, *F. O. Matthiessen*, 107–13.

33. Rackliffe, ed., *The Responsibilities of the Critic*, 5.

34. Matthiessen must have been aware that many of the literary radicals of the 1930s were publicly renouncing their commitments to any form of Marxist criticism and were publicly announcing their commitment to a liberty found in American capitalism. See, for example, the analysis in William L. O'Neill, *A Better World: The Great Schism, Stalinism, and the American Intellectuals* (New York: Simon and Schuster, 1982).

4. Elegies for the National Landscape

1. Early discussions of the development of American studies are Cecil F. Tate, *The Search for Method in American Studies* (Minneapolis: University of Minnesota Press, 1973) and Gene Wise, *American Historical Explanations: A Strategy for Grounded Inquiry* (Homewood, Ill.: Dorsey Press, 1973). David R. Shumway, *Creating American*

Civilization: A Genealogy of American Literature as an Academic Discipline (Minneapolis: University of Minnesota Press, 1994), discusses the relationship of American literary studies in the 1930s and 1940s and the development of American studies as a discipline.

2. A group of essays that discuss the symbol-myth school are to be found in Lucy Maddox, ed., *Locating American Studies: The Evolution of a Discipline* (Baltimore: The Johns Hopkins University Press, 1999); Leo Marx, *The Machine in the Garden: Technology and the Pastoral Ideal in America* (New York: Oxford University Press, 1964); Henry Nash Smith, *Virgin Land: The American West as Symbol and Myth* (Cambridge: Harvard University Press, 1950); and R. W. B. Lewis, *The American Adam: Innocence, Tragedy, and Tradition in the Nineteenth Century* (Chicago: University of Chicago Press, 1955). Bruce Kuklick, "Myth and Symbol in American Studies," *American Quarterly* 24 (October 1972): 438–50, was an early criticism of the symbol-myth school. Shumway, *Creating American Civilization,* discusses Smith, Lewis, and Marx in his chapter 9, "Civilization 'Discovered.'"

3. Tate, *The Search for Method in American Studies,* has a discussion of the centrality of holism for the symbol-myth school.

4. Smith, *Virgin Land,* 4.

5. Ibid., 137–38.

6. See my discussion of Cooper in David W. Noble, "Cooper, Leatherstocking, and the Death of an American Adam," *American Quarterly* 16 (fall 1964): 419–31.

7. Smith, *Virgin Land,* 89.

8. Ibid., 119.

9. Ibid., 191, 205–6.

10. Ibid., 224.

11. Ibid., 249.

12. Ibid., 260.

13. Ibid., 260.

14. Lewis, *The American Adam,* 1, 5.

15. Ibid., 91.

16. Ibid., 113.

17. Ibid., 152.

18. Ibid., 144.

19. Ibid., 9.

20. Ibid., 195.

21. Ibid., 198.

22. Marx, *The Machine in the Garden,* 3.

23. Ibid., 9.

24. Ibid., 88.

25. Ibid., 143, 144.

26. Ibid., 242.

27. Ibid., 252.

28. Ibid., 264.

5. The New Literary Criticism

1. Vincent B. Leitch, *American Literary Criticism from the Thirties to the Eighties* (New York: Columbia University Press, 1988) provides an overview of this development.

2. John A. Macy, *The Spirit of American Literature* (Garden City, N.Y.: Doubleday, Page Company, 1913). Van Wyck Brooks, *America's Coming-of-Age* (New York: B. W. Huebsch, 1915).

3. V. F. Calverton, *The Liberation of American Literature* (New York: C. Scribner's Sons, 1932), xii. Granville Hicks, *The Great Tradition: An Interpretation of American Literature since the Civil War* (New York: The Macmillan Company, 1933).

4. *I'll Take My Stand: The South and the Agrarian Tradition, by Twelve Southerners* (New York and London: Harper & Brothers, 1930). Hicks, *The Great Tradition,* 282. Books about the southern agrarians are John M. Bradbury, *The Fugitives: A Critical Account* (Chapel Hill: University of North Carolina Press, 1958); James L. Stewart, *The Burden of Time* (Princeton: Princeton University Press, 1965); Alexander Karanikas, *Tillers of a Myth: Southern Agrarians as Social and Literary Critics* (Madison: University of Wisconsin Press, 1966); Mark Jancovich, *The Cultural Politics of the New Criticism* (Cambridge: Cambridge University Press, 1993); Mark G. Malavasi, *The Unregenerate South: The Agrarian Thought of John Crowe Ransom, Allen Tate, and Donald Davidson* (Baton Rouge: Louisiana State University Press, 1997); Thomas A. Underwood, *Allen Tate: Orphan of the South* (Princeton: Princeton University Press, 2000); and Randy Hendricks, *Lonelier Than God: Robert Penn Warren and the Southern Exile* (Athens: University of Georgia Press, 2000).

5. Allen Tate, *Collected Essays* (Denver: Alan Swallow, 1959).

6. John Crowe Ransom, *Poems about God* (New York: H. Holt and Company, 1919); *Chills and Fever: Poems* (New York: A. A. Knopf, 1924); *Grace after Meat* (London: Hogarth Press, 1924); *Two Gentlemen in Bonds* (New York: A. A. Knopf, 1927). Donald Davidson, *Southern Writers in the Modern World* (Athens: University of Georgia Press, 1958), 21–22.

7. Allen Tate, *The Fathers* (New York: G. P. Putnam's Sons, 1938).

8. Robert Penn Warren, *All the King's Men* (New York: Harcourt, Brace & World, 1946).

9. Herbert Agar and Allen Tate, eds., *Who Owns America? A New Declaration of Independence* (Boston: Houghton Mifflin, 1936).

10. T. S. Eliot, *Selected Essays* (New York: Harcourt Brace, 1950), 4

11. Grant Webster, *The Republic of Letters: A History of Postwar American Literary Opinion* (Baltimore: The Johns Hopkins University Press, 1979).

12. Cleanth Brooks and Robert Penn Warren, *Understanding Poetry* (New York: Henry Holt, 1938). Grant Webster, *The Republic of Letters.* See also William E. Cain, *The Crisis in Criticism: Theory, Literature, and Reform in English Studies* (Baltimore: The Johns Hopkins University Press, 1984). Thomas S. Kuhn, *The Structure of Scientific Revolutions* (Chicago: University of Chicago Press, 1962).

13. William K. Wimsatt Jr. and Cleanth Brooks, *Literary Criticism: A Short History* (New York: Knopf, 1957), 749.

14. Cleanth Brooks and Robert Penn Warren, *Understanding Fiction* (New York: F. S. Crofts, 1943).

15. John Crowe Ransom, *The New Criticism* (Norford, Conn.: New Directions, 1941), 41–42. Robert Penn Warren, "Notes on the Poetry of John Crowe Ransom at His Eightieth Birthday," *Kenyon Review* 30 (1968): 319–49.

16. Cleanth Brooks, "My Credo: The Formalist Critics," *Kenyon Review* 13 (winter 1951): 75. Allen Tate, "The Present Function of Criticism" (originally 1940), in *Collected Essays,* 7.

17. Cleanth Brooks, "New Criticism," in Alex Preminger et al., eds., *Princeton Encyclopedia of Poetry and Poetics* (Princeton: Princeton University Press, 1974), 567–68. Tate, *Collected Essays,* 15.

18. Tate, *Collected Essays,* 535.

6. The Vanishing National Landscape

1. Art historians were slower than literary critics and historians to participate in the paradigm revolution that replaced the aesthetic authority of a national landscape home to Anglo-Protestants with the aesthetic authority of a variety of landscapes and a variety of cultures within the political boundaries of the United States. Some of the books that mark this paradigm shift are Vivien Green Fryd, *Art and Empire: The Politics of Ethnicity in the United States Capitol, 1815–1860* (New Haven: Yale University Press, 1992); Stephen Daniels, *Fields of Vision: Landscape Imagery and National Identity in England and the United States* (Princeton: Princeton University Press, 1993); Angela Miller, *The Empire of the Eye: Landscape Representation and American Cultural Politics, 1825–1875* (Ithaca: Cornell University Press, 1993); and David M. Lubin, *Picturing a Nation: Art and Social Change in Nineteenth-Century America* (New Haven: Yale University Press, 1994).

2. The last major synthesis of the tradition in art history of seeing the beauty of the national landscape as an inspiration to "American" painters was Barbara Novak, *Nature and Culture: American Landscape and Painting, 1825–1875* (New York: Oxford University Press, 1980). Angela Miller, "Everywhere and Nowhere: The Making of the National Landscape," *American Literary History* 4 (summer 1992): 207–29.

3. See Larzer Ziff, *The American 1890s* (New York: Viking Press, 1966). He describes the writers and artists of this decade as a lost generation.

4. Quoted in Lloyd Goodrich, *Thomas Eakins: His Life and Works* (New York: Whitney Museum of American Art, 1933), 139.

5. Robert Henri, *The Art Spirit* (Philadelphia and London: J. B. Lippincott Company, 1930), 217.

6. Jerome Myers, *An Artist in Manhattan* (New York: American Artists Group, 1940), 36–37.

7. Quoted in Charles C. Alexander, *Here the Country Lies: Nationalism and the Arts in Twentieth-Century America* (Bloomington: University of Indiana Press, 1980). Alexander's book was a major influence as I developed the concept of the national landscape.

8. Randolph Bourne, "Twilight of Idols," *Seven Arts* 2 (October 1917): 689. See also Stuart I. Rochester, *American Liberal Disillusionment in the Wake of World War I* (University Park: Pennsylvania State University Press, 1977).

9. See the discussion in Alexander, "Thorough Malcontents," chap. 3 in *Here the Country Lies.*

10. Charles Burchfield, "On the Middle Border," *Creative Art* 3 (September 1928): xxix.

11. Erika Doss discusses Benton's relationship to a complex New York artistic community in *Benton, Pollock, and the Politics of Modernism: From Regionalism to Abstract Expressionism* (Chicago: University of Chicago Press, 1991).

12. Thomas Hart Benton, *An Artist in America*, 4th ed. (Columbia: University of Missouri Press, 1983), 314.

13. Thomas Hart Benton, *An American in Art: A Professional and Technical Autobiography* (Lawrence: University Press of Kansas, 1969), 149.

14. Thomas Hart Benton, "Confessions of an American," part 3, "Class Rule vs. Democracy," *Common Sense* 6 (September 1937): 20.

15. Thomas Hart Benton, *An Artist in America*, 326–27.

16. Quoted in Doss, *Benton, Pollock, and the Politics of Modernism*, 319.

17. See the discussion in Doss, *Benton, Pollock, and the Politics of Modernism.*

18. Letter from Jackson Pollock to Louis Bounce, June 2, 1946, quoted in Doss, *Benton, Pollock, and the Politics of Modernism*, 391. It is Doss's theory that the abstract expressionists emerged because of the collapse of the republican tradition represented by men like Benton. I agree, but I see the republican tradition itself as an expression of the belief in the national landscape.

19. The co-opting of abstract expressionism by the new political, economic, and cultural leadership committed to the international marketplace is discussed in Serge Guilbaut, *How New York Stole the Idea of Modern Art: Abstract Expressionism, Freedom, and the Cold War*, trans. Arthur Goldhammer (Chicago: University of Chicago Press, 1983); Max Kozloff, "American Painting During the Cold War," *Artforum* 11 (May 1973): 43–54; Eva Cockcraft, "Abstract Expressionism: Weapon of the Cold War," *Artforum* 12 (June 1974): 39–41; Jane de Hart Matthews, "Art and Politics in Cold War America," *American Historical Review* 81 (October 1976): 762–87; and David Shapiro, "Abstract Expressionism: The Politics of Apolitical Painting," *Prospects* 3 (1977): 175–214.

20. Arthur C. Danto, *After the End of Art: Contemporary Art and the Pale of History* (Princeton: Princeton University Press, 1997).

21. Eleanor Heartney, *Critical Condition: American Culture at the Crossroads* (Cambridge, New York: Cambridge University Press, 1997).

22. Tyler Cowen, *In Praise of Commercial Culture* (Cambridge: Harvard University Press, 1998).

23. Jonathan Freedman, *The Temple of Culture: Assimilation and Anti-Semitism in Literary Anglo-America* (Oxford, New York: Oxford University Press, 2000).

24. William L. Anthes, "Indian Style: Primitivism, Nationalism, and Cultural Sovereignty in Twentieth-Century American Art" (Ph.D. diss., University of Minnesota, 2000).

25. Hal Foster, *The Return of the Real: The Avant-Garde at the End of the Century* (Cambridge: MIT Press, 1996), 197.

26. Arif Dirlik, *The Postcolonial Aura: Third-World Criticism in the Age of Global Capitalism* (Boulder, Colo.: Westview Press, 1997). See the discussion in Anthes, "Native American Cultural Sovereignty," chap. 5 in *Indian Style.* See also Steven Leuthold, *Indigenous Aesthetics: Native Art, Media, and Identity* (Austin: University of Texas Press, 1998).

27. Quoted in Anthes, *Indian Style*, 191–92.

28. Lewis Mumford, *Sticks and Stones: A Study of American Architecture and Civilization* (New York: W. W. Norton, 1924) and *The Golden Day: A Study of American Literature and Culture* (New York: Boni and Liveright, 1926, 1983). Discussions of Mumford are T. P. and A. C. Hughes, eds., *Lewis Mumford: Public Intellectual* (New

York: Oxford University Press, 1990), and Mark Luccarelli, *Lewis Mumford and the Ecological Region: The Politics of Planning* (New York: The Guilford Press, 1995).

29. Louis Sullivan, *The Autobiography of an Idea* (New York: Dover Publications, 1956, 1924), 98. Sullivan is discussed in Sherman Paul, *Louis Sullivan: An Architect in American Thought* (Englewood Cliffs, N.J.: Prentice-Hall, 1962); Hugh Dalziel Duncan, *Culture and Democracy: The Struggle for Form in Society and Architecture in Chicago and the Middle West During the Life and Times of Louis H. Sullivan* (Totowa, N.J.: Bedminster Press, 1965); Hugh Morrison, *Louis Sullivan: Prophet of Modern Architecture* (New York: Museum of Modern Art and W. W. Norton & Co., 1935); Narcisco G. Menocal, *Architecture as Nature: The Transcendental Idea of Louis Sullivan* (Madison: University of Wisconsin Press, 1981); David S. Andrew, *Louis Sullivan and the Polemics of Modern Architecture: The Present against the Past* (Urbana: University of Illinois Press, 1985); and James F. O'Gorman, *Three American Architects: Richardson, Sullivan, and Wright, 1865–1915* (Chicago: University of Chicago Press, 1991).

30. Sullivan, *The Autobiography of an Idea*, 98.

31. Ibid., 275–76.

32. Ibid., 248–49.

33. Ibid., 313.

34. Quoted in Paul, *Louis Sullivan*, 93.

35. Ibid., 283.

36. Ibid., 325.

37. See the discussion of Wright's childhood in Robert Fishman, *Urban Utopias in the Twentieth Century: Ebenezer Howard, Frank Lloyd Wright, and Le Corbusier* (New York: Basic Books, 1977). Other books discussing Wright are Norris Kelly Smith, *Frank Lloyd Wright: A Study in Architectural Content* (Englewood Cliffs, N.J.: Prentice-Hall, 1966); Robert C. Twombly, *Frank Lloyd Wright: An Interpretive Biography* (New York: Harper & Row, 1973); Brendan Gill, *Many Masks: A Life of Frank Lloyd Wright* (New York: Putnam, 1987); Donald Leslie Johnson, *Frank Lloyd Wright versus America: The 1930s* (Cambridge: MIT Press, 1990); and H. Allen Brooks, *The Prairie School: Frank Lloyd Wright and His Midwest Contemporaries* (Toronto: University of Toronto Press, 1972).

38. Louis Sullivan, *Kindergarten Chats and Other Writings*, ed. Isabella Athey (New York: Wittenborn, Schultz, 1947), 30. Alan Crawford, "Ten Letters from Frank Lloyd Wright to Charles Robert Ashbee, *Architectural History* 13 (1970): 64.

39. Frank Lloyd Wright, *An Autobiography* (New York: Duell, Sloan and Pearce, 1943), 79.

40. Ibid., 162, 168. Frank Lloyd Wright, *The Disappearing City* (New York: W. F. Payson, 1932), 28.

41. Frank Lloyd Wright, *The Living City* (New York: New American Library, 1963, 1958), 153.

42. *Taliesin Square Paper* 6 (October 1941), quoted in Fishman, *Urban Utopias in the Twentieth Century*, 150.

43. Frank Lloyd Wright, *Genius and the Mobocracy* (New York: Duell, Sloan Pearce, 1949), 38.

44. These changing patterns are discussed in Robert Venturi, *Complexity and Contradiction in Architecture* (New York: Museum of Modern Art, 1966); Kenneth

Frampton, *Modern Architecture: A Critical History* (New York: Oxford University Press, 1980); James Sloan Allen, *The Romance of Commerce and Culture: Capitalism, Modernism, and the Chicago-Aspen Crusade for Cultural Reform* (Chicago: University of Chicago Press, 1983); Todd A. Marder, ed., *The Critical Edge: Controversy in Recent American Architecture* (New Brunswick, N.J.: Jane Voophees Zimmerli Art Museum; Rutgers: State University of New Jersey; Cambridge: MIT Press, 1985); Heinrich Klotz, *The History of Postmodern Architecture,* trans. Radka Donnell (Cambridge: MIT Press, 1986); and Magali Sarfatti Larson, *Behind the Postmodern Façade: Architectural Change in Late Twentieth-Century America* (Berkeley and Los Angeles: University of California Press, 1993).

45. Alexander, *Here the Country Lies,* discusses the crisis in Anglo-American music as he also discusses the Anglo-American crises in painting and architecture at the end of the nineteenth century. By the 1890s it became of great importance to Anglo-American composers to prove their independence from Europe. Older histories that were aware of this tension are Gilbert Chase, *America's Music from the Pilgrims to the Present* (New York: McGraw Hill, 1955), and Wilfred Mellers, *Music in a New Found Land: Themes and Development in the History of American Music* (London: Barrie and Rocklift, 1964). Specific studies of the crisis of national identity expressed by Anglo-American composers in the 1890s are Barbara A. Zuck, *A History of Musical Americanism* (Ann Arbor: UMI Research Press, 1980) and Alan Howard Levy, *Musical Nationalism: American Composers' Search for Identity* (Westport, Conn.: Greenwood Press, 1983).

46. MacDonald Smith Moore, *Yankee Blues: Musical Culture and American Identity* (Bloomington: Indiana University Press, 1985), analyzes this concern with overcoming class divisions. Laurence Levine, in *High Brow/Low Brow: The Emergence of Cultural Hierarchy in America* (Cambridge: Harvard University Press, 1990), discusses the growing cultural divisions in late nineteenth-century America. Henry Pleasants, *The Agony of Modern Music* (New York: Simon and Schuster, 1955), alerted readers to the transnational aspect of this crisis. This also was true of Eric Salzman, *Twentieth-Century Music: An Introduction* (Englewood Cliffs, N.J.: Prentice-Hall, 1967); Peter Yates, *Twentieth-Century Music: Its Evolution from the End of the Harmonic Era to the Present Era of Sound* (New York: Pantheon Books, 1967); and Samuel Lipman, *Music after Modernism* (New York: Basic Books, 1979).

47. See the discussion in Moore, *Yankee Blues,* 10–43, and also in Rosalie Sandra Perry, *Charles Ives and the American Mind* (Kent, Ohio: Kent State University Press, 1974), 1–18.

48. Aaron Copland, *Music and Imagination* (Cambridge: Harvard University Press, 1952), 101.

49. Mellers, *Music in a New Found Land,* 27–30, 456.

50. Charles Ives, "Berceuse for Voice and Piano," 1900, and "Marie," 1921, text after Rudolf von Gottschall. Charles Ives, *114 Songs, 1884–1921* (privately printed by Ives, 1922) and *50 Songs* (privately printed by Ives, 1923), and John Kirkpatrick, "A Temporary Mimeographed Catalogue of the Music MSS and Related Materials of Charles Edward Ives" (published by Kirkpatrick, 1960) are standard sources for Ives's songs. See additional song publication sources in Henry Cowell and Sidney Cowell, *Charles Ives and His Music* (New York: Oxford University Press, 1955), 210–11. Some useful World Wide Web sources are Lied and Song Texts (http://www.rec-

music.org/lieder), All Music Guide, Classical Search (http://www.allclassical.com), Broadcast Music, Inc. (http://www.bmi.com), and The Charles Ives Society (http://www.charlesives.org). See Moore, *Yankee Blues*, 1–10.

51. Cowell and Cowell, *Charles Ives and His Music*, 203. Studies of Ives include Frank R. Rossiter, *Charles Ives and His America* (New York: Liveright, 1975); J. Peter Burkholder, *Charles Ives: The Ideas behind the Music* (New Haven: Yale University Press, 1985); Philip Lambert, ed., *Ives Studies* (Cambridge, U.K., New York: Cambridge University Press, 1997); and Stuart Feder, *The Life of Charles Ives* (Cambridge, U.K., New York: Cambridge University Press, 1999).

52. Charles Ives, *Essays before a Sonata and Other Writings*, ed. Howard Boatwright (New York: W. W. Norton, 1920, 1964), 29.

53. Charles Ives, *Memos*, ed. John Kirkpatrick (New York: W. W. Norton, 1972), 44.

54. Quoted in Cowell and Cowell, *Charles Ives and His Music*, 96–97.

55. Ives, *Essays before a Sonata*, 8.

56. Ibid., 84.

57. Charles Ives, "West London for Voice and Piano," 1912, text by Matthew Arnold.

58. Charles Ives, "Majority," 1914 /1921.

59. Charles Ives, "A Farewell to Land for Voice and Piano," 1909, text by George Gordon, Lord Byron.

60. Henry Pleasants, *Serious Music and All That Jazz! An Adventure in Music Criticism* (New York: Session and Schuster, 1969), argued that, as the music of white composers in European countries and the United States became dissonant, they lost audiences, who turned both in Europe and the United States to jazz. Neil Leonard, in *Jazz and the White Americans: The Acceptance of a New Art Form* (Chicago: University of Chicago Press, 1962), pointed out that most white critics in the United States refused to consider jazz and American music until the 1940s. This is also a major theme in Moore's *Yankee Blues*.

61. Daniel Gregory Mason, *Tune in, America* (New York: Alfred A. Knopf, 1931), 160.

62. Recent studies of Copland include Howard Pollack, *Aaron Copland: The Life and Work of an Uncommon Man* (New York: Henry Holt, 1999); Gail Levin and Judith Tick, *Aaron Copland's America: A Cultural Perspective* (New York: Watson-Guptill, 2000); Aaron Copland and Vivian Perlis, *Copland: 1900 through 1942* (New York: St. Martin's Press, 1984) and *Copland: Since 1943* (New York: St. Martin's Press, 1989). See the discussion of Gershwin in Alexander, *Here the Country Lies*, 128–42, and in Moore, *Yankee Blues*, 130–50.

63. Copland, *Music and Imagination*, 99–100.

64. Quoted in Moore, *Yankee Blues*, 141.

65. The fullest discussion of these groups is in Michael Denning, *The Cultural Front: The Laboring of American Culture in the Twentieth Century* (London, New York: Verso, 1996).

66. Aaron Copland, "Workers Sing!" *New Masses* 10 (June 5, 1934): 28.

67. Again, the best discussion of the Popular Front is to be found in Denning, *The Cultural Front*.

68. See the discussion in Alexander, *Here the Country Lies*, 167–72, and in Zuck, *A History of Musical Americanism*.

69. Copland, *Music and Imagination*, 110.

70. Quoted in Mellers, *Music in a New Found Land,* 187. Cage is discussed in Michael Nyman, *Experimental Music: Cage and Beyond* (London: Studio Vista, 1974); Richard Kostelanetz, *Conversing with Cage* (New York: Limelight Editions, 1987); David Revill, *The Roaring Silence: John Cage, A Life* (New York: Arcade Publishing, 1992); and Christopher Shultis, *Silencing the Sounded Self: John Cage and the American Experimental Tradition* (Boston: Northeastern University Press, 1998).

71. Quoted in George E. Lewis, "Improvised Music since 1950; Afrological and Eurological Perspectives," *Black Music Research Journal* 16 (spring 1996): 106, 118.

72. Quoted in Lewis, "Improvised Music since 1950," 98.

73. Richard Hofstadter, *Social Darwinism in American Thought, 1860–1915* (Philadelphia: University of Pennsylvania Press, 1944). Hofstadter later turned against Dewey as he had turned against Beard. See his criticism of Dewey in *Anti-Intellectualism in American Life* (New York: Alfred A. Knopf and Random House, 1963).

74. See the discussion of logical positivism in Robert B. Westbrook, *John Dewey and American Democracy* (Ithaca: Cornell University Press, 1991), 402–10.

75. John Dewey, "From Absolution to Experimentation," in George P. Adams and William P. Montague, eds., *Contemporary American Philosophy: Personal Statements* (New York: The Macmillan Co., 1930), 19. Robert M. Crunden, in his *Ministers of Reform: The Progressives' Achievement in American Civilization, 1889–1920* (New York: Basic Books, 1982), interprets Dewey as part of a generation, including Ives, that was engaged in a religious revival comparable to those associated with Protestantism. Discussions of Dewey are found in David Marcell, *Progress and Pragmatism: James, Dewey, Beard, and the American Idea of Progress* (Westport, Conn.: Greenwood Press, 1975); Cornel West, *The American Evasion of Philosophy: A Genealogy of Pragmatism* (Madison: University of Wisconsin Press, 1989); Robert B. Westbrook, *John Dewey and American Democracy* (Ithaca: Cornell University Press, 1991); John Patrick Diggins, *The Promises of Pragmatism: Modernism and the Crisis of Knowledge and Authority* (Chicago: University of Chicago Press, 1994); Thomas M. Alexander, *John Dewey's Theory of Art, Experience, and Nature: The Horizons of Feeling* (Albany: State University of New York Press, 1987); Alan Ryan, *John Dewey and the High Tides of American Liberalism* (New York: W. W. Norton, 1995); Paul Jay, *Contingency Blues: The Search for Foundations in American Criticism* (Madison: University of Wisconsin Press, 1997); and Philip W. Jackson, *John Dewey and the Lessons of Art* (New Haven: Yale University Press, 1998).

76. John Dewey, *Moral Principles in Education* (Boston, New York: Houghton Mifflin Company, 1909), 38, and *Individualism: Old and New* (New York: Minton, Balch & Company, 1930), 149.

77. John Dewey, *Intelligence in the Modern World* (New York: The Modern Library, 1939), 353.

78. John Dewey, *The Influence of Darwin on Philosophy and Other Essays in Contemporary Thought* (New York: Henry Holt and Company, 1910), 287.

79. John Dewey, *The Quest for Certainty: A Study of the Relation of Knowledge and Action* (New York: Minton, Balch & Company, 1929), 245.

80. John Dewey, "My Pedagogic Creed," vol. 1 of *The Early Works, 1882–1898* (Carbondale: Southern Illinois Press, 1967–1972), 94–95.

81. John Dewey, "The Schools and Social Progressivism," vol. 10 of *The Middle Works, 1899–1924,* ed. Jo Ann Boydston (Carbondale: Southern Illinois Press, 1976–1983), 193.

82. See my discussion of Veblen, Beard, and Dewey and their eagerness to enter World War I in David W. Noble, *The Progressive Mind, 1890–1917* (Chicago: Rand McNally, 1970), 30–80.

83. John Dewey, *German Philosophy and Politics* (New York: C. P. Putnam's Sons, 1915).

84. John Dewey, "What Are We Fighting For?" vol. 2 of *Middle Works*, 102.

85. John Dewey, "Our National Dilemma," vol. 12 of *Middle Works*, 3.

86. Books to consider here by John Dewey are *Reconstruction in Philosophy* (New York: H. Holt and Company, 1920); *Human Nature and Conduct: An Introduction to Social Psychology* (New York: H. Holt and Company, 1922); *Experience and Nature* (Chicago, London: Open Court Publishing, 1925); *The Public and Its Problems* (New York: H. Holt and Company, 1927); *The Quest for Certainty: A Study of the Relation of Knowledge and Action* (New York: Minton, Balch & Company, 1929); *Individualism: Old and New* (New York: Minton, Balch & Company, 1930); *Philosophy and Civilization* (New York: Minton, Balch & Company, 1931); *Art as Experience* (New York: Minton, Balch & Company, 1934); *A Common Faith* (New Haven: Yale University Press, 1934); *Liberalism and Social Action* (New York: G. P. Putnam, 1935); *Experience and Education* (New York: The Macmillan Company, 1938); and *Logic: The Theory of Inquiry* (New York: H. Holt and Company, 1939).

87. John Dewey, "Progress," *The International Journal of Ethics* 26 (1916): 820–30. Dewey, *Reconstruction in Philosophy*, ix.

88. Dewey, *Human Nature and Conduct*, 55.

89. Dewey, *The Quest for Certainty*, 83.

90. Dewey in the 1930s shared the admiration for Thomas Jefferson expressed by the Beards in their *The Rise of Civilization*. Like them, he ignored Jefferson's role as a slaveholder and militant enemy of Native Americans. See John Dewey, "Presenting Thomas Jefferson," in *The Later Works, 1925–1953*, ed. Jo Ann Boydston (Carbondale: Southern Illinois University Press, 1981–1990, 1940), 14: 202, 213–18.

91. Dewey, *A Common Faith*, 14.

92. Dewey, *Art as Experience*, 15–16.

93. Ibid., 5–6.

94. Ibid., 274.

95. See the discussion of Dewey's *Liberalism and Social Action* and of his political activities in Westbrook, *John Dewey and American Democracy*, 452–62.

96. See the discussion of Dewey's views on communism in Westbrook, *John Dewey and American Democracy*, 463–95.

97. John Dewey, introduction to "The Problems of Men and the Present State of Philosophy" in his *The Later Works*, 15: 154–59.

7. The Disintegration of National Boundaries

1. Bill Readings, *The University in Ruins* (Cambridge: Harvard University Press, 1996).

2. Russell J. Reising, *The Unusable Past: Theory and the Study of American Literature* (New York: Methuen, 1986).

3. Ibid., 17.

4. Lionel Trilling, *The Liberal Imagination: Essays on Literature and Society* (New York: Viking Press, 1950). Reising, *The Unusable Past,* 97.

5. Richard Poirier, *A World Elsewhere: The Place of Style in American Literature* (New York: Oxford University Press, 1966). Reising, *The Unusable Past,* 187.

6. Jonathan Freedman, in *The Temple of Culture: Assimilation and Anti-Semitism in Literary Anglo-America* (New York: Oxford University Press, 2000), discusses the irony that, just as Jews were permitted to enter national culture in the 1940s, that culture was itself disintegrating. He describes the ways in which many (but not all) in this first generation of Jewish scholars in literary studies tried to hold that national culture together. Other books that discuss the difficult and complex relationship of Jews to the academy are Rael Meyerowitz, *Transferring to America: Jewish Interpretations of American Dreams* (Albany: State University of New York Press, 1995); Susanne Klingenstein, *Jews in the American Academy, 1900–1940: The Dynamics of Intellectual Assimilation* (New Haven: Yale University Press, 1991); and Susanne Klingenstein, *Enlarging America: The Cultural Work of Jewish Literary Scholars, 1930–1990* (Syracuse: Syracuse University Press, 1998).

7. Trilling, *The Liberal Imagination;* Daniel J. Boorstin, *The Genius of American Politics* (Chicago: University of Chicago Press, 1953); Richard Hofstadter, *The Age of Reform: From Bryan to F.D.R.* (New York: Knopf, 1955); Louis Hartz, *The Liberal Tradition in America: An Interpretation of American Political Thought since the Revolution* (New York: Harcourt, Brace, 1955); Leslie A. Fiedler, *An End to Innocence: Essays on Culture and Politics* (Boston: Beacon Press, 1955); Daniel Bell, *The End of Ideology: On the Exhaustion of Political Ideas in the Fifties* (Glencoe, Ill.: Fress Press 1960).

8. Freedman, *The Temple of Culture.*

9. Mary Louise Pratt, "Women, Literature, and National Brotherhood" in Emilie Bergman, et al., *Women, Culture, and Politics in Latin America: Seminar on Feminism and Culture in Latin America* (Berkeley and Los Angeles: University of California Press, 1989), 48–73.

10. Ibid., 52.

11. Nina Baym, *Women's Fiction: A Guide to Novels by and about Women in America, 1820–1870* (Ithaca: Cornell University Press, 1978). Nina Baym, "Melodramas of Beset Manhood: How Theories of American Fiction Exclude Women Authors," *American Quarterly* 33 (summer 1981), 123–39, 126.

12. Baym, "Melodramas of Beset Manhood," 129.

13. Ibid., 131. Annette Kolodny, *The Lay of the Land: Metaphor as Experience and History in American Life and Letters* (Chapel Hill: University of North Carolina Press, 1975).

14. Baym, "Melodramas of Beset Manhood," 138.

15. Harold Bloom, *The Anxiety of Influence: A Theory of Poetry* (New York, Oxford: Oxford University Press, 1973). Edward W. Said, *Beginnings: Intention and Method* (New York: Basic Books, 1975).

16. Jane Tompkins, *Sensational Designs: The Cultural Work of American Fiction, 1790–1860* (New York: Oxford University Press, 1985).

17. Ibid., xvi.

18. Ibid., xii.

19. Ibid., 25.

20. Ibid., 200.

21. Amy Kaplan, "Manifest Domesticity," *American Literature: A Journal of Literary History, Criticism, and Bibliography* 70, no. 3 (September 1998): 581–606.

22. Houston A. Baker Jr., *Blues, Ideology, and Afro-American Literature: A Vernacular Theory* (Chicago: University of Chicago Press, 1984).

23. Tompkins, xv.

24. Paul Jay, *Contingency Blues: The Search for Foundations in American Criticism* (Madison: University of Wisconsin Press, 1997); Giles Gunn, *The Culture of Criticism and the Criticism of Culture* (New York, Oxford: Oxford University Press, 1987).

25. Giles Gunn, *Thinking across the Grain: Ideology, Intellect, and the New Pragmatism* (Chicago: University of Chicago Press, 1992); Richard Poirier, *The Renewal of Literature: Emersonian Reflections* (New York: Random House, 1987); Richard Poirier, *Poetry and Pragmatism* (Cambridge: Harvard University Press, 1992).

26. Mary Louise Pratt, *Imperial Eyes: Travel Writing and Transculturalism* (London, New York: Routledge, 1992), quoted in Jay, *Contingency Blues,* 154.

27. Carolyn Porter, "What We Know That We Don't Know: Remapping American Literary Studies," *American Literary History* 6 (1994): 467–526. Peter C. Carafiol, *The American Ideal: Literary History as a Worldly Activity* (New York: Oxford University Press, 1991).

28. Sacvan Bercovitch, *The American Jeremiad* (Madison: University of Wisconsin Press, 1978).

29. Philip Fisher, ed., *The New American Studies: Essays from Representations* (Berkeley and Los Angeles: University of California Press, 1991).

30. Ibid., 71, 72, 97.

31. Ibid., 86.

32. Ibid., xiv.

33. Gregory S. Jay, "The End of 'American' Literature: Toward a Multicultural Practice," *College English* 53 (1991): 264–81. See also Gregory S. Jay, *American Literature and the Culture Wars* (Ithaca: Cornell University Press, 1997); Donald E. Pease, ed., *National Identities and Post-Americanist Narratives* (Durham: Duke University Press, 1994); Priscilla Wald, *Constituting Americans: Cultural Anxiety and Narrative Form* (Durham: Duke University Press, 1995); John Carlos Rowe, *At Emerson's Tomb: The Politics of Classic American Literature* (New York: Columbia University Press, 1997).

central texts

34. Porter, "What We Know That We Don't Know," 467.

35. José David Saldívar, *The Dialectics of Our America: Genealogy, Cultural Critique, and Literary History* (Durham, N.C.: Duke University Press, 1991).

36. José Martí, "La Conferencia monetaria de los republica de America" (1891) in *Obras Completas* 6 (La Habana: Editorial Nacional de Cuba, 1963). See also Jeffrey Belnap and Raúl Fernandez, eds., *José Martí's "Our America": From National to Hemispheric Studies* (Durham: Duke University Press, 1998).

37. See, for example, the essay by Annette Kolodny, "The Integrity of Memory: Creating a New Literary History of the United States," *American Literature* 57 (1985): 291–305, and the essay by Janice Radway, "What's in a Name?" *American Quarterly* 51 (March 1999): 1–32. José David Saldívar, *Border Matters: Remapping American Cultural Studies* (Berkeley and Los Angeles: University of California Press, 1997). Mary Helen Washington, "Disturbing the Peace: What Happens to American Studies If

You Put African-American Studies at the Center?" *American Quarterly* 50 (March 1998): 1.

38. Paul Gilroy, *The Black Atlantic: Modernity and Double Consciousness* (Cambridge: Harvard University Press, 1993).

39. Stelamaris Coser, *Bridging the Americas: The Literature of Paula Marshall, Toni Morrison, and Gayle Jones* (Philadelphia: Temple University Press, 1995).

40. Lisa Lowe, *Immigrant Acts: On Asian American Cultural Politics* (Durham: Duke University Press, 1996).

41. N. Scott Momaday, *House Made of Dawn* (New York: Harper & Row, 1968).

42. Louis Owens, *Other Destinies: Understanding the American Indian Novel* (Norman: University of Oklahoma Press, 1992). Bill Ashcroft, Gareth Griffiths, and Helen Tiffin, *The Empire Writes Back: Theory and Practice in Post-Colonial Literatures* (London, New York: Routledge, 1989).

43. Cheryl Walker, *Indian Nation: Native American Literature and Nineteenth-Century Nationalism* (Durham: Duke University Press, 1997). Craig S. Womack, *Red on Red: Native American Literary Separatism* (Minneapolis: University of Minnesota Press, 1999), 4.

44. Ibid., 11.

45. See, for example, Vine Deloria Jr., *God Is Red* (New York: Grosset & Dunlap, 1973), and Vine Deloria Jr., *Red Earth, White Lies: Native Americans and the Myth of Scientific Fact* (New York: Scribner, 1995).

8. The End of American History

1. John Higham, *Strangers in the Land: Patterns of American Nativism, 1860–1925* (New Brunswick, N.J.: Rutgers University Press, 1955).

2. Kenneth M. Stampp, *The Peculiar Institution: Slavery in the Antebellum South* (New York: Knopf, 1956).

3. Thomas F. Gossett, *Race: The History of an Idea in America* (Dallas: Southern Methodist University Press, 1963). Leon F. Litwack, *North of Slavery: The Negro in the Free States, 1790–1860* (Chicago: University of Chicago Press, 1961). Eugene H. Berwanger, *The Frontier against Slavery: Western Anti-Negro Prejudice and the Slavery Extension Controversy* (Urbana: University of Illinois Press, 1967). Winthrop D. Jordan, *White over Black: American Attitudes toward the Negro, 1550–1812* (Chapel Hill: University of North Carolina Press, 1968). George M. Fredrickson, *The Black Image in the White Mind: The Debate on Afro-American Character and Destiny, 1817–1914* (New York: Harper & Row, 1971).

4. W. E. B. DuBois, *Black Reconstruction: An Essay toward a History of the Part Which Black Folk Played in the Attempt to Reconstruct Democracy in America, 1860–1880* (New York: Harcourt, Brace, 1935). Joel Williamson, *After Slavery: The Negro in South Carolina During Reconstruction, 1861–1877* (Chapel Hill: University of North Carolina Press, 1965). Eric Foner, *Reconstruction: America's Unfinished Revolution, 1863–1877* (New York: Harper & Row, 1988).

5. Edmund S. Morgan, *American Slavery, American Freedom: The Ordeal of Colonial Virginia* (New York: Norton, 1975).

6. Francis Jennings, *The Invasion of America: Indians, Colonialism, and the Cant of Conquest* (Chapel Hill: University of North Carolina Press, 1975).

7. Richard Slotkin, *Regeneration through Violence: The Mythology of the American Frontier, 1600–1880* (Middletown, Conn.: Wesleyan University Press, 1973). Richard Drinnon, *Facing West: The Metaphysics of Indian Hating and Empire Building* (Minneapolis: University of Minnesota Press, 1980). Russell Thornton, *American Indian Holocaust and Survival: A Population History since 1492* (Norman: University of Oklahoma Press, 1987). Alfred W. Crosby Jr., *The Columbian Exchange: Biological and Cultural Consequences of 1492* (Westport, Conn.: Greenwood Press, 1972). David E. Stannard, *American Holocaust: Columbus and the Conquest of the New World* (New York: Oxford University Press, 1992). Ian K. Steele, *Warpaths: Invasions of North America* (New York: Oxford University Press, 1994). Kerwin Lee Klein, *Frontiers of Historical Imagination: Narrating the European Conquest of Native America, 1890–1990* (Berkeley and Los Angeles: University of California Press, 1997).

8. Gary B. Nash, *Red, White, and Black: The Peoples of Early America* (Englewood Cliffs: Prentice-Hall, 1974). James Axtell, *The Invasion Within: The Contest of Cultures in Colonial North America* (New York: Oxford University Press, 1985). James H. Merrill, *The Indians' New World: Catawbas and Their Neighbors from European Contact through the Era of Removal* (Chapel Hill: North Carolina Press, 1989). Matthew Dennis, *Cultivating a Landscape of Peace: Iroquois-European Encounters in Seventeenth-Century America* (Ithaca: Cornell University Press, 1993). William Cronon, *Changes in the Land: Indians, Colonists, and the Ecology of New England* (New York: Hill & Wang, 1983). Anthony F. C. Wallace, *The Death and Rebirth of the Seneca* (New York: Knopf, 1969).

9. Richard White, *The Middle Ground: Indians, Empires, and Republics in the Great Lakes Region, 1650–1815* (Cambridge, New York: Cambridge University Press, 1991).

10. Robert F. Berkhofer Jr., *The White Man's Indian: Images of the American Indian from Columbus to the Present* (New York: Knopf, 1978). Reginald Horsman, *Expansion and American Indian Policy, 1783–1812* (East Lansing: Michigan State University Press, 1967). Bernard W. Sheehan, *Seeds of Extinction: Jeffersonian Philanthropy and the American Indian* (Chapel Hill: University of North Carolina Press, 1973). Peter S. Onuf, ed., *Jeffersonian Legacies* (Charlottesville: University Press of Virginia, 1993).

11. Robert W. Tucker and David C. Hendrickson, *Empire of Liberty: The Statecraft of Thomas Jefferson* (New York: Oxford University Press, 1990). Bradford Perkins, *The Creation of a Republican Empire, 1776–1865* (Cambridge: Cambridge University Press, 1993). William E. Weeks, *Building the Continental Empire: American Expansion from the Revolution to the Civil War* (Chicago: Ivan R. Dee, 1996). Frank L. Owsley Jr. and Gene A. Smith, *Filibusters and Expansionists: Jeffersonian Manifest Destiny, 1800–1821* (Tuscaloosa: University of Alabama Press, 1997). Lawrence S. Kaplan, *Thomas Jefferson: Westward the Course of Empire* (Wilmington, Del.: SR Books, 1999). Anthony F. C. Wallace, *Jefferson and the Indians: The Tragic Fate of the First Americans* (Cambridge: Harvard University Press, 1999).

12. Edward Pessen, *Riches, Class, and Power before the Civil War* (Lexington, Mass.: D.C. Heath, 1973). Charles G. Sellers, *The Market Revolution: Jacksonian America, 1815–1846* (New York: Oxford University Press, 1991).

13. Reginald Horsman, *Race and Manifest Destiny: The Origins of American Racial Anglo-Saxonism* (Cambridge: Harvard University Press, 1981). Ronald T. Takaki, *Iron Cages: Race and Culture in Nineteenth-Century America* (New York:

Knopf, 1979). Alexander Saxton, *The Rise and Fall of the White Republic: Class, Politics, and Mass Culture in Nineteenth-Century America* (London, New York: Verso, 1990). Eric Lott, *Love and Theft: Blackface Minstrelsy and the American Working Class* (New York: Oxford University Press, 1993). David R. Roediger, *The Wages of Whiteness: Race and the Making of the American Working Class* (London, New York: Verso, 1991).

14. Edward W. Said, *Orientalism* (New York: Pantheon Books, 1978). Stanley M. Elkins, *Slavery: A Problem in American Institutional and Intellectual Life* (Chicago: University of Chicago Press, 1959). George M. Fredrickson, *White Supremacy: A Comparative Study in American and South African History* (New York: Oxford University Press, 1981).

15. Ivan Hannaford, *Race: The History of an Idea in the West* (Washington, D.C.: Woodrow Wilson Center; Baltimore: The Johns Hopkins University Press, 1996).

16. Louis Hartz, *The Founding of New Societies: Studies in the History of the United States, Latin America, South Africa, Canada, and Australia* (New York: Harcourt, Brace & World, 1964).

17. Bernard Bailyn, *The Ideological Origins of the American Revolution* (Cambridge: Harvard University Press, 1967). J. G. A. Pocock, *The Machiavellian Moment: Florentine Political Thought and the Atlantic Republican Tradition* (Princeton: Princeton University Press, 1975). Ian K. Steele, *The English Atlantic, 1675–1740: An Exploration of Communication and Community* (New York: Oxford University Press, 1986). Daniel W. Howe, *American History in an Atlantic Context: An Inaugural Lecture Delivered before the University of Oxford on 3 June 1993* (Oxford: Clarendon Press; New York: Oxford University Press, 1993).

18. Carole Shammas, *The Pre-Industrial Consumer in England and America* (Oxford: Clarendon Press; New York: Oxford University Press, 1990). Richard L. Bushman, *The Refinement of America: Persons, Houses, Cities* (New York: Knopf, 1992). John Brewer and Roy Porter, eds., *Consumption and the World of Goods* (London, New York: Routledge, 1993).

19. David Hackett Fisher, *Albion's Seed: Four British Folkways in America* (New York: Oxford University Press, 1989). James Horn, *Adapting to a New World: English Society in the Seventeenth-Century Chesapeake* (Chapel Hill: University of North Carolina Press, 1994).

20. Gerald W. Mullin, *Flight and Rebellion: Slave Resistance in Eighteenth-Century Virginia* (New York: Oxford University Press, 1972). Peter H. Wood, *Black Majority: Negroes in Colonial South Carolina from 1670 through the Stono Rebellion* (New York: Knopf, 1974). Sidney W. Mintz and Richard Price, *The Birth of African-American Culture: An Anthropological Perspective* (Boston: Beacon Press, 1992). David C. Littlefield, *Rice and Slaves: Ethnicity and the Slave Trade in Colonial South Carolina* (Baton Rouge: Louisiana State University Press, 1981). Allan Kulikoff, *Tobacco and Slaves: The Development of Southern Cultures in the Chesapeake, 1680–1800* (Chapel Hill: University of North Carolina Press, 1986. Marvin L. Michael Kay and Lorin Lee Cary, *Slavery in North Carolina, 1748–1775* (Chapel Hill: University of North Carolina Press, 1995).

21. Mechal Sobel, *The World They Made Together: Black and White Values in Eighteenth-Century Virginia* (Princeton: Princeton University Press, 1987). Michael Mullin, *Africa in America: Slave Acculturation and Resistance in the American South and the British Caribbean, 1736–1831* (Urbana: University of Illinois Press, 1992).

John Thornton, *Africa and Africans in the Making of the Atlantic World, 1400–1680* (Cambridge, New York: Cambridge University Press, 1992).

22. Patricia Seed, *Ceremonies of Possession in Europe's Conquest of the New World, 1492–1640* (New York: Cambridge University Press, 1995). Anthony Pagden, *Lords of All the World: Ideologies of Empire in Spain, Britain, and France, c. 1500–c. 1850* (New Haven: Yale University Press, 1995). William H. McNeill, *Polyethnicity and National Unity in World History* (Toronto and Buffalo: University of Toronto Press, 1986). William H. McNeill, *The Global Condition: Conquerors, Catastrophes, and Community* (Princeton: Princeton University Press, 1992). Marshall G. S. Hodgson, ed., *Rethinking World History: Essays on Europe, Islam, and World History* (Cambridge, New York: Cambridge University Press, 1993). Paul Costello, *World Historians and Their Goals: Twentieth-Century Answers to Modernism* (DeKalb, Ill.: Northern Illinois University Press, 1993). Bruce Mazlish and Ralph Buultjens, eds., *Conceptualizing Global History* (Boulder, Colo.: Westview Press, 1993).

23. Jack D. Forbes, *Black Africans and Native Americans: Color, Race, and Caste in the Evolution of Red-Black Peoples* (Oxford, UK, and New York: Blackwell, 1988). Daniel H. Usner Jr., *Indians, Settlers, and Slaves in a Frontier Exchange Economy: The Lower Mississippi Valley before 1783* (Chapel Hill: University of North Carolina Press, 1992). Gerald M. Sider, *Lumbee Indian Histories: Race, Ethnicity, and Indian Identity in the Southern United States* (Cambridge, New York: Cambridge University Press, 1993). Naomi Zack, ed., *American Mixed Race: The Culture of Microdiversity* (Lanham, Md.: Rowman & Littlefield Publishers, 1995.)

24. Gary B. Nash, *Race and Revolution* (Madison: Madison House, 1990). Sylvia R. Frey, *Water from the Rock: Black Resistance in a Revolutionary Age* (Princeton: Princeton University Press, 1991). M. Thomas Hatley, *The Dividing Paths: Cherokees and South Carolinians through the Era of Revolution* (New York: Oxford University Press, 1993). Colin G. Calloway, *The American Revolution in Indian Country: Crisis and Diversity in Native American Communities* (Cambridge, New York: Cambridge University Press, 1995).

25. See, for example, Elizabeth V. Spellman, *Inessential Women: Problems of Exclusion in Feminist Thought* (Boston: Beacon, 1988), and Louise Michelle Newman, *White Women's Rights: The Racial Origins of Feminism in the United States* (New York: Oxford University Press, 1999).

26. Kathleen M. Brown, "Beyond the Great Debates: Gender and Race in Early America," in Louis P. Masur, ed., *Reviews in American History* 26: *The Challenge of American History* (Baltimore: The Johns Hopkins University Press, 1998), 96–123. A new self-consciousness of dramatic changes in the paradigms used by historians led to two other collections of essays on "new" history in the 1990s: Eric Foner, ed., *The New American History* (Philadelphia: Temple University Press, 1997), and Anthony Molho and Gordon S. Wood, eds., *Imagined Histories: American Historians Interpret the Past* (Princeton: Princeton University Press, 1998).

27. Mary Beth Norton, *Founding Mothers and Fathers: Gendered Power and the Forming of American Society* (New York: Alfred A. Knopf, 1996). Nancy Shoemaker, ed., *Negotiators of Change: Historical Perspectives on Native American Women* (New York: Routledge, 1995). David Barry Gaspar and Darlene Clark Hine, eds., *More Than Chattel: Black Women and Slavery in the Americas* (Bloomington: University of Indiana Press, 1996).

28. Kenneth A. Lockridge, *On the Sources of Patriarchal Rage: The Commonplace Books of William Byrd and Thomas Jefferson and the Gendering of Power in the Eighteenth Century* (London, New York: New York University Press, 1992).

29. Cornelia Hughes Dayton, *Women before the Bar: Gender, Law, and Society in Connecticut: 1639–1789* (Chapel Hill: University of North Carolina Press, 1995). Deborah A. Rosen, *Courts and Commerce: Gender, Law, and the Market Economy in Colonial New York* (Columbus: Ohio State University Press, 1997).

30. George L. Mosse, *Nationalism and Sexuality: Middle-Class Morality and Sexual Norms in Modern Europe* (Madison: University of Wisconsin Press, 1985, 1988).

31. Robert J. Corber, *Homosexuality in Cold War America: Resistance and the Crisis of Masculinity* (Durham: Duke University Press, 1997). Eric Marcus, *Making History: The Struggle for Gay and Lesbian Equal Rights, 1945–1990: An Oral History* (New York: HarperCollins Publishers, 1992). Lisa Duggan and Nan D. Hunter, *Sex Wars: Sexual Dissent and Political Culture* (New York: Routledge, 1995). Carl F. Stychin, *A Nation by Rights: National Culture, Sexual Identity Politics, and the Discourse of Rights* (Philadelphia: Temple University Press, 1998). Diane Helene Miller, *Freedom to Differ: The Shaping of the Gay and Lesbian Struggle for Civil Rights* (New York: New York University Press, 1998).

32. Deborah Gray White, *Ar'n't I a Woman: Female Slaves in the Plantation South* (New York: W. W. Norton, 1987). Jacqueline Jones, *Labor of Love, Labor of Sorrow: Black Women, Work, and the Family from Slavery to the Present* (New York: Basic Books, 1985). Tera W. Hunter, *To 'Joy My Freedom: Southern Black Women's Lives and Labors after the Civil War* (Cambridge: Harvard University Press, 1997). Laura F. Edwards, *Gendered Strife and Confusion: The Political Culture of Reconstruction* (Urbana: University of Illinois Press, 1997). Elizabeth Clark-Lewis, *Living In, Living Out: African American Domestics in Washington, D.C., 1910–1940* (Washington, D.C.: Smithsonian Institution Press, 1994).

33. Oscar Handlin, *Boston's Immigrants: A Study in Acculturation* (Cambridge: Belknap Press of Harvard University Press, 1979) and *The Uprooted: The Epic Story of the Great Migrations That Made the American People* (Boston: Little Brown, 1951).

34. Rudolph J. Vecoli, "Contadini in Chicago: A Critique of the Uprooted," *The Journal of American History* 51 (December 1964): 407–17. John Bodnar, *The Transplanted: A History of Immigrants in Urban America* (Bloomington: University of Indiana Press, 1985). Walter Nugent, *Crossings: The Great Transatlantic Migrations, 1870–1914* (Bloomington: University of Indiana Press, 1992). Mark Wyman, *Round Trip to America: The Immigrants Return to Europe, 1890–1930* (Ithaca: Cornell University Press, 1993).

35. Donna Gabaccia, *From the Other Side: Women, Gender, and Immigrant Life in the United States, 1820–1990* (Bloomington: University of Indiana Press, 1994). Rodolfo Acuña, *Occupied America: A History of Chicanos* (New York: Harper & Row, 1981, 1988). Ronald T. Takaki, *Strangers from a Different Shore: A History of Asian-Americans* (Boston: Little Brown, 1989). Gary Y. Okihiro, *Margins and Mainstreams: Asians in American History and Culture* (Seattle: University of Washington Press, 1994). Dirk Hoerder, ed., *Labor Migration in the Atlantic Economies: The European and North American Working Classes During the Period of Industrialization* (Westport, Conn.: Greenwood Press, 1985). Jan Lucassen and Leo Lucassen, eds., *Migration, Migration History: Old Paradigms and New Perspectives* (Bern, New York: Peter Lang,

1997). Wang Gungwu, ed., *Global History and Migrations* (Boulder, Colo.: Westview, 1997).

36. Laurence Veysey, "The Autonomy of American History Reconsidered," *American Quarterly* 31 (autumn 1979): 455–77. Ian Tyrrell, "American Exceptionalism in an Age of International History," *American Historical Review* 96 (October 1991): 1031–55. David Thelen, "Of Audiences, Borderlands, and Comparisons: Toward the Internationalization of American History," *The Journal of American History* (September 1992): 432–62. Joyce Appleby, "Recovering America's Historic Diversity: Beyond Exceptionalism," *The Journal of American History* 79 (September 1992): 419–31. James E. Cronin, "Neither Exceptional Nor Peculiar: Towards the Comparative Study of Labor in Advanced Society," *International Review of Social History* 38 (1993): 59–75. George M. Fredrickson, "From Exceptionalism to Variability: Recent Developments in Cross-National Comparative History," *The Journal of American History* 82 (September 1995): 587–604. Daniel T. Rogers, "Exceptionalism," in Anthony Molho and Gordon S. Wood, eds., *Imagined Histories: American Historians Interpret the Past* (Princeton: Princeton University Press, 1998), 21–40.

37. Thomas Bender, "Wholes and Parts: The Need for Synthesis in American History," *The Journal of American History* 73 (June 1986) 120–36. Michael McGerr, "The Price of the 'New Transnational History,'" *The American Historical Review* 96 (October 1991) 1056–67. Michael Kammen, "The Problem of American Exceptionalism: A Reconsideration," *American Quarterly* 45 (March 1993): 1–43. John Higham, "The Future of American History," *The Journal of American History* 80 (March 1994): 1289–1309.

Epilogue

1. When the aesthetic authority of bourgeois nationalism disintegrated in the 1940s, Western anthropologists suddenly were able to see that they had been agents of Western nations who had been imposing their power on non-Western peoples. Examples of their dramatic paradigm shift are Johannes Fabian, *Time and the Other: How Anthropology Makes Its Object* (New York: Columbia University Press, 1983); Immanuel Wallerstein, *Unthinking Social Science: The Limits of Nineteenth-Century Paradigms* (Cambridge, Mass.: B. Blackwell, 1991); J. M. Blaut, *The Colonizer's Model of the World: Geographical Diffusionism and Eurocentric History* (New York: The Guilford Press, 1993); Nicholas Thomas, *Colonialism's Culture: Anthropology, Travel, and Government* (Princeton: Princeton University Press, 1994); Ella Shohat and Robert Stam, *Unthinking Eurocentrism: Multiculturalism and the Media* (London, New York: Routledge, 1994). After the paradigm that world history was a movement toward the universal hegemony of bourgeois national culture broke, an alternative paradigm that the world was inevitably characterized by cultural pluralism began to be powerful. Several of the important expressions of this paradigm are Bill Ashcroft, Gareth Griffiths, and Helen Tiffin, eds., *The Empire Writes Back: Theory and Practice in Post-Colonial Literatures* (London, New York: Routledge, 1989); Samir Amin, *Delinking: Towards a Polycentric World,* trans. Michael Wolfers (London and New Jersey: Zed Books, 1990); Ulf Hannerz, *Cultural Complexity: Studies in the Social Organization of Meaning* (New York: Columbia University Press, 1992); Arif Dirlik, *The Postcolonial Aura: Third World Criticism in the Age of Global Capitalism* (Boulder, Colo.: Westview Press, 1997); Fawzia Afzal-Khan and Kalpana Seshadri-Crooks,

eds., *The Pre-occupation of Postcolonial Studies* (Durham: Duke University Press, 2000); Philip D. Curtin, *The World and the West: The European Challenge and the Overseas Response in the Age of Empire* (Cambridge and New York: Cambridge University Press, 2000). But the leaders of the nation-states and of multinational corporations, who had been constructing the aesthetic authority of the international marketplace since the 1940s, believe that the variety of human cultures does not threaten the harmony of that space. Their cultural hegemony rested on the faith that the space of the international marketplace is eternal and immortal. It built on the faith that this sacred space will expand forever. Within this vision, varieties of cultures are only minor impediments to the rational expansion of the marketplace. When the national landscape became terminally ill in the 1940s, scholars everywhere in the Western world wrote elegies for the idea of progress. But a number of scholars were now helping to revitalize an idea of progress that was linked to the immortality of the marketplace. See, for example, Arthur M. Melzer, Jerry Weinberger, and M. Richard Zinman, eds., *History and the Idea of Progress* (Ithaca: Cornell University Press, 1995). Aihwa Ong was an anthropologist who was aware of the confidence held by the cultural leaders of the international marketplace that the variety of cultures would not hinder global economic expansion. See her *Flexible Citizenship: The Cultural Logics of Transnationality* (Durham: Duke University Press, 1999).

2. Robert N. Bellah, *The Broken Covenant: American Civil Religion in a Time of Trial* (New York: Seabury Press, 1975).

3. Robert Bellah et al., *Habits of the Heart: Individualism and Commitment in American Life* (Berkeley and Los Angeles: University of California Press, 1985).

4. Godfrey Hodgson, *The World Turned Right-Side Up: A History of Conservative Ascendancy in America* (Boston: Houghton Mifflin, 1996).

5. Michael J. Sandel, *Democracy's Discontent: America in Search of a Public Philosophy* (Cambridge, Mass.: Belnap Press of Harvard University Press, 1996). Michael Schudson, *The Good Citizen: A History of American Civic Life* (New York: Martin Kessler Books, 1998).

6. George Lipsitz, *The Possessive Investment in Whiteness: How White People Profit from Identity Politics* (Philadelphia: Temple University Press, 1998).

7. Several books that discuss the continuation of the imperial power of capitalism in the new era of globalism are Robert Ross and Kent C. Trachte, *Global Capitalism: The New Leviathan* (Albany: State University of New York Press, 1990); Leslie Sklar, *Sociology of the Global System* (New York: Harvester Wheatsheaf, 1991); Arif Dirlik, *After the Revolution: Waking to Global Capitalism* (Hanover: The University Press of New England, 1994); and Giovanni Arrighi, *The Long Twentieth Century: Money, Power, and the Origins of Our Times* (London, New York: Verso, 1994).

8. See, for example, Roger M. Smith, *Civic Ideals: Conflicting Visions of Citizenship in U. S. History* (New Haven: Yale University Press, 1997).

9. Analyses of the growing gap between rich and poor are found in Kevin Phillips, *The Politics of Rich and Poor: Wealth and the American Electorate in the Reagan Aftermath* (New York: Harper Perennial, 1991); Graef S. Crystal, *In Search of Excess: The Overcompensation of American Executives* (New York: W. W. Norton, 1991); and Robert H. Frank and Philip J. Cook, *The Winner-Take-All Society: How More and More Americans Compete for Fewer and Bigger Prizes, Encouraging Economic Waste, Income Inequality, and Impoverished Cultural Life* (New York: The Free Press, 1995).

10. See, for example, Susan Jeffords, *The Remasculinization of America: Gender and the Vietnam War* (Bloomington: Indiana Press, 1989); James William Gibson, *Warrior Dreams: Paramilitary Culture in Post-Vietnam America* (New York: Hill and Wang, 1994); and David Savran, *Taking It Like a Man: White Masculinity, Masochism, and Contemporary American Culture* (Princeton: Princeton University Press, 1998). Michael Lind, *Up from Conservatism: Why the Right Is Wrong for America* (New York: The Free Press, 1996), discusses the increasing racism in the United States. Richard J. Herrnstein and Charles Murray, *The Bell Curve: Intelligence and Class Structure in American Life* (New York: Free Press, 1994).

11. See, for example, Russell Jacoby, *The Last Intellectuals: American Culture in the Age of Academe* (New York: Basic Books, 1987), and *The End of Utopia: Politics and Culture in an Age of Apathy* (New York: Basic Books, 1999).

12. John Gray in *Enlightenment's Wake: Politics and Culture at the Close of the Modern Age* (London: Routledge, 1995) and *False Dawn: The Delusions of Global Capitalism* (New York: The New Press, 1998) criticizes global capitalism for its utopian expectations. Thomas Frank, *One Market under God: Extreme Capitalism, Market Capitalism, Market Populism, and the End of Economic Democracy* (New York: Doubleday, 2000), captures the mythic power of the space of the marketplace that, because it is supposed to be sacred, is beyond criticism.

13. Books that emphasize the instability of international capitalism and its destructive ecological consequences are Herman E. Daly, *The Case against "Free Trade": GATT, NAFTA, and the Globalization of Corporate Power* (San Francisco: Earth Island Press; Berkeley: North Atlantic Books, 1993); Paul Hirst and Grahame Thompson, *Globalization in Question: The International Economy and the Possibilities of Governance* (Cambridge, U.K.: Polity Press; Oxford, U.K.; Cambridge, Mass: Blackwell Publishers, 1996); Daniel Drache and Robert Boyer, eds., *States against Markets: The Limits of Globalization* (London: Routledge, 1996); Jerry Mander and Edward Goldsmith, eds., *The Case against the Global Economy: And for a Turn Toward the Local* (San Francisco: Sierra Club Books, 1997); William Greider, *One World, Ready or Not: The Manic Logic of Global Capitalism* (New York: Simon and Schuster, 1996); Catherine Caufield, *Masters of Illusion: The World Bank and the Poverty of Nations* (New York: Henry Holt, 1996); Richard C. Longworth, *Global Squeeze: The Coming Crisis for First-World Nations* (Lincolnwood, Ill.: Contemporary Books, 1998); Giovanni Arrighi and Beverly J. Silver, *Chaos and Governance in the Modern World System* (Minneapolis: University of Minnesota Press, 1999); Michael E. Latham, *Modernization as Ideology: American Social Science and "Nation Building" in the Kennedy Era* (Chapel Hill: University of North Carolina Press, 2000); Richard Hofrichter, ed., *Reclaiming the Environmental Debate: The Politics of Health in a Toxic Culture* (Cambridge: MIT Press, 2000); and William A. Schutkin, *The Land That Could Be: Environmentalism and Democracy in the Twenty-First Century* (Cambridge: MIT Press, 2000).

14. Bourgeois nationalism is a threat to local cultures because it imagines a universal national. The culture of international capitalism is a threat to the local because it imagines a universal in which all individuals will find their identities as consumers in a worldwide marketplace. The recognition that international capitalism is characterized by cultural imperialism as well as by economic imperialism is a major focus of Arif Dirlik's *The Postcolonial Aura.* Earlier analyses and criticisms of the cultural imperialism of international capitalism are Pierre Clastres, *Society against*

the State: Essays in Political Anthropology, trans. Robert Hurley (New York: Zone Books; Cambridge, Mass: MIT Press, 1987); Calvin Martin, ed., *The American Indian and the Problem of History* (New York: Oxford University Press, 1987); Henry A. Giroux, *Border Crossings: Cultural Workers and the Politics of Education* (New York: Routledge, 1992); M. Annette Jaimes, ed., *Fantasies of the Master Race: Literature, Cinema, and the Colonization of American Indians* (Monroe, Maine: Common Courage Press, 1992); Roger Moody, ed., *The Indigenous Voice: Visions and Realities* (Utrecht: International Books, 1993); and Ward Churchill, *Struggle for the Land: Indigenous Resistance to Genocide, Ecocide, and Expropriation in Contemporary North America* (Monroe, Maine: Common Courage Press, 1993).

Index

David W. Noble is professor of American studies at the University of Minnesota. He has written several books, including *The End of American History* and (with Peter Carroll) *The Free and the Unfree.*